Forgotten Fights

Little-Known Raids and
Skirmishes on the Frontier,
1823 to 1890

*Gregory F. Michno and
Susan J. Michno*

2008
MOUNTAIN PRESS PUBLISHING COMPANY
Missoula, Montana

All photographs are by the authors unless otherwise indicated.

Library of Congress Cataloging-in-Publication Data
Michno, Gregory, 1948–
    Forgotten fights : little-known raids and skirmishes on the frontier,
    1823 to 1890 / Gregory F. Michno and Susan J. Michno.
        p. cm.
    Includes bibliographical references and index.
    ISBN 978-0-87842-549-5 (pbk. : alk. paper)
    1. Indians of North America—Wars—West (U.S.) I. Michno, Susan,
    1947– II. Title.
    E81.M53 2008
    970.004'97—dc22
                                        2008029823

Mountain Press Publishing Company
P.O. Box 2399
Missoula, Montana 59806
406-728-1900

Contents

Preface

The stories in this compilation of lesser-known incidents of the nineteenth-century Indian Wars are intended to give readers varied glimpses into the unpredictable lives of the frontiersmen, traders, emigrants, homesteaders, soldiers, and Indians of the western American frontier. These were people whose everyday existence could erupt without warning into violent confrontations that plunged them, unwillingly, into an evolving historical drama.

This book is meant both to stand alone and to supplement one of our previous books, *Encyclopedia of Indian Wars: Western Battles and Skirmishes, 1850–1890* (Mountain Press, 2003). Readers familiar with the earlier work will find this volume constructed in a similar manner. Feedback from readers of *Encyclopedia of Indian Wars* indicated that its concept and coverage were good, but they wanted us to expand both the number of entries and the time span covered. In this volume, we included more than 300 additional incidents, choosing 1823 as the starting date, the year of the first Plains Indian war. The ending date, 1890, is the same, the year the Census Bureau declared the closing of the frontier. This study encompasses many unique and memorable episodes.

Setting aside discussion of the larger and more famous battles allows a sharper focus on some of the innumerable small-scale, personal confrontations that defined the Indian Wars. The detailed discussions in these entries illustrate that victims and villains existed on both sides and that noncombatants often suffered more than soldiers and warriors.

ARIZONA

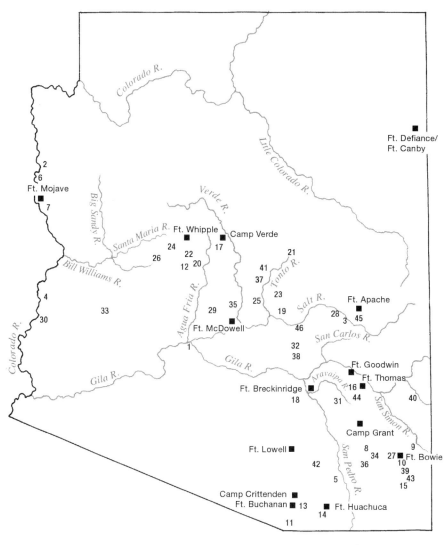

ARIZONA

CALIFORNIA

Ft. Bidwell

Ft. Jones

Ft.
Humbolt) Ft. Gaston
        6 g
      5 13
     12

Ft. Crook

Ft. Bragg

8

Presidio
        2

4

10

11

3
  7
14

Ft. Tejon

1

Ft. Yuma

CALIFORNIA

COLORADO

1   (19 June 1848) Manco Burro Pass
2   (23 July 1848) Cumbres Pass
3   (25 August 1868) Dietemann Massacre
4   (25 August 1887) Colorow's War

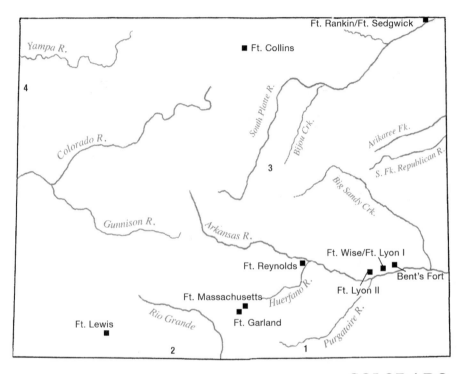

COLORADO

IDAHO

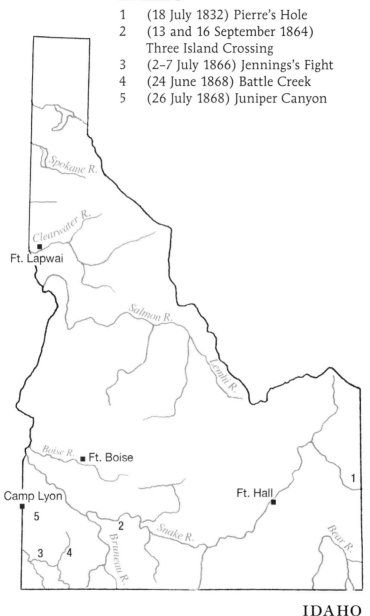

1   (18 July 1832) Pierre's Hole
2   (13 and 16 September 1864)
     Three Island Crossing
3   (2–7 July 1866) Jennings's Fight
4   (24 June 1868) Battle Creek
5   (26 July 1868) Juniper Canyon

Spokane R.

Clearwater R.

Ft. Lapwai

Salmon R.

Lemhi R.

Boise R.   Ft. Boise

Camp Lyon   Ft. Hall

5

2   Snake R.   Bear R.

3   4

Bruneau R.

IDAHO

KANSAS

1 (4 July 1843) Owl Creek
2 (12 May 1847) Pawnee Fork
3 (28 May 1847) Walnut Creek
4 (26 June 1847) Plain Encampment/Love's Defeat
5 (20 July 1847) Easton's Fight
6 (1 August 1847) Ash Creek
7 (Ca. 10 August 1847) Coon Creek Crossing
8 (16 November 1847) Fort Mann
9 (18 June 1848) Coon Creek
10 (9 July 1848) Battle of the Cimarron
11 (20 July 1848) Jones's Fight
12 (9 September 1860) Peacock Massacre
13 (15 May 1863) Verdigris River
14 (20–22 July 1864) Cow Creek
15 (1 August 1864) Wagon Bed Spring
16 (6 August 1864) Moffitt Massacre
17 (21 August 1864) Cimarron Crossing
18 (12 June 1865) Fort Dodge
19 (18 May 1866) Little Cheyenne Creek
20 (21–27 June 1867) Union Pacific Railroad
21 (30 May 1869) Spillman Creek Raids
22 (Ca. 25 August 1874) Lone Tree Massacre

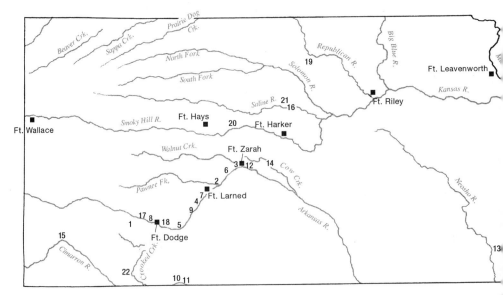

KANS

MONTANA

1   (4 May 1823) Smith River
2   (31 May 1823) Immell-Jones Massacre
3   (14 October 1832) Vanderburgh Massacre
4   (Winter 1833) Death of Hugh Glass
5   (16 April 1868) Fort C. F. Smith
6   (Winter 1875–76) Fort Pease
7   (5 April 1879) Mizpah Creek
8   (8 March 1880) Rosebud Creek
9   (17 August 1880) Little Missouri River
10 (19 April 1883) Wild Horse Lake

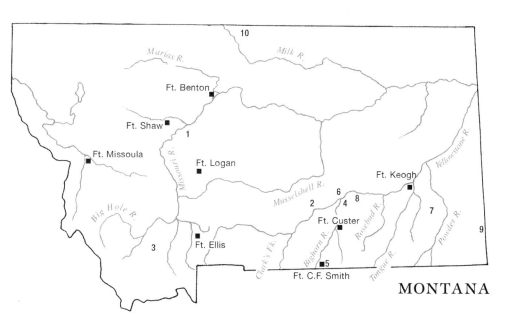

NEVADA

1   (Ca. 7 September 1833) Barren River Massacre
2   (September 1862) Gravelly Ford Massacre
3   (22 March 1863) Eight Mile Station
4   (4 May 1863) Duck Creek
5   (6 May 1863) Cedar Swamp
6   (6 July 1863) Egan Canyon Station
7   (Ca. 15 August 1863) Steptoe Valley
8   (Ca. 15 March 1865) Granite Creek Station
9   (6 April 1865) Cottonwood Creek
10 (26 July 1865) Willow Point
11 (31 July 1865) Cottonwood Canyon
12 (3 September 1865) Table Mountain
13 (13 September 1865) Willow Creek
14 (17 November 1865) Leonard Creek
15 (12 January 1866) Battle Creek
16 (15 February 1866) Guano Valley
17 (18 January 1867) Eden Valley
18 (15 February 1867) Black Slate Mountain
19 (22 March 1867) South Fork Owyhee
20 (29 April 1868) Deep Canyon

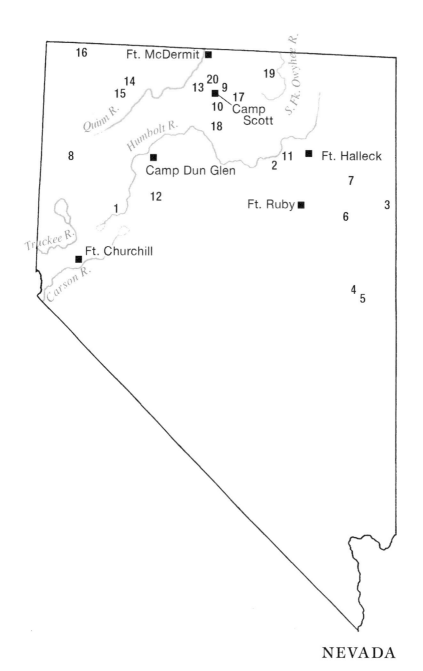

16

Ft. McDermit ■

19

14
15

13 20 9
■
17
10 Camp
Scott

Quinn R.

Humbolt R.

S. Fk. Owyhee R.

18

8

11 ■ Ft. Halleck

Camp Dun Glen ■

2

7

12

Ft. Ruby ■

3

1

6

Truckee R.

Ft. Churchill ■

4
5

Carson R.

NEVADA

NEW MEXICO

1   (28 October 1846) Isleta
2   (19 January 1847) Turley's Mill
3   (13 March 1849) El Cerro de la Olla
4   (16 August 1849) Santa Rita Copper Mines
5   (25 January 1852) Laguna del Muerto
6   (13 June 1858) Guadalupe Mountains
7   (29 August 1858) Ojo del Oso
8   (29 May 1860) Santa Rita del Cobre
9   (27 August 1861) Cooke's Canyon/Ake's Fight
10 (28 August 1861) Mastin's Fight
11 (27 September 1861) Pinos Altos
12 (8 September 1863) Mimbres River
13 (1 July 1865) San Andreas Pass
14 (17 September 1865) Mimbres Mountains
15 (17 January 1866) Oak Grove
16 (Ca. 1 August 1867) Loving's Fight
17 (8–10 September 1877) San Francisco River
18 (17 September 1878) Bear Creek
19 (10 September 1879) McEver's Ranch
20 (Ca. 5 March 1880) Palomas
21 (14 May 1880) Old Fort Tularosa
22 (24 January 1881) Canada Alamosa
23 (18 August 1881) Gold Dust
24 (1 June 1882) Cloverdale Canyon
25 (9 December 1885) Lillie's Ranch

3

2

Ft. Union ■

Ft. Marcy ■

Ft. Bascom ■

1

Ft. Sumner ■

■ Ft. Wingate II
7

■ Ft.Tularosa
21

22

■ Ft. Craig

Ft. Stanton
■

17

25

Ft.West
18

■ Ft. McRae
5

14

20

11
8

Ft. Bayard 4

23

Ft. Thorn

12

19

13

Ft. Cummings

Ft. Selden

9, 10, 15

6

16

24

NEW MEXICO

NORTH DAKOTA

1   (26 May 1865) Fort Rice
2   (20 August 1868) Fort Buford
3   (26 August 1872) Fort McKean
4   (3 and 4 October 1872) Heart River
5   (2 and 14 October 1872) Fort McKean
6   (7 May and 15 and 17 June 1873) Fort Abraham Lincoln

SOUTH DAKOTA

1   (2 June 1823) Ashley's Fight
2   (9–10 August 1823) Arikara Villages
3   (26 June 1864) Little Cheyenne River
4   (1 August 1876) Red Canyon

NEBRASKA

1   (29 October 1849) Fort Kearny
2   (Ca. 26 August and ca. 5 September 1856) Babbitt's Wagon Train
3   (Ca. 24 August 1869) Nelson Buck Massacre

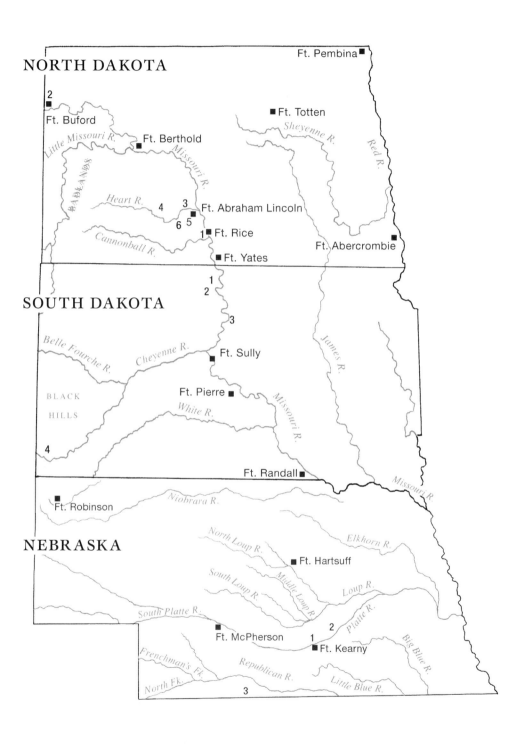

NORTH DAKOTA

Ft. Pembina

2
Ft. Buford

Ft. Totten

Little Missouri R.

Sheyenne R.

Red R.

Ft. Berthold

Missouri R.

BADLANDS

Heart R. 4   3   Ft. Abraham Lincoln

6   5

Cannonball R. 1   Ft. Rice

Ft. Yates

Ft. Abercrombie

SOUTH DAKOTA

1
2

3

Belle Fourche R. *Cheyenne R.*

James R.

Ft. Sully

BLACK

Ft. Pierre

HILLS

White R.

Missouri R.

4

Ft. Randall

Missouri R.

Ft. Robinson

Niobrara R.

NEBRASKA

North Loup R.

Elkhorn R.

South Loup R. *Middle Loup R.* Ft. Hartsuff

Loup R.

South Platte R.

Platte R.

Ft. McPherson 2

1   Ft. Kearny *Big Blue R.*

Frenchman's Fk.

Republican R.

Little Blue R.

North Fk. 3

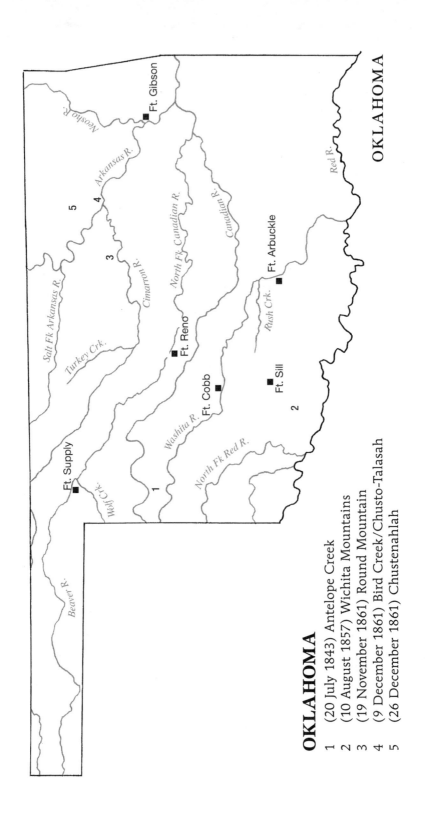

OKLAHOMA

1 (20 July 1843) Antelope Creek
2 (10 August 1857) Wichita Mountains
3 (19 November 1861) Round Mountain
4 (9 December 1861) Bird Creek/Chusto-Talasah
5 (26 December 1861) Chustenahlah

OREGON

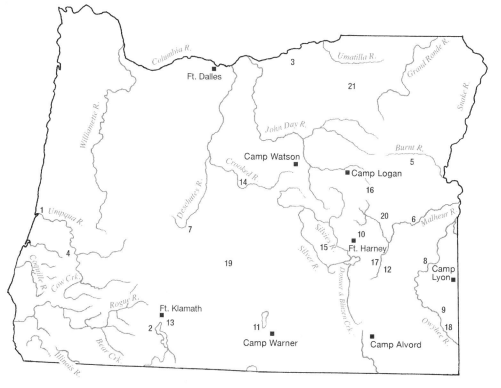

OREGON

TEXAS 1823–1850

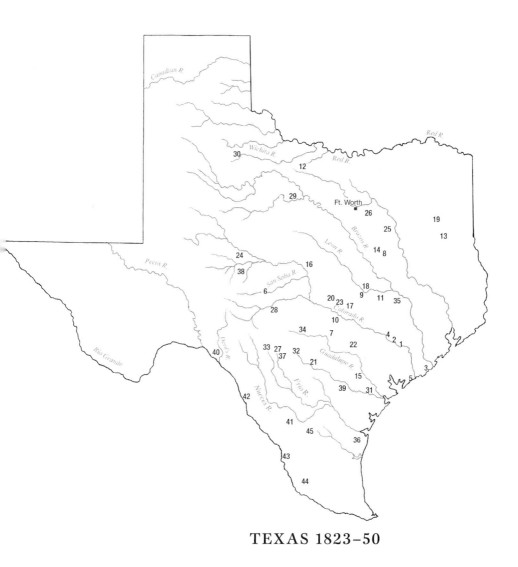

TEXAS 1823–50

TEXAS 1851–1890

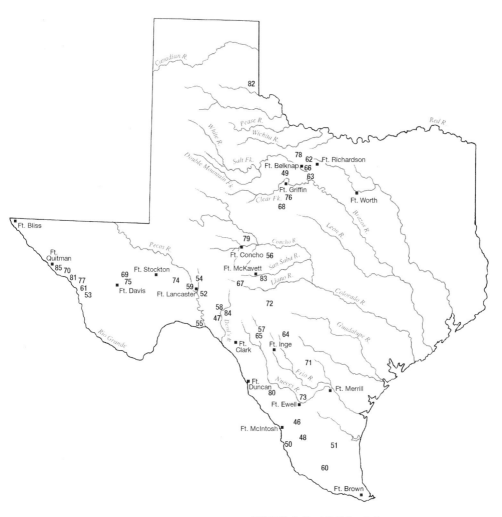

TEXAS 1851–90

82   (7 September 1874) Whitefish Creek
83   (21 November 1874) Menard
84   (Ca. 10 February 1875) Beaver Lake
85   (9 August 1880) Quitman Canyon

UTAH

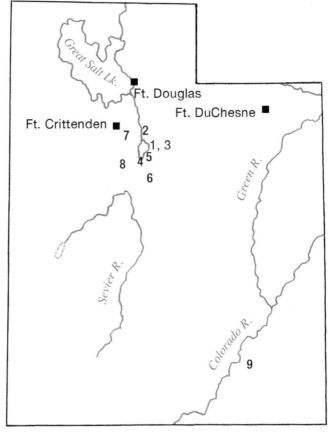

UTAH

WASHINGTON

WYOMING

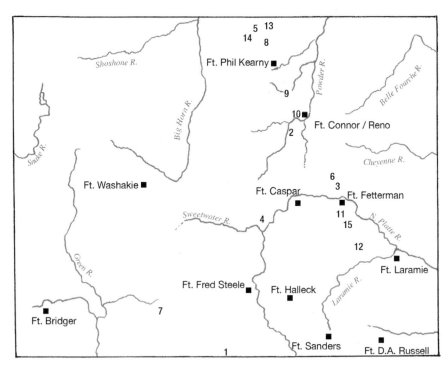

WYOMING

— 1823 —

Spring 1823
SKULL CREEK *(Eagle Lake, Texas)*

Among the first Americans to discover that colonizing Texas would be a long, difficult process were John C. Clark, John Alley, and a man named Loy. They were part of the "Old Three Hundred," the name given to the settlers who received land grants in Stephen F. Austin's first colony. In January 1821 Austin's father, Moses Austin, received a permit from the Spanish to settle 300 families in Texas, but he died before he could realize his plans. Taking his father's place, Stephen traveled to San Antonio and finalized plans with the Spanish governor. Austin quickly found willing colonists, and by the end of the summer of 1824, most of the Old Three Hundred had moved in. These and other early Texas settlers fought with local Indians almost from the day they arrived. At this time, hostile Indians in the area were not Comanches, but Wacos, Tawakonis, Karankawas, Ionis, and Anadarkos.

A drought in the spring of 1823 made farming difficult, so Clark, Alley, and Loy had to bring in food supplies from the Gulf Coast. Ascending the Colorado River with a canoe load of corn, the men got as far as the mouth of Skull Creek, near present-day Eagle Lake, when a band of Karankawa Indians attacked them. Alley and Loy were killed instantly. Clark was wounded seven times, but he managed to swim to the opposite bank and escape.

Later that day, colonist Robert Brotherton unluckily encountered the same band of Indians. Believing them to be friendly Tonkawas, he rode up to them. When he got close, the Karankawas grabbed him. Brotherton struggled and managed to escape, but not before taking an arrow in his back. Reaching the nearest settlement, Brotherton spread news of the assault.

Colonist Robert Kuykendall gathered about twelve men, plus the Tonkawa chief Carita, and rode after the Karankawas. That evening, Kuykendall's posse found the Indians camped in a thicket near the mouth of Skull Creek, pounding briar root, seemingly oblivious to the possibility of a pursuit. Kuykendall placed his men in a semicircle around the camp, cutting off the Indians' escape route to the swamp, and waited until dawn.

When the first warrior arose, the settlers charged in, firing left and right. About ten warriors were killed on the spot. Of the remaining dozen who broke for the marsh, about ten more were killed. Only a few made it through, and they may have been wounded. Kuykendall destroyed the encampment and returned home. The Karankawas vacated the area and left the colonists alone for a time. Later Karankawa raids would be made with more stealth and precaution.[1]

4 May 1823
SMITH RIVER *(Great Falls, Montana)*

The Blackfeet's bitter resentment toward arriving Americans dated back to a fight between men of the Lewis and Clark expedition and the Blackfeet on the Marias River in present-day Montana in 1806. The capture of trapper John Colter two years later, and his subsequent escape, marked the onset of a relentless thirty-year conflict. As more brigades of fur trappers hunted the upper reaches of the Missouri River, collisions with the Blackfeet inevitably increased.

During the winter of 1822–23, some of Andrew Henry's trappers camped on the Missouri River at the mouth of the Musselshell, about 180 miles upstream from Fort Henry, on the Yellowstone. In April, when the river became navigable, the trappers set out. On 6 April, eleven of Henry's men took two dugout canoes up the Missouri. They wound their way past the Judith and Marias Rivers, setting traps as they traveled upstream toward Three Forks.

On 4 May, while the trappers were deep in Blackfeet territory, warriors attacked them near the mouth of the Smith River, twelve miles above present-day Great Falls, Montana. The Indians killed four of Henry's men. The seven survivors, still determined to salvage some business if they could, buried 172 more traps, in addition to the 30 they had already set, before fleeing 450 miles back down the Missouri to Fort Henry.[2]

31 May 1823
IMMELL-JONES MASSACRE *(Huntley, Montana)*

Only a few weeks after the Blackfeet attacked Henry's men (see previous entry), they hit the Immell and Jones brigade about 180 miles southeast of the site of the Smith River fight. In the fall of 1822, Michael Immell and Robert Jones, working for the Missouri Fur Company, led a party of about forty-five men to the Yellowstone River. They had a good hunt, getting thirty packs, or about 1,500 beaver. Caching the packs, they proceeded to the Missouri, where they discovered that the Blackfeet had already made the beaver pickings slim. During the winter, thirteen men deserted the party. Nevertheless, Immell and Jones collected about twenty more packs.

On the Jefferson River, the trappers encountered a band of thirty-eight Piegan Blackfeet, a band that was somewhat less hostile to Americans than other Blackfeet. After uneasily smoking and parleying with the Piegans, Immell and Jones headed back to the Yellowstone and traveled downstream to a point about ten miles from a friendly Crow camp, where they figured they were nearly out of harm's way. In a gorge of the river near Pryor's Fork, however, they ran into an ambush by a band of Blood Blackfeet.

The narrow river trail the trappers were following at the time led along the base of a steep hill, requiring them to walk single file and making them more vulnerable. The Indians came at the twenty-nine men with axes, knives, and lances. They killed Immell and Jones in the first rush, and before the rest could escape, another five were killed and four were wounded. In addition, the trappers lost their horses, equipment, traps, and beaver packs, totaling about $12,000 worth of goods.

The surviving trappers swam or floated on logs down the river and made it to the Crow camp, where company clerk Charles Keemle built skin canoes for the party to leave in. The trappers recovered the cached beaver packs from the fall hunt and floated downriver. As the trappers passed an Arikara village on the Missouri in present-day South Dakota, Indians fired on them, and they experienced another narrow escape. More trouble with the Arikaras would follow.[3]

2 June 1823
ASHLEY'S FIGHT *(Mobridge, South Dakota)*
On 30 May 1823 William H. Ashley and an entourage of ninety engagés were on a trapping expedition with two keelboats, the *Yellowstone Packet* and the *Rocky Mountain*, and their crews of French Canadian voyageurs and "St. Louis gumboes." They set anchor in a narrow river channel opposite two Arikara villages on the Missouri above the confluence of Grand River. The Arikaras had constructed a breastwork on a sandbar at the mouth of Cottonwood Creek, and the channel, less than 100 yards wide, was fortified on both sides to constrict river passage.

Ashley had stopped because he wanted to trade with the Arikaras for some horses, which he hoped to take overland to Henry's Fort, at the mouth of the Yellowstone. He proceeded cautiously, for he knew two of the tribe's warriors had been killed during a recent altercation with the Missouri Fur Company at Cedar Fort, and he did not know how he would be received. Chiefs Grey Eyes and Little Soldier met Ashley on the beach below the lower village, where the trapper gave them gifts and explained he wanted to trade for horses. Grey Eyes accepted the gifts, but Little Soldier refused, and the two chiefs went to confer with the tribal council to determine their course of action.

Grey Eyes and some of his tribesmen appeared on the beach that evening. Ashley and his interpreter, Edward Rose, met with them, and the chief agreed to a trade. Ashley would receive nineteen horses and more than 200 buffalo robes in exchange for twenty-five muskets, powder, shot, and some trinkets. One chief wanted to continue bartering for more guns and ammunition, but Ashley refused. Leaving a party of forty men onshore, Ashley went back to the keelboat. The men onshore set up camp and posted a guard over the horses.

On 31 May the trappers brought in some goods to proceed with the trade, but a fierce thunderstorm interrupted the exchange until the following evening. That afternoon, Bear, a chief from the upper village, invited Ashley to his lodge. Accompanied by his interpreter, Edward Rose, Ashley listened as Bear and Little Soldier warned him of a possible attack on his group by the lower-village Indians. In response, Ashley doubled the guard onshore. That night, despite the chief's warning, Rose and another trapper, Aaron Stephens, decided to go to the lower village, where they had previously been offered an invitation to have sex with the women.

About 3:30 the following morning, three Arikara warriors boarded the *Rocky Mountain* and tried to murder Ashley, but he and his men awoke in time to repel the attackers. Rose then arrived with word that there was a great commotion in the village. Warriors were whooping and brandishing weapons; Rose had been driven out and Stephens had been killed. Ashley quickly reinforced his shore guard and waited for dawn to pull out. In the meantime, the men ashore demanded the return of Stephens's body for burial; one Indian said he would deliver the body in exchange for a horse. The trappers agreed, but the Indian returned without the remains, stating that the body had been decapitated and mutilated.

At first light, the Indians began firing on the beach company from the picketed palisades surrounding the lower village. Their first barrage killed men and horses alike. Ashley ordered his keelboat to rescue the men on the beach, but the *Rocky Mountain* crew panicked and refused.

The *Yellowstone Packet* set out, but it ran aground on a sandbar, so Ashley ordered his boatmen to take two skiffs to attempt the rescue. They rescued some men, but when they went back for more of them, Indians killed the oarsmen. About seven of the remaining shore party swam to the skiff, which then got caught in the current and drifted downstream. The rest of the company onshore held the Indians off for another fifteen minutes, then swam for the keelboats.

Ashley's keelboat drifted downstream and finally ran ashore. Ashley proposed they regroup, run the gauntlet, and continue on to Henry's Fort, but he gave up the idea when all but thirty of his men threatened to desert. While the boat was anchored, James Clyman stumbled aboard, having evaded the Indians. He and Reed Gibson had climbed into a skiff, reached shore, and then separated, Clyman going over the plains and Gibson sneaking along the riverbank. Three Arikaras chased Clyman, but he outran them. Later the trappers learned that Gibson had been badly wounded but had managed to crawl to the river and paddle downstream. The keelboat finally found him, but he soon died. Ashley had lost fifteen men, and nine were wounded.

One of the trappers, Jedediah Smith, and a French Canadian companion volunteered to make the trek to Henry's Fort to get reinforcements. Ashley and the rest of his company floated downriver seventy-five miles to an island near the mouth of the Cheyenne River, where they set up a base on 7 June. Ashley sent the *Yellowstone Packet* to Fort Atkinson with five wounded men and forty-three others who decided to quit. They arrived on 18 June and informed Col. Henry Leavenworth of the situation. Leavenworth would soon arrive to rescue Ashley and confront the Arikaras (see Arikara Villages, 9–10 August 1823).[4]

July 1823
TUMLINSON'S REVENGE *(Columbus, Texas)*

Early Texas settler John Jackson Tumlinson and a companion, Joseph Newman, were on their way to San Antonio to secure ammunition for Lt. Moses Morrison's militia company when they were attacked by a band of Karankawas and Wacos near the present-day town of Seguin on 6 July 1823. The Indians killed Tumlinson, but Newman, on a fleeter horse, got away. Tumlinson's body was never found.

Upon hearing of the attack, Tumlinson's son, John Jackson Jr., sought swift vengeance. He rounded up a posse of eleven young Texans, including his teenage brother, Joseph, who would act as a scout. The young men set off after the Indians, following a trail that led northeast. Young Joseph discovered a camp of about thirteen Wacos concealed in the trees on the east bank of the Colorado River, about fifteen miles above present-day Columbus, Texas. Late that evening, the posse crept up to the camp. The plan was to surround the Indians and wait for dawn, but when Joseph saw a warrior stand up very close to him, he fired. The Waco let out a loud scream as he fell, and the other warriors all jumped up. Tumlinson's posse blasted away. In a few minutes, twelve Indians were dead, only one having escaped into the brush.[5]

9–10 August 1823
ARIKARA VILLAGES (*Mobridge, South Dakota*)

On 22 June 1823 Col. Henry Leavenworth departed Fort Atkinson with 230 officers and soldiers of the Sixth U.S. Infantry, determined to punish the Arikara Indians for their assault on William H. Ashley and his fur trappers (see Ashley's Fight, 2 June 1823). Leavenworth's entourage included five regular infantry companies, one rifle company, three keelboats of supplies, ten boatmen, and two six-pounder howitzers. Maj. Abram Woolley commanded the flotilla. Two days behind Leavenworth, two additional keelboats carried Joshua Pilcher of the Missouri Fur Company with about fifty men, a five-inch howitzer, and more supplies. Leavenworth and Pilcher combined their forces on 27 June, and three days later they joined with Ashley, his partner Andrew Henry, and their eighty men at the Cheyenne River camp.

The trappers divided into two companies of forty men each, with Jedediah Smith and Hiram Smith as captains. Pilcher, designated major by Leavenworth, also formed his men into companies. Pilcher's officers included Capt. William Henry Vanderburgh, two lieutenants, and Angus McDonald, in command of the Indian auxiliaries. The latter included 500 Sioux warriors and 250 of their family members; one-third of the warriors were armed with muskets.

On 9 August Leavenworth prepared to attack the Arikaras. He ordered the mounted Sioux to stop the Arikaras if they tried to leave the villages. Vanderburgh's men poled the five keelboats upstream while Leavenworth formed his lines, placing Ashley and the trappers on the extreme right, four companies of infantry in the center, and Capt. Bennet Riley and his riflemen on the far left. All were poised to attack the unsuspecting Arikaras, who were going about their business in the fields outside the fortified villages. But the Sioux advance party, who were scattered in front of the troops, obstructed Leavenworth's line of fire. The Sioux fought the Arikaras for an hour before the troops could get into a clear firing position. By then, the Arikaras had taken refuge behind the palisades of their villages, with the Sioux close on their heels. Leavenworth halted his line 400 yards in front of the villages.

The Sioux had killed from ten to fifteen Arikaras and suffered two killed and seven wounded. They were gloating over the Arikaras' apparent weakness and mutilating their enemy's bodies as Leavenworth approached. One Sioux woman pummeled an Arikara body; a warrior, mimicking a bear, crawled up to another body and tore mouthfuls of flesh from the man's chest.

The boats with the artillery arrived at the scene near nightfall. Day two began with Leavenworth's assault on the villages. Riley's riflemen and one company of infantry led by Lt. John Bradley took on the upper village. They also had one six-pounder, commanded by Sergeant Perkins. Leavenworth went after the lower village with the remainder of the soldiers. Ashley and his trappers were on the far right; Lt. William W. Morris with the other six-pounder and the howitzer were next to Ashley. The rest of the Sixth Infantrymen and the Indian auxiliaries brought up the rear. The first shells overshot the village and landed in the river, but corrections soon brought the shells on target. In the lower village, Chief Grey Eyes was killed and many structures were damaged.

In the end, however, Leavenworth proved to be an ineffective commander. He proposed that Riley assault the upper village, breach the stockade to check out the defenses, and withdraw to attack later with the full strength of the troops. Meanwhile, the trappers under Ashley were to distract the lower village by firing on it. The strategy—sending in a risky partial assault just to test the enemy's capabilities, then intentionally withdrawing—made little sense.

Leavenworth had second thoughts, fearing that if the Sioux saw Riley withdrawing from the upper village, they might think the whites were admitting defeat, possibly causing the Sioux to desert or join the Arikaras. Although he had already positioned his troops, Leavenworth canceled the assault. As the artillery intermittently fired on both villages, with unclear results, the colonel continued to vacillate for two days. The Sioux, losing interest, plundered the Arikaras' crops while they waited for something to happen.

Leavenworth finally decided to attack the lower village, but he discovered that Morris's troops had run out of round shot, so he withdrew

Riley's men from the upper village to support the assault. When he told the Sioux his new plan of action, they disappeared. Later Leavenworth spotted them conferring with the Arikaras and joined the parley, where he learned that the Arikaras wanted peace.

Leavenworth negotiated with Chief Little Soldier and some other lower-village chiefs. The Arikaras promised to return five hostages as well as Ashley's stolen property. In addition, they agreed to allow unmolested navigation of the Missouri and to treat Americans entering Arikara lands as friends. As it turned out, however, the only items Ashley got back were three rifles, a horse, and eighteen robes. Leavenworth demanded that Chief Little Soldier return the rest. Unable to comply—most of Ashley's horses and pelts were long gone—Little Soldier begged for peace, even offering to act as an informant.

While all this was taking place, the troopers and trappers were losing patience with their commander's inaction. A scuffle ensued between Pilcher's half-Sioux interpreter, Colin Campbell, and an Arikara. The Indians broke off talks and retreated to their village. Leavenworth was in a quandary. At the urging of his officers, the colonel agreed to resume the attack if the Indians did not accept the peace terms. But he never got the chance. That night, the Arikaras abandoned the villages and fled. Even the Sioux rode away, but not before stealing several horses and mules from the soldiers and trappers. In the abandoned villages, Leavenworth found only Chief Grey Eyes's aged mother, about fifty dogs, and one rooster.

The Missouri Fur Company men left on 15 August. In defiance of Leavenworth's wishes, two of Pilcher's men, Angus McDonald and William Gordon, set fire to the empty villages. An angry Leavenworth denounced the trappers and reprimanded Pilcher. Pilcher responded with equal fervor, "You have by the imbecility of your conduct and operations, created and left impassable barriers" to peace with the Indians.[6]

After the expedition, Leavenworth estimated that about fifty Arikaras had been killed. According to Pilcher, the total was closer to twenty. Leavenworth deemed the operation a success, stating, "The blood of our countrymen has been honorably avenged, the Arikarees humbled, and in such manner as will teach them and the [other] Indian tribes to respect the American name and character."[7] Most of the men disagreed with his assessment and viewed the operation as a fiasco.[8]

— 1824 —

September 1824
JONES CREEK *(Jones Creek, Texas)*

Stephen Austin's colonists faced numerous Indian raids while establishing their new homes on the Texas Gulf Coast. After Karankawas attacked a group of settlers in the summer of 1824, Austin authorized a retaliation. Capt. Randal Jones and twenty-three men canoed down the Brazos in pursuit of the raiders. Near Matagorda Bay they learned from some Karankawas that the band responsible had gone upstream to Bailey's Store, about five miles west of present-day Angleton, Texas, to get supplies and ammunition. Jones sent a few local colonists to Bailey's to learn the raiders' whereabouts and to recruit more volunteers.

The settlers who lived near Bailey's Store were already worried that the Karankawa band had bought the ammunition to use against them. They formed an armed band, and at dawn they fired on the Indians' camp, killing and wounding a few of them and driving the rest away.

In the meantime, Jones was bivouacked on a stream about half a mile from present-day Jones Creek, Texas, unaware that the main Karankawa camp was nearby. When the Indians involved in the fight at Bailey's returned to the main camp, they began lamenting their dead and wounded. The cries were so loud that Jones was able to pinpoint the camp's location. He crossed the creek about half a mile above the camp and waited for daybreak.

Jones's dawn attack surprised the warriors, but they quickly recovered, hiding in the tall marsh grass and returning fire. In a short while, the Texans found they were in trouble. The warriors kept up a withering fire from the marsh; Singer, Bailey, and Spencer were killed, and many were wounded. After weighing the Texans' chances, Jones decided to retreat.

Jones estimated that they had killed fifteen warriors. The battle was later said to have made the Karankawas "more hostile and troublesome."[9]

October 1824
PROVOST'S HOLE *(Provo, Utah)*

Born in 1785, Etienne Provost was one of the older mountain men to establish himself as a trapper in the southern Rockies. With partner Francois LeClerc, he set up business in Taos in 1822. But the area had a glut of trappers and traders, and the beaver population was declining, so in 1823 the partners went north to try their luck on the Green River

9

in the Uinta Basin. The venture was a success, and they returned the following year.

In September 1824 the Provost-LeClerc brigade set up camp near the junction of the White and Green Rivers, then Provost led a party of ten men west over the Wasatch Mountains. In October Provost and his men stopped on the shores of Utah Lake, near the town and river that would later take Provost's name, anglicized to Provo. As they worked their way along the Jordan River, between Utah Lake and Great Salt Lake, the trappers met a band of Shoshones who were camped in the area. A recent confrontation with Hudson's Bay Company trappers had soured the Indians' mood: that summer, in a skirmish with Alexander Ross, one of their chiefs had been killed. Unknown to the trappers, the Indians planned revenge.

Some of the Shoshones, led by a chief whose name was rendered as Bad Left-Handed One, discovered Provost's men along the Jordan River. The chief came up with a plan. He invited the trappers into a council lodge to smoke the peace pipe. There he explained that sacred custom prohibited metal objects in the room during the ceremony. The trappers obligingly stacked their arms outside. As the pipe was passed, the chief signaled, and his warriors drew hidden knives and lunged at the trappers. Within seconds the melee was over. Eight trappers were killed; only Provost and one companion managed to escape into the mountains, eventually making it back to their base camp.[10]

— 1826 —

4 April 1826
ROSS CREEK (*LaGrange, Texas*)
In March 1826 a band of Towakonis rode into the area along the Colorado River in present-day Fayette County, Texas. Reportedly they were there hunting for Tankawa enemies, who were said to be cannibals. Eventually, the Tawakonis stole some horses and killed a Mexican resident. When word of this got around, Colorado militia captain James Ross assembled a party of thirty-one militiamen—including John J. Tumlinson Jr., John Cryer, and S. A. Anderson—to look for the Indians.

To protect themselves from a cold northern wind, the band of sixteen Tawakonis had made camp in a wooded bend of Ross Creek near its junction with the Colorado, about seven miles downriver from present-day LaGrange. Not expecting trouble, several were lying down, a few were parching corn, and a few others were later described to have been "dancing around with their scalps."[11] In a flash, Ross's militiamen killed eight Indians, and they believed they wounded seven of the eight who escaped. The men set fire to the bodies, leaving the smoldering bones to bleach in the creek bed.[12] A later settler recalled finding the skeletons lying "grim and ghastly on the green grass."[13]

— 1827 —

January 1827
YOUNG'S FIGHT ON THE GILA *(Phoenix, Arizona)*

Trapping and trading partners Ewing Young and William Wolfskill had been ranging throughout the Taos country for about four years when they concluded that the area was overrun with competition. Eager to seek new horizons, Young proclaimed, "I want to get outside of where trappers have ever been."[14]

In the fall of 1826, Young and Wolfskill organized an expedition of some twelve to eighteen men to follow the Gila River to its junction with the Colorado. Near Santa Fe, Young, who was ill, remained behind while Wolfskill led the brigade, which included Thomas L. Smith and Milton Sublette, down the Gilato to its junction with the Salt River. Here a scuffle with some Apaches ensued. The Indians shot Sublette in the leg with an arrow and stole the party's traps. As Smith rescued Sublette, Wolfskill retreated. Meanwhile Alexander Branch reportedly killed two Apaches with one bullet.

In January, the expedition pushed out again from the Santa Rita River, this time with Young in the lead. Young intended not only to take beaver, but also to punish the Indians for the autumn attack. Near the junction of the Gila and Salt, they found three members of Miguel Robidoux's trapping party, including Robidoux and James Ohio Pattie, survivors of a recent fierce assault. Pattie identified the attackers as Papagoes, but they were more likely Apaches or Yavapais. Soon afterward, the trappers discovered the mutilated bodies of Robidoux's men and vowed revenge.

A few days later, Young found an Indian village, probably Apache. During the night, he deployed his men around the village, and at sunrise, the trappers somehow lured the warriors into a trap. As soon as the first Indian appeared, Tom Smith fired and killed him, then ran forward to scalp him. The other trappers opened fire, killing several more warriors.

The rest of the villagers escaped to the mountains. The next day, a few of the Indians appeared, offering to make peace. Young, satisfied with his revenge, departed down the Gila believing that he had taught the Indians a lesson. In fact, fighting between whites and the Apaches and Yavapais would go on for another six decades.[15]

March 1827
YOUNG'S FIGHT ON THE COLORADO
(Mohave Valley, Arizona)

After making "peace" with the local Indians (see previous entry), Ewing Young divided his trappers into two divisions. One ventured upstream on the Salt River, the other went upstream on the Gila. Both then worked their way back down to meet at the rivers' junction. The reunited brigade trapped down the Gila to the Colorado. Encountering no trouble with the Yuma Indians in the area, they moved leisurely up the Colorado, finding good hunting along the way.

When the trappers reached the Mojave villages across the river from present-day Needles, California, however, tensions increased. The Indians were apparently friendly by day, but Young sensed it was a facade. One night, Indians fired arrows into the trappers' camp, riddling the sleeping gear of James O. Pattie with sixteen barbs but without striking him. Convinced of the Indians' animosity, Young had his men build a wooden stockade around the camp. The Mojaves visited the white men daily, and one day the Indians challenged the trappers to a shooting contest. When one chief shot an arrow into a small tree, Young split the arrow with a bullet from his rifle, and the Indians sullenly departed.

The next morning, Mojave warriors attacked the stockade, but Young and his men were ready and waiting. They fought the charging Indians, killing sixteen, wounding several others, and sending them into retreat. Regardless of his victory, Young knew he could not stay in the area any longer.

The trappers traveled upriver for four days, keeping a watchful guard at night. The next night Young relaxed his vigilance, and sure enough, the Mojaves attacked, this time killing two trappers and wounding two others. The eighteen remaining trappers pursued the Indians on horseback. They caught up with their attackers and killed a small number of them. In an attempt to discourage further aggression, they hung the Mojaves' bodies from trees. Young and his party then departed Mojave country, leaving ill will in their wake.[16]

18 August 1827
MOJAVE MASSACRE *(Needles, California)*

On 13 July 1827 a group of eighteen fur trappers, led by Jedediah Smith, left the Bear Lake Rendezvous, in present-day Utah, to head back to California, where they had left the other men in their brigade the previous year.[17] Following portions of the Old Spanish Trail, Smith reached the Colorado River, where he met a band of Mojave Indians he had traded with in the past. The trappers decided to stop for a few days to trade with the seemingly friendly Indians for fresh horses and some supplies. Their visit to the first village was uneventful, and at the second village, Smith and his men built some cane-grass rafts, which they planned to use to cross the river.

At dawn on 18 August, Smith and eight of his men loaded supplies on the rafts and started across the Colorado. The rest of the men waited at the Indian village with all the horses and the remaining supplies, which were to be ferried across on a second trip. Suddenly, onshore, a few hundred Mojaves charged in and attacked the men on the bank. Ten trappers, caught completely unawares, were immediately killed.[18] The raiders also took some of the village women prisoner.

From the middle of the river, Smith watched helplessly. Thinking quickly, he landed the rafts on a sandbar and told his men to spread out most of their goods on the ground, hoping the Indians would stop there to collect the booty. Then, hastily packing whatever essential supplies they could carry on their backs, the trappers fled. The trappers had traveled only about half a mile when the Indians began to close in. They retreated to a cottonwood thicket and hurriedly constructed a frail breastwork out of nearby saplings. The party had only five guns; several of the men constructed makeshift lances from their hunting knives. Smith ordered that only three weapons should be fired at a time, and then only if the target was certain.

The Indians approached the barrier cautiously, remaining mostly hidden except to intentionally draw fire. Nevertheless, Smith's marksmen killed two Mojaves and wounded another, which quickly dampened the Indians' eagerness to attack. Two of the trappers, Isaac Galbraith and Thomas Virgin, were wounded in the fighting. Although the Mojaves still hovered, as night fell, the trappers crept out and made their escape. Fleeing to the desert, they traveled for nine days, finally reaching a ranch in the San Bernardino Valley on 28 August.

The overseer of the San Bernardino Rancho was hospitable, and Smith was able to obtain horses for all his men. The wounded trappers stayed behind to heal as Smith took off for another expedition.[19]

— 1828 —

14 July 1828
UMPQUA MASSACRE *(Reedsport, Oregon)*

After his experience with the Mojaves, Jedediah Smith (see previous entry) decided to head back east on a different route, exploring and trapping in the Oregon country along the way. On 13 July 1828 Smith and his nineteen men reached the Umpqua River, just above its mouth, and set up camp on a tributary that was later named for Smith. Some Kuitsh (lower Umpqua) Indians approached the encampment to trade. Smith was circumspect, since he had recently had an uncomfortable encounter with a chief of this tribe. The chief had stolen an ax from Smith, and Smith had tied him up and demanded he return the item. The chief complied and was released unharmed but greatly humiliated. Smith cautioned his men to be on guard.

The next day, Smith, John Turner, Richard Leland, and an Indian guide took a canoe upriver to find a suitable crossing. As soon as they departed, the remaining trappers, despite Smith's warning, allowed approximately 100 Indians into the camp to trade. When Smith returned from his excursion near midday, the camp appeared to be abandoned. The Indian guide suddenly sprang forward in the canoe, grabbed Smith's rifle, and dove into the river. Simultaneously, a number of Indians appeared on the shore and opened fire on the three trappers in the canoe. The three paddled furiously for the opposite bank and raced into the woods. Looking back on the campsite from a nearby hill, Smith concluded that his men must have been overrun. Smith and his two companions headed for Fort Vancouver, about ninety miles north, hoping for help from the Hudson's Bay Company.

Meanwhile, one trapper, Arthur Black, had survived the massacre. After stumbling through the woods, he finally emerged on the beach. He scuffled with an Indian who tried to take his knife, but Black got away. Later seven warriors relieved the trapper of his clothing, then began to argue over his fate; while the Indians were thus distracted, Black bolted for the woods and escaped. He ran north until he reached Tillamook Bay, where some friendly Indians provided him with a guide. On the night of

8 August, Black arrived at Fort Vancouver, where he told John McLoughlin of the attack. McLoughlin sent out a party to search for survivors.

Smith and his companions arrived at Fort Vancouver two days later, and Black recounted to them what had happened. He said that while the men were cleaning and drying their guns after a severe thunderstorm, 100 warriors rushed them. Two of the Indians, trying to wrest Black's gun from him, slashed his hands with their knives. One tried to ax him in the head, but he lunged away, and the ax instead landed in his back. Dropping his gun, Black bolted for the woods. During the fight, he had seen several of his fellow trappers axed to death.

On 28 October the men from Fort Vancouver, led by Alexander R. McLeod, arrived at the battlesite, where they found eleven skeletons. This left four men unaccounted for. Later they heard a rumor that four trappers had been taken prisoner by the Cahoose Indians. While this may have been the case, the four were never heard from again. After five months of scouring the countryside, McLeod returned with about 700 beaver skins, thirty-nine horses, and two journals—but no rescued survivors.[20]

— 1829 —

October 1829
SALT RIVER *(Fort Apache, Arizona)*

When Ewing Young returned to Taos from the 1826–27 trapping season, which he'd spent in Mexican territory, the governor of New Mexico seized all his furs. At that time, U.S. citizens were not allowed to trap in Mexico. Undaunted, Young arranged for another party to the Gila River in 1828. This time, Apaches drove the trappers back to Taos.

In August 1829 Ewing Young tried again to trap in Mexico, this time with a brigade of forty men, including Americans, Frenchmen, and Canadians. To fool the governor, Young went north fifty miles into Colorado's San Luis Valley, as if he were leaving Mexico, then turned southwest and headed for the Zuni Pueblo. From there, he continued southwest to the junction of the Black River and the White River, which form the Salt River in the vicinity of present-day Fort Apache, Arizona. Indians had attacked trappers in this area the previous year, so the men kept their eyes open as they worked their traps along the majestic orange and yellow canyons of the Salt.

One day the trappers spotted some approaching Indians, so Young ordered most of his men to hide behind bushes, under blankets, and among the pack saddles. According to one of the trappers, a young apprentice named Kit Carson, there on his first expedition, "The hills were covered with Indians, and seeing so few of us they concluded to make an attack and drive us from our position." At Young's command, his men rose from their hiding places and blasted the charging Apaches, who stopped in their tracks and turned to retreat, but not before, as Carson reported, "having fifteen or twenty warriors killed and a great number wounded."[21]

After this victory, their way temporarily cleared, Young's men continued trapping down the Salt to the Verde River, where they worked their way upstream. Along much of the trappers' trek up the Verde, however, Indians frequently crept into their camp to steal traps, occasionally killing a horse or mule. At the head of the Verde, the brigade divided, half taking the furs back to Taos and the other half heading to California.[22]

Canyon of the Salt River, Arizona

— 1830 —

August 1830

MISSION SAN JOSE *(San Jose, California)*

After splitting up his brigade of fur trappers in the fall of 1829 (see previous entry), Ewing Young led half of his men west and north to hunt in California's San Joaquin Valley. The streams flowing west out of the Sierra Nevada were once well stocked with beaver, but in the spring of 1830, a large brigade from Hudson's Bay Company had thinned them out. Young's company went north for a while to trap up the Sacramento Valley, then traveled back down to San Francisco Bay.

In the summer of 1830, hoping to expedite selling his furs to ocean-going traders in the bay, Young decided to ingratiate himself with the Mexican authorities at the San Jose Mission. He thought of a way that he and his men might be of service to the Mexicans. Mission Indians at San Jose had recently rebelled against Father Narciso Duran's strict physical and spiritual directives and fled to the Sierra Nevada foothills. A small contingent of Mexican soldiers had tried but failed to find the renegades. Young's men, experienced frontiersmen, might be able to help track them down.

Young sent twelve men, including the young Kit Carson, to accompany a second contingent of Mexican soldiers. They soon found the runaway's camp and stopped to planned their strategy. In Carson's words: "We returned to the village and made an attack and fought for one entire day. The Indians were routed, and lost a great number of men. We entered the village in triumph, set fire to it, and burned it to the ground."[23] They recovered the escapees and returned them to the mission, pleasing Father Duran.

Young used the goodwill to approach trader Don Jose Acero, whose schooner was in the bay. Young sold his furs to Acero and in turn bought horses from him, and the trappers readied to head out. But before they left, a small band of Indian raiders attacked their camp and ran off sixty horses, many of which Young had just purchased. The angry trappers recovered fourteen of their stock in the morning, then rode out to get the rest. An armed party of twelve trailed the raiders about 100 miles to the Sierra Nevada. Carson recounted the episode: "We surprised the Indians while they were feasting off some of our animals they had killed. We charged their camp, killed eight Indians, took three children prisoners and recovered all our animals, with the exception of six that were eaten."[24]

With all business finished, Young's brigade finally left the mission on 1 September and headed back to Taos.[25]

— 1831 —

Date unknown, ca. 1831
LIVE OAK BAYOU/BATTLE ISLAND
(Matagorda, Texas)

Elisha Flowers and Charles Cavina (or Cavanaugh), along with their families, were among the first emigrants to join Stephen Austin's colony. Both families settled near Live Oak Bayou, which empties into East Matagorda Bay. In 1831 about seventy Karankawa Indians attacked the area.[26] They ransacked Cavina's cabin after killing his wife and three daughters. Flowers's wife, who had been visiting the Cavinas, was also killed. A little girl, perhaps the daughter of Flowers, survived despite a serious arrow wound.

Charles Cavina, returning from a trip with two of his slaves, witnessed the Indians plundering his cabin. Being unarmed, he ran off to warn Flowers, but he arrived too late. The Karankawas had already murdered Elisha Flowers and the remainder of his family.

Cavina immediately set out to raise a militia to pursue the Karankawas. About sixty men gathered, choosing Aylett C. Buckner—a soldier of fortune, filibusterer, and duelist—as their captain. This company trailed the Karankawas west to an island near the mouth of the Colorado River, near present-day Matagorda. One of the militiamen, Moses Morrison, crept up to a high bank overlooking the Indians' position. When he leaned over for a better look, the ledge crumbled, sending him tumbling down about forty feet into the camp. Though dazed, Morrison quickly recovered and shot at the nearest warrior. He then dove into a hole in the riverbank, from which he fended off the Indians.

Buckner heard the shots and swept into the fight with the remaining men. Some Karankawa warriors scrambled to save their families, giving Buckner's men an advantage. Buckner's party killed many Indians on the island and others in the river; women and children were hit in the process. A militiaman named Williams recalled shooting a warrior who sprang up from behind some driftwood. When he later investigated, he discovered to his "surprise and regret" that he had in fact killed a woman with a baby on her back.[27]

By the time the fighting ended, between forty and fifty Karankawas were dead. The Colorado River was said to be "literally red with blood."[28] Later, a treaty was signed at the site, which the locals named Battle Island.[29]

22 November 1831
BOWIE'S SAN SABA FIGHT *(Menard, Texas)*

Renowned frontiersman and adventurer James Bowie arrived in Texas in 1830. He soon became interested in the "lost" Los Almagres Mine, said to be located somewhere around the Santa Cruz de San Saba Mission ruins west of San Antonio, near present-day Menard. After Bowie obtained permission from Mexican authorities to enter the country, his brother Rezin rode in from Louisiana to join the search. On 2 November 1831, they left San Antonio with nine companions: Robert Armstrong, David Buchanan, Jesse Wallace, Thomas McCaslin, Matthew Doyle, Caiaphas K. Ham, James Coryell, and two servants.

The "lost" silver mine the Texans sought was believed to be guarded by Indians, whose ancestors had killed previous adventurers who had

San Saba Mission ruins, Menard, Texas

come to the area in 1758. The prospectors unknowingly passed the mine site, in the Riley Mountains in present-day Llano County, while heading for the old smelting site at the San Saba Mission.

Nineteen days after the group left San Antonio, Bowie learned from some friendly Comanches that a war party of about 160 Wacos, Caddos, and Tawakonis was following them, intending to kill them all. The men pushed on toward the old mission, camping that night in an oak grove six miles from their destination.[30] Keeping an eye out for the Indians, they carved out a defensive position amid a thicket of small trees and prickly pears. They saw no sign of their enemies overnight, but as they packed to move out the next morning, the warriors struck.

At sixteen-to-one, the odds were not promising for the Texans, so Rezin Bowie and Buchanan signaled to the Indians for a parley. They walked to within forty yards of the Indians when the warriors rose up and fired at them, wounding Buchanan in the leg. Rezin fired his shotgun, then hurried his companion back toward the camp. Buchanan was hit twice more on the retreat.

Some of the warriors charged the camp with tomahawks, but the Texans' rifles held them off, killing four and chasing away the rest. When the Indians charged again, Ham hit a mounted warrior who appeared to be the chief. The other Texans shot him down, along with several others who came to bear his body away. Jim Bowie killed another mounted warrior, and the Indians fell back once more.

The battle heated up again when a new wave of warriors crept up along a creek bank in the Texans' rear. Firing from forty yards away, the Indians shot Doyle through the chest, then hit McCaslin as he came out to rescue his comrade. Bowie had his men pull back to the cactus and thickets by the riverbank, where they drove off the nearest warriors. Bowie had his men shoot, then roll several yards to a new spot to shoot again, hoping to baffle the Indians as to the men's numbers and positions. After a few hours, the Indians tried to burn them out, but the Texans cleared the grass around them and piled up rocks as a fire barrier, then threw sand at the flames. When the wind shifted, the miners beat the flames out with buffalo hides and blankets.

With most of their cover burned away, the Texans were left with little defense but their earth-and-rock perimeter. Nevertheless, the Indians had become discouraged. They had been fighting for thirteen hours, and still the Texans kept up a steady fire. At sunset the Indians finally backed off. Bowie's men heard baleful wails of mourning throughout the night.

Sunrise brought no new attack. When they crept out to investigate, the Texans found forty-eight bloody spots on the ground where the Indians had camped the night. Bowie's men figured they had killed and wounded about eighty, and the Indians reported fifty-two killed. Bowie had his men remain where they were for eight days, until the wounded recovered enough to be moved. The friendly Comanches, not believing that Bowie's men could have survived the attack, had already spread word that they had all perished. When all eleven of them arrived in San Antonio, it was as if they had returned from the dead. Their astounding victory was celebrated with great rejoicing.[31]

— 1832 —

18 July 1832
PIERRE'S HOLE *(Victor, Idaho)*
After the July 1832 rendezvous at Pierre's Hole, a valley on the west side of the Trois Tetons, the traders and trappers dispersed. Milton Sublette and Henry Fraeb, together with twenty-two other trappers, joined up with Alexander Sinclair and his fifteen men, plus Nathaniel J. Wyeth and his ten eastern greenhorns. They traveled southwest, planning to traverse the Snake River Mountains and wend their way to the Humboldt River to start their fall hunt.

On 18 July, about eight miles from the rendezvous site, the party spotted 150 to 200 Gros Ventres emerging from a mountain gap directly ahead. Two of the trappers immediately returned to Pierre's Hole for reinforcements. The women and children in the Indian group ran for shelter in the nearby mountains as the warriors got ready to attack the trappers.

In a commonly used maneuver to gain time to prepare for battle, a chief carrying a peace pipe walked forward to greet the trappers. Antoine Godin, a mixed-blood Iroquois in Sublette's employ, and a Flathead scout rode out to meet the chief. Realizing the peace gesture was a ploy, Godin firmly grasped the chief's extended hand and yelled "Fire!" to his companion, who killed the chief instantly. Godin and the Flathead scalped the chief, took his colorful blanket, and sprinted back with their trophies.

The Indians ran to a nearby marsh of willows and cottonwoods, threw up a breastwork of timber, and set the women to work digging trenches behind the barrier. The trappers believed the position was too well defended to attempt an immediate charge, so they chose to begin shooting at long range. Meanwhile, Sublette and his men fortified themselves in a nearby natural trench, and Wyeth secured his inexperienced men behind packs they'd removed from the mules.

Before long, the reinforcements arrived, including William Sublette, brother of Milton, and more than 100 trappers, along with 400 Nez Perces and Flatheads, enemies of the Gros Ventres, all ready to fight. The newly arrived Sublette plunged into the grove with Wyeth, Sinclair, Robert Campbell, and about sixty other men. Sinclair was shot dead while Sublette, spying an Indian peering from behind the fortification, shot the warrior in the eye and received a bullet in the arm in return. The trappers formed a crescent on two sides of the Indians' breastwork. In spite of cross-fire danger, Milton Sublette successfully attacked the Gros Ventres' rear while Flatheads and Nez Perces attacked their flanks.

Some Flatheads breached the fortification and emerged with a blanket and a few other spoils. One of Fraeb's men, slightly intoxicated, indulged an impulse to scale the breastwork; two bullets struck him in the cranium. When ammunition ran low, the trappers started to set the timber that surrounded the Gros Ventres on fire. The allied Indians were displeased, for this meant the booty they wanted would go up in flames, and they convinced the trappers to cease.

Fearing defeat, the Gros Ventres yelled out that although they might perish, they had 400 lodges nearby who would retaliate. Their taunts were mistranslated: the trappers thought the rendezvous site was already being attacked. Most of the trappers raced to Pierre's Hole to lend assistance, while a small number remained to guard the Gros Ventres. A few hours later, after nightfall, the trappers returned, somewhat worse for wear.

At daybreak the trappers discovered the Gros Ventres had escaped. Investigating behind the breastwork, the company found about thirty dead horses, nine dead Gros Ventres, a wounded Indian woman—who was readily slain by a Flathead—and an unknown wounded white man, who soon died. The nearby woods were littered with other Gros Ventre bodies. The Gros Ventres later claimed that only twenty-six of their tribe had been killed. On the trappers' side, five trappers and seven allied Indians were killed; six trappers and seven allied Indians were wounded.[32]

14 October 1832
VANDERBURGH MASSACRE *(Alder, Montana)*
The Rocky Mountain fur trade was developing into a cutthroat business, and independent traders were slowly losing out to large companies. The Rocky Mountain Fur Company, formed in 1830 by Thomas Fitzpatrick,

Milton Sublette, Jim Bridger, Henry Fraeb, and Jean Gervais, was being dogged by the larger American Fur Company, owned by John Jacob Astor. Astor sent William Henry Vanderburgh and Andrew Drips to trace Fitzpatrick and Bridger's footsteps and learn the locations of their prime beaver lands. Crossing and recrossing the mountains and rivers of Montana, the American Fur men trapped all their rival's streams. Fitzpatrick and Bridger tried time and again to shake Astor's men off their tail, but they couldn't do it. Finally, realizing that both companies were losing the entire trapping season playing hide-and-seek, the competitors agreed to split up the territory and get back to business.

Vanderburgh left the Three Forks area to trap the Madison River, Drips went to the Jefferson, and Fitzpatrick and Bridger moved up the Gallatin. After some fruitless trapping, Vanderburgh turned west to team up with Drips. His small brigade crossed the Greenhorn Range and headed down Alder Creek. Somewhere in the vicinity of present-day Alder, Montana, they ran into trouble. On 14 October, a trapper found a butchered buffalo, which alerted the party that Indians were in the area. The understandably nervous trappers wanted an investigation, so Vanderburgh and six men set out to look for Indians. Nearby they found a campfire and another butchered buffalo. As Vanderburgh and his men crossed a small gully to reach a grove of trees, a large band of Blackfeet jumped them.

"Suddenly the lightning and thunder of at least twenty fusils burst upon our astonished senses from the gully," wrote Vanderburgh's clerk, Warren Ferris. Vanderburgh's horse was shot and fell on him, but he pulled himself free and called out, "Don't run, boys!" as he shot the nearest Indian. The warriors fired a volley at him and he fell. "They uttered a loud and shrill yell of exultation," Ferris recalled, "and the noble spirit of a good and brave man had passed away forever."[33] After the trappers fled, the Blackfeet stripped Vanderburgh's flesh from his bones, chopped off his arms, and threw his remains into the stream.

The trappers were lucky to escape with relatively few casualties. Only Vanderburgh and one Canadian trapper were killed, and two were wounded, including Ferris, who took a bullet in the shoulder. The trappers made it back to camp, then hastily moved to safer territory. The Rocky Mountain Fur Company now had one less rival.[34]

— 1833 —

Winter 1833

DEATH OF HUGH GLASS *(Bighorn, Montana)*

The legendary trapper Hugh Glass is remembered mainly for his survival story following a grizzly attack. As part of William H. Ashley's trapping expedition of 1823, Glass was severely mauled by a bear in present-day South Dakota. While the rest of the brigade continued on, John S. Fitzgerald and a seventeen-year-old James Bridger stayed behind to care for Glass and give him a decent burial when he died. Shortly afterward, however, they changed their minds. Tired of waiting and worried about Indians, the pair abandoned him. Regaining consciousness, Glass crawled 300 miles along the Grand River to the Missouri, eventually reaching safety at Fort Kiowa, where he vowed vengeance. He later found Bridger while traveling to the Yellowstone River, but Glass spared him because of his youth.

In 1832 Glass was employed by Kenneth McKenzie of the American Fur Company at Fort Cass, a trading post for the Crow Indians on the east bank of the Yellowstone, three miles below the mouth of the Bighorn River. Samuel Tulloch, in charge of the fort, sent Glass, Edward Rose, and a man called Menard to carry a message to the company headquarters at Fort Union, near the junction of the Yellowstone and Missouri Rivers. The three knew the territory well; Rose had lived with the Crows sporadically since 1807.

At the time, the Arikaras, who had a long-standing feud with white trappers and traders, had penetrated Crow country. As Glass, Rose, and Menard crossed the ice-covered Yellowstone River, thirty Arikara warriors attacked them from the opposite bank. The usually alert mountain men were completely surprised and overwhelmed. Out on the ice, they had nowhere to hide. The Arikaras killed and scalped the three men and took their clothes and supplies.

Sometime later, trapper Johnson Gardner and his men, camping on Powder River, discovered a band of Arikaras trying to steal their horses. After a brief scuffle, the trappers captured three of them. Gardner noticed that one of the warriors had a distinctively decorated knife that had belonged to Glass. Soon afterward, a group of Arikaras—one of whom had another of Glass's belongings, a rifle—approached the trappers to barter for the return of the captives. Gardner demanded that his stolen horses be returned, but the Indians refused and left, sealing the fate of their captive tribesmen. The three captives began their soulful death songs, then attempted to run for their lives. One managed to escape, but the other two were gunned down, and Gardner scalped them. Later he would make a gift of one of the scalps to visiting dignitary Maximilian of Wied-Neuwied.[35]

Ca. 7 September 1833
BARREN RIVER MASSACRE *(Lovelock, Nevada)*

Born in Tennessee in 1798, Joseph Reddeford Walker was described by one historian as possibly the greatest of all mountain men. In 1832 Walker joined Benjamin L. E. Bonneville's new fur-trading operation. After an unsuccessful first year, Bonneville sought to recoup his losses by sending Walker on a trapping and exploring expedition to California. The Walker expedition proved to be one of the most valuable explorations of the West in history.

Walker left the Green River, in present-day Wyoming, on 27 July 1833 with about forty men. At the Bear River about twenty free trappers joined him for the adventure. The combined party included Joe Meek, Bill Craig, Bill Williams, Alexis Godey, George Nidever, Antoine Janise, and Zenas Leonard. During the trip, the men explored the shores of Great Salt Lake and ultimately debunked the notion of a fabled river, the Buenaventura, thought to lead from the lake to the Pacific Ocean.

After talking with some Bannocks, Walker decided to head directly west from the lake, seeking a shorter route to California. About 1 September, Walker and his party found a river they dubbed the Barren River, so named because, as Leonard put it, "You may travel for many days on the banks of this river, without finding a stick large enough to make a walking cane."[36] This waterway, later called the Humboldt River, would eventually become the main overland route for emigrants to California.

As the expedition traveled downriver, Paiute Indians began stealing the party's beaver traps. The Paiutes, a poor tribe, had taken to pilfering whatever they could from passersby. Many later travelers through the area derisively called them "Digger Indians." But Walker's party may have been the first whites these Indians had ever seen. The Paiutes' continual stealing finally led a few trappers to shoot a couple of the culprits away from Walker's main camp. The Indians naturally sought vengeance, but they had little idea of the destruction that could be wrought by the white men's firearms.

About 7 September, Walker's men reached what would later be called the Humboldt Sink, where the river waters spread over the valley and seep into the sand. Suddenly, several hundred angry Paiutes appeared on all sides of them. Walker ordered his men to make a breastwork out of their packs and supplies, then the trappers took defensive positions and waited. The Indians came to within 150 yards of the little fortification, and five chiefs advanced. Through sign language, they asked to be allowed into the camp to smoke and parley, but Walker refused. The chiefs indicated that they would come in anyway and started forward. Walker signed to them that his men would kill them if they came any closer. The Indians laughed, thinking it impossible to kill anyone from such a distance. Walker realized that they had no conception of firearms. To make his point, Walker gave a shooting demonstration, killing a number of ducks on a nearby pond. The awed Paiutes withdrew.

Walker hoped that this display would dissuade the Paiutes from further harassment, but it did not. As the trappers headed out the next morning, a band of "saucy and bold" warriors appeared in front of them as if to cut them off. Walker determined to get rid of them once and for all. After making one more attempt to disperse them, Walker ordered an attack. Thirty-two of his men dismounted, loaded their weapons, and charged the nearly 100 warriors who blocked their path. The unprepared Indians had no chance. Leonard described the fight:

> We closed in on them and fired, leaving thirty-nine dead on the field—which was nearly half—the remainder were overwhelmed with dismay—running into the high grass in every direction, howling in the most lamentable manner. Captain Walker then gave orders to some of the men to take the bows of the fallen Indians and put the wounded out of misery. The severity with which we dealt with these Indians may be revolting to the heart of the philanthropist; but the circumstances of the case altogether atones for the cruelty.[37]

No one in Walker's party was killed. The expedition continued unmolested to the Sierra Nevada.[38]

— 1835 —

Spring 1835
RIO BLANCO *(Wimberley, Texas)*
In 1833 Missourian John Castleman moved to Texas with his wife, four children, and his wife's mother, settling on the frontier about fifteen miles west of Gonzales. Castleman's homestead, which was protected by

a palisade, became a refuge for travelers on the road between Gonzales and San Antonio.

Castleman owned four ferocious hunting dogs that kept guard over his place. One evening, when a band of Indians crept up to the cabin, the dogs attacked them. Though the Indians killed the dogs, they retreated empty-handed. Castleman found blood all over the area where the dogs had wrecked havoc on the intruders.

In the spring of 1835, a Frenchman named Geser, his two partners, and ten Mexican muleteers and wagoners stopped at Castleman's for the evening. Though Castleman offered to shelter them inside, warning them that he had spotted signs of Indians that day, Geser declined, saying that his men were well armed and could take care of themselves. The party camped at a nearby pond.

The next morning, Comanches attacked. The traders put up a good fight from behind their carts and wagon boxes, but the Indians tightened their circle, and soon Geser and all his men were dead. Watching the fight from his fortified cabin, Castleman wanted to shoot, but his wife insisted that the Indians would leave them alone if he did not kill any of them. As the Comanches left with their booty, Castleman counted eighty warriors ride by. The Indians shook their lances at his cabin, but they did not attack him.

As soon as the Indians were gone, Castleman took his family to Gonzales and spread the alarm. The following morning, thirty volunteers joined up to track the raiders. Some of this posse would become major players in Texas history, including Matthew Caldwell, Daniel McCoy, James C. Darst, Almaron Dickinson, Andrew J. Sowell, David Hanna, and William S. Fisher. Bartlett D. McClure was chosen captain. The Indians' trail led up the Guadalupe River, then north toward present-day San Marcos. The trail was easy to follow because, for unknown reasons, the Indians had tied thread to their horses' tails, letting the spools unwind across the prairie.

After four days the Texans were in the rough country bordering the Rio Blanco, near present-day Wimberly. In the foggy river valley, they heard the whoop of an Indian war cry cutting through the morning mist. McClure ordered a rapid advance in the direction of the sound, but a dense thicket slowed them down, and they had to dismount. They snaked forward in single file, emerging into a small clearing near the river. Just then, shots rang out. "Charge up, boys!" McClure shouted. "Here they are!"[39]

In front, Dickinson, Darst, and McCoy walked right into about fifty warriors and turned around to run. One Indian caught McCoy by the flap of his long-tail coat, but the Texan kept running, throwing his arms back and pulling free of the garment while shouting, "Take it, damn you!"[40]

As the other two came rushing back, they ran into their comrades' line of fire. They dove aside, allowing the others a chance to shoot. McClure killed the leading Indian and Castleman shot the next, but Sowell's flintlock misfired. The Indians ran. The Texans charged after them, chasing them into the clearing. The fighting was chaotic, with men running, leaping, shooting, and dodging. Some of the volunteers recalled that the Indians' whooping was louder than the gunshots.

Most of the warriors seemed more interested in getting their stolen goods across the river than in fighting the Texans. After they had crossed over, most of the Indians kept running, but a few stayed behind to fire from the opposite bank. Sowell, having finally fixed his musket, shot one Comanche as he tried to clamber up a steep bank.

After the fight was over, McClure's men gathered up the stolen property the Indians had dropped and returned to Gonzales. The Texans had suffered only a few minor wounds in the skirmish. The Indians' poor showing was attributed to their having used all their arrows in the attack on Geser's men—several quivers found after the battle were empty or nearly so.[41]

11 July 1835
TEHUACANA SPRINGS (*Tehuacana, Texas*)

Notable pioneer, Indian fighter, and eventual Texas senator George B. Erath once wrote that the war with the Indians began in 1835.[42] That year marked the unfortunate killing of Caddo chief Canoma, which incited many of the region's tribes. Canoma, who had helped Texas settlers on several occasions, was captured in June 1835 under suspicious circumstances, accused of killing a small party of emigrants and stealing their horses. The posse that caught up with Canoma and his companions was divided in opinion as to the Indians' guilt, but it was decided that the captives should be killed, whereupon half the group left in disgust. Canoma's wife was set free, however, and her description of the bloody episode inflamed the Caddos and other Texas tribes.

A short time later, to protect the region's settlements, several companies of militia, or rangers, were raised. One of them was under the command of Robert M. Coleman, who was among the men who had carried out the executions of Canoma and his companions. On 4 July 1835 Coleman, on patrol with about eighteen Robertson Colony volunteers, crossed the Brazos and headed for a Tawakoni village near Tehuacana Springs. Coleman's alleged purpose was to hold a peace council to stop the border fighting, but the Tawakonis, along with some Caddos and Ionis who were camped with them, doubted Coleman's intentions and were on guard.

Versions of the story differ: either Coleman, with no intention of talking to the Indians, instigated the fight, or the Indians fired upon him from a fortified position. One participant, Jesse Halderman, recalled Coleman ordering him to make a stealthy approach and give the attack signal. When some dogs discovered him and began barking, Halderman fired the signal shot and Coleman's men attacked. To their surprise, the Texans found themselves facing a village of about 100 people. After a fight described by some witnesses as "desperate" and lasting several hours, Coleman retreated south, across the Navasota River, to the security of Parker's Fort.

One Texan, John Williams, was killed. Halderman and two others, named Bliss and Wallace, were badly wounded. Coleman reported that he and his men had killed several Indians.[43]

12 November 1835
TAYLOR FAMILY FIGHT *(Little River, Texas)*

By 1833 settlers in Robertson Colony had pushed northwest to the area of present-day Temple, Texas. One of them, Joseph Taylor, had built his place near the Three Forks of the Little River, on the region's outermost frontier. His bride, Nancy Frazier Taylor, along with her two grown daughters and two sons from a previous marriage, moved into Joe's "dogtrot" home—a double log cabin with a covered walkway between the structures. The parents and girls slept in one cabin and the boys in the other.

On the moonlit evening of 12 November, just after the family had gone to bed, a band of eleven Kickapoos approached the home.[44] The Indians, who had recently lost some horses, had been told by some Tonkawas that Joe Taylor had stolen them. The Taylors' dog began barking, but the Kickapoos silenced it with an arrow. Still, the barking had been enough to wake the family. An English-speaking warrior called to Taylor through one of many gaps in the walls, demanding to know how many men were inside. "We have plenty of men, well armed and ready to fight," Joe answered. The Kickapoo looked through the crack and said, "You lie, one man!"[45] Joe jabbed at the Indian's face with a board.

As Nancy pulled open the bedroom door and called to her boys, a shower of arrows and bullets blasted into the room through the gaps. Incredibly, no one was hit. Nancy pushed a table against the cabin door, and her twelve-year-old son climbed on it to fire out from a vent above the door.

Throughout the night, the two girls sat in a safe corner and molded bullets. The Kickapoos circled the cabin, trying to find a convenient crack in the walls through which to fire. When a warrior seized an ax from the shed and entered the breezeway to batter the door, Nancy's younger boy shot him dead. Another warrior tried to retrieve the body, but Joe shot him. Finally the Indians set the back of the cabin on fire, and the flames quickly spread.

Joe thought they should all run outside, figuring that he could bait the Indians while his wife and the children got away in the night. But Nancy refused to run—she would rather her children die than be captured. With the fire progressing, Nancy climbed up on the table and removed some boards and shingles from the roof, then asked the children to hand her cans of milk and vinegar, which she threw onto the advancing flames.

As Nancy worked to extinguish the fire, the Indians tried to steal the family's horses. Joe and his fourteen-year-old stepson, Stephen Frazier, fired from the windows and wounded one or two of them. Then Nancy, spotting a warrior trying to break through a chink by the chimney, threw a shovelful of live coals into his face.

With two warriors dead and several wounded, the Kickapoos finally departed. About an hour later, the family cautiously stepped out of their charred home. They traveled about seven miles to their nearest neighbor, who put them up for a few weeks. The episode had a profound effect on the young Stephen Frazier, who would join a ranger company two months later to seek revenge on the Indians.[46]

— 1836 —

20 January 1836
TUMLINSON'S FIGHT *(Austin, Texas)*

Sarah Creath McSherry Hibbins Stinnet Howard experienced more than her share of Indian trouble. Over a period of thirteen years, she lost three husbands and a child to Indian violence and was herself taken captive once. Born near Brownsville, Illinois, about 1812, Sarah Creath married John McSherry around 1828, and the couple moved to Dewitt's Colony in Texas. Early in 1829, Sarah gave birth to a son, John Jr.

Later that year, Sarah's life was shaken when Indians killed her husband while he was fetching water at a nearby spring. A few years later the young widow married John Hibbins and had another child. While traveling in February 1836, Sarah, John, and the children, along with Sarah's brother, George Creath, camped on Rocky Creek, only about fifteen miles from the Hibbins cabin. Without warning, thirteen Comanches swept down on the camp, and in a few minutes George Creath and John Hibbins were dead. After stealing what they wanted from the settlers' wagon, the Indians tied Sarah, John Jr., and the baby to mules and headed northwest with their captives. The second night out, the younger boy, tired and hungry, began to cry. An angry warrior took the child from Sarah and killed him.[47]

The next day the party camped on Walnut Creek, where the city of Austin now stands. The Indians, perhaps believing that they were too far from a settlement for the captives to escape, let Sarah and her surviving son sleep without a close guard. Sarah saw her chance. She thought her best hope would be to slip away alone, find help, and return to rescue her boy. When the Indians were asleep, she tucked John Jr. under a buffalo robe and slipped away. The night was bitter cold, but she waded down an icy creek so she'd leave no tracks.

Sarah had been following the twisting gullies for about two hours when she heard a cry that sounded like "Mama!" Was it her son? After all her walking, was she still so close to the camp, or were the Indians following her? She turned away from the sound and hurried off in the direction she hoped was south, which would lead her back to the settlements.[48]

After walking for nearly twenty-four hours, her feet frozen and her arms and legs scratched from brambles, Sarah had covered only about ten miles. Ready to drop from exhaustion, she followed some cows to the farmhouse of Jacob Harrell. There she opened the door and collapsed. When she had recovered and was able to tell her story, Harrell hurried her to the nearby cabin of Reuben Hornsby, where a company of sixty Texas Rangers under Capt. John J. Tumlinson Jr. had just arrived and were preparing supper. As ranger Noah Smithwick described the bedraggled Sarah, "her clothes [were] hanging in shreds about her torn and bleeding body."[49]

Sarah told the men what had happened and implored them to find her son. After she described the Indian party and the direction they were traveling, Hornsby guided the rangers northwest up the Colorado River. The men continued on the Indians' trail until it was pitch black, then camped for the night. At first light they were on the move, and they quickly picked up the trail. The Indians must have spent a good deal of the previous day searching for their missing captive, for they had not traveled very far. Nor had they hurried, which indicated that they did not expect to be pursued. "They did not seem to be at all alarmed about the consequence of her escape," Smithwick wrote. "It was about 10 o'clock in the morning when we came upon them, just preparing to break camp."[50]

The rangers charged. Smithwick, on a fleet horse, rode right into the fleeing Indians. A warrior fired at the ranger from behind a tree, but he missed. Having trouble controlling his horse, Smithwick jumped off and chased the Indian on foot. "I fired on him and had the satisfaction of seeing him fall," Smithwick recalled. "My blood was up and, leaving him for dead, I ran on." The Indian was not dead, however; he rose up and fired at Tumlinson, narrowly missing him and killing his horse. Ranger Conrad Rohrer killed the warrior with the butt of his rifle.

Most of the Indians escaped into a thick canebrake. Suddenly a mule carrying something or someone wrapped in a buffalo robe ran past the rangers, and they gave chase. Assuming the robed form was an Indian, Rohrer rode up to the mule, placed his rifle barrel against the robe, and pulled the trigger. The gun misfired. He tried again, with the same result. Before he could attempt it a third time, "one of the other boys, perceiving with horror the tragedy about to be enacted, knocked the gun up, it firing clear, sending a ball whistling over the head" of the intended target, Smithwick reported.[51] Inside the robe, the men discovered, was young John Jr.

Four Comanches were killed. Among the rangers, Elijah Ingram and Hugh M. Childress were wounded. Tumlinson's Fight was the first recorded skirmish between the Texas Rangers and the Comanches.

Late in the afternoon, the rangers rode into Hornsby's, where Lt. Joseph Rogers presented John Jr. to his mother. Tumlinson remembered, "The scene which here ensued beggars description. . . . Not an eye was dry. She called us brothers, and every other endearing name. . . . She hugged the child—her only remaining treasure—to her bosom as if fearful that she would again lose him."

Sarah got married a third time, this time to Claiborne Stinnett, who was also later killed by Indians. After she married her fourth husband, Phillip Howard, in 1840, her son John was nearly captured by the Comanches again. In 1842 the family moved to Lavaca County, where Sarah experienced no more Indian attacks.[52]

26 February 1836
GRAVES'S FIGHT *(Cameron, Texas)*

Land claims were still in dispute in Robertson Colony in 1836, and surveyor Thomas A. Graves hoped to help remedy the situation. In February 1836 he organized a ten-man crew and began surveying the lands along Brushy Creek and the Little River. Most of his party were themselves residents of Robertson Colony, so they were eager to set the record straight about their own land claims.

On Thursday, 25 February, Graves and his men pitched camp in post oak country about eight and a half miles from the confluence of Brushy Creek and Little River. Because they had seen no signs of Indians previously, the surveyors "laid down carelessly as we had done before," Graves later wrote. Shortly before daylight the next morning, a large band of Indians attacked. "There could not have been less than one hundred," he reported. The Indians, who may have been Caddos, charged up to within twenty paces and discharged fifteen to eighteen shots among the abruptly aroused surveyors. James Drake was killed, as was a black servant of Bernard W. Holtzclaw. Montgomery Shackleford was wounded in the thigh, and James Shaw in the knee.

Graves and his men scattered for cover into the closest timber. The warriors rode out of range, but after fifteen minutes they charged in again. This time, the surveyors were more prepared, although in their haste to take cover, they had left a few rifles and shot pouches behind. Said Graves, "[A]mong the whole we only had four guns that we could have shot more than once."

After taking several shots at the Indians, which seemed to make them hesitate, Graves told his men to flee. Normally, running away from mounted Indians was not the way to increase one's survival chances, but apparently the warriors were more interested in the goods the crew had abandoned than in pursuing the men. As the surveyors made their escape, only Holtzclaw took a bullet, which went through his trousers without breaking the skin. They made it to Little River, boarded a raft, and floated nearly thirty miles downriver to the nearest settlement. Although Graves was lucky to have escaped with his life, he was furious about losing a thousand dollars' worth of equipment and all his survey notes.[53]

— 1837 —

10 November 1837
STONE HOUSES FIGHT *(Windthorst, Texas)*

On 13 October 1837, a detachment of sixty-eight Texas Rangers departed Fort Smith, also known as the Little River Fort, south of present day Temple, Texas. They were in pursuit of Indians who had stolen some settlers' horses. The detachment included Capt. William M. Eastland from Fort Colorado, southeast of Austin; Capt. John Bowyer's men from Houston, commanded by Lt. A. B. Vanbenthuysen and Lt. Alfred H. Miles; and Maj. William Henry Smith's battalion, under the command of Lt. John Lynch. On 1 November, with their search proving fruitless, the officers had reached a stalemate about the wisdom of persisting, so they agreed to split the forces. Vanbenthuysen and Miles continued on with sixteen rangers, while Eastland and Lynch returned to Fort Colorado.

Vanbenthuysen and Miles headed out from Pecan Bayou, northeast toward the Brazos River. On 3 November they crossed the path of a Cherokee trading party. The Texans saw a lone Kichai, who was in fact a guide for the Cherokees, but Vanbenthuysen's men assumed he was a threat and demanded that the Kichai surrender. The Indian instead fired at Miles, and a second later, Pvt. Felix McCluskey shot the warrior dead. McCluskey scalped his victim and helped himself to a large chaw of tobacco from the Indian's pocket.

Too late, the Cherokees hurried to inform Vanbenthuysen that the Kichais were their guides and that Indian agent Jesse Watkins had made a treaty with them. They also mentioned that they themselves were en route to trade with the Comanches. Vanbenthuysen insisted that the Cherokees must not trade powder and lead to the Comanches, and he instructed them to return to their village. The Indians withdrew peacefully, and the rangers continued on.

On 10 November the rangers approached a distinctive rock formation known as the "Stone Houses," near the headwaters of the West Fork of the Trinity River. Knowing that Indians could be about, Vanbenthuysen scurried up the rock mound, where he spotted 150 mounted Kichais. He quickly positioned his men in trees and utilized a deep ravine for protection. At 3 p.m., the Indians charged, and soon they completely surrounded the rangers. During the conflict, a private who could speak Kichai was sent to try to parley. The Indians demanded that the rangers turn over their warrior's murderer, but Vanbenthuysen refused and the fight continued.

One of the Indian chiefs rode his pony up and down the ravine to draw the Texans' fire, and one of the rangers' bullets knocked him dead off his horse. The conflict became more heated. The Indians' position was tactically sound, as they were concealed in thick woods and undergrowth. The rangers, although hidden in a ravine, had to climb up to an exposed position in order to fire. The Indians fired volleys at each of the Texans' feeble sorties. About 4:30 p.m. the firing ceased and the Indians withdrew. Four rangers had been killed.[54]

Fifteen minutes later, the Indians returned and set the prairie afire. With flames on three sides of them and the fourth side guarded by mounted warriors, Vanbenthuysen figured they'd have to make a break for it right through the Indians, run up a hill, and head for a thicket beyond. Their horses were wild and uncontrollable because of the approaching flames, so the remaining fourteen rangers burst out of the tightening circle on foot.

The Texans' sudden charge broke through the blocking horsemen, but their run to the thicket proved deadly: six were killed and three were wounded.[55] Only Vanbenthuysen, James O. Rice, Felix McCluskey, Oliver Buckman, and John Hobson escaped unscathed. When the rangers reached the thicket, the Indians appeared reluctant to charge after them. Estimating that the Kichais had suffered fifty casualties, Vanbenthuysen supposed they were weary of fighting.

For four days the survivors followed the West Fork of the Trinity River with no provisions—only their guns and ammunition. On the fourth day they shot four buffalo. The wounded men used the buffalo tallow to salve their injuries. On 20 November the party ran into an Indian and followed him to his camp at the junction of the West and Elm Forks of the Trinity River. The Indians at the camp were wary, and it took some serious persuasion for the Texans to get permission to stay one night. The next day, the rangers crossed the Trinity River at Three Forks and found some friendly Kickapoos, who fed them and gave them directions to Martin Lacy's trading post on the Old San Antonio Road. While most of the rangers remained at Lacy's, Vanbenthuysen, Rice, and McCluskey continued on to Houston.[56]

5 October 1838
KILLOUGH MASSACRE *(Jacksonville, Texas)*

The Killough Massacre, which took place on 5 October 1838, was the largest single Indian depredation in east Texas. The extended Killough family had emigrated from Alabama in 1836, settling in Cherokee County. Due to rising Indian tensions during the summer of 1837, most settlers in the area moved to Nacogdoches County to be out of harm's way. Many of them, including the Killoughs, returned to their homes in the fall of 1837. Friendly Indians warned the settlers not to return because many hostile bands were still wandering in the area, but the settlers paid no attention. By Christmas 1837 Isaac Killough Sr., his four sons and two daughters, and their families were at home on what was then called Killough Creek, about seven miles northwest of Jacksonville, Texas.

Over the subsequent months, the Killoughs cleared and developed their land, built homes and fences, and planted crops. In August, when the corn was nearly ready for harvest, they received word of an insurrection led by a disgruntled Mexican named Vincente Cordova and involving various bands of Indians. The settlers of Cherokee County once again fled to Nacogdoches, but because the revolt was far away, near the Rio Grande, they soon returned to harvest their crops.

On 5 October, as the men were returning from the fields, a large band of Caddos, Coushattas, Kichais, and Mexicans attacked the Killough farm. The raiders killed several settlers immediately, including Isaac Killough Sr. and his son-in-law, while the remainder scattered to their homes, trying to warn the others. When the marauders hit Allen Killough's home, he, his wife, and their five children were all killed or captured. Most of the family of the elder Killough daughter, Mary "Polly" Williams, escaped. The senior Isaac Killough's wife, Urcey, either escaped or was released and made her way to Lacy's Fort, about forty miles south. After the attack, a militia force under Thomas J. Rusk trailed the raiders and, finding some of them at an old Kickapoo village near Frankston, killed an estimated eleven of them.

In all, about eighteen members of the Killough, Woods, and Williams families were either murdered or captured. The names of most of the victims were not recorded, and their ultimate fate is unknown.[57]

8 October 1838
BATTLE CREEK *(Dawson, Texas)*

The Battle Creek Fight, also known as the Surveyors' Fight, began to unfold when a party of approximately twenty-three surveyors and assistants arrived in Franklin, present-day Navarro County, to record land grants for soldiers who had served in the Texas Revolution. After camping for a day at Parker's Fort, the surveyors continued north. On the way they encountered a band of Kickapoos, who warned them that the Ionis would attack them if they persisted in their course. The party, under Capt. J. Neil and surveyor William F. Henderson, did not heed the warning.[58] The next day, more Kickapoos implored the white men to leave, saying that if the surveyors were attacked, the Kickapoos themselves would be blamed. The men again ignored the Indians' words.

The party commenced surveying along a stream that would later be called Battle Creek. Following breakfast on the third day, 8 October, the surveyors went to work about a mile away from the camp. About fifty Indians, probably Tehuacanas, Ionis, Wacos and Caddos, began to fire on them from a ravine about forty yards away. The surveyors charged the warriors, drove them out, and took their own position in the ravine, as more Indians kept appearing. Nearly 300 warriors swarmed in, and the surveyors were trapped.

One of the surveyors, Euclid M. Cox, whom his colleagues later called "a gallant gentleman," seemed to be everywhere, exposing himself to danger. He climbed up an isolated tree to better fire at the Indians. After a few hours, having killed a few Indian snipers, Cox was hit in the spine and plummeted to the ground. Walter Lane ran to his wounded companion and dragged him back into the ravine.

A surveyor named Davis tried to go for help, but the Indians immediately caught and killed him. The Indians charged several times, but the surveyors repulsed them each time. The fighting sputtered on until nearly midnight, at which point the surveyors decided to make a break for it. About fifteen were already dead and a few were wounded. Cox was still alive, but there was no way they could transport him. Cox told his friend, a man named Button, to leave him behind. Button refused at first, but Cox insisted. He told Button to take one of his two pistols and give it to his wife; he would keep the other one to take out a few Indians before he was killed. Button bade him farewell.

The surveyors waited until the moon clouded over and then burst out of the trap, riding double on the three remaining horses, heading for the river bottom about a quarter of a mile away. Lane believed the Indians to be only about thirty yards behind them the whole way. Neil was shot in the back and fell. He called to his companions to help him onto a riderless horse that just galloped up. They did so, but Neil had gone hardly twenty paces when a spray of Indian bullets killed him along with the horse. Lane sped off, taking a bullet in the leg before he reached the timber.

In the black night, somewhere in a thicket, Lane found Henderson and Button, the only men who weren't wounded. The three crawled down a cutbank to the creek, where Henderson tied a cloth around Lane's bleeding leg. The surveyors hid motionless in a ditch while a dozen warriors passed by, "so close I could have touched them," Lane later wrote. Eventually they found a log on the bank and paddled across to an island, where they lay hidden all the next day. Lane, in a semiconscious state from pain and loss of blood, heard Button tell Henderson to leave him behind, for he could never make it. Lane woke from his stupor and cursed Button, saying he would beat him in a race back to Franklin. With the help of some Kickapoos along the way, the three reached Franklin, about thirty miles south of the battle site, five days later.

Later, a party of settlers rode back to bury the bodies. Sixteen surveyors had been killed in the fight, and of the seven who escaped, five were wounded. An estimated thirty Indians had been killed.[59]

October 1838
LOCKHART-PUTMAN INCIDENT
(Dewitt County, Texas)

The Lockhart family emigrated from Illinois to Texas in 1828, settling on the Guadalupe River in what is now DeWitt County.[60] They abandoned their home during the "Runaway Scrape" in 1836, when Texans fled from the approaching Mexican army, returning in the summer of 1837. Accompanying the Lockharts was the family of Mitchell Putman, who had just been honorably discharged from the army.

When the pecans ripened in the fall, the children of both families went along the bottomland to gather the nuts. Thirteen-year-old Matilda Lockhart was the oldest of the group, and the four Putman children, James, Rhoda, Elizabeth, and Juda, ranged from about ten to two and a half years of age.[61] Their buckets full, the children emerged at the edge of the prairie, where they were surprised by a band of Comanches.

At first sight, Matilda dropped her bucket and ran for the house. She might have escaped but for the crying of the youngest Putman girl, who pleaded with Matilda not to leave her behind. All of the children were captured. The Indians strapped them to horses with rawhide thongs and rode off to the northwest. As evening approached, the Lockharts and Putmans began to worry about their children. After dark, a signal fire was built, horns were blown, and guns were fired. By morning, the parents were disconsolate, fully realizing that their children had been taken by Indians.

A company of settlers pursued the raiders upriver to the mouth of the Comal, but they lost the trail when it entered the hill country. Andrew Lockhart, Matilda's father, wanted to continue, but his companions finally talked him out of it with the promise that they would get more men and try again.[62]

— 1839 —

15 February 1839
SPRING CREEK *(San Saba, Texas)*

In January 1839, a few months after the Lockhart-Putman incident (see previous entry), a band of friendly Lipans discovered a Comanche camp near the headwaters of the San Gabriel River, about fifty miles northwest of Waterloo, Texas—the village that would soon become Austin. When the Lipans reported their find, settlers from Bastrop and LaGrange organized ranger companies. Andrew Lockhart eagerly joined the LaGrange Company. On 26 January, sixty-three rangers and sixteen Lipans, under the leadership of Col. John H. Moore, set out for the San Gabriel. As they rode west, a norther swept in, pelting them with snow and rain for three days. Some of the horses died of exposure, supplies ran low, and Ranger Wilson was seriously wounded in the chest by an accidental rifle discharge. There was talk of abandoning the expedition, but Moore insisted they continue.

The Lipans finally spotted the village, probably a camp of Penetekas under Chief Muguara, near Spring Creek, in a valley just south of the Colorado River and north of the San Saba. On the morning of 15 February, Moore arranged his companies to hit the large village from three sides, and the Texans charged in. Over the sound of horses' hooves and a few rounds of opening gunfire, the shouts of Andrew Lockhart were distinctly heard by many. "Matilda Lockhart! Oh my child! If you are here, run to me. I am your father!"[63]

Lockhart continued to call out until the sounds of battle drowned him out. Matilda was indeed there and she did hear him, but some

Comanche women stopped her from running, lashing her and driving her back into the thickets along Spring Creek. The rangers reached the center of the camp, shooting down quite a few Indians as they emerged from their lodges and capturing several others. Most of the villagers, however, were able to flee to the cutbanks along the creek, where the warriors formed up for a counterattack. Moore, realizing that his men were disorganized and vulnerable, called for a retreat to a line of timber. He did so just in time, for the Comanches charged out and nearly broke Moore's line. The rangers repulsed several attacks, fighting until about ten in the morning, at which point the Comanches pulled back to surround Moore's men and open up with long-range firing. Moore estimated that he was facing between 300 and 500 Indians.

About noon a Comanche warrior and a captive Lipan woman with a white flag approached the Texans. Moore went out with a Lipan to talk while the captive woman translated. The Comanches offered to trade prisoners. According to the Lipan woman, the Comanches had a middle-aged white woman, a girl of about fifteen, and three younger children.[64] Moore probably would have made the swap, but he had just learned that his Lipan allies had already killed the Comanche prisoners. When Moore indicated there would be no trade, the Comanches warned him that they had a great number of warriors, with more arriving all the time. Moore put up a bold front, saying that the Texans would gladly fight even if outnumbered. With that, the parley ended.

The Texans awaited the next attack, but none came. The Comanches had probably taken enough casualties—Moore estimated about thirty killed and fifty wounded. Seeing the Comanches pull back, Moore prepared to go. The Lipan chief Castro, disgusted that the rangers were leaving, withdrew with his warriors. One of the seven wounded Texans was Andrew Lockhart, who was no doubt disappointed that no further effort would be made to rescue his daughter.

The Comanches would keep Matilda another fourteen months, until a fateful meeting in San Antonio when a negotiation went bad, developing into a major incident in Texas history (see Council House Fight, 19 March 1840).[65]

19 February 1839
BRUSHY CREEK (Taylor, Texas)

Robert M. Coleman and his family settled on the north bank of the Colorado River in 1830, near today's Webberville, about a dozen miles southeast of present-day Austin, Texas. Coleman, originally from Kentucky, had fought against the Caddos in 1835 (see Tehuacana Springs, 11 July 1835). In 1837 Coleman drowned, leaving his wife, Elizabeth, to raise three sons and two daughters alone. Her nearest neighbor was about 500 yards away.

The Colemans lived within the hunting grounds of the Peneteka Comanches, who had carried off five white children four months before and had fought a battle with the rangers who were trying to rescue them (see previous entry). Following their victory over the Texans, nearly 500 Comanches swept down the Colorado River in another raid. About ten o'clock in the morning on 18 February, Elizabeth Coleman and her five-year-old son Thomas were outside doing chores.[66] Albert, age fourteen, was in the house with his two little sisters, ages eleven and nine. James, the eldest, was out working in the fields with a hired man. The Indians appeared so suddenly out of the dense woods that there was little time to react. A large number of warriors cut James and the hired man off from the house. They immediately ran downstream to try to warn the neighbors.

Elizabeth saw the Indians and ran toward the house, but at the doorstep she turned to look for Thomas, and an arrow struck her in the throat. She collapsed inside, and Albert barred the door. Outside, the Indians snatched Thomas, then turned their attention to the cabin. Albert grabbed one of the two or three loaded guns in the cabin, shot out the window, and hit a warrior on the doorstep.

Elizabeth, choking and bleeding profusely, propped herself up on a chair near a window and tried to aim a rifle. Before firing, she attempted to pull the arrow out of her throat. The barb tore a gaping wound—she fell from the chair and soon bled to death. Albert picked up the rifle and fired, hitting another warrior. When the Indians backed off, Albert pulled up some boards covering a storage space under the floor. He ordered his sisters to crawl in, admonishing them not to make a sound until they heard white voices.[67] Then, furiously reloading, Albert kept shooting from various windows and apertures, hoping that the besieging Indians would think there were several defenders inside.

After a short time, however, some warriors crept up to the house. One of them thrust a lance through a wall opening, stabbing Albert, while others blasted away into the cabin, hitting him with bullets. The fatally wounded boy dragged himself over to his mother's body, lay down, and died. His sisters remembered Albert's final words to them as:

"Father is dead, mother is dead, and I am dying, but something tells me God will protect you."[68]

Inexplicably, the warriors, either thinking there were still armed defenders inside or hearing whooping coming from the house down the road, left the Coleman place and ran off, taking the little boy and some of the settlers' slaves. The two girls were eventually found safe under the floorboards.

After the incident, settlers around the nearby town of Bastrop quickly organized a retaliatory expedition. Capt. Jacob Burleson and twenty-five men joined with Capt. James Rogers's twenty-seven men, and the two companies rode off to follow the Indians' trail. Riding hard, they caught up with the Indians the next forenoon at Post Oak Island, near present-day Taylor, Texas, about twenty-five miles north of the Coleman house.

Seeing the whites coming, the Indians took position in a line of trees. Burleson hurried forward to open the attack before the Indians were ready. He dismounted and ordered his men to open fire, but only a few obeyed. The rest, seeing that they were seriously outnumbered, retreated. Burleson, having only a few men standing with him, had no choice but to flee. As he mounted his horse, a bullet caught him in the back of the head. He tumbled to the ground, and the Indians set upon him. His body was later found scalped and mutilated, and the Comanches had cut out his heart and taken it.

The Texans fell back three miles and halted, probably pondering their shameful conduct and wondering what to do next. The answer came when Jacob Burleson's brother, Edward, rode up with thirty-one more men. The combined force of about eighty-four men rode back to fight. Burleson divided the command in half to hit the Comanches on each flank. The plan was good, but because the approaches to the Comanche position led through open areas, it was too dangerous to attack in daylight. Instead, Burleson later wrote, "We were forced to select safe positions . . . and whenever an Indian showed himself, to draw down on him and send the messenger of death to dispatch him."[69]

The battle turned into a sniping contest. When darkness ended the fight, four white men were dead or mortally wounded: besides Jacob Burleson were John Walters, Edward Blakey, and James Gilleland. Seven others had lighter wounds.

In the morning Burleson attacked the Comanche position, but the Indians were gone. They still had little Thomas Coleman and most of the slaves. One slave was found still alive but pierced with nine arrows.

He said that the Indians, having lost about thirty killed and wounded, decided to slip away during the night. Capt. Jesse Billingsley took off with thirty men to pursue them, but the Texans found that the Indians had split up and headed in all directions, so Billingsley called off the pursuit.

As for Thomas Coleman, little else is known. According to some sources, he was held by the Indians until he was almost grown. His relatives reportedly went to great expense trying to find him. One of his cousins enlisted the aid of several Texas frontiersmen and the Delaware guide John Connor to search throughout Indian territory. Thomas was eventually found and, after the utmost persuasion, he agreed to come back to his relatives. But the boy had lived too long with his Indian family, and he could not adapt to white society—he soon returned to the Indians.[70]

26 May 1839
BIRD'S CREEK *(Temple, Texas)*
Tennessean John Bird, who fought with Andrew Jackson in the War of 1812, moved to Texas in 1830. As a captain in the Austin Colony militia, Bird commanded a unit of Texas cavalry against the Mexicans near San Antonio in 1835 and led sixty volunteers in defense of the Brazos frontier in 1836. In April 1839 he was elected captain of a ranger company, which he took to Fort Milam at the falls of the Brazos after hearing of Indian forays around the unprotected settlements to the west, around Little River Fort.

On 25 May Bird and about thirty-five rangers arrived in the vicinity of Little River, where a few Comanches had been seen skinning buffalo just a few hours earlier. The Indians fled but returned the following morning and stampeded a herd of buffalo through the rangers' camp. After pursuing the Comanches for four miles, Bird and his men discovered about twenty-seven more warriors, again skinning buffalo. The Indians scattered and fled in different directions. Bird chose the largest group and galloped after them. The chase led north to a little stream, later known as Bird's Creek, that flowed southwest into the Leon River. There the rangers abruptly halted—they had run right into a trap laid by an estimated 300 Comanche, Caddo, and Kickapoo warriors. The Texans attempted to fall back to Little River Fort but after a quarter-mile run, at about 3 p.m., they were overtaken. The rangers made for a nearby ravine and prepared to make the Indians pay dearly for the Texans' lives. Bird called out to his men, "Stand and fight like men—or die like dogs!"[71]

The Indians formed a battle line, started a yell that traveled from one end of the line to the other, and charged. Bird's men blasted away at them, deflecting one charge after another. Bird was killed early in the fight, taking an arrow through the heart, and several other rangers were hit. After the Texans repulsed several mounted charges, the Indians tried to take them on foot, charging along the ends of the ravine, but that attack was also driven back.

By early evening the rangers, exhausted, talked of fleeing, every man for himself. But young James Robinett, who had taken command, stepped forward to rally his men, swearing that he would kill the chief in the next charge. As fate would have it, the next charge was led by Buffalo Hump, adorned with his horned war bonnet. Robinett placed himself at the head of the ravine and, waiting until the warriors nearly ran him over, took careful aim and fired. Buffalo Hump dropped from his horse. The charge stopped, and about ten warriors hurried to carry his body away.

The fight ended there. The Indians withdrew, "yelling like devils," according to one survivor. Five rangers had been killed, including Privates Gale, Nash, and Weaver, and three were wounded. One ranger said of Bird, "He was the bravest of the brave, and died encouraging his men to fight like heroes."[72] Comanche deaths were estimated at between thirty and seventy-five.

The next morning the Texans hastily made their way back to Little River Fort. With reinforcements, the rangers went back to the battleground to retrieve their comrades' bodies, which they found badly mutilated. Bird and the other fallen rangers were buried near the fort, though their exact resting places are unknown.[73]

15–16 July 1839
BATTLE OF THE NECHES *(Tyler, Texas)*

In the late 1830s, after about twenty years of relative peace between the Cherokees and the people of Texas, various misunderstandings, suspicions, and depredations—as well as the fact that the Cherokees inhabited prime lands that Texans wanted—ultimately led to a confrontation. For one thing, Texans believed that Cherokees had been involved in the appalling Killough Massacre (see 5 October 1838).

Upon taking office in December 1838, Texas president Mirabeau B. Lamar, convinced that the Cherokees were in treasonable correspondence with the Mexicans, launched a campaign to drive them from Texas, along with the Alabamas, Shawnees, and Coushattas. An incident in May 1839 seemed to confirm Lamar's belief. After battling a party of Mexicans near Brushy Creek, rangers found on the body of one of the Mexicans correspondence indicating a plot to unite all the Texas Indians for an attack upon the Texans. Cherokee chief Bowles (Duwali) was immediately threatened with expulsion, but the chief vowed that his people would not leave without a fight, even if it meant their own destruction.

Last-minute negotiations failed, and Chief Bowles used the delays to prepare his warriors. Finally in July the Texans, about 700 men under Kelsey H. Douglass, Edward Burleson, and Thomas J. Rusk, moved to drive the Cherokees out. Also present were Texas vice president David G. Burnet and Texas Secretary of War Gen. Albert Sidney Johnston. The battle began on 15 July a few miles west of present-day Tyler, in Henderson County, near the Neches River. Chief Bowles, who aspired to live like the white man, imitated the military by forming his 700 warriors into battle lines. It was to prove a mistake.

Burleson attacked a screen of Cherokee warriors and drove them back into a thicket, where their main force lay. Rusk led in 400 men for support, and the battle spread along the line. When Rusk took the center, Burleson spotted a Cherokee attempt to circle around the Texans' rear to get their horses. He moved 300 men to the Cherokees' right flank to check their approach, while companies under Capts. Mark B. Lewis and James Ownsby assaulted the Indians' left. The spirited fight lasted about an hour and a half. It was a very hot day, and all participants suffered from heat and thirst.

Finally Douglass, in overall command, ordered a simultaneous assault, and the Indian line broke. The Cherokees ran for a mile back into the swamps along the river, pursued and taking losses all along the way. Near the Indians' village, in the cornfields and fence rows, Chief Bowles rallied his men, but it was only a temporary stand. The chief was shot off his horse. Later, on the prairie near the river, Capt. Robert W. Smith found the wounded chief still brandishing a pistol, unwilling to surrender. Smith shot him in the head. The battle continued the next day, as the Texans followed fleeing bands of Indians north into Van Zandt County, shooting them down without mercy.

About 100 Cherokees were killed and wounded. Texan losses were five killed or mortally wounded and thirty wounded less seriously. Both Vice President Burnet and General Johnston were cited in the commander's report for gallant action on the field. Public reaction to the battle and the Cherokee expulsion was mixed.[74] Many contemporary commentators did not see the justice in the affair. "All the Indians were not bad," one recorded, "nor were all the whites good. Their expulsion, thus resolved into the necessity of self-preservation, is not without shades of sorrow."[75]

1 October 1839
WEBSTER MASSACRE *(Leander, Texas)*

In 1837 John Webster and his family left their Virginia home for Texas, seeking land, good soil, and a milder climate. The Websters, along with the Flesher and Stillwell families, settled in Bastrop, on the Colorado River, where they stayed for nearly two years. In 1839, John Webster purchased some military land to the north, near the San Gabriel River, and with typical pioneering spirit, the families moved on.

The two-wagon ox train left on 27 September 1839. The party included John Webster and his wife, Dolly; their children, Booker, age ten, and Patsy, age three; their servant, Nelson; the Stillwell, Flesher, and Morton families; and eight young men. A few days after they passed Austin, the emigrants were heading west between the forks of the San Gabriel. Unknown to them, Comanches were watching them from atop Pilot Knob, several miles ahead and across the North Fork. Near the North Fork, two of the young men rode ahead to hunt, but they heard Indians across the stream and hurried back to alert the rest of the train. The men met to discuss their options. Some wanted to retreat, but others said that "they would rather die than go back and be laughed at as cowards."[76]

John Webster volunteered to ride ahead and see if he could determine the Indians' intentions, but the others dissuaded him. Finally, after two hours of arguing, the party agreed to turn back. The train traveled most of the night, hoping to be far away from the Indians before daybreak. After the moon set, no longer able to see their way, they stopped to camp by a lower ford of the San Gabriel. The next morning, 1 October, they got an early start and traveled for two hours before coming to a narrow prairie with thick timber along both sides. Suddenly, sixteen Comanches rode up to their rear, shouting and shooting. The thirteen mounted men in the Webster train charged after the Indians, firing and hitting two.

The attack had been a ruse, however. As soon as the mounted men were distracted, about 150 Comanches attacked the front of the train. Benjamin Reese, an experienced Indian fighter, instructed the others to turn the oxen loose and pull the wagons together. As the Indians charged by on horseback, the emigrants fired at them, but they hit very few. Most of the party were unused to firing weapons, so only about ten men defended the little corral.

Morton was hit next, then Perry Reese. John Webster took a ball in the chest and went down, then two others were killed. Nelson Flesher, Dolly Webster's nephew, fell with a gunshot to the thigh. Warriors were about to scalp Webster when one shouted, "blanco, blanco," apparently reluctant to take his white hair. Stillwell was killed, but he was bald, so the Indians took only his wig. Dolly Webster was wounded. In a short while, the last two men went down. Only Dolly and her two children were still alive. Dolly saw the warriors scalp and mutilate the dead before she fainted.

The Comanches plundered the wagons and destroyed what they could not carry off. They seemed most interested in the gold watches and mirrors; more than $1,300 in coins was discarded. Dolly was stripped of her clothes, beaten, and dragged off by her hair. The Indians took her and her children to their camp, where they were held with several other white captives from previous raids.

Dolly and her children attempted to escape in November 1839, but they were recaptured. In March 1840, when the Comanches left to trade one of their captives, Matilda Lockhart (see Spring Creek, 15 February 1839), for ransom, Dolly was able to grab Patsy and make a second escape. This time she made it to San Antonio, nine days after the Comanches were defeated in the Council House Fight (see next entry). The Indians brought in Booker Webster the following month.[77]

— 1840 —

19 March 1840
COUNCIL HOUSE FIGHT *(San Antonio, Texas)*

The Peneteka Comanches had been raiding in the San Antonio area for years. By January 1840, they held perhaps twenty Texans and many more Mexicans captive. After a foray into Mexico went badly, however, the Indians decided to ask the Texans for a cessation of hostilities. From a large Indian village on the Frio River, a delegation of Comanches and a Mexican captive went to San Antonio to see Col. Henry W. Karnes, who commanded the southern military region. The Indians claimed to have turned down offers by other Indians and Mexicans to unite for a general war on the Texans and said they wanted peace on any terms. Karnes later stated: "These statements may be true; but their known treachery and duplicity, induces me to put little faith in them."

Karnes treated the delegates well and sent them away with presents, but he warned that "the government would not enter into any Treaty without the release of the American captives, and the restoration of all stolen property."[78] The Comanches agreed to comply and to come back within thirty days. In his report to Secretary of War Albert Sidney Johnston, Karnes suggested that the secretary send a few commissioners to San Antonio to treat with the Indians, as well as a force of soldiers sufficient to seize the Comanches as hostages should they not deliver the captives as promised.

Taking Karnes's suggestion, Johnston ordered Lt. Col. William S. Fisher, First Infantry, to take three companies to San Antonio. Texas president Mirabeau B. Lamar appointed Quartermaster General Col. William G. Cooke and Adjutant General Col. Hugh McLeod as commissioners. Their instructions stipulated that any treaty must contain terms in which the Indians must: return the captives; stay west of a line drawn through central Texas; keep away from settlements; and not interfere with white attempts to settle on vacant lands. In addition, the practice of giving presents was to end. For their own part, the Comanches were confident that they also held bargaining chips. They believed that the Texans were eager for peace and would pay handsomely for the white prisoners. Chief Muguara argued that the captives should be taken in one by one to get the most out of every transaction.

The captives included Matilda Lockhart and the three Putman children captured seventeen months earlier in DeWitt County (see Lockhart-Putman Incident, October 1838). The Comanches took one of the children, James Putman, to San Antonio to see if Muguara's plan would work. They hoped to trade the boy for a supply of powder and lead. The Indians reached San Antonio before Lieutenant Colonel Fisher, the commissioners, and the First Infantry companies had arrived. The Texans' response was just what Muguara had believed it would be, and James Putman was ransomed for ammunition.

The jubilant Comanches returned to their camp. Although they again promised that they would bring in all the captives the next time, the plan was to take in Matilda Lockhart next, to see what she would bring. On 15 March Muguara and twelve other chiefs, along with some fifty warriors, women, and children, left for San Antonio. The only captives they brought were Matilda and a Mexican woman named Leno.

The Comanches proudly rode into town on 19 March. They had been to San Antonio many times before, and no Texans or Mexicans had ever dared to molest them. The fact that they had brought their women and children along indicates that they believed this time would be no different. They met the commissioners at the old courthouse with Matilda in tow. The girl appeared to have been severely abused and even disfigured by her captors. At the first opportunity, she poured out her story, telling the commissioners that the Indians were holding many other captives in the village and were planning to sell them one at a time. Hearing this news, Lieutenant Colonel Fisher had his troops surround the courthouse.

Still, the Comanches were not alarmed. When the commissioners asked where the other prisoners were, Muguara responded, "We have brought in the only one we had; the others are with other tribes." It was an obvious lie, and the commissioners were stunned into a momentary silence. Perhaps overestimating his position, Muguara curtly added, "How do you like the answer?"

"I do not like your answer," Fisher replied sternly. He signaled for Capt. George T. Howard to bring his company in, and the soldiers took position at the doors and windows. Fisher delivered his orders to the Comanches: "Your women and children may depart in peace and your braves may go and tell your people to send in the prisoners. When those prisoners are returned, your chiefs here present may likewise go free. Until then we will hold you as hostages."[79]

The Comanche interpreter paled and refused to translate the ultimatum, knowing what the result would be. When the commissioners insisted, the interpreter translated the message and bolted from the room. The Comanches pulled out their weapons. Fisher ordered that the soldiers prepare to fire.

A chief dashed for a doorway and stabbed the soldier who barred his way. With this, a melee broke out. Bullets and arrows flew, knives flashed, and rifles were used as clubs. A few chiefs fought their way out the door. Muguara stabbed Captain Howard in the side, then he was shot to death. The commotion aroused the rest of the Comanches in the plaza. The surrounding streets, alleys, and backyards became a battleground. It was after midnight when the last two Indians were burned out of a backyard kitchen in which they had taken refuge.

Thirty-five Comanches were killed, including three women and two children, and twenty-seven Indian women and children were captured. Seven Texans were dead, and eight were wounded. The captured Indians were locked up as hostages except for one woman, who was given a horse and provisions and told to take the army's message to the tribe.

After the battle, several townswomen got together to care for Matilda Lockhart. "She was in a frightful condition, poor girl," wrote one of the women, Mary Maverick. "Her head, arms and face were full of sores and bruises, and her nose actually burned off. . . . Ah, it was sickening to behold, and made one's blood boil for vengeance." Matilda herself "was very sad and broken hearted. She said she felt utterly degraded, and could never hold her head up again—that she would be glad to get back home, where she would hide away and never permit herself to be seen."[80]

Matilda's abuse enraged the Texans, and they were determined to get back the remaining white captives. The Comanches, however, looked upon the Council House incident as another example of Texan treachery. The Indians pulled back into the hill country northwest of San Antonio and planned their next move.[81]

12 August 1840
PLUM CREEK *(Lockhart, Texas)*

After the Council House fight in March 1840 (see previous entry), the Comanches were eager to take revenge on the Texans. More than 500 Indians, mostly Comanches, with some Kiowas and a few Mexicans, descended from the hill country north of San Antonio and west of Austin. They headed for the coast, following the San Marcos and Guadalupe Rivers, intent on bringing destruction to settlements all along the way. On 6 August, they attacked Victoria, killing two settlers and wounding several others. A hastily organized defense kept the Indians from overrunning the town. The raiders captured about 1,500 horses and mules and rode on. The next day, near Nine Mile Point, they captured Nancy Crosby, a granddaughter of Daniel Boone, and her small child. Later, when the child's crying apparently irritated the warriors, they threw it to the ground and killed it with a spear.

On 9 August, the Indians attacked Linnville, at the northwest end of Lavaca Bay. Most of the inhabitants rushed to the bay, where they sought safety in boats or waded neck-deep into the water. Indians killed about twenty-three settlers, including Maj. Hugh Watts and two of his slaves. The raiders captured the major's wife, Juliet Constance Watts, along with a black nurse and a child, as they tried to escape in the water. After plundering and burning the town, the Indians headed for home.

The Texans were determined not to let the Indians get away without a fight. While some mounted settlers trailed the retreating raiders, others gathered along Plum Creek near present-day Lockhart, Texas, where they believed the Indians would pass. The volunteers included Lafayette Ward and twenty-two men, Matthew Caldwell and thirty-nine men, and Capt. James Bird with thirty men from Gonzales. Ben McCulloch and his companions joined the group, as did Col. Edward Burleson with eighty-seven volunteers from the Bastrop area. Thirteen Tonkawa Indians, enemies of the Comanches, also joined them. Gen. Felix Huston of the Texas Militia arrived from Austin, but no one was charged with overall command of the entire group of volunteers. On 12 August, the group of 200 confronted the Comanches on the prairie along Plum Creek.

The Indian cavalcade moved across the open fields, with warriors decked out in stolen clothes, driving about 2,000 stolen horses. When the Texans moved out to attack, the Comanches appeared undecided whether to fight or run. They took a middle course, forming a line between the Texans and the plundered horses, and commenced a fighting retreat for about five miles. Some of the Indians formed up in a stand of oaks at Kelley Springs, where they fought for half an hour. When a Comanche chief in a large headdress rode out to challenge the Texans, several rifles blasted at him, knocking him to the ground. "Now, General," Caldwell said to Huston, "is your time to charge them! They are whipped."[82]

The Texans dashed forward and the Comanches broke. Many Indians were killed in their flight across creeks and marshes as the Texans pursued them for a dozen miles. The Indians abandoned most of their stolen horses and other plunder. They killed Nancy Crosby and tried to kill Juliet Watts, but the steel-ribbed corset she wore deflected the arrow just enough to prevent a mortal wound.

About eighty Comanche warriors were killed, while the Texans lost two killed and six wounded. The Plum Creek fight was a severe blow to the Comanches. They never again made such a large raid, although they did perpetrate smaller raids on settlements for decades to come. The Texans drew an important lesson from the fight: a charge on horseback was more likely to succeed than a dismounted fight.[83]

August 1840
KENNEY'S FORT *(Round Rock, Texas)*

In the summer of 1839, Dr. Thomas Kenney moved from Bastrop County to Williamson County, Texas, settling at the junction of Brushy and

Dyer Creeks. After building a few substantial cabins, Kenney was joined by several other families. The settlers built a rectangular stockade around the perimeter of their homes.

One August morning in 1840, as he worked outside the stockade, Joseph Weeks became alarmed when he heard "owls" hooting in the woods. They sounded more human than avian, and he grew more anxious when the hoots were answered by other calls. Weeks alerted the other settlers, who had no sooner gotten inside when Indians rushed the fort. The stockade was not yet complete, but Week's quick thinking bought them enough time to mount a defense. A volley of musketry from the stockade walls blasted the charging Indians, and they fell back. Realizing they could not overwhelm the settlement, the raiders dropped back and began long-range firing.

During the siege, a courier dashed through the Indian position to get help from the nearest settlements. The Indians stayed only a short while, however. They soon gathered up their dead and wounded and left the area. Only one man at Kenney's Fort was wounded. Fifty men arrived the next day, only to find the Indians had long gone.[84]

24 October 1840
RED FORK COLORADO/MOORE'S FIGHT
(Colorado City, Texas)
In September 1840, following the Battle of Plum Creek (see 12 August 1840), Col. John H. Moore received orders to organize a volunteer force and attack the Comanches in their home country. On 5 October, with about ninety Texans and a dozen or more Lipan scouts under Chief Castro, Moore left Austin and headed up the Colorado River. Bad weather dogged the march, and a norther hit the party near the Concho River. Several men became sick, and one died.

Along what some called the Red Fork of the Colorado, Moore noted curious rock art and hieroglyphics. Seeing frequent signs of Indians, the Lipans went out to reconnoiter on 23 October. The scouts returned late that night with news that they had found a village. Moore took his men out that very night, marching about ten miles to the Colorado River, then about eight miles upstream, stopping just short of the village.[85]

The Lipans estimated there were 60 tipis and about 125 warriors in the village, which was at a horseshoe bend of the river. At daylight, Moore moved in. Capt. Thomas J. Rabb rode on the right, Lt. Clarke L. Owen in the center, and Capt. Nicholas M. Dawson took the left. Within 200 yards of the camp, they broke into a charge. The sleeping Indians were taken completely by surprise. Halfway through the village the Texans dismounted, firing as they walked. The battle lasted half an hour. Some Comanches were killed while trying to cross the river. Those who made it across were met by Lieutenant Owen and fifteen mounted men who had circled around to prevent the retreat. The volunteers chased the rest of the warriors about four miles across the prairie.

The Texans made an effort to spare the women and children, but some were killed during the fight. One woman clubbed Capt. Isaac N. Mitchell off his mount, then came at him with a knife. "Kill her, Mitchell!" his men shouted, but he replied, "Oh no, boys, I can't kill a woman!" He finally had to knock her down and wrestle the knife from her. A Comanche boy of about fourteen fought so well that the Texans decided to spare him "for his bravery and pluck."[86]

The Comanches had received their greatest defeat to date. Moore reported forty-eight Indians killed in the village area and another eighty killed at the river and beyond. Only two volunteers were wounded. The Texans took thirty-four prisoners, and they recovered two Mexican captives the Comanches had taken about three months earlier. In the village they found a great deal of plunder taken from Linnville the previous summer. Moore rounded up 500 horses, collected all the goods he could carry, and burned the village. They left standing one large tipi, where several women remained with the wounded of the village. Moore arrived back in Austin on 7 November. The residents of Austin held a dinner and celebratory ball for Moore and his men.[87]

— 1841 —

21 April 1841
PECAN CREEK *(Corsicana, Texas)*

One Texas militia company, organized in Robertson County in March 1841, was led by Capt. Eli Chandler, a forty-two-year-old South Carolinian who had come to Texas in 1835. In early April, Indians raided along the Navasota River, killed a man, and chased off eight horses. Chandler pursued the raiders unsuccessfully. On 16 April, Chandler got word of a group of Indians living on Pecan Creek, a tributary of the Trinity River, in present-day Navarro County. He and his forty-five-man company from Franklin marched north. They were later joined by seven more volunteers.

On the night of 20 April, the Texans discovered a deserted village of twenty-eight lodges. The next morning they followed the Indians' trail about five miles up Pecan Creek, where they ran into eight or ten Comanches. When the Indians veered off, Chandler gave chase, but after about three miles they eluded him. Realizing the trail was a fake, Chandler countermarched back to the main trail and returned to the abandoned village, where he took up a smaller trail. After one mile the volunteers ran into the same Indians, this time on the real trail to the new village.

In pursuit of the Comanches, Chandler led one column down the trail, while Lt. William M. Love took another detachment along a path that followed a ridgeline between two parallel creeks. With little space to maneuver, the Texans chased the warriors for five more miles. The Indians outraced them, but not by much, and they got to the village barely in time to shout a warning. It was enough, however, and many of the Indians got away before the Texans opened fire. The village was surrounded by nearly impenetrable thickets, so Chandler had his men dismount. The Texans scoured the brush for the fleeing Comanches, but nearly all of them escaped.

Chandler reported three Indians killed and several wounded. Only one Texan was wounded. The militia collected nine mules and twenty-three horses, along with powder, lead, axes, pelts, and other items, in total worth more than $3,000. They burned the village and rode back to Franklin.[88]

24 May 1841
VILLAGE CREEK (Arlington, Texas)
Village Creek, which today forms the boundary between Arlington and Fort Worth, Texas, flows north into the West Fork Trinity River. In the early 1840s the creek was home to numerous bands of Caddos, Cherokees, Wacos, Kickapoos, and Anadarkos who were believed to be raiding frontier settlements. After an Indian attack on the Ripley cabin, in Titus County, in April 1841, in which half a dozen settlers were killed, locals formed a retaliatory expedition.

In early May, citizens gathered around Fort Johnson, near what is now Denison, Texas, where they organized a company of about sixty-nine men. Capt. James Bourland and Lt. William C. Young led the volunteers, with John B. Denton and Henry Stout in command of several scouts. Edward H. Tarrant, brigadier general of the Fourth Texas Militia, was in titular command by virtue of his rank. The party marched southwest to the West Fork of the Trinity River and followed an Indian trail downstream, finding a few deserted villages along the way. The scouts captured a lone Indian, who revealed the location of the current villages. Tarrant moved the men across the Trinity near the mouth of Fossil Creek, then took them along an old buffalo trail south to Village Creek. The scouts reported villages about three miles ahead, and the Texans prepared for battle.

On Village Creek the men encountered a few Indian women cooking in a glade. The women began shouting and running toward their camp, and the Texans charged after them. As Tarrant later reported, "The village was taken in an instant." The village, however, turned out to be only the first of several. After the Texans had chased the fleeing Indians along the creek for a mile, they ran into a larger village. Bourland circled to the right with half the men, while Sgt. Lemuel M. Cochran took another detachment to the left. They took this village as well, but many of the Indians fled downstream. Eight men crossed the creek in pursuit. They soon spotted a third village and saw more beyond. "There was no distinction of villages," Tarrant recalled, "but one continuous village for the distance of one mile and a half."[89]

Tarrant and Bourland agreed that the men should stay put until they could reorganize. Denton, however, convinced Tarrant to allow him to take ten men and follow the retreating Indians. Bourland took ten other men and rode with Denton. The Texans, with Denton's party in front, eventually reached a big thicket in the bottomland, where Denton halted his men to wait for the others. Stout rode up to him and said, "If you are afraid to go in there, I am not."[90] His bravery challenged, Denton, declaring that he was willing to go to "the infernal regions" in pursuit of the enemy, rushed into the thicket.[91] Only a few hundred yards in, shots rang out; Stout was wounded and Denton fell dead, pierced by three bullets. The survivors hastily retreated to the main command.

Back at Tarrant's camp, Bourland took twenty-four men to recover Denton's body then returned to camp. Bourland and Tarrant realized they had bitten off more than they could chew when they learned from a captured Indian that another thousand or so warriors were waiting farther downstream. Tarrant had already counted 225 lodges in the combined villages—far too many Indians for the Texans to challenge. They wisely decided to get out while they could. At five p.m. the Texans backtracked twelve miles and recrossed the Trinity in the darkness. Along

Fossil Creek, likely somewhere in present-day Haltom City, they buried John Denton.

About eight militiamen were wounded in the village raids, while twelve Indians were killed and another score wounded. The Texans seized thirty-seven horses, six cattle, hundreds of pounds of ammunition, and numerous other items. Tarrant captured one Indian child, whom he returned to its mother at a council the following year. With the Village Creek incident, the Indians' formerly secure position was compromised. When Tarrant returned in May with 400 men, he found the area deserted.[92]

24 June 1841
UVALDE CANYON *(Utopia, Texas)*

On 24 June 1841, Texas Ranger John Coffee (Jack) Hays gathered a force of sixteen Texans and twenty Mexicans under Captain Flores to pursue Comanches who had been stealing horses in the San Antonio area. The party picked up the Indians' trail, which headed west. After a few

Sabinal River near site of Uvalde Canyon battle, Utopia, Texas

days, the tracks led up the Sabinal River into Canyon de Uvalde, south of present-day Utopia, Texas. Here a circling flock of buzzards caught the rangers' attention, as the birds often gathered near Indian camps. Within two miles of the canyon, Hays and a Mexican dismounted and crept closer, finding a band of about twelve Indians.

Hays returned to his company, ordered the men to mount up, and led them to charge the camp. At the first shots, the Comanches fled into a nearby thicket, but the rangers and Mexicans barreled right in after them. "The Indians had but one gun," Hays reported, "and the thicket being too dense to admit their using their arrows well, they fought under great disadvantage but continued to struggle to the last, keeping up their warsongs until all were hushed in death."[93] During the three-hour fight, an arrow clipped Hays's finger and two more rangers were wounded. The Texans killed ten Indians and captured two, one a wounded warrior and the other a woman. The trail continued on to what appeared to be a larger camp, but with tired horses and loaded with plunder, Hays decided to return to San Antonio. There he would enlist a larger expedition to continue pursuit of the Comanches.[94]

Ca. 24 July 1841
BATTLE OF THE LLANO *(Junction, Texas)*

After returning from the fight with the Comanches in Uvalde Canyon (see previous entry), Capt. Jack Hays added to his expedition about fifteen men from Gonzales and ten Lipan warriors, including the chief Flacco, increasing his force to around fifty men. Returning to the site of the Uvalde Canyon fight, the party picked up a trail that led up the Balcones Escarpment and north to the Frio River. The trail, which grew wider as they progressed, eventually led to the headwaters of the Llano River, in the vicinity of present-day Junction, Texas.

Hays and his men found an encampment of nearly 200 Indians, packing up and just about ready to move. As the Texans approached, the Comanches, seeing that they outnumbered the rangers, formed up in a line in front of the village to shield their families. Hays, unintimidated, moved his rangers forward to attack.

Hays himself was riding a mule and could not keep up with his men, who had already begun firing on the Indians. Spotting a ranger on a fine horse, Hays asked him to exchange mounts. The ranger agreed but warned Hays that the horse was spirited and might run away with him. Hays took the chance.

In a minute, Hays was in the front line, but there was no stopping the horse. Despite Hays's best efforts to rein him in, the steed barreled through the Indian line. Flacco joined Hays in punching through the line, circling around the Indians, then coming back along the flank. Both men, armed with five-shot pistols, were able to keep the Comanches at bay. Finally the rest of the rangers forced their way through and divided the Indian force, who then melted away and fled.

The Texans estimated that they had killed ten Indians and wounded several others. In the abandoned camp, the rangers found the body of a Mexican prisoner, who had been shot, lanced, and left hanging by his heels.[95] Flacco was no coward, but he felt that Hays's conduct was rash. He said that "Captain Jack" was "bravo too much."[96]

3 August 1841
ERATH'S FIGHT *(Palo Pinto, Texas)*
Austrian-born George B. Erath, for whom Erath County, Texas, was named, came to America in 1832. He fought in many Indian engagements, as well as at the Battle of San Jacinto in 1836. In July 1841 Erath gathered his Milam County militia, met with Capt. Eli Chandler's men from Robertson County, and went looking for Indians. They made slow progress up the Brazos River, having to deal with many sick men.

In the western Cross Timbers region, the Texans passed several abandoned villages. At the edge of the Cross Timbers, with supplies running low, the command was about to turn back when they spotted several Indians. Erath took twenty men to follow them, pushing hard along a trail that led into the mountains west of present-day Palo Pinto. Suddenly Indians, either Cherokees or Kickapoos according to Erath, opened fire on the men from behind a rocky cliff. Hidden within the rocks, the Indians were nearly impossible to see, and the canyon was narrow, giving Erath little room to maneuver.

Capt. A. J. Smith was killed in the first volley. Erath formed his men up in a little grove and returned fire for half an hour before Capt. William M. Love arrived with reinforcements. The combined forces charged the bluffs and drove the Indians from their position; the rough country made further pursuit impossible, however. The Texans buried Smith and headed home.

Erath figured that the Texans had killed and wounded several Indians. On 7 August, Erath and Chandler parted ways and Erath made his way home to Fort Bryant, south of present-day Temple, Texas.[97]

20 August 1841
BATTLE CREEK/FRAEB'S FIGHT *(Savery, Wyoming)*

By 1841 the era of the mountain man was nearly over. The beaver were about trapped out and the first large emigrant train, the Bidwell-Bartleson party, was crossing the plains to California, opening a new chapter in the westward movement. On their way back from California in July, a large party of mountain men that included Henry Fraeb, Jim Bridger, and Joe Walker stopped to trade with the Bidwell party on the Green River.

As the emigrants passed on, Fraeb and thirty-two trappers moved southeast. They stopped to trap on the Little Snake River, a tributary of the Yampa, on the present-day Wyoming-Colorado border. Fraeb sent ten men out from their camp to drive in some buffalo ranging on the nearby plains. While out, the detachment encountered a large party of Lakota and Cheyenne. The Indians attacked, and the ten trappers circled up to defend. One trapper, who was wounded early on, sent his horse running back toward camp, hoping it would alert Fraeb.

Battle Creek, Wyoming —Courtesy Robert and Elizabeth Rosenberg

The horse reached camp, and Fraeb got the message. He mounted up his remaining men and raced toward the fight. The battle was close, but Fraeb and the others, all excellent shots, succeeded in holding the Indians at bay. About a dozen Indians were killed. The surviving Indians set fire to the forest as they retreated to the mountains. The trappers lost four dead, including old Henry Fraeb.[98] Wrote trapper Jim Baker: "When he was killed he never fell, but sat braced against the stump, a sight to behold."[99]

30 August 1841
QUITAQUE CREEK *(Flomot, Texas)*

In 1841 Mirabeau B. Lamar, president of the Republic of Texas, wanted Texas to have a piece of the trade from the Santa Fe Trail and to establish Texas jurisdiction over the Santa Fe area. To accomplish this, Texans organized a political-military-commercial expedition to Santa Fe in June.

Volunteer soldiers gathered to transport and protect a large group of merchants and their goods. Brig. Gen. Hugh McLeod led the expedition, with Maj. George T. Howard second in command. They organized the recruits into five companies of infantry and one of artillery. Journalist George Wilkins Kendall and Englishman Thomas Falconer accompanied the 321-man expedition as guests. Twenty-one ox-drawn wagons carried supplies and merchandise valued at $200,000.

The company set out from Kenney's Fort, on Brushy Creek, on 19 June 1841. They headed north across the Brazos to the western Cross Timbers in present Parker County and continued north to the Wichita River, traveling upstream to its headwaters. On 17 August the company's Mexican guide deserted; they stumbled generally northwest, looking for the best paths. Along the way, Kiowas lurked about menacingly and stole some of their horses. Kendall recorded that on 28 June the Texans asked a Spanish-speaking Kiowa for directions, but he and his tribesmen gave only equivocal answers and said they knew nothing about the Colorado or Red Rivers. Soon the expedition began to run short of provisions and water.

In August, on Quitaque Creek in present Motley County, McLeod was unable to find a route for the wagons to ascend the caprock, so he sent out several parties to search for a path. Early in the morning of 30 August, Lt. George Hull and four men were riding north looking for water when about twenty Kiowas ambushed them. Hull formed a tight defensive circle and fought the charging Indians as well as he could, killing at least one Kiowa, called Adalhabakia (Sloping Hair). Another

Texan saw the attack and sped back to the main camp, shouting a warning. About fifty volunteers mounted up and rode toward the sound of the gunfire, while the wagons formed up in a square. But before the Texans could reach the scene, the fight had ended and the Kiowas were gone. Hull and his four men lay dead in their tight circle, the bodies scalped and mutilated. Hull had thirty arrow and lance wounds in his body, and another man's heart had been cut out.

The Texans were furious, wrote Kendall, "and madly did our men spur their horses in pursuit, with the vain hope of avenging the death of their companions."[100] The Kiowas kept just out of reach during the entire chase, until finally the Texans gave up. They buried Hull and his men on the prairie and continued their march to Santa Fe. About two weeks later, upon reaching New Mexico, the whole company was captured by New Mexican soldiers and marched to prison in Mexico City. Most were eventually released, but the episode increased the tensions between the United States and Mexico, which would ultimately erupt into the Mexican War.[101]

— 1842 —

April 1842
HANNUM'S FIGHT *(Fannin, Texas)*

In March of 1842, Gen. Antonio de Santa Anna sent an army under Gen. Rafael Vasquez, on an expedition north of the Rio Grande, during which Mexican forces easily captured San Antonio, Refugio, and Goliad. Families in west Texas fled east, and Texas president Sam Houston moved the government from Austin to Houston. One of these families were the Gillelands. Johnstone and Mary Barbour Gilleland moved from Pennsylvania to Texas in 1837, eventually settling in northern Refugio County, where Johnstone served with Capt. John J. Tumlinson's Texas Rangers. Johnstone and Mary's daughter Rebecca Gilleland, ten years old at the time of the Vasquez invasion, remembered how her family "frequently had to flee through blinding storms, cold and hungry, to escape . . . . The whole country was in a state of excitement. Families were in constant danger and had to be ready at any moment to flee for their lives."[102]

In the Gillelands' case, however, it was Indians, not the Mexican army, they had to fear. Taking advantage of the confusion, Comanches and other Indians began raiding out toward the Texas coast. One warm spring evening in April 1842, the Gillelands and their two children, Rebecca and her younger brother William, were outside their home when a war party of Comanches surprised them.[103] Johnstone ran for his rifle, but he was killed before he could reach it. Mary clutched Rebecca and William to her side and prayed for a moment before a warrior cut her down. The Indians dragged the children away, and a white renegade Texan riding with the Comanches threatened to cut off their hands and feet if they did not stop crying.

The raiders took what they wanted from the home and rode north. Recent incursions of the Mexican army had alerted the settlers and caused many local militia companies to organize. Lt. A. B. Hannum and Dr. A. T. Axsom of the Matagorda Riflemen were near the lower San Antonio River with men of other units, waiting for the Mexican army's next move. Also among the party was Albert Sidney Johnston, who would later become a Confederate general. When news of the Gilleland raid arrived, Hannum quickly obtained reinforcements and followed a broad, fresh trail he had recently spotted, headed north.

The Comanches never stopped moving. Carefully avoiding settlements, they crossed the river and rode through the night. In the morning, figuring it was finally safe to do so, they halted to rest near present-day Fannin, the site of the an 1836 battle during the Texas Revolution, in present Goliad County. No sooner had they stopped than the volunteers caught up with them. The Comanches saw the soldiers approaching and formed a battle line.

As one ornately dressed warrior pranced out in front on his pony, Hannum shot him off his horse, and the remaining Indians took to the woods. The volunteers dismounted and ran after them, planning to battle them from tree to tree. The Indians never stopped running, however, even leaving behind weapons, shields, and horses. Rather than bother with their captives, the Indians clubbed Rebecca on the side of her head and lanced William. Rebecca shook off her blow and made her way over to her badly wounded brother. Praying ardently, she carried him to the edge of the woods. Seeing horsemen approaching and believing they were Indians, she went back to hide in the timber. Then she heard friendly voices calling her name. Gathering up her strength, she carried the nearly lifeless William out to the prairie, where Hannum and his men found them.

The boy was in bad shape; blood flowed from his wound every time he breathed. Back at camp, Dr. Axsom immediately got to work and was miraculously able to patched the child up. He later published the details of the operation in the *New Orleans Medical Journal*. Dr. Axsom continued to care for William for some time, while Rebecca stayed with a Presbyterian minister, Dr. William Blair, in Victoria. The children later went to live with an aunt in Galveston. William recovered from his wounds and grew up to become a prominent Austin citizen. Rebecca Gilleland Fisher gained fame as president of the Daughters of the Republic of Texas. She was known as the "Mother of Texas" for her work in education, politics, and religion.[104]

— 1843 —

May 1843
BANDERA PASS *(Bandera, Texas)*

In the spring of 1843, Texas Ranger Jack Hays and his company of about forty men were camped on Leon Creek, west of San Antonio.[105] Leaving on a scout for Indians, the company headed northwest, stopping on the Medina River at present-day Bandera, Texas. From there, Hays planned to travel north to the Guadalupe Valley by way of Bandera Pass. At the same time, a band of about a hundred Comanches were heading in the opposite direction, intending to use the pass to raid in the Medina Valley.

Hay's Fight memorial at Bandera Pass, Texas

Hays arrived late in the morning at the south entrance of the long, wide pass, which was bounded by rock walls fifty to seventy-five feet high. The Comanches had arrived at the pass just ahead of the rangers and, seeing the Texans coming, they left their horses in the rear and hid themselves among the rocks and bushes on both sides of the canyon. The rangers suspected nothing until bullets and arrows started raining down on them. The attack threw them into temporary confusion, and when the Indians charged into them, the scene became a melee of bucking horses, thrown riders, wild shooting, and hand-to-hand fighting.

Hays, who had never before been caught in a trap, called out, "Steady there, boys; dismount and tie those horses; we can whip them; no doubt about that."[106] The rangers tethered most of their horses near the south entrance and formed a rough defensive perimeter facing north, but the Comanches were already upon them. A bullet pierced Sam Luckey's chest, and Ben Highsmith caught him as he fell. Highsmith tried to stop Luckey's bleeding with one hand as he fired with the other. While Highsmith covered Luckey, he was hit in the leg with an arrow, but he continued to shoot. Meanwhile, a warrior charged in and grappled with Sgt. Kit Ackland. The two men shot each other, then both fell to the ground and wrestled, each with a knife in his hand. After a long struggle in the dirt, it was Ackland who stood up, smeared with mud and blood.

Many of the rangers had Colt five-shooters, which made up for their smaller numbers and undoubtedly saved their lives. They finally drove off the Comanches, who were able to carry off most of their considerable number of dead and wounded. The Comanches buried their dead at the north end of the pass and rode back into the Guadalupe Valley. The rangers lost five killed, among them Peter Fohr (or Fore) and George Jackson. Their six wounded included Luckey, Ackland, Highsmith, Tom Galbreath, and James Dunn. Hays pulled back to a water hole at the south entrance of the pass, where the Texans spent the night burying their dead and taking care of the wounded. In the morning, they headed back to San Antonio.[107]

4 July 1843
OWL CREEK *(Cimarron, Kansas)*

The embarrassment of Texans over the failures of the Santa Fe Expedition of 1841 and the Mier expedition of 1842, as well as Mexican general Adrian Woll's 1842 raid on San Antonio, led Texan Jacob Snively to petition the Republic of Texas for permission to retaliate. On January 28, 1843, he requested approval for an expedition to capture Mexican caravans passing through territory claimed by Texas along the Santa Fe Trail. With permission granted, nearly 200 Texans gathered at Fort Johnson, near Coffee's Station on the Red River. Calling themselves the Battalion of Invincibles, they organized themselves into four companies and chose Snively as their commander.

The force, about 190 strong, crossed the Red River and traveled northwest across present-day Oklahoma, finally reaching the Arkansas River. Snively kept his force hidden south of the river for one month, hoping to pounce on passing Mexican wagon trains. On one occasion, they battled a force of a hundred Mexican soldiers, killing seventeen and capturing the others, but the rest of the time was spent waiting. The long days of inactivity soon brought discontent, and many of the men wanted to return home. On 28 June, the battalion was disbanded and the prisoners were released.

The men divided into two groups, designated the "Mountaineers" and the "Home Boys." The latter group of about seventy-six men selected Eli Chandler, who had opposed many of Snively's actions, as their leader. The companies marched separately to the Arkansas River. On 30 June U.S. Dragoons under Capt. Philip St. George Cooke, who had been sent to protect the Mexican caravans, discovered and disarmed the Mountain-eers, leaving them with only ten muskets. Most of the Texans, however, had hidden their good weapons when they saw the Dragoons, and they gave Cooke only the arms they had captured from the Mexicans. About forty-two of Snively's men accepted Cooke's offer to escort them back to Independence, Missouri, rather than retrace their steps through danger-ous Indian country. Snively and the rest rejoined Chandler on 2 July.

On 4 July, the company camped at a little stream called Owl Creek, which does not appear on modern maps but may have been near present-day Cimarron, Kansas. There, more than a hundred Comanches attacked the Texans and stampeded about fifty of their horses. After fighting off the attack, about thirty mounted Texans tenaciously pursued the raiders until nightfall. Finally catching up with the Indians, the Texans killed about twelve warriors and recovered some of the stock. They lost one of their own men in the fight, however, and several were wounded.

With men wounded, horses lost, and ammunition getting low, the Texans knew they were running out of options. When a large Mexican caravan appeared on the Santa Fe Trail on 13 July, the Texans followed it for a while but soon realized that its escort was too large to fight. The reunited companies, under Snively, finally turned toward home.[108]

20 July 1843
ANTELOPE CREEK *(Roll, Oklahoma)*

The expedition under Jacob Snively (see previous entry) was now reduced to about 140 men, divided into two commands under Snively and Eli Chandler. A lack of horses and the difficulty of transporting wounded men slowed their progress. Near the Antelope Hills the company camped on Antelope Creek, a small stream flowing into the Canadian River in present-day Roger Mills County, Oklahoma.

Frontiersman James O. Rice moved ahead to scout a path across the boggy creek when five Indians, probably Comanches or Kiowas, surprised him. They chased Rice into a dogwood thicket and captured his mule. While the warriors kept Rice pinned down, a few hundred more Indians attacked the camped Texans. Snively and Chandler were prepared, however, having built a solid defensive perimeter around the camp. The Indians circled the Texans, keeping up a desultory fire, but then pulled back. During the lull in the fighting, Rice crept out of the dogwoods and made it back to the camp, where the Texans cheered him—having seen his riderless mule return to camp, they had assumed he was dead.

The Texans repulsed a second attack from the Indians, after which a chief advanced with a flag, indicating he wanted to talk. Snively met with him, and the conference was friendly. They talked, smoked a pipe, and shook hands, then the chief walked away. The Texans had hardly heard the news of "peace" when the Indians charged them once more. The renewed fighting led to more deaths for the Indians. A chief again signaled for a parley, and Snively went out for another talk while the Indians removed their dead and wounded from the field. Immediately after the parley, however, the Indians launched yet another attack. The alternate shooting and talking went on until sunset, when a chief called out to the Texans: "We all now go to sleep—you go to sleep, and in the morning we get up—all have big smoke and all go home."[109]

Snively correctly figured that the chief only meant to delay things so the Indians could fetch reinforcements. Snively tried to move the company out that night, but the Indians heard them and attacked, though the Texans drove them off. Finally Snively sent Rice to find a quiet escape route, then, as silently as possible, the Texans crept away in single file. Upon reaching a grassy, open plain, they double-timed their way south. In the distance they could hear the Indians yelling at the discovery that the Texans were gone. The exhausted men made it to Bird's Fort, on the Trinity River, on 6 August.

During the repeated fights, the Texans suffered only a few men wounded. Although the Indians' losses were uncertain, their casualties must have been significant considering all the charges the warriors made.[110]

— 1844 —

April 1844

NUECES CANYON *(Camp Wood, Texas)*

After Comanches raided the country west of San Antonio, John C. (Jack) Hays took his Texas Rangers out to find them. His fifteen men included Kit Ackland, Mike Chevalier (or Chevaille), Creed Taylor, Tom Galbreath, Noah and Sam Cherry, and a new Irish recruit named Paddy. They headed west to the Nueces River, upstream into the Balcones Escarpment, and onto the Edwards Plateau. Reaching the headwaters of the river and finding no sign of Indians, Hays turned back downstream.

On the second day's ride, someone spotted a beehive in a tree. Honey was a welcome addition to the men's rations, and since it was getting to be about noon anyway, Hays had the rangers unsaddle the horses while Noah Cherry climbed the tree to get some honey. Up in the tree, Cherry noticed Indians coming down the valley. "Je-ru-sa-lem!" Cherry called out. "Captain, yonder comes a thousand Indians!"

Hays ordered his men to ready themselves and the horses. Galbreath estimated there were 200 Indians, who quickly spotted the rangers and charged. Hays told the men to hold their ground. The Texans' first volley knocked down several Indians, who split their charge left and right around the rangers. They probably expected the rangers to stay standing for better defense, but Hays told them to mount up. "After them, men!" he called. "Crowd them! Powder-burn them!"[111]

The rangers charged right behind the galloping Comanches, shooting at them continually. The Indians, unable to rally, scattered in all directions. Hays chased one group for three miles; Kit Ackland got so close he was lanced three times. Finally, the Texans gave up the chase and rode back. Several rangers were wounded, but none seriously except Ackland.

As the company regrouped, Paddy pointed to a brushy ravine, where he had seen a wounded Indian crawling. Hays warned, "If you go in there where he is, he will kill you before you see him."[112] Paddy declared he was not afraid of a wounded Indian and clambered into the thicket. A minute later, the Texans heard a sharp cry, followed by silence. Four rangers rushed in to find Paddy with an arrow through his heart. They saw the wounded Comanche hiding under some leaves and quickly killed him. The rangers buried Paddy beneath the bee tree and, forgetting about the honey, packed up and headed for home.

Years later, a friendly Delaware Indian reported that the chief who had led the Comanches that day said that many of his warriors were killed, and he never wanted to fight the rangers again. "They had a shot for every finger on the hand," the chief had said.[113] The comment was a tribute to the effectiveness of the Texans' newly acquired five-shot Colts. The Nueces Canyon battle may have been the first time the Colt had been used in a major fight.[114]

27 April 1844
AGUA DE TOMASO *(Baker, California)*

In April 1844 John Charles Fremont, on his way back to the States after his second expedition to explore and map the West, was camped on the Mojave River near present-day Harvard, California. On 23 April two Mexicans, Andreas Fuentes and an eleven-year-old boy, Pablo Hernandez, approached Fremont and asked him to help them get their horses back to the caravan they'd been traveling with. The pair and four others—two men and two women—had been traveling ahead of a larger Mexican caravan when about a hundred Indians attempted to capture their thirty-horse herd. Fuentes and the boy, who were guarding the herd at the time, drove the horses directly through the Indians, with arrows flying everywhere. To evade the raiders, the two drove the herd sixty miles to the water hole known as Agua de Tomaso, today called Bitter Spring. Assuming they'd evaded the Indians, they left the horses there and set off to find the caravan. When they came upon Fremont's camp, the Americans offered to help them.

Two days later, Fremont and his group followed Fuentes to Agua de Tomaso, about twenty miles east of present-day Baker. The horses were gone and the Indian trail was fresh. The next morning, Christopher H. "Kit" Carson and Alexis Godey volunteered to go after the Indians with Fuentes. Later that day, Fuentes's horse gave out and he returned to Fremont's camp. Godey and Carson continued on, traveling into the night. They stopped to camp but lit no fire for fear of giving away their position.

At sunrise Godey and Carson picked up the trail, soon spotting about thirty Indians, probably Chemehuevis, roughly two miles ahead. The two dismounted and walked quietly toward the Indians. They were able to creep right in among the stolen horses before a warrior spotted them, whereupon they boldly charged the Indians. Carson's first shot killed one warrior, Godey felled another, and the other twenty-eight ran for the hills. Godey was trying to scalp the Indian he'd shot when the warrior sprang up and fired an arrow through Godey's shirt collar. When the Indian collapsed again, Godey finished him off. The two victors rounded up fifteen horses (five had already been killed) and drove them back to Fremont's camp.

After the horses were recovered, Fremont and his men, along with Fuentes and Pablo, proceeded northeast to Archilette (today's Resting Springs), about four miles east of Tecopa, California, where Fuentes had last seen his four companions. Upon their arrival, an eerie silence greeted them. They found the bodies of the two men, Hernandez (Pablo's father) and Santiago Giacome, naked and mutilated—Hernandez with his legs cut off, and Giacome pierced with arrows. Pablo's dog had remained with the corpses and was ecstatic to see Pablo. The party saw no sign of the two women—Fuentes's wife and Pablo's mother—indicating they had probably been captured. Pablo cried in horror, "Mi padre—mi madre!" Fremont was outraged by the murders and apparent kidnappings. In honor of Pablo's father, he named the spot Agua de Hernandez. Later, another party found the bodies of the two women, mutilated and staked to the ground.[115]

8 June 1844
WALKER CREEK *(Sisterdale, Texas)*
In the spring of 1844, Maj. John C. (Jack) Hays led fourteen Texas Rangers out of San Antonio to scout for Indians in the hill country to the northwest. Among the company were several men who would become famous in ranger history, including Samuel H. Walker and Richard A. Gillespie. Hays's rangers were armed with the new Paterson Colt .36-caliber five-shooters. The rapid-shooting revolvers, along with the rangers' tight discipline, would give the Texans equal footing against mounted Indian warriors.

Hays led his men to the headwaters of the Pedernales River without finding any Indians; on the way back to San Antonio, however, the rangers discovered an Indian trail. While the company paused on Walker Creek, about thirteen miles north of present-day Boerne, Texas, Hays's rear guard came riding in to report that Comanches were right behind them. The rangers mounted and turned on the Indians, who leisurely retreated toward a thicket, exposing their role as decoys. When Hays did not follow them, more than sixty warriors rode out and confronted him. The rangers formed a line and moved slowly forward, whereupon the Comanches withdrew up a brush-covered slope and dismounted, taunting the Texans in Spanish.

Hays was not about to charge uphill against four times his number. Instead, he rode down a shallow ravine out of the Indians' sight, rode up the ridge, then charged the Comanche line from the flank. The rangers fired first with their rifles, then their five-shooters, blasting away at the startled Indians. Recovering from their surprise, the Comanches formed up and countercharged. Hays maneuvered his men into a tight circle, with the horses rump to rump, and repelled the Comanche charges from all angles. Walker and Gillespie took lance wounds, but the near-constant fire of the five-shooters decimated the Comanches. The Indians fled.

The Texans pursued them for two miles, then it was the Comanches' turn to rally. A chief loudly exhorted his warriors to fight. Hays shouted, "Any man who has a load, kill that chief!"[116] Gillespie, despite his wound, dismounted, took careful aim, and fired. When the bullet hit

Site of Walker Creek Battle, near Sisterdale, Texas

the chief, the Comanches suddenly lost their resolve. They pulled back, but still hovered about the ranger position.

Hays, with little ammunition remaining, could not go after the Indians again, nor did he feel he could retreat with his wounded, so he sent a man named Threadgill to get help. Back in San Antonio, however, Hays's lieutenant, Ben McCulloch, had already decided on his own to ride out with twelve more men to find Hays. When McCulloch arrived, the Comanches finally vacated the area. They left behind twenty-three warriors dead on the field, and Hays estimated that thirty more had been wounded. Two rangers had been killed and five were wounded.[117]

July 1844
BATTLEGROUND PRAIRIE *(Caldwell, Texas)*
Kentucky native William P. Oldham participated in many of Texas's formative episodes, including the siege of Bexar and the Somervell Expedition. He was also one of the few escapees of those captured in the Mier Expedition of 1842. Eventually Oldham built a homestead in what is now eastern Burleson County. Known as Fort Oldham, it sometimes served as a refuge for area settlers during Indian attacks.

In the summer of 1844, Oldham may have thought his fighting days were over, but when Indians raided the area he was called back into action. A small band of seven or eight Comanches had swept down through Milam County, where a small number of settlers discovered and pursued them along Cedar Creek. The Indians finally stopped in a strong defensive position along the creek. The settlers surrounded them, but they concluded they needed some help and sent for "Colonel" Oldham, who lived nearby.

Oldham, swiftly raising about thirty volunteers, hurried to the scene. The Indians, however, had slipped away. The combined force, with a number of good hunting dogs, found the Indians at what would become known as "Battleground Prairie," about twelve miles north of Caldwell, Texas. The Comanches had dug breastworks in the swampy creek bottom and were hiding partially buried in the dirt, but the dogs picked up the scent and bayed furiously. Two Texans, named Reed and Bingham, followed the dogs and spotted the Indians. Reed and a warrior fired almost simultaneously, and both bullets hit their target, Reed taking a fatal shot in the chest. Oldham and the volunteers poured shots into the marsh, but with little effect. The Indians returned fire, this time killing Bingham.

Oldham, bold as he might have been in his younger days, decided that the Indians were too well posted to be driven out without the Texans taking more casualties. He pulled his men back, and at nightfall, the Indians escaped. A few of the settlers returned the next morning to bury Reed and Bingham. The Indians' retreat was more or less permanent, and Battleground Prairie was the last major Indian fight in Burleson County.[118]

Ca. 15 July 1844
AGUA DULCE CREEK *(Orange Grove, Texas)*

Learning that Mexicans may have been planning an armed incursion into Texas, Capt. Jack Hays took fifteen Texas Rangers from Bexar to the Nueces River, continued to the lower Rio Grande, and rode back north to Corpus Christi, all without gathering proof of an intent to invade. While resting in Corpus Christi in mid-July, Hays received word that Comanches were raiding west of the city. He took twelve men and rode to the scene.

On Agua Dulce Creek, the rangers overtook and attacked about seventy-five Comanches. The warriors fought bravely, but the firepower of the Texans' five-shot Colts came as an unpleasant surprise. After roughly thirty Indians were killed and wounded in about fifty minutes, the Comanches fled the field. Hays took several wounded rangers back to Corpus Christi for medical attention, then rode with the rest of his men back to San Antonio.[119]

— 1845 —

April 1845
SABINAL CANYON *(Utopia, Texas)*

In February 1845, enlistments for several companies of Texas Rangers ended and new companies were mustered in for six months' service. Four reorganized units operated in south Texas; one of them, under a Captain Warfield, with William Knox as first lieutenant, was headquartered on the Seco River near present-day D'Hanis, Texas. The company's main purpose was to protect the settlers of Castroville and the surrounding countryside.

In the spring, Knox took a thirteen-man detachment, including John and Doc Saddler, Jim Fell, Doc Huffman, Josiah Cass, John Eastwood, Harrison Dougherty, and John Wesley Deer, on a scout into Sabinal Canyon. The trip was proving uneventful, so the rangers spent a few days hunting bears.

One cold night, Deer, the youngest and least experienced of the party, was on guard duty when he stopped to stir the campfire. A single shot rang out, piercing Deer's heart, and he fell back onto the bedrolls of Knox and Cass. The attackers, Lipan Apaches, charged, but the rangers, instantly alert, immediately pumped shots at them. John Saddler shot the first Lipan he could see, receiving an arrow in the chest in return. Another arrow pierced Huffman's hat. But the Texans' furious response soon drove the Indians away.

The rangers doused the fire and sat at the ready the rest of the night. Daylight revealed that eight Indians had been killed in the fight. Lashing Deer's body to a horse, the Texans rode back to their camp on the Seco, where they buried him. Saddler recovered from his wound.[120]

— 1846 —

Ca. 12–13 March 1846
PAINT ROCK *(Paint Rock, Texas)*

In February and March 1846, Comanches swept down off the Edwards Plateau and raided southwest of San Antonio, hitting the new settlements near Castroville and Quihi. In response, Maj. Jack Hays led forty Texas Rangers from their Medina River camp to go after the raiders. The trail led north through Bandera Pass; at Enchanted Rock, in Llano County, the rangers found a fresh trail going northwest. Hays figured the Indians were headed for Paint Rock, a favorite campsite and watering place nearly 100 miles away. He abandoned the meandering trail and, playing his hunch, headed straight for Paint Rock.

Hays stopped to rest his men at midnight, and the next day he drove them almost continuously. At one o'clock in the morning, the rangers arrived near Paint Rock, where Hays concealed his men in a willow grove not far from the small lake. At dawn, the Indians unsuspectingly passed by. At Hays command, the rangers blasted them with a volley. In the poor light, however, they hit only a few Indians, while more rode up. The Texans were badly outnumbered, perhaps fifteen to one. As the Comanches attacked from the northeast, Hays advised his men to "pick a warrior facing you and aim carefully!" One young recruit, F. W. Harrison, was nervous, and the old hands tried to calm him with jokes, such as "[Those] Injuns look too pretty to shoot." There appeared to be nearly 600 Comanches around them. Harrison remembered, "I saw the long line of painted savages coming and felt the hair rise on my head."[121]

When the Indians were within fifty yards, the rangers fired, knocking many down. The charge split in two. The Comanches regrouped and charged from the west, with the same result. They couldn't break into the willow thicket to dislodge the Texans. The Indians kept up the fight all day, attacking from different directions. Because the lake was within range of the rangers' weapons, the Comanches couldn't get to the water, so many eventually left to find another source.

The next morning, the Comanches attacked from all sides, trying to smash their way into the thicket, but the Texans forced them to break and retreat in the very first wave. Their next strategy was to shoot long-range arrows from the top of Paint Rock, but this tactic, too, was ineffective. By the third day, the Indians had realized they faced the hated "Devil Jack" Hays, and they began taunting him to come out and fight.

After a while a chief rode in close to the thicket, and when he turned to urge his warriors forward, his thick buffalo-hide shield shifted enough to leave an opening for Hays to squeeze off a good shot. The bullet hit the chief in the side and knocked him over, at which point a ranger leapt on his horse, rode out and lassoed the body, and dragged it back into the willows. This impudent action enraged the Comanches. The Indians made one last charge, but the Texans beat them off again. Finally they fled the area, departing so quickly that six Indians who were herding some stolen horses nearby were left behind, unaware that the fight was over. They were still waiting for their tribesmen when the rangers caught them and killed them, recovering about fifty horses.

The exhausted rangers picked up a few souvenirs from the battlefield and hurried back to San Antonio. The Texans had counted nearly a hundred dead Comanches on the ground. Of the rangers, only Emory Gibbons was wounded in the arm by an arrow.[122]

9 May 1846
KLAMATH LAKE *(Klamath Falls, Oregon)*
In 1846 John Charles Fremont, captain of the Army Corps of Topographical Engineers, was on his third expedition of the West. This time he was exploring the Great Basin, the mountains and deserts that stretch from the Columbia Plateau to the Mojave Desert. He was also hoping to survey and map a wagon road from Independence, Missouri, to the Pacific Ocean via the Great Salt Lake. At the time, a war with Mexico appeared likely; the government unofficially asked Fremont and his group of sixty

well-armed men to maintain a presence in California and be ready to act in a military capacity if necessary.

On 8 May 1846 Fremont and his men were in the Oregon Country, encamped in a stand of cedars on the west side of Upper Klamath Lake. Samuel Neal, who had been a member of Fremont's earlier expedition into California, and Sigler, Neal's employee, rode into the camp to tell Fremont that a courier from the United States, Lt. Archibald Gillespie, had messages for him. Anxious for news, Fremont took ten men (Kit Carson, Alexis Godey, Lucien Maxwell, Richard Owens, Basil Lajeunesse, Bill Stepp, an Iowa mixed-blood named Denny, and Delawares named Sagundai, Swanok, and Crane) and set off with Neal and Sigler to meet with Gillespie, who was camped about a day's ride south.

The party found Gillespie at the lower end of Klamath Lake with Peter Lassen and a few others from Sutter's Fort. Fremont read letters from his wife, Jessie; his father-in-law, Senator Thomas Hart Benton; the U.S. consul in California, Thomas O. Larkin; and Secretary of State James Buchanan. He also listened to a memorized message from President Polk bringing him up to date on the political situation in California. That night Fremont and his party camped near Ball Bay, on the northwestern end of Upper Klamath Lake, about seventeen miles northwest of present-day Klamath Falls. Believing the spot to be peaceful, the captain did not set a guard over the camp. He stayed up late that night rereading the correspondence and pondering his mission. Suddenly he heard noises among the mules and horses tethered near the lake and grabbed his revolver, stepping out to investigate. Finding nothing amiss, Fremont went back to his blankets. As he recalled in his memoirs, "I had barely fallen to sleep when I was awakened by the sound of Carson's voice calling to Basil [Lajeunesse] to know 'what the matter was over there?'"[123] The query was soon answered with shouts from Carson and Owens: "Indians!"

In a flash, the Klamath raiders split open Lajeunesse's head with an ax and shot Denny with several arrows. Fremont's Delawares grabbed their rifles and took cover. Fremont, Carson, Godey, Stepp, and Owens ran to their aid just as the Klamaths charged into the open ground. In the dim light, Fremont could see Crane springing from side to side, defending himself with the butt end of his unloaded gun, but the Delaware soon fell with five arrows in his torso. One of Fremont's men shot down the Klamath's chief, who dropped in front of Crane's body. The death of their chief sent the Indians fleeing for the woods, where they kept up a barrage of arrows and tried to retrieve the chief's body.

Fremont's group returned fire, making it so hazardous for the Klamaths that they finally gave up. Fremont and his men spent the remainder of the night with rifles at the ready, expecting another attack.

At dawn the explorers saw that the Klamaths had disappeared; their tracks indicated that there had been fifteen or twenty of them. Fremont remembered, "It was a sorrowful sight that met our eyes in the gray of the morning. Three of our men had been killed: Basil, Crane, and the half-breed Denny, and another Delaware had been wounded; one-fourth of our number."[124] Gillespie recognized the dead Klamath chief as one who had given him a salmon at the lake a day before. Carson split the chief's skull to bits with an ax, and Sagundai scalped him. The creek by the encampment was named Denny Creek in memory of the Iowa mixed-blood.

The next morning Fremont was marching for his main camp when it appeared that Klamaths might attack them again. He and his men had been carrying the bodies of their three dead companions, but at this point Fremont decided it best to bury them. The attack never came, however. The following morning Fremont, knowing the Klamath warriors would return to the battle site for their chief's remains, permitted Sagundai and Swanok to return there and wait to ambush the raiders in revenge for Crane's death. A few hours later, the two Delawares caught up with Fremont carrying two fresh scalps.

Further retribution occurred on 12 May, when Carson and ten men found a Klamath encampment of fifty lodges at the northeast corner of Klamath Lake, near the mouth of the Williamson River. They charged into the village, and within a short time, fourteen Indians lay dead. Carson and his companions torched the village and reduced the Klamath canoes to toothpicks. The Delawares, still avenging Crane's death, took the scalps of the dead Klamaths.[125]

28 October 1846
ISLETA *(Isleta, New Mexico)*
In the summer of 1846, at the start of the Mexican War, Gen. Stephen W. Kearny left Santa Fe and marched to California. Following in October was Capt. Philip St. George Cooke and his Mormon Battalion. On 25 October at Valencia on the Rio Grande, Navajo raiders killed two shepherds and ran off more than 5,000 sheep from the ranch of Don Antonio Jose Otero. The next day, Cooke, camped at Los Lunas, across the river from Valencia, learned of the depredation. Unable to chase the

marauders himself, Cooke sent word to Capt. John Henry K. Burgwin, First Dragoons, who was camped near Albuquerque. Burgwin and a detachment of two companies had been sent out to escort some American traders to Chihuahua. After the raid, most of the Pueblo Indians in the area were already out looking for the Navajos, so Burgwin and his poorly mounted dragoons went to help protect the people of Los Lunas and Valencia.

Meanwhile, the Navajos returned to make another raid, this time taking livestock and capturing a woman and five children at Isleta Pueblo, about six miles upriver from Los Lunas. Burgwin sent Capt. William N. Grier and Lt. Clarendon Wilson, with portions of Companies D and G, to pursue the raiders. The troops, only partially mounted, chased the Indians west for sixteen miles, recovering some straggling stock on the way. Most of the men, on exhausted mounts, eventually dropped back. By day's end, only Grier, Wilson, and two soldiers were still on the chase.

When the four dragoons saw four Navajos enter a ravine ahead, they spurred on to catch the Indians before nightfall. Suddenly, the four Navajos became fifty, and the Indians turned to attack. Grier, who was in the lead, stopped and fired, killing two Navajos. He kept up a fighting retreat until the rest of the dragoons caught up with him. The soldiers killed one more Navajo and wounded several, with one dragoon getting slightly wounded in the process. When the dragoons advanced, the Navajos fled. Grier's men rescued the captives and recovered some of the stock. They scalped the three dead Navajos and later presented the scalps to the Pueblo Indians of Isleta. A few nights later, the Pueblos held a celebratory dance with the three scalps.[126]

— 1847 —

19 January 1847
TURLEY'S MILL *(Arroyo Hondo, New Mexico)*
Former trapper Simeon Turley lived about a dozen miles north of Taos, on the banks of the Rio Hondo, where he had built a gristmill and distillery. His "Taos Lightning," a fiery wheat whiskey, was famous among the area's trappers, traders, and Indians. Adventurer George F. Ruxton, who visited Turley in mid-January 1847, described the place and its residents as prosperous and happy. Ruxton noted that Turley, along with his family members and Indian and Mexican employees, were always

Ruins of Turley's Mill, Arroyo Hondo, New Mexico

willing to feed the hungry and aid the poor. Ruxton left Turley's Mill on 16 January; three days later, the place was destroyed and most of its inhabitants were killed.

The people at Turley's Mill were victims of the Taos uprising. In August 1846, at the beginning of the Mexican War, American soldiers under Col. Stephen W. Kearny had seized and occupied New Mexico, but having met little resistance, Kearny moved most of the soldiers out a few weeks later. The conquered Mexicans and Indians plotted a revolt, and in January 1847 they rose up to kill or drive out the remaining Americans.

On 18 January in Taos, Mexicans, Pueblo Indians, and possibly some Jicarilla Apaches and Navajos killed New Mexico territorial governor Charles Bent and several other officials and ransacked the town. That evening, a rider sped by Turley's Mill with a warning. Turley considered himself a friend to the local Mexicans and Indians, and he even had a Mexican wife, but he was an American and had American employees. Just in case, Turley and his American men decided to barricade themselves in the distillery.

At sunrise the next morning, a mob of Mexicans and Indians appeared at the mill. Approaching the distillery, one of them called out to Turley, asking who was inside. Turley replied that there were eight other Americans with him. The mob leader said that they would spare Turley if he came out, but they were going to kill every other American in the valley. "I will never surrender my house or my men," he replied. "If you want them you'll have to come and get them."[127]

With that, the Indians began shouting and dancing. John Albert, firing from an upper window, shot one down, and the battle was on. Billy Austin killed another warrior, and Albert shot a third. The Indians scattered. A moment later, however, the Mexicans and Indians encircled the two-story adobe building, taking cover in the trees and among the boulders of the surrounding canyon. From there they fired a barrage of bullets, which thudded into the distillery's thick walls but failed to hit any of the defenders. By nightfall, several Mexicans and Indians had been shot, but not one American had received a scratch. Though the besieging force had grown to more than 500, and some of them kept up an intermittent fire all night, the Americans held them off, pouring out bullets and keeping up their defense.

At one point some Indians crept up to the distillery and tried to chop through a wall, but it didn't work. As the warriors ran back across the open corral, an American fired through a loophole and hit one of them. When another Indian tried to drag the body away, he too was shot. Then a third was killed. Three more ran out after the bodies, but the Americans blasted them. Seeing six Indians lying dead in the corral, the attackers finally made a concerted rush. A hundred guns blazed. For the first time, two trappers were hit and mortally wounded.

At first light, there was a lull in the battle. By now the Americans were dangerously low on ammunition. In the midafternoon the fighting picked up, and Turley was hit in the shoulder. The Americans hoped to hold out until dark, then make a run for it. But when dusk fell, the Indians rushed up to the distillery and started several fires. The flames eventually took hold and spread over the wooden roof. As thick smoke poured into the building, the men on the second floor realized they had to go downstairs. Just then, part of the roof collapsed. The men raced down the stairs, but falling timbers blocked two of them. Tom Tobin, trapped in a back room, kicked out some loose bricks in the wall and squeezed out into the corral. Finding no Indians posted there, Tobin crept away into the night.

Downstairs, some Indians broke down the front door. After shooting the intruders, the remaining Americans rushed out into the yard with guns blazing and knives flashing. During the melee, all of the Americans were killed except one. Only John Albert broke through and disappeared in the dark, heading north to Colorado.[128]

Meanwhile Tobin ran to his house to get his Mexican wife and his family. But his wife urged him to escape without them, assuring him that the insurgents would not harm them. Tobin mounted his best mule and took off for Santa Fe to alert the U.S. forces there. When Col. Sterling Price organized a punitive expedition, Tobin was among the first civilians to join up.[129]

12 May 1847
PAWNEE FORK *(Larned, Kansas)*

On 12 May 1847, 100 Comanche Indians led by Chief Ikanosa (Red Sleeve or Red Arm) and 100 Kiowas led by Chief Satank were searching for their Pawnee enemies. Unsuccessful in their quest, they spotted a wagon train on the Santa Fe Trail, traveling eastbound on the south side of the Pawnee River. Ikanosa proposed an attack, but Satank felt bound to honor a peace treaty made in 1837. Ikanosa slung insults of cowardice at Satank and his warriors, demanding that they watch as he and his Comanches attacked the train.

The wagon train, property of New Mexico governor Manuel Armijo's family, consisted of fifty-four men with eighteen mule-drawn wagons and a large herd of mules and horses. Providing protection were fourteen newly discharged Missouri Volunteers who had served in the Army of the West during the Mexican War. The Comanches appeared on a hill west of the trail and north of the Pawnee River. Seeing the war-painted Indians, the wagonmaster arranged his train into a square. The Indians crossed the river and began to circle the wagons, but the teamsters and soldiers held their fire until the raiders got closer. When Ikanosa's Comanches tightened the circle and charged the train, the rifles of the teamsters and Missourians exploded in a well-planned volley. The first Indian hit was Chief Ikanosa. The bullet passed through his thigh and penetrated his horse's spine. The horse fell, pinning the chief to the ground. The Indians wavered, then retreated, gathering their wounded as they left.

Ikanosa lay too close to the enemy for his tribesmen to rescue him. He screamed for Satank to help, but the Kiowa, still angry at Ikanosa's recent insults, did nothing to save him. When the men of the wagon train realized the Indians would not launch a second attack, they ran out to the trapped chief and shot him dead. The Kiowas and Comanches rode away.

The raid had been a partial success, however, for the attack had diverted the defenders while the Comanches rounded up many of the train's horses and mules. No one in the train had been hit, but they did lose 105 of their livestock. The train continued its journey with no further trouble from Indians, reaching St. Louis on 28 May.

On 22 June another eastbound party, camped on the south bank of the Pawnee River, discovered the badly decomposed body of an Indian. One of the travelers, Lewis H. Garrard, wrote, "I found the skull and skeleton of an Indian. The sinews, well gnawed by the wolves, were not yet dry and the skin and hair still graced the head, which, passed from hand to hand by the curious, was, at last, tossed into . . . Pawnee Fork."[130] Thus was the unceremonious end of Chief Red Sleeve.[131]

28 May 1847
WALNUT CREEK *(Great Bend, Kansas)*

In the spring of 1847, Indian attacks along the Santa Fe Trail were at their zenith. An eastbound wagon train owned by Bent, St. Vrain & Company and commanded by Frank De Lise passed Fort Mann, Kansas, on 24 May. Three days later, De Lise selected a campsite at Walnut Creek Crossing. Walnut Creek, in the midst of the buffalo plains, was a shallow stream feeding into the Arkansas River. With its steep banks lined with scrub trees, it was an ideal camp spot and an equally good spot for Indian ambushes.

The next morning, De Lise and another trader, William Tharp, went on a buffalo hunt while the livestock were let out of the corral to graze. Suddenly, mounted Indians attacked the circled wagons, the livestock, and the hunters all at once. The raiders ran off sixty of Tharp's mules, forty of Bent and St. Vrain's mules and oxen, and nine other horses and mules. Only 200 yards from camp, four groups of Indians attacked the two buffalo hunters from all directions. Although caught by surprise and vastly outnumbered, De Lise and Tharp held their ground and put up a staunch defense. They shot down five Indians before Tharp was killed and scalped. He was buried at Walnut Creek Crossing.[132]

26 June 1847
PLAIN ENCAMPMENT/LOVE'S DEFEAT
(Garfield, Kansas)

In June 1847, 1st Lt. John Love and Company B, First Dragoons, were ordered to escort the paymaster, Maj. Charles Bodine, from Fort Leavenworth,

Kansas, to Santa Fe, New Mexico Territory. Bodine's twelve-wagon train was carrying $350,000 in specie. At Pawnee Fork on 23 June, two more wagon trains joined Love's group for protection. One was government wagonmaster Capt. Charles Hayden's thirty-wagon train, and the other was a thirty-wagon train led by a man named Fagan.

Earlier that day, Indians had attacked Hayden and Fagan, wounding three or four of Fagan's men. A Mr. Smith, from Van Buren County, Missouri, was lanced seven times, but he managed to shoot and kill his attacker as he lay bleeding. The same Indians had also attacked another train, led by a Mr. Bell and Col. William H. Russell, and its fifteen-man guard from the California Battalion, commanded by Second Lieutenant Brown. The raiders had driven off and slaughtered 160 of that train's oxen. Love assured Bell and Russell that he would seek revenge.

On 24 June, the expanded party spent the day getting the wagons across the Pawnee River. The next day, Love ordered the trains to stay close together. Fagan was fine with that directive, but Hayden stubbornly rode ahead, forcing the others to travel until nightfall to catch up. Love camped next to the Arkansas River for better access to grass and water;

Site of Plain Encampment/Love's Defeat, Garfield, Kansas

the spot also appeared to be fairly safe from attack. Fagan's train camped in the rear. This campground, later known as Plain Encampment or Grand Prairie, was five miles southwest of present-day Garfield, Kansas, near the Big Coon Creek Crossing.

Saturday morning, 26 June, was a clear day with a gentle southerly breeze. Both Hayden and Fagan, believing there was no danger, let their oxen out to graze under the watchful eyes of the herdsmen. Love was surveying the area with his telescope from a high point overlooking the camps when he heard some war whoops coming from the direction of Hayden's camp. A group of mounted Comanches rose out of some tall grass nearby, while others charged from the ravine near Big Coon Creek. The sight and noise of charging horsemen caused the oxen to stampede. About 250 Comanches rode among the animals, lancing several. The herders, helpless to stop the stampede, placed themselves between the warriors and the livestock, but the Indians charged right through. Three herdsmen were wounded.

Seeing this, Love hurried back and ordered his dragoons to pursue the Indians. Just then, 200 more Comanches appeared south of the river, directly across from the dragoon camp. The lieutenant deployed twenty-five dragoons around the camp to protect the paymaster's wagons and sent Sgt. Ben Bishop to take twenty-five mounted men in pursuit of the original raiders and the stolen oxen.

Bishop's detachment crossed Coon Creek and saw the Comanches 150 yards in front of them. Bishop charged, expecting that Hayden's teamsters and herders would join him, but seeing that their side was outnumbered about tenfold, Hayden's men fled back to camp. The dragoons fought bravely in hand-to-hand combat for twenty minutes. After five soldiers were killed and six wounded, Bishop ordered a retreat.[133] The Comanches scalped three of the fallen soldiers, cut the throat of one, and sliced off the ears of the last. The dragoons estimated a dozen or more Comanche casualties. About 160 oxen were driven off.

After the attack, Love had all members of the party camp together for protection. He sent a messenger to Fort Leavenworth to inform officials of their plight and requested that supplies and new oxen for the trains be sent to Fort Mann, a nearby post that, though abandoned, could still provide a degree of protection. To allow the wounded time to stabilize, Love waited until 2 July before traveling to Fort Mann. Six days later, Love and his dragoons, the paymaster and his entourage, and Fagan's train left the fort, reaching Santa Fe on 6 August. Hayden and his train had to wait at Fort Mann until a party arrived with more oxen. Finally, on 23 July, with 360 head of oxen yoked to his wagons, Hayden headed for Santa Fe.[134]

20 July 1847
EASTON'S FIGHT *(Ford, Kansas)*

Lt. Col. Alton R. Easton, with three infantry companies and one company of cavalry (Missouri Mounted Volunteers), set out from Council Grove on 5 July escorting thirty-three wagons and teamsters, 200 mules, 100 horses, 600 loose cattle, and 30 mounted herdsmen to Fort Mann. The party was bringing oxen to Capt. Charles Hayden's wagon train, to replace those stolen in a raid on 26 June (see previous entry). On 20 July the company stopped to camp along the Arkansas River about twenty-five miles downstream of Fort Mann, approximately seven miles east of present-day Ford, Kansas.

While camped, about twenty-five to fifty greenhorn infantrymen went to gather wood from a grove of cottonwoods on the opposite bank of the river, unwisely leaving their weapons behind. Suddenly, the same Comanches who had attacked Hayden's train appeared at the edge of the sand dunes near the river and ambushed the unarmed soldiers. The Indians killed eight soldiers and wounded four others before anyone was able to come to their aid. The Comanches lost one warrior. The Indians scalped four of the dead soldiers and buried all the bodies in a mass grave.[135]

Easton arrived at Fort Mann on 23 July, where he resupplied Hayden's thirty-wagon train with oxen, enabling Hayden to continue his journey to Santa Fe. Easton himself departed Fort Mann on 26 July and arrived in Santa Fe on 22 August.[136]

1 August 1847
ASH CREEK *(Pawnee Rock, Kansas)*

Lt. Christopher "Kit" Carson departed Fort Leavenworth on 17 July to deliver dispatches from President James K. Polk to Col. Sterling Price in Santa Fe and Gen. Stephen W. Kearny in California. Lt. Stephen D. Mullowny and fifty men of Company D, Third Regiment, Missouri Mounted Volunteers, escorted Carson. On 1 August Carson and his entourage camped at Ash Creek, near the famous landmark of Pawnee Rock. On the same evening, Capt. Benjamin W. Smithson's Company I, Third Regiment, Missouri Volunteers, which was escorting a large wagon train, was camped 300 yards away.

As morning dawned, Smithson's inexperienced men led their horses and livestock out to graze. Suddenly, war whoops shattered the calm, and from the brush by the riverbank 400 Comanches appeared and charged the livestock, causing them to stampede in all directions. Most of the animals ran toward Carson's camp, and Kit and some soldiers cut between the stock and the charging Indians. They held off the attackers until troopers from both camps converged and drove the Indians back. Smithson lost thirty-six cattle, and Carson lost two horses.

About six or eight Comanches were killed and about the same number were wounded. Three of Mullowny's men were wounded. Carson reached Santa Fe on 27 August without further Indian engagements.[137]

Ca. 10 August 1847
COON CREEK CROSSING *(Garfield, Kansas)*

In the summer of 1847, with troops needed to fight in the Mexican War, Col. Edward W. B. Newby and his regiment of Illinois Infantry Volunteers prepared to leave Fort Leavenworth for Santa Fe. He divided his regiment into three detachments and staggered their march. Traveling west on the Santa Fe Trail, Newby led one detachment, comprising Companies D, F, and G, along with a supply train. Just before Newby reached the Great Bend of the Arkansas River, traders Alexander Barclay and Louis Tharp and their seven-wagon train joined the group. Near Pawnee Rock the party passed Col. Sterling Price, who was headed east to Fort Leavenworth. Price's men were leading some traders' horses they had recently recovered from Indian raiders.

After passing Price, Newby continued on, stopping to camp at Coon Creek Crossing. The infantrymen tried to build a fire with buffalo chips, but a recent rain had soaked the fuel, which produced little more than acrid smoke. Several of the men decided to wade over to a nearby island in the Arkansas River to look for firewood. One of the volunteers had a gun, but he dropped it in the water, rendering it inoperable.

Upon reaching the island, the soldiers were immediately attacked by some Indians who had been hiding in the brush. As the volunteers fled for the northwest bank, two were killed and one was wounded; all three were scalped. Alerted by the screams and war whoops, twenty-five armed men from the camp rushed out to pursue the Indians, who were thought to be Comanches or Arapahos. The Indians mounted and fled southeast toward some sand hills. The soldiers chased the attackers for five miles, but the Indians escaped without a trace.

On 20 August, another of Newby's detachments joined the party at Lower Cimarron Spring. Newby regrouped, then continued on to Santa Fe, arriving in mid-September without further incident. The wounded and scalped soldier survived; in Santa Fe, he was sent home with an eastbound wagon train.[138]

16 November 1847
FORT MANN *(Howell, Kansas)*

Fort Mann was established in April 1847 as a midpoint on the Santa Fe Trail between Fort Leavenworth and Santa Fe. In November 1847 several companies of Missouri Volunteers of the Indian Battalion were garrisoned at the fort, including Capt. William Pelzer and Company C, his all-German foot artillery; Capt. Paul Holtzscheiter and the all-German Infantry Company D; and Capt. Napoleon Koscialowski with Infantry Company E. Pelzer was characterized by Indian agent Thomas Fitzpatrick as a man with not the slightest savvy in dealing with Indians.

In the middle of the afternoon on 16 November, a Pawnee chief and three warriors approached the fort. Pelzer, Lt. Caleb S. Tuttle, and a six-man guard went outside the fort to parley with them. The chief handed Pelzer a letter declaring they were peaceful, so the captain let them inside. After smoking a peace pipe with the chief, Pelzer fired a howitzer to impress his guests. Meanwhile, he sent a detail to bring the chief's sixty other Pawnees into the fort.

Pelzer was still suspicious of the Indians, however, and planned to disarm and hold them until Lt. Col. William E. Gilpin of the Indian Battalion, who was camped at the Big Timbers with two other companies, could give him instructions. When the other Pawnees arrived, Pelzer told the guards not to let them leave. The Indians, assuming they were going to be fed, seated themselves in a circle around the flagpole.

Around this time, a sentry alerted Pelzer that another 300 or more Indians were gathered on the opposite bank of the Arkansas River. Several Pawnees were still waiting outside the fort, and Pelzer ordered a guard to bring them in. Fearful that the Indians at the river would try to free those in the fort, Pelzer asked the chief in sign language if they were with him. The chief said no, but Pelzer accused him of lying. The captain hurriedly conferred with Lt. Henry L. Rouett about what to do next. Rouett wanted to release the Indians, but Pelzer snapped back that he would rather "butcher" them all.

It is uncertain whether the Pawnees understood Pelzer's threat, but the chief no doubt had already sensed trouble, and he signaled for his tribesmen to run for their lives. Pelzer ordered his men to fire. One warrior was killed and two were wounded in the first volley. While most of the Pawnees escaped through the open gate, three of them ran into Pelzer's quarters for cover. The soldiers fired into the building. One of the warriors fled, making it over the fort walls, but he was soon killed. The other two gathered all the combustible goods they could find and started a fire. The soldiers shot through the door and windows, leaving both Indians "perfectly riddled with balls."[139]

Four Pawnees were killed in the melee, and about twenty were wounded. Three soldiers, including Captain Holtzscheiter, were wounded. Newspapers blamed Pelzer for the bloody fiasco.[140]

— 1848 —

24 February 1848
SAND HOLLOW *(Boardman, Oregon)*

In November 1847, rebellious Cayuse Indians killed a dozen people and took forty-nine captives at Marcus Whitman's mission in southeastern Washington. The following month, the provisional legislature of Oregon Territory authorized the governor to raise a regiment of riflemen, not to exceed 500 men, for ten months of service. The Oregon Rifles, 441 strong, under Col. Cornelius Gilliam, marched for the Walla Walla country in February 1848. Their objective was quasimilitary, being charged only with apprehending the Cayuses involved in the massacre.

The first major contact with the Cayuses was made about noon on 24 February, east of Willow Creek and about fifteen miles southeast of present-day Boardman, Oregon. Peace commissioners rode in front of the soldiers carrying a white flag, but a large group of Cayuses suddenly appeared on the surrounding hills and waved the commissioners away. The battle was on.

The forces were about equal in number, both just under 500. Along with the Cayuses rode some Walla Wallas, Palouses, and Umatillas; watching the fight nearby were bands of Coeur d'Alenes, Flatheads, and Kalispels. The Indians probably thought their experience on the uneven terrain would benefit them, but many of the Oregon Volunteers were frontiersmen, and the officers handled the situation well. Gilliam deployed the men in two diverging lines to protect the supply train and cattle. In the northeast quarter of the field, the enthusiastic soldiers advanced in double time, shouting louder than the Cayuses.

The Indians fired a volley then retreated, and the soldiers advanced. The Cayuses fired another volley and retreated. The tactic was apparently meant to draw the soldiers away from the main command, but the troops never outran their support, keeping together remarkably well for new, untrained recruits. Riding up close to the soldiers, Chiefs Gray Eagle and Five Crows called out that they were big medicine men; Gray Eagle claimed he could swallow bullets. Capt. Tom McKay, who knew Gray Eagle, heard the chief's boast. "Then let him swallow this one," he said, and he shot Gray Eagle through the head. Interpreter Baptiste Dorion ran out and stomped on Gray Eagle's head to underscore the point. At the same time, Lt. Charles McKay shattered Five Crows's arm with another bullet. As the wounded chief fled, Lieutenant McKay chased him, but Five Crows's fleeter pony swept him to safety.

Seeing that the Americans could fight, the Cayuses finally broke and fell back. The Indians had lost eight killed and five wounded; five of Gilliam's men were wounded, including Lt. Col. James Waters.[141]

Ca. 13–14 March 1848
TOUCHET RIVER *(Waitsburg, Washington)*

Col. Cornelius Gilliam and his Oregon Rifles continued their march to the wrecked Whitman Mission (see previous entry), near present-day Walla Walla, Washington, arriving there 2 March 1848. Finding that animals had dug up the victims' bodies, the soldiers reburied many of them in a common grave. The men stayed to rebuild some of the destroyed buildings into a fortification they called Fort Waters. During this time, a few Indians tried to make peace overtures, but Gilliam was so angry about the massacre that he would hold no council.

On 7 March Gilliam learned from some friendly Nez Perces that the guilty Cayuses were camped about thirty miles north, near the mouth of the Tucannon River. Four days later, after sending the peace commissioners and some ill soldiers back with an escort to the Willamette Valley, Gilliam and 268 men marched north. The Cayuse chief Sticcas met Gilliam and told him that as an offer of peace he had tried to capture Joe Lewis, a mixed-blood who had been an instigator in the Whitman murders, but Lewis had escaped. Gilliam, unimpressed, hurried on his way. When the soldiers reached the Tucannon River, they discovered that the Cayuses had fled across the Snake River. The men rounded up some stray livestock and headed back to Fort Waters.

As the Oregon Rifles marched south over the divide between the Tucannon and Touchet Rivers, about 400 Palouse Indians attacked them. Gilliam kept his outnumbered soldiers moving in a fighting retreat. The bold Indians charged close to the troops several times, but the soldiers drove them away each time. That night, Gilliam camped without fires or food. The Indians would not let the soldiers rest, however, peppering the campsite with gunfire throughout the night. Hoping to appease them, Gilliam released the cattle, but it was to no avail.

As Gilliam set out the next morning, the Palouses followed along, firing as they had done the previous day. Finally, two angry and frustrated companies from Yamhill and Washington Counties went after some Palouses who had come too close, going to a hilltop and challenging the Indians to fight. Their stand enabled the rest of the soldiers to move closer to the Touchet River, though they had to fight their way past a small Indian fortification, where several soldiers were wounded. Capt. William Shaw took twenty mounted men and dashed ahead to take a key hill above the river, where they could command the immediate terrain and secure a passage for the troops.

When Gilliam finally reached the Touchet, the Palouses yielded to the wishes of their women and stopped fighting. It was a lucky break for Gilliam. Although he had lost only a few killed and several wounded, he was nearly out of supplies and ammunition. On the Palouse side, four had been killed and fourteen wounded.

Gilliam reached Fort Waters on 16 March. Shortly afterward he left with half his force to get supplies at The Dalles. While camped near the Umatilla River on 20 March, Gilliam reached into a wagon for a rope, which caught the trigger of a loaded rifle. The bullet killed him instantly.[142]

18 June 1848
COON CREEK (Kinsley, Kansas)

On 5 June 1848, Lt. William B. Royall of William Gilpin's Santa Fe Battalion left Council Grove with seventy-one recruits, headed for Fort Mann. The company was escorting a sixty-wagon government train that included paymaster Maj. Thomas S. Bryant with the soldiers' wages, as well as civilian wagonmaster Fagan's 425 cattle, which were being driven to Santa Fe. Civilians named Burnham and Fulton led the train. Near

Walnut Creek, Lt. Phillip Stremmel and sixty-four artillerymen of Gilpin's Battalion joined Royall's party.

On 17 June the train camped between the Arkansas River and Coon Creek, a few miles northeast of present-day Kinsley, Kansas. Bryant and twenty-five men guarded the southern edge of the camp. The paymaster's wagons were set up directly north of Bryant, adjacent to Royall's recruits; Fagan's wagons and the beef herd filled in the gaps. The cattle and horses were corralled or picketed under the supervision of guide Tandy Giddings. Stremmel's artillery completed the circle, with howitzers placed at the north and south ends of camp. Signs of Indians had been seen all day, and the campsite was well known for ambushes, so Royall doubled the guard.

At 5:20 a.m. on 18 June, the shout of "Injuns!" rang through the camp. The troopers scrambled for their weapons. Two Comanches had been seen on the southeast bank of the river, shaking their lances and shouting war whoops. Then, to the west, 200 to 300 war-painted Comanches approached. To the north were another 200 warriors, and to the south, 200 more.

This was the first battle in which the soldiers used their new breech-loading carbines, whose one-ounce balls could be fired five times a minute with a range of almost 400 yards. When the Comanches galloped within range, Royall's men fired their first volley, but most of the bullets bounced off the Indians' war shields. At 300 yards the troopers fired again, with similar results. Finally at 200 yards, the Indians suffered some damage. As the charge neared forty yards, the soldiers were ordered to shoot the horses. The painful cries of the ponies caused the Indians to turn and retreat. The soldiers fired again, and more Comanches fell.

A new group of Indians appeared from the dry bed of Coon Creek and tried to charge through Bryant's tents, but Royall's men repulsed them. Bryant moved a howitzer into position beyond the picket line and directed its firing, killing two warriors and their horses. The Indians galloped through Royall's tents, but the soldiers' fire was intense, and several warriors were killed. As the Comanches reached Fagan's wagons on the far side of the camp, they met a barrage of fire from the teamsters. When Burnham shot and killed one of the Indians, the warrior's pony dragged his body into the corral, where the Comanches were unable to retrieve it.

Stremmel fired his howitzer from the tents on the north side of the camp. The Indians charged into the picket line and attempted to stampede the animals, but the damage was contained and Lt. William Khulow was able to recover most of the stock. The Comanches finally withdrew, crossing the Arkansas River. Bryant shot two of the retreating Indians with his howitzer, and one of Royall's sharpshooters killed another with a long-distance carbine shot.

Almost miraculously, not one soldier was killed or wounded in the fight, though twenty horses and four mules were stolen. Nine Indians were killed and an unknown number were wounded. While most of the soldiers continued the march to Fort Mann with the wagon train, Royall and thirty-eight men pursued the Indians to recover the animals. Royall's detachment rode north and crossed the Arkansas two miles below the campsite. There Royall saw about 100 warriors fleeing southeast into the sand hills and began to gallop after them. About two miles from the river, as the troopers plodded through the sand, about 600 Comanches encircled them.

Royall ordered his men to charge up a high sand dune to the south. The soldiers caught the Indians off guard, killing four or five of them, and nearly broke out. In the initial charge, one soldier, Smith P. Carter, dropped his carbine and fell from his horse as he tried to pick it up. A Comanche brandishing a war club saw the trooper's predicament and charged him. Royall interposed himself and fired, but he missed. The warrior then turned on Royall, charging him several times with his lance. On one pass he pierced the lieutenant's hat. A Sergeant Northcutt, seeing the attack, shot and killed the Indian. Meanwhile, Carter was rammed by an Indian's horse, which bruised his shoulder, but he escaped and joined the others on the dune.

Pvt. James Roop also had a close call when a Comanche charged him with a lance. The weapon struck Roop's iron belt buckle and stuck fast. Roop held the lance with one hand and shot the Indian with the other. Though seriously wounded, Roop joined his detachment at the top of the dune. There, Royall formed a perimeter to protect his position from all sides. The Comanches attacked, but the soldiers killed or wounded several warriors on the first pass. The Indians regrouped and charged a few more times, but they suffered casualties on each attempt. Finally the Comanches retreated just beyond the dune. From there they sent a barrage of arcing arrows that wounded several soldiers. Royall replied with carbine fire, and the Indians finally quit the field.

Royall estimated that fourteen Comanches were killed and twenty-eight were wounded, and that the troopers had killed ten Indian ponies.

Remarkably, only four troopers were wounded.[143] Royall's command arrived at Fort Mann on 20 June. The soldiers rested there for two days then struck out for Santa Fe with the wagons and the cattle herd. Bryant delivered the pay to the troopers at Fort Mann and left for Fort Leaven-worth on 1 July.[144]

19 June 1848
MANCO BURRO PASS *(Trinidad, Colorado)*

A westbound merchant train left Missouri for Santa Fe in May 1848. Among the traders were Preston Beck, Sam Wethered, Elliott Lee, G. Estes, Thomas O. Boggs, H. O'Neil, Peter Joseph de Tevis, and Smith Towne. They traveled together to the Middle Crossing of the Arkansas River, where most of the party took the Dry Route, but Lee, Towne, Tevis, and about twelve others took the Mountain Route.

At Bent's Fort, the smaller group met up with Charles Towne (Smith's brother); mixed-blood trader Pascual Riviere, nicknamed Blackhawk; a Delaware called Little Beaver; a man named Piles; and frontiersman, trader, and guide Lucien Maxwell. Just a week earlier, some of these men had been attacked by Indians while trying to cross the Raton Mountains,

Manco Burro Canyon, Colorado

so they decided to try a different route. The combined group left Bent's Fort about 16 June, and headed for Manco Burro Pass, which Charles Towne described as "a perfectly easy route" through the mountains. The party included the young children of William Tharp, a trader who had been killed by Indians the previous year (see Walnut Creek, 28 May 1847). The second party of traders, friends of Tharp, had agreed to take six-year-old Mary and four-year-old James to their grandparents in Taos.

At noon on 19 June, the travelers stopped for lunch in a little valley at the top of the pass, elevation 8,430 feet, about a dozen miles southeast of present-day Trinidad, Colorado. While the stock grazed and the party sat down to eat, about 150 Jicarilla Apaches, possibly aided by Utes, attacked them. The Indians ran off the animals then swept by the camp, firing bullets and arrows. The traders drove the raiders away, but they returned, this time setting fire to the grass. Despite the flames, the traders stayed put and fought for about four hours. In that time, one was killed and five were wounded. They finally decided they had to break out of the circle and climb up the mountain walls. As they fled, Lee was hit in the hand and thigh, but he continued on. Charles Towne was hit in the thigh, the bullet breaking his leg, and according to Lee, he "was left to the mercy of the Indians."[145] Both of the Tharp children were captured in the escape attempt.

Besides Towne, three other traders were killed in the attack: Jose Cortez, Jose Carnuel, and Pascual Riviere. Of the escapees, eight out of nine had been wounded, but by nightfall they felt they were safe. They traveled through the night, and at daylight they rested, hiding under dirt and rocks to ward off the cold and hide from Apache searchers. As the men continued their trek, Lee's wound slowed him down so much that the others left him behind. As his companions moved ahead, Lee called out to them, but they did not respond. He walked and crawled toward Taos, eating some food he found in an abandoned Indian camp. On the seventh day, he met up with a small party of miners, one of whom was Thomas Boggs, who had taken the Dry Route when the original train split up at Middle Crossing and was now on his way to Taos. They stopped in Mora, where Lee recuperated for a time before making his way to Taos.

Meanwhile the rest of the survivors struggled through the mountains until Tevis, the only one not wounded, went ahead to Taos for help. There, frontier guide Dick Wootton was informed of the situation, and he led a party of forty soldiers out to rescue the survivors, who arrived in Taos much the worse for wear. One, Andres Fernandez, soon died of his wounds, but the others recovered. About three months later, Taos merchants ransomed back the Tharp children for $160, but Mary died shortly afterwards. The Manco Burro Pass incident resulted in increased military activity against the Jicarillas.[146]

9 July 1848
BATTLE OF THE CIMARRON *(Protection, Kansas)*

On 7 July 1848, Capt. John C. Griffin and 101 men of Companies A, B, C, and D of William Gilpin's Indian Battalion, with one six-pound howitzer, set out to scout for Comanches who had been causing chaos on the Santa Fe Trail. Their march began from the cavalry camp (Camp Gilpin) across the Arkansas River from Fort Mann. They traveled south to Crooked Creek, which they followed down to the Cimarron River. They marched east along the Cimarron about eight miles and camped on the south bank, in present-day Harper County, Oklahoma. From a high point, Griffin spotted a large grove of trees at the mouth of Clark Creek, about twelve miles ahead, possibly sheltering Indians.

The morning march on 9 July revealed that the grove had indeed been home to a Comanche village. While the soldiers watered their horses, they spotted a mounted Indian, and Lt. Joseph C. Eldridge, Company B, took twenty men to investigate. As the detachment rode east, a Mexican boy rode up to them. Eldridge took the youngster to Griffin, who suspected that he could be a Comanche spy.[148] The boy revealed that the Comanches were camped about nine miles downstream. Griffin ordered a pursuit.

After a three-hour trek, Griffin reported, the soldiers "came in sight of their warriors, about 600 strong, posted on a well-chosen piece of ground on the north side of the Cimar[r]on."[149] The Indians formed into a double-lined battle formation, with their flanking wings thrown forward. The left wing was on the ridge of a low sand dune, and the right wing was on a higher ridge behind the left wing. Griffin ordered his men to the center of the Comanche line. The artillery crew unlimbered the howitzer in a dry arroyo nearby and fired at a cluster of Indians while the cavalry prepared for a charge. Griffin sent some mounted men toward the Indians' left wing. At the same time, Lieutenant Benson, Sergeant Clark, and twenty soldiers attacked some warriors to the left of the arroyo. Benson's soldiers pushed the

Indians to the crest of the embankment. At the top, however, Benson was surprised by 200 mounted Comanches poised to charge. The soldiers dismounted and formed a line, loosing a barrage of fire that drove the Indians back. More Comanches appeared in the soldiers' rear and fired at them ineffectually with small arms.

Griffin had meanwhile crossed the arroyo with his remaining men and the howitzer, while Eldridge and twenty men went to strengthen Benson's position. When a new group of Indians threatened Benson's rear, Griffin blasted away at them with the howitzer. The Comanches' right flank gave way, and their left flank retreated to its original position in the sand dunes. Eldridge pursued the retreating Indians, with Benson providing support. Griffin fired a few long-range howitzer shells, killing two Indians. From a hill, Griffin saw the fleeing Comanches about six miles downstream. Two groups of cavalry pursued but could not catch them.

At a cost of only slight arrow wounds to Eldridge's hand and Gibson's head, the soldiers estimated thirty Indians were killed in the three-hour battle. Griffin and his exhausted troops set up camp on the river next to the battlefield. The next day, they marched north toward Mulberry Creek, but for two days they found no water. Late on 11 July, they reached the dry creek, but it took another hour to find a water hole and relieve their extreme thirst. They reached Fort Mann the next day.[150]

20 July 1848
JONES'S FIGHT *(Protection, Kansas)*

Lt. Col. William Gilpin wanted confirmation that the hostile Indians had been removed from the vicinity of the Santa Fe Trail and no longer posed a threat to travelers. On 15 July 1848, Gilpin ordered Capt. Thomas Jones, Company B, Indian Battalion, to take 113 cavalry, civilian guides, and a six-pound howitzer to scout for any remaining Indians.

Jones left the Arkansas River at its south bend and headed south along Bluff Creek to the Cimarron River, camping there on 19 July. At dawn the next day, the company marched west up the north bank of the Cimarron. At 10 a.m. civilian guide Micheau Duvall spotted Indians upriver. Jones organized his men for an attack and proceeded to a densely vegetated spot near the mouth of Willow Creek, about twelve miles south of present-day Protection, Kansas. A Lieutenant Bain took thirty cavalrymen to inspect the grove, whereupon a band of Comanches sprang out and attacked them. Jones, seeing Bain's predicament, sent Lt. Joseph C. Eldridge to the other end of the grove with thirty additional troopers. Eldridge approached from the south, trapping the Comanches between the two detachments. The battle was fought hand-to-hand for a while, but the troopers finally managed to get into shooting positions and overwhelm the Indians with their superior firepower.

The soldiers counted forty-one Indians in total, and only six were seen to get away. They found twenty-one Comanche bodies; Jones assumed the remaining fourteen were dead or dying in the thick brush, but he didn't stay around long enough to police the woods. Five soldiers were severely wounded, one of them Eldridge, whose wound was his second in eleven days (see previous entry).[151]

After tending to his men's wounds, Jones trekked along the Cimarron to the mouth of Snake Creek, where he discovered the remains of an Indian village near the site of the Battle of the Cimarron (see previous entry). Jones returned to Fort Mann to get medical care for his wounded, arriving there on 23 July. The army's two recent victories appeared to have driven the Comanches away from the Santa Fe Trail, at least for the time being.[152]

23 July 1848
CUMBRES PASS *(Cumbres, Colorado)*

In 1848, after the Mexican War, the Third Regiment of Missouri Mounted Volunteers was stationed in the Santa Fe and Taos area. Before the Missourians were mustered out, they were employed to protect the local settlers and travelers. The infamous borderlander and scalp hunter James Kirker signed on with the Missourians as a guide and spy. In mid-June, Kirker led a battalion of fifty Missourians under Capt. A. S. Boake into the Raton Mountains. They caught up to a band of Jicarillas north of the mountains, near the Purgatoire River. The Indians fled, and Boake recovered thirty-two stolen horses and mules, some of them belonging to the Lee-Townes train, which had been attacked several days earlier (see previous entry).

On 18 July, Kirker, along with frontiersmen Bob Fisher, Levin Mitchell, and Bill Williams, left Taos with a larger expedition of 150 Missourians under Maj. William W. Reynolds. They crossed the mountains to the upper Purgatoire, where they picked up a trail of perhaps 400 Indians. The track cut across the San Luis Valley to the upper Chama River in New Mexico Territory. The Missourians found a band of Indians and opened fire, but the Indians fled without any substantial damage to either side. Kirker and the other mountain men trailed one of the scattered bands to a strong defensive position in Cumbres Pass, in the southwest corner of present-day Conejos County, Colorado. The ensuing battle was hard fought, and the result was devastating to the Jicarillas and Utes. The Missourians lost two men, but they killed thirty-six Indians and wounded many more. The battalion then returned to Taos.[147]

11 October 1848
ESCONDIDO CREEK *(Kenedy, Texas)*

For several years prior to 1848, the Texas counties of Gonzales, DeWitt, and Karnes saw relatively few Indian attacks. That changed in October, when a band of about forty Lipan Apaches came down the Cibolo River and raided Sandies Creek in western Gonzales County, in the process killing two settlers, Dr. George W. Barnett and the son of Rev. John S. McGehee. Then, along Ecleto Creek in Karnes County, they killed two more, a man named Lockhart and the son of Thacker Vivian.

The raid sent a shock wave through the area. In western DeWitt County, thirty-two men and boys gathered under the command of Capt. John York, for whom the village of Yorktown, Texas, was later named. York, a native of Kentucky, had fought in many battles during the Texas Revolution. Among the men accompanying York were his son-in-law, John M. Bell; his own son, James York; Richard H. Chisholm; James H. Sykes; Hugh R. Young; and guide Joseph Tumlinson. On 11 October, York's command picked up the Indians' trail on Cabezo Creek and followed it to the junction of Escondido Creek and the San Antonio River. Crossing to the west side of the river, they found an abandoned campsite with letters and other possessions of the Apaches' recent victims. Judging by their trail, the Indians, driving many horses, were leaving the region.

Even though York and his men had been tracking the Indians for nearly twenty hours with hardly any rest, they hurried on. After following Escondido Creek for about five miles, the Texans ran into an ambush. The Lipans, hidden in a small patch of trees, screamed and fired at Tumlinson and York's advance men, throwing them into confusion. Even so, Tumlinson tried to hold. When the main command came up, the Texans made one rush at the Lipans, but the Indians' close, accurate fire took a toll. Sykes was shot and killed as he dashed up to the thicket. Two Lipans rushed out to scalp him, but the Texans shot them. John Bell, York's son-in-law, was shot down on the open prairie between the lines. As York ran to him and picked him up, he was shot through the kidneys. Both men fell in a death embrace.

The surviving Texans, in a panic, retreated to a small grove about sixty yards away. The Lipans came out to pin them down, and for the remaining hour of daylight, both sides kept blasting. Finally, darkness ended the fighting, and both sides, tired, hurt, and low on ammunition, moved off in opposite directions.

The Texans lost three killed and about six wounded, including Tumlinson, Young, and York's son James. The latter was shot through both cheeks, which left him severely disfigured. The Texans believed they had killed or wounded half a dozen Indians. The Lipans' October rampage was the last Indian raid in that part of the country. John York and John Bell were buried in the same grave, in a cemetery eight miles east of Yorktown.[153]

— 1849 —

28 February 1849
BATTLE CREEK (Pleasant Grove, Utah)

Since Brigham Young entered the Great Salt Lake Valley in July 1847, the Mormons had remained at peace with the Indians. Though Young recognized that the Indians had a rightful claim to the land and tried to coexist peacefully with them, he did take a stab at turning them into farmers. The peace lasted until early in 1849, when a band of discontented Timpanogos Utes began raiding south of Salt Lake City and around Utah Lake.

Immediately after the raids, Capt. John Scott left Salt Lake City with about forty men of the Nauvoo Legion, a temporary volunteer force who formed up in times of crisis. Scott took his men south to where Utes had recently killed stock and stolen horses around Willow Creek and present-day Draper, Utah. From there they went to the east side of Utah Lake and met the Timpanogos Little Chief. The chief told Scott that the renegade band was camped by a creek a short distance to the north. Little Chief's son led Scott to the stream, where they saw the Indians' campfires in a deep ravine amid dense willows. Scott divided his command into four sections, surrounded the camp, and charged.

The small band, under Kone and Blue Shirt, numbered only seventeen people, just four of them warriors. Even so, they put up a tough fight that lasted more than three hours. After all four men were finally killed, Scott captured the women and children and took them to Salt Lake City on 6 March. The captives were well cared for during their captivity, and they were soon released.

After this and similar incidents, Brigham Young decided that punishing the Indians was more trouble than it was worth. He wanted to teach them to farm, but, he concluded, "They prefer idleness and theft." Intermittent fighting would flare up for years.[154]

13 March 1849
EL CERRO DE LA OLLA *(Cerro, New Mexico)*

Until 1849, the Utes had remained generally peaceful with the white trappers and traders in what is now northern New Mexico and southern Colorado. Early that year the Arapahos defeated the Utes in a devastating battle on the plains, destroying many of their livestock. To recoup their losses, the Utes began stealing stock from Mexican settlements in the Taos area. In March Lt. Joseph H. Whittlesey, stationed in Santa Fe, was ordered to chastise the guilty Utes.

Whittlesey gathered fifty-seven men from Companies G and I of the First Dragoons and marched north, guided by frontiersmen Bill Williams, Charles Autobees, Asa Estes, and others. A short distance from Santa Fe, the scouts located a fifty-lodge Ute village near the 9,475-foot peak known as Cerro de la Olla, ten miles west of present Cerro, New Mexico. Whittlesey attacked the village, killing ten warriors, capturing three women and children, and destroying the lodges and supplies. Two dragoons were killed in the fight.

The defeated village was left even more destitute than before. The Indians claimed they would make a reparation for the stolen stock at some point in the future. Later that month, the Utes exacted some revenge by killing "Old Bill" Williams in the Colorado Rockies.[155]

1 May 1849
FORT NISQUALLY *(Dupont, Washington)*

Fort Nisqually, the first European settlement on Puget Sound, was established by the Hudson's Bay Company in 1833. The original site was above the Nisqually River delta in the present town of DuPont. The fort had a twenty-foot-high stockade around it with three-story bastions at the northwest and southeast corners. The 1846 boundary treaty between the United States and Great Britain placed the fort in American territory, increasing American settlement in the area. By 1849, with the fur trade declining and competition from American merchants rising, the fort was of little importance. Nevertheless, its presence, along with the influx of settlers, alarmed the local Indians.

One of the most vocal Indians was Patkanin of the Snoqualmies, who was exhorting the tribes to rise up and kill the Americans before their numbers became too great. Patkanin wanted to attack the small settlement at Tumwater, but he met opposition from Nisqually chief Gray Head. Instead they planned to kill some white men on Whidby Island. The men, however, were forewarned and escaped. Next Patkanin decided he would try his luck at Fort Nisqually. Using the pretext that he wanted to chastise one of the Indians at the fort, the Nisqually Lachalet, for allegedly beating his Snoqualmie wife, Patkanin arrived at the post with 100 Snoqualmie, Snohomish, and Skokomish warriors. Patkanin reckoned on interference by the men at the fort, giving him an excuse to attack them.

When so many warriors appeared at the fort, the Hudson's Bay Company factor, Dr. William F. Tolmie, asked them why they were there, and he was given the story about Lachalet's wife beating. To defuse the situation, Tolmie invited Patkanin into the fort for a council, while the other chiefs were given tobacco and told to wait outside. One of them, Quallawout, refused his, believing it to be poisoned. Two other men, the Nisqually Gohome and Louis Thibeault, got their weapons and stood by the gate.

A short time later, Gohome fired his musket—whether it was done in jest, by accident, or as a signal is not known. With the shot, many jittery Nisquallies and a few Americans ran toward the fort for protection, followed by Patkanin's warriors. A warrior named Kassas (or Cussas) shoved Gohome aside and got in. The company clerk, Walter Ross, ordered him to leave, but Kassas cursed at him. When Ross tried to push him outside, the warrior pulled his dagger and thrust it at Ross.

Several Indians inside began scuffling with the whites. Gohome closed the gate, but another employee, Charles Wren, was still outside, so Ross ordered Gohome to let him in. When he did, several more Indians squeezed in. Wren grabbed an Indian's gun and wrestled it from him. The gun dropped in the gateway and prevented the gate from being closed. The Snoqualmie Quallawout fired at Wren but missed. Kassas fired at Ross, missed him, and hit another employee. After several shots and knife thrusts, the Indians, realizing that they did not have enough warriors inside to take over the post, rushed to the gate to get away. During the excitement, Patkanin, who had been inside talking with Tolmie, ran outside, scaled the stockade, and escaped.

The Indians rushing out met three Americans trying to get in. Kassas shot and killed trader Leander Wallace, and a man named Walker was wounded. A man named Lewis made it to safety after bullets pierced his vest and trousers and another grazed his arm. Hudson's Bay men climbed the bastions and fired at the retreating Indians, killing a Skokomish medicine man and wounding two Snoqualmies.

Ross later expressed that he was certain that if the Indians had succeeded in killing the men in the fort, they would have murdered all the whites along the sound. Patkanin had accomplished several things he certainly did not want. The Hudson's Bay men were now enemies, as were the white settlers. Blockhouses were built at Tumwater and Cowlitz Prairie, and more soldiers arrived in the area. In October, six Indians were arrested and brought to trial at Fort Steilacoom. Four were acquitted, but Kassas and Quallawout were convicted of murder and hanged.[156]

June 1849
DEADMAN'S PASS *(Comstock, Texas)*

A train of five wagons, owned by a Dr. Lyons and Nat Lewis of San Antonio, left El Paso in late June 1849 headed for home. Among the thirteen men in the train were Ben Sanford, Emory Givens, John Crowder, Charley Hill, Jerry Priest, Charles Blawinsky, Nick Andres, and men named Brown and McDonald. John L. Mann, who had been along the route several times, served as guide. Eight men on horseback rode along with them, but at Devil's River these men left the slower wagons and rode on. This brought the party's number back to thirteen, which some of the men considered a bad omen.

Deadman's Pass, Texas

At Deadman's Pass, north of present-day Comstock, Texas, a band of Comanches allowed the riders to go through, waiting for the slower wagons. Mann saw a lone man in the road far ahead, but he thought it was one of the riders and no cause for alarm. Walking in front were Priest and an unnamed blacksmith. The latter was apparently of unsound mind; the others thought he was crazy, but harmless. When the wagons reached the pass, the Indians attacked from both sides of the road. Priest ran back to the others, but the blacksmith just stood in the road. He was killed in his tracks.

Brown, an old Indian fighter, calmly stood by his wagon and fired, knocking a warrior from his horse thirty yards away. A bullet fatally struck Brown. Blawinsky, whom the men called "Polander," fought near Brown and was also mortally wounded. Some men from the next wagon ran out and pulled Blawinsky back with them. Andres climbed into the wagon bed and was about to shoot over the rim when a bullet hit him in the throat and killed him. An unnamed old man who was with Andres picked up the dead man's gun and ran to the next wagon, but he went down with a bullet in the knee. Crowder and Givens were both wounded in the arm. Mann took a minor wound when a bullet tore through his hat and grazed his scalp. During the fighting, the Indians ransacked Mann's wagon, stealing his best rifle. The warriors also captured the wagon in which Andres lay and took the dead man's scalp.

The Indians besieged the wagon train's survivors until about two in the morning. When the defenders began to hear fewer shots, Mann expressed confidence that the Indians were running out of ammunition and assured his companions that the rest of them would all survive. Sure enough, the Indians pulled off about 400 yards, built a fire, and roasted the beef from Mann's wagon. At daylight they were gone. Though Charley Hill, walking up a hill to see if the raiders had left, was chased back to the wagons by four mounted warriors, no further damage was done. About 9 a.m. seven mounted Mexicans riding in advance of a small wagon train appeared. When Mann explained the situation, the Mexicans combined their train with Mann's to form a secure corral. They readied for another attack, but none came.

The Mexicans sent a rider north and up Devil's River to a detachment of soldiers at Beaver Lake. The soldiers arrived the next day and took up the Indians' trail, but they never caught up with them. Two wagons were lost in the fight, a few oxen were killed, and several animals were stolen. The four dead men were buried at the pass.[157]

16 August 1849
SANTA RITA COPPER MINES *(Cobre, New Mexico)*

Gold seekers heading to California quickly wore out their tentative welcome while crossing through Apache lands in New Mexico Territory. When some of them tried to work the old mines abandoned by the Mexicans at Santa Rita del Cobre, hostilities increased. Capt. Enoch Steen, First Dragoons, arrived in Santa Fe from Fort Leavenworth in July 1849 and marched down the Rio Grande to Dona Ana, where he established a post on 1 August. Stationed at Dona Ana during its first few months were Companies D, F, and H of the First Dragoons and Company B of the Third Infantry.

Only a week after the post was established, Apache raiders under Mangas Coloradas came through the area. Steen led about fifty dragoons of Company H in pursuit. The Indians' trail led northwest past the Mimbres River to the foot of the Pinos Altos Range and the old copper mines.[158] There Steen met a large band of Apaches and got the worst of the encounter. Three dragoons were wounded, while the Indians may have taken no casualties. Steen was severely wounded by a man known as "Apache Jack" Gordon, a white renegade who had lived with the Chiricahuas for several years. The dragoons marched back to Dona Ana and claimed they had defeated the Indians, but the Apaches continued to raid in the area nearly unchallenged.[159]

29 October 1849
FORT KEARNY *(Kearney, Nebraska)*

Fort Kearny, on the Platte River, was a busy place in 1849. Upwards of 30,000 emigrants and "Forty-Niners" would head to the Pacific coast by year's end. By midsummer, about 4,400 wagons had already rolled past the fort on their way west. Travelers were required to stop at the fort to register the names of those in the party, along with the number of wagons, the number of animals, and so on. Many emigrants purchased supplies while they were there and made repairs at the blacksmith shop. The number of emigrants on the road almost guaranteed confrontations with the Indians.

The local Pawnees, who often passed the fort on their way to buffalo hunts or raids against the Cheyennes, were accused of stealing emigrants' stock. When Capt. Robert H. Chilton, Company B, First Dragoons, took over as commander of Fort Kearny in July, he constantly sent his men out on scouts, vainly attempting to keep the peace. In October, south of the fort on the headwaters of the Little Blue River, Chilton's men clashed with a band of Pawnees. Later that month, Chilton received news of some Pawnees camped on an island in the Platte, only a few miles north of the fort. Hoping to secure the safety of the new wave of emigrants expected the next spring, Chilton planned to capture the Indians, thus inducing their chiefs to come in for a peace conference.

Chilton rode out to the island camp with a detachment of Company B. He ordered his men not to shoot, which would be a nearly impossible directive to follow if plans went awry. As the dragoons maneuvered through the tall grass, wild grapes, and willows trying to surround the Indians, the Pawnees naturally thought they were being attacked. Sergeant Martin, Corporals Haff and Cook, and Bugler Peel confronted four Indians and tried to get them to put down their weapons. One of the warriors ran, and Haff chased after him and shot him. Another Pawnee ran to a cottonwood, with Cook close behind. As the two men, only twenty feet apart, trained their guns on each other, Cook signed to

Fort Kearny, Nebraska

the Indian to drop his weapon. Instead the warrior threw back his blanket, preparing to shoot. He and Cook fired at the same time. The Indian missed, but Cook's bullet hit, slicing through the warrior's mouth.

Cook was reloading when Chilton rode up and asked him who had killed the Indian. "I did," Cook replied. Chilton demanded to know why he had violated the mandate. The corporal was flabbergasted but said nothing. Just then, Peel rode up and reported that Martin was dead. Peel explained that Martin had chased a Pawnee to try to make him surrender his weapon, but the Indian had turned on him. Peel, nearby, had fired and hit the Indian, but after falling the warrior raised himself up and shot Martin through the heart.

The enlisted men were angered over the results of Chilton's order, which they believed was foolish. Now Martin and two Indians were dead, and the Pawnees were probably convinced that the soldiers meant to kill them all. The dragoons placed Martin's body across his horse and took it back to Fort Kearny for burial.[160]

— 1850 —

8–9 February 1850
PROVO RIVER *(Provo, Utah)*

For several months, the Mormon settlers at Fort Utah, on the south side of the Provo River, had endured the depredations of a band of Ute Indians led by Chief Walker (Wakara). Each day, the Indians became bolder, despite warning shots from the fort's cannon. The settlers, afraid that the Indians were trying to push them out, appealed to their church leaders in Salt Lake City for aid. At the meeting of the church's high council on 31 January 1850, Willard Richards stated that the troublesome Utes in the Utah Valley should be exterminated, and Brigham Young agreed. Gen. Daniel H. Wells, commander of the Utah Territorial Militia, ordered a company of fifty minutemen under Capt. George D. Grant and thirty more under Capt. Andrew Lytle to go to Fort Utah and put an end to the siege. Wells told them to take no prisoners and "let none escape but do the work up clean."[161]

Grant and Lytle arrived at the fort on 7 February. They met with fort commander Capt. Peter W. Conover and his officers to plan the initial attack for the next morning. The warring Utes had secured themselves in a redoubt of felled cottonwoods in the river bottom a mile above the fort. Across from the Indians' fortified village was the log home of prominent settler James A. Bean, occupied by the Indians after Bean fled to the fort.

On 8 February at 9 a.m., Wells's militiamen and thirty men from Fort Utah moved up the east side of the river. Artillerymen commanded by Lt. George W. Howland of the Regiment of Mounted Rifles, who was assisting the Mormons in their campaign, positioned the cannon on the east side of the river as close as possible to the Indian camp. Conover and sixty infantrymen crossed to the west side of the river and positioned themselves opposite the Indian fortification, hiding in the undergrowth on the bank. When all the troops were in place, Grant took some of his militiamen and interpreter Dimick B. Huntington to the Indian camp to propose a peaceful surrender. While peace chief Ope-Carry spoke with Huntington, Chief Old Elk and his men, still within the redoubt, opened fire on Grant's men. The battle had begun.

The artillerymen fired the cannon at the Indians, but this was not very successful, as the Indians were partially protected by the riverbank and the cannon was too close—most of the shots carried overhead. One Indian woman was killed, her legs cut off by chain shot (two cannon-balls connected by a chain). Artilleryman George Mayer later wrote: "The Indens Returnd the fire with Rifils and the boolets wised among us like hale, and Severl of our men ware wooned."[162] The cannon was moved back to a spot near Miles Weaver's cabin, half a mile southwest of Bean's house. The officers had selected the cabin as their field headquarters.

Still on the west riverbank, Conover saw an opportunity to capture about half a dozen Ute ponies. With Lt. Robert Egbert and Sgt. Robert T. Thomas, Conover waded through the frigid waters of the Provo to seize the horses. On the way back, a Ute spotted them and fired, grazing Conover's cheek. Conover returned fire and struck the warrior, also in the cheek. (The Ute, named Fisherman, survived the wound and later became Conover's good friend.)

As a bitterly cold night descended, the militia retreated to the fort. Mormon settler William Hickman reported that when the militia withdrew, the "Indians set up such a yell of victory that one would think 10,000 devils had been turned loose."[163] But the Indians had not won yet. The next morning, Grant ordered the militiamen up both sides of the river as before. While he commanded the men on the east bank, Conover and frontiersman Edmund Ellsworth concentrated their troops on the west. Fighting in the morning was heaviest on the west side, moving to the east side in the afternoon.

One of the Fort Utah militiamen, Lt. Alexander Williams, begged the commanders to give him ten men to implement a plan: taking a position on the west bank, he would fire from an angle that would force the Indians from their fortification. His request was granted, but the Utes spotted the detachment and held them at bay with their own rifle fire. Williams was shot through the shoulder, and nineteen-year-old Joseph Higbee was shot in the neck and killed.[164]

Howland also implemented a plan, constructing two movable barricades that would permit the militia to move in closer to the Indians' redoubt. The sight of these portable "forts" slowly closing in on them frightened the Utes, and they opened a heavy barrage of gunfire against them. Later Grant ordered Lt. William H. Kimball to choose fifteen men to charge and capture Bean's house, which the Utes had just abandoned. Kimball's men included Robert T. Burton, Lot Smith, James Ferguson, John R. Murdock, Ephraim K. Hanks, A. J. Pendleton, Orson K. Whitney, Barney Ward, Henry Johnson, and Isham Flyn. The mounted detachment moved up the river, approached the house from the rear, and charged. The Indians fired on the horsemen as they crossed a small slough, wounding Flyn, but the remaining attackers reached the rear of the house. The front door was exposed to Ute fire from the redoubt; Smith and Burton dashed inside while the rest of the group huddled behind the structure. The Indians fired at them from their fortification and killed half of the horses, but the volunteers escaped unscathed.

Grant sent ten infantrymen under the command of Jabez B. Nowlin (or Nowlan) to chop their way into the back of the house with axes. Nowlin, who had an extremely large nose, had been teased by his wife prior to the fight that any wound he got would be in his nose. Her prediction came true; a few moments after reaching Bean's house, Nowlin was clipped in the nose by a bullet.

That night, the Indians withdrew under the cover of darkness. The next morning, the militia found eight dead bodies left behind—three men, four women (one of them elderly), and a child. Higbee was the only militiaman killed, and seven were wounded.[165]

14 February 1850
TABLE MOUNTAIN *(Table Point, Utah)*
Gen. Daniel H. Wells, commander of the Utah Territorial Militia, arrived at Fort Utah on 11 February to learn that the Utes had fled (see previous

entry). He ordered two detachments to go after them. Capt. George D. Grant led one force to Rock Canyon, known as "the House of God" to the Utes, who considered it holy ground. Grant figured the Utes had no way out of the canyon's steep walls, ice, and snow, so he simply left a detail at the canyon's mouth to keep an eye on them, then he went to help Wells pursue the other Utes.

Not until 17 February did Wells send militia, under Capt. Andrew Lytle and Capt. Andrew L. Lamoreaux, into the canyon. Upon seeing the troops, the Utes began to scale the massive cliffs surrounding them. Old Elk's wife fell to her death as she attempted to climb a sheer rock face. (Though she may not have fallen from "Squaw Peak," it was named in her memory.) The militia fired at the retreating Utes and killed six, one of them Old Elk. Atop the mountain the militia discovered deserted Ute lodgings (near present-day Rock Canyon Campground), where they spotted two Indians. They killed one and captured the other. Despite the Utah Militia's certainty that no one else could have escaped over the mountain, in fact eight warriors (including the wounded chief Ope-Carry and Patsowet, who had shot Joseph Higbee at Provo River), six women, and seven children successfully got away.[166]

On 12 February Wells and the main body of cavalry, about 110 men, left to follow the larger band of Indians toward a Ute encampment that Lt. D. S. Carn had found on Spanish Fork River. By the time they arrived, the Utes had already fled. Wells started on the Indians' trail toward Peteetneet Creek, but facing snow and frigid temperatures, he soon ordered the troops back to the camp at Spanish Fork. The next morning the general took his men to Table Mountain, now called West Mountain, at the south end of Utah Lake. He divided his command, going with Lytle to the east and south sides of the mountain and sending Grant to the west side.

Grant discovered the Utes on the north side of the mountain, near Table Point. Wells's forces hurried to meet Grant, while Lytle took a detachment to search for more Indians along Peteetneet Creek. At the creek, Lt. Robert T. Thomas and twelve men discovered three Indian men, one of whom was blind. They decided not to bother with them and returned to the camp at Spanish Fork. Upon learning of Thomas's decision to spare the three Utes, Wells was perturbed, wishing the lieutenant had killed them.

At Table Mountain, Grant obtained the surrender of some of the Indians, but others retreated up the slopes. Those who surrendered refused to relinquish their weapons, so Grant posted a guard around them. Wells's cold and hungry men arrived at Table Mountain late that night. The next day, 14 February, a conflict erupted, though the particulars of the incident are uncertain. As Wells described it, "We encountered the Indians [on the mountain] and completely defeated them."[167] Lt. John W. Gunnison of the Topographical Engineers, who heard the story from a participant, gave a different version: "[The Indians] were guarded in camp until morning, and then ordered to give up their weapons. They refused to do this, and acting in a sullen and hostile manner, were fired upon and nearly all killed immediately. A few broke through the line of sentinels and endeavored to escape by crossing [Utah] lake on the ice, but were chased down by horsemen and 'ceased to breath[e].'"[168]

After the prisoners were killed, an old Indian man came into the militia camp and asked to be shot so he could die with his tribesmen. His wish was granted. Eleven Ute men were killed and fifteen to twenty women and children were captured. The militia took the women and children to Salt Lake City, where most of them eventually perished.

When Brigham Young received news of the encounter, he instructed Wells to remain vigilant: "If the Indians sue for peace, grant it to them, according to your discretionary judgment in the case—If they continue hostile pursue them until you use them up—Let it be peace with them or extermination."[169] The day after the Table Mountain episode, Wells sent Lamoreaux to hunt down the three Utes whom Thomas had left on Peteetneet Creek. Lamoreaux divided his fifteen men into three groups, hoping to drive the Indians into the open. But the Utes remained in the underbrush, so the troops went in after them. One warrior shot an arrow at Lt. Reddick N. Allred, striking a button of his coat. Allred fired back and shot the warrior through the head. Soon, all three Utes were dead, including the blind man.

On 14 February a reconnaissance detachment led by Captain Lytle discovered five mounted Ute spies on the edge of Utah Lake. The militiamen gave chase over the frozen lake, and in the ensuing running fight, three Utes were killed and one was wounded, while one escaped.

In a macabre epilogue, on 17 February army surgeon James Blake decided to collect some Ute heads for his scientific study. He, James Orr, and Abner Blackburn rode a sleigh across the frozen Utah Lake to Table Point, where they decapitated the Ute bodies that still lay there. They made no effort to bury the remains.[170]

24 February 1850
LAS RAICES CREEK *(Artesia Wells, Texas)*

In January 1850 Tawakoni Indians came down into the areas between Laredo and Eagle Pass from the north on a horse-stealing expedition. About twenty miles north of Laredo, they captured two Mexican boys, who were themselves out looking for horses. One of the boys was killed and the other was held captive. On 23 January a Tawakoni warrior went to the stables at Fort McIntosh to assess his chances of stealing the government animals, but the stock was well protected. Angry, he shot one of the horses dead and ran off in the night.

The next morning, Lt. Walter W. Hudson took a twelve-man mounted detachment of Company G, First Infantry, in pursuit of the intruder. A mile north of the post, Hudson spotted the trail of two mounted Indians accompanied by one on foot. The track meandered north through dense chaparral. The soldiers followed it until about one in the afternoon, when the trail changed, revealing that another thirteen Indians on ponies had joined the group. At the same time, another twelve-man detachment of soldiers, who had been trailing the thirteen mounted Indians, appeared and joined Hudson.

At 5 p.m. the party, about fifty miles north of Fort McIntosh, saw twenty to thirty warriors on a hill to the north. The Indians, seeing the soldiers' approach, fired first. "I returned their fire," Hudson later wrote, "wounding one of them slightly, when upon a signal from their Chief they fled."[171] Hudson ordered the other detachment to try to cut the band off at their right flank, but the Indians having favorable ground and fresher horses, got away. Hudson pursued them for three miles before his mounts gave out; one of the horses even collapsed and died.

When Hudson and his company returned to the site of the first encounter, they found the Mexican boy the Indians had captured; he had escaped during the melee. The boy informed Hudson that there were about sixty Tawakonis altogether, and he told him where their camp was. The next day, Hudson followed the trail to the campsite and beyond, but the Indians were long gone.[172]

3 March 1850
CHACON CREEK *(Eagle Pass, Texas)*

Troops were spread thin in south Texas in the early 1850s, with only 1,868 in the entire state. Fort Duncan, in present-day Eagle Pass, was home to four companies of the First Infantry, and Fort Inge, near present-day

Uvalde, housed two companies of the Eighth Infantry and several companies of the Second Dragoons.

In late February 1850, four men of Company C, Second Dragoons, under a Private Phitzeer escorted a merchant train from Fort Inge to Fort Duncan. As they prepared to return, Lt. Charles J. Whiting placed in their charge his ambulance wagon, for use by the Mexican wife of an unarmed, discharged soldier who rode along with the dragoons.

On 3 March, the party reached Chacon Creek, about midway between the two forts. Here more than fifty Lipans, most on horseback, attacked them. At the first fire, a Private Cater was shot through the head and killed. The Mexican woman got out of the ambulance wagon and ran, only to be captured. The four remaining dragoons, unable to control the mules, abandoned the ambulance and ran for their lives.

About six miles up the road, the survivors came upon a detachment under Capt. Charles G. Merchant, Eighth Infantry, escorting a civilian family to Fort Duncan. Keeping three of the dragoons to augment his force, Merchant unsuccessfully chased the Lipan raiders while Phitzeer went on to Fort Inge to report the attack.[173]

15 June 1850
BENEVIDES'S RANCH *(San Ygnacio, Texas)*

Early in June 1850, Comanches raided in Webb County, Texas, in the vicinity of Laredo, and many Mexican settlers fled to town for protection. Capt. John S. Ford ordered Lt. Andrew J. Walker out to intercept the raiders. Walker made camp near Laredo, where he got word of another depredation, said to have occurred farther down the Rio Grande.

Walker hurried downstream with about twenty rangers. He picked up an Indian trail that led to Don Basilio Benevides's Ranch, about twenty miles south of Laredo and about a dozen miles north of present-day San Ygnacio. When the rangers arrived, seven Comanches were still near the ranch, using Benevides's own corral to select their remounts then herding them along a bend in the river. When Walker charged, the Indians headed east, away from the river.

After a chase of one and a half miles, Walker caught up to the raiders. Ed Stevens, a former sheriff of Bexar County, rode up to one warrior, who turned and shot an arrow into Stevens's head at the same time as Stevens shot the Indian in the face. Jose Morales chased down another, dismounted warrior and rode over him with his horse three times before shooting him dead.

The pursuit continued for a few more miles, with the rangers killing or fatally wounding all seven Comanches. Morales helped Stevens pull the arrow from his head, which had pierced his scalp and bent around the curve of his skull. The blood gushed out of what appeared to be a fatal wound, but Morales bound the area tightly with his handkerchief and stopped the blood flow. Stevens survived.

The rangers caught one badly wounded Indian and took him to Benevides's home with the intention of trying to save him. Both of his hips were smashed, however, and the Texans figured he would not recover. None of the rangers wanted the job of putting him out of his misery, so a Mexican muleteer named Lorenzo performed the task. Most of Benevides's horses were recovered, and the rangers received thanks from many of the locals.[174]

26 June 1850
SAN ANTONIO VIEJO *(Guerra, Texas)*

In February 1850 the Texas Rangers decided to reorganize. Capt. John S. Ford moved some of his men from the Corpus Christi area to a new camp at San Antonio Viejo, in present-day southwestern Jim Hogg County. The camp, at the southern edge of a large sand belt extending across Nueces, Texas, was built in a stand of oaks, near several large natural wells of clear water.

When Ford learned of Walker's fight (see previous entry), he decided to take part of his force to link up with Walker in Laredo. He left Lt. Malcijah B. Highsmith in command of the camp, which comprised ten rangers and various employees and teamsters, for a total of twenty-six men. He instructed the lieutenant to keep a constant watch for Indians. A week after Ford left, the camp was indeed attacked. Ford's servant, Don Francisco de la Garza Falcon, whom the rangers called "Monkey" and who often regaled them with his imaginary feats of heroism, heard cattle bellowing up near the wells. When he went out to investigate, he saw the dust of about 200 fast-approaching Comanches. The rangers made a hasty barricade and took defensive positions around their square of tents.

As the Comanches circled, Ranger Hardy fired first, bringing down a warrior. The Indians pulled back and began a long-range siege. Luckily the Texans had recently restocked their water supply and had plenty of provisions. The Comanches stole ten horses and five mules, but they could not break into the rangers' camp as the outnumbered defenders held their perimeter. Falcon and mule driver August Harmuth climbed the little barricade and taunted the Indians to come and fight. Falcon closed his eyes and fired blindly several times, asking after each shot, "Did I kill one?" With each negative response, Falcon cursed his pistol.[175]

The siege lasted a few days. The Indians left at the approach of Capt. Joseph H. La Motte with a detachment of First U.S. Infantry from Ringgold Barracks. La Motte came to the rescue after the rangers' Carrizo Indian guide broke away from the besieged camp and rode hard to the barracks, which were about forty-five miles south. As he headed out, La Motte sent word upriver to Ford in Laredo. When Ford learned about the siege, he and his rangers hurried the nearly seventy miles back to the camp, but once there he found the situation already under control.[176]

12 August 1850
OAKES'S FIGHT *(South Texas)*

From late June through August of 1850, Capt. William J. Hardee was in command of a large-scale expedition consisting of ten companies of Second Dragoons and First Infantry and two companies of Texas Mounted Volunteers. They staged their forays out of Fort Inge, scouring up and down the Nueces River and west to the Rio Grande for raiding Comanche and Lipan Apache Indians.

Scouting along the Nueces, Capt. James Oakes with Company G, Second Dragoons, pursued a party of Indians. On 11 July they killed two Indians and captured twenty-two horses and mules. On 12 August, near the banks of the Nueces, Oakes attacked a band of Comanches and found them to be tough adversaries. The soldiers killed three Indians, but Oakes took two severe wounds, which would continue to trouble him for more than twenty-five years.[177]

— 1851 —

25 January 1851
GATO CREEK *(Freer, Texas)*

In 1850 Texas Rangers under Capt. John S. "Rip" Ford established a temporary camp at Los Ojuelos (Little Springs), about thirty miles east of Laredo, a site of good water, wood, and grass in an otherwise barren plain. Rangers at Los Ojuelos could cover both roads from Laredo, one going east to Corpus Christi and the other going south to San Antonio Viejo and Ringgold Barracks.

In January 1851, while Ford was getting medical treatment in Laredo, Lt. Andrew J. Walker led an eighteen-man scout. Along Gato Creek, about thirty miles north of Los Ojuelos and about twenty miles west of present-day Freer, Texas, he discovered a Comanche campsite. Finding hobbled horses and stores of supplies, Walker deduced that the Indians had cached items there before going out to raid in Mexico, and he was sure they would come back. He positioned his rangers in a covered spot on a rise about two miles away, from which point they could observe the Indian camp. Among Walker's men were Robert Rankin, David Steele, Andrew Gatliff, Marvin and Wallace McNeill, John E. Wilson, Alfred Wheeler, Albert Gallatin, Volney Rountree, and Sgt. David M. Level.

Walker waited a few days. When no Indians appeared, his men began grumbling, saying that the Comanches had probably taken a different route, but Walker was convinced they would return. At 4 p.m. on 25 January, the sixth day of their vigil, the Indians came in sight. Two advance scouts led the way, but Walker let them go by. Fifteen more Comanches soon followed, driving 50 horses and 150 mules. Seizing the moment, Walker's rangers charged the unsuspecting Comanches. A chief blew on a bone whistle, and half his warriors tried to form up in a line to face the Texans, but the rangers burst through the line, firing left and right as the Indians broke out. The chief again blew his whistle, and his warriors tried again to form up. Again the Indians' line did not hold, and a bullet knocked the chief off his horse, but the Comanches kept fighting nonetheless.

A knot of warriors attacked Walker, Level, Wilson, Wheeler, and Wallace McNeill. Walker shot the closest Comanche while another one charged him with a long knife. Wheeler shot the charging warrior through the head. McNeill shot another one then stripped him of his weapons and rigging. Level, dismounting, was holding onto his saddle-horn with one hand when an arrow hit his hand and pinned it to the saddle. Another arrow killed the horse, and Level fell, trapped. A warrior charged him. "Boys," Level called out, "don't you see that infernal Indian coming to lance me?"[178] Running to Level's aid, Wilson fired a ball into the charging Indian's side.

Meanwhile, as Rountree leaned over in his saddle to avoid an arrow, his stirrup broke and he tumbled to the ground. His horse ran off, taking his weapons with it, so Rountree found a mule and climbed on. As he rode to catch up with his companions, he passed a seemingly dead

Comanche who suddenly sprang to life and shot arrows at him, forcing him to abandon his mule and run for cover. The Indian caught the mule and rode off.

During the fight, a captive Mexican boy of about thirteen sat on his mule and cried out, "Estan Buenos Americanos!" Most of the Indians finally dispersed and escaped into the chaparral. Four were killed, their bodies left on the field, and about six were wounded. Walker lost one man killed and one wounded. The rangers recovered about seventy mules and horses, as well as the Mexican boy.

Walker turned the recovered livestock over to the U.S. quartermaster at Fort McIntosh. A month later, a lawyer called on Rip Ford, stating that his client had lost thirty-five mules, but he got back only twenty-eight—he was going to file suit for the other seven animals. The angry Ford told the lawyer, "I consider your client a very lucky man. If I were in Lieutenant Walker's place, and you were to bring any such suit against me, I would cut off your ears."[179] The lawyer's client decided not to sue.[180]

Ca. 15 May 1851
YOSEMITE VALLEY *(Mariposa, California)*

A string of robberies and murders between settlers and local Indians in California's Central Valley and around the Sierra Nevada mines led to a short but sharp conflict called the Mariposa War. The war had few large battles with great casualties; the ultimate defeat of the Indians—Chowchillas, Yokuts, and Yosemites—came mainly from their being worn down and starved into submission by the destruction of their villages, crops, and supplies.

Between January and April of 1851, militia leader James Savage led men of the Mariposa Battalion to defeat some of the Yokuts and Chowchillas. During the same period, the Indians seized from the settlers and miners about half a million dollars' worth of livestock and goods. In mid-May a detachment of the Mariposa Battalion under Capt. John Boling defeated a combined Indian force of about 600 warriors on the upper San Joaquin River. The charging soldiers, pursuing the Indians through dense chaparral, completely routed them. The next day, under a flag of truce, one of the chiefs suggested that the Americans must have been drunk to have charged as they did. Boling assured him that his men had been sober. The discouraged Indians figured they could not defeat such intense fighters, and because their leader, Jose Rey, had died in the battle, they surrendered.

The last holdouts of the Mariposa War were a band of Yosemites under old Chief Tenaya, who retreated far up the Merced River into an area of sheer cliffs and towering waterfalls. Boling's men pursued them, killing and capturing many of them in minor skirmishes. In one fight, Tenaya's son was captured and afterward allowed to "escape," whereupon he was shot down in the act. Soon after, Tenaya was caught. When he saw the body of his son and learned the circumstances of his death, he told Boling in Spanish: "Kill *me*, sir captain. Yes, *kill me*, as you killed my son; as you would kill my people if they would come to you!"[181]

Tenaya then put a curse on the whites, saying that he would forever follow them into the trees, rocks, and rivers, and his unseen spirit would make them grow cold from fear. Boling's scouts from other tribes were spooked by Tenaya's words. They were already afraid of the valley, which they believed was inhabited by witches. Despite his rage, Tenaya agreed to guide the soldiers into the valley to round up the rest of his tribe. Boling's detachment was the first group of white men ever to enter what would become Yosemite National Park. The Yosemites themselves were placed on the Fresno Reservation.[182]

17 November 1851
SITGREAVES'S FIGHT *(Poston, Arizona)*

In the summer of 1851 Capt. Lorenzo Sitgreaves of the Corps of Topographical Engineers organized a party of men in Santa Fe to seek out a practical route across New Mexico to the Colorado River and on to California. The expedition included Lt. J. G. Parke, engineer; Dr. S. W. Woodhouse, naturalist; R. H. Kern, naturalist; Antoine Leroux, guide; and five American and ten Mexican packers. They were ready to leave the Rio Grande on 1 August, but Col. Edwin V. Sumner, who was about to begin an expedition against the Navajos, directed Sitgreaves to wait for him so he could provide protection during part of Sitgreaves's journey.

Sitgreaves waited at the Zuni villages along the present-day New Mexico–Arizona border until 24 September. Finally, Capt. Henry L. Kendrick, Second Artillery, and thirty men arrived to escort Sitgreaves the rest of the way to California. By then, the expedition had already used up many of their supplies.

Sitgreaves headed west, down the Little Colorado River and past the San Francisco Mountains, roughly following the future path of Route 66. He and his party spoke with some Yavapai Indians, who indicated that the country of the Mojaves, which the expedition would have to pass through, was one day's journey west from the Colorado River. On 1 November, unknown Indians fired into Sitgreaves's camp, killing three mules. An arrow struck Leroux a glancing blow on the head, which was painful but not serious. The soldiers returned fire and wounded one Indian.

On 5 November the expedition climbed Union Pass and got their first glimpse of the Colorado River. In the valley below they saw fires from a large village. Near the river they met a group of Mojaves, who were reluctant to get close enough for questioning. Sitgreaves moved downriver, where Leroux found "Indian hieroglyphics" that he interpreted as warnings to turn back. Soon, many more Indians appeared, and Sitgreaves eventually induced them to join him. In the evening the Indians brought in items to trade. They seemed friendly, but Leroux and a few others were not convinced. On 8 November, so many Indians appeared in camp that Sitgreaves had to restrict their number for safety reasons, an arrangement that he said "gave [them] great dissatisfaction."[183] More Indians, some of them armed, infiltrated the camp until Sitgreaves had to have them physically ejected. On 9 November, while Sitgreaves was preparing to march, several Mojaves shot arrows into camp. One struck Dr. Woodhouse in the leg. Sitgreaves packed up and moved quickly down the river, out of Mojave territory.

Sitgreaves and his company would soon discover that they had stepped out of the proverbial frying pan and into the fire. On 16 November, now in Yuma territory, they came upon a large settlement near present-day Poston, Arizona. A Yuma who spoke Spanish told them they were about eight days' march from the Gila River. Sitgreaves traded with the Yumas but refused to allow a large number of them near his camp. The next day, Leroux advised Captain Kendrick to avoid a trail that passed through some willows near the river; he suggested they stay on a road that was rougher but back from the water. It was good advice, for out of the willows emerged about sixty Yumas, who surprised a straggling soldier named Jones. They caught him and clubbed him to death with weapons "shaped like a potato masher."[184]

The Yumas then charged the main party. Kendrick ordered the Mexican packers to run forward and fire a volley, then fall back to the soldiers' line. The tactic stopped the initial charge, but the Indians were still close enough to shoot arrows. The warriors held their ground, said Sitgreaves, "against the fire of our rifles and musketoons for some fifteen minutes."[185] When a bullet pierced the chest of one Yuma, presumed to be a chief, it seemed to unnerve the Indians and they fled the field, leaving four dead on the ground but carrying off several wounded. A few warriors, however, dogged Sitgreaves's men for several miles with the musket they'd captured from Jones. Though they fired from a distance of half a mile, the harassment hurried the company on its way.

The weary and hungry expedition, with its mules dying of starvation and exhaustion, finally reached Camp Yuma on 30 November. There Sitgreaves obtained supplies for the last leg of the journey to San Diego.[186]

— 1852 —

25 January 1852
LAGUNA DEL MUERTO
(Truth or Consequences, New Mexico)
In September 1851, Henry Skillman was granted a contract by the Postmaster General to carry mail from San Antonio to Santa Fe, via El Paso. Trouble with the Indians began promptly. In January 1852, the second westbound mail stage from San Antonio was ambushed in Quitman Canyon in west Texas. When the stage became overdue, searchers set out, but they found only ashes and some charred wagon wheels.

The Apaches struck next along the barren stretch of road known as the Jornada del Muerto, the Journey of Death, east of the Rio Grande and south of Socorro. At dawn on 25 January, the northbound stage left camp at Laguna del Muerto, northeast of present-day Truth or Consequences, on its way to Santa Fe. Riding along with the stage was a small escort of Second Dragoons. The stage had gone only a short distance when, despite the presence of the soldiers, Apache raiders struck. After a twenty-minute fight, three dragoons were killed and one was wounded. The survivors abandoned the stage and retreated south. Troops from Fort Conrad took up a pursuit, but the Indians were gone.[187]

9 September 1852
PAINTED CAVES *(Comstock, Texas)*
Because of Indians, the mail run between Leona Station (Fort Inge), Texas, and Fort Fillmore, New Mexico Territory, was a very dangerous undertaking. One of Henry Skillman's drivers who proved equal to the task was William A. "Bigfoot" Wallace. On 9 September, Wallace, accompanied by eight men, made an early-evening camp near the Painted Caves of Devil's River. They drove the stage to a dense chaparral next to the water hole, and while some of the men prepared supper,

others went to sleep under the coach. Feeling uneasy, Wallace left his men and went to inspect the area from a small hill fifty yards ahead. Several animals running by alerted him that someone was approaching. Hurrying back to camp, he woke everyone and warned them to prepare for Indians. Seconds later, about twenty-three Comanches charged in.

According to Wallace, the defenders hit a few Indians on the first charge. The Comanches fell back, then "circling around us [they] took possession of a Big Bluff, directly over our camp, and then the *fandango* began."[188] The warriors fired down from the bluff, answered by the accurate shooting of Wallace and his party. A man named Fry was wounded and one of the pack mules was killed, while the stage drivers knocked four warriors off their ponies. The Indians fell back, waiting to see if the stage would try to leave. Wallace placed his men under the coach and in the chaparral, keeping them quiet and hidden. Finally the Indians' curiosity got the best of them and they came in for a closer look. Wallace waited until several showed themselves before opening fire. Once again, the Indians were forced back.

Before dark, a party of about forty Comanches rode up, signaling for a parley. Wallace went out and spoke with one of them in Spanish, boasting that he could ride his stage through "the whole Comanche nation." He said he intended to continue his journey as soon as his men finished supper. The Indians pulled back, no doubt waiting for the coach to begin to roll. Instead Wallace packed up his men and the coach, and when dusk fell, he retreated as fast as he could, keeping a sharp watch. "I could not by any means pass the Indians with the mail on mule back," he wrote.[189] He and his men made it safely back to San Antonio, but they realized that future mail coaches would need a larger escort to have any hope of getting through.[190]

— 1853 —

Ca. 15 March 1853
CHARCO LARGO (*Escobas, Texas*)
In early 1853 Lt. Jerome Napoleon Bonaparte, cousin of the Emperor of France, was leading Company F, Mounted Rifles, in a series of scouts south of the Nueces River. In mid-March, the company was camped at Redmond's Ranch, near present-day Zapata, Texas, when a party of Comanches crept into camp and stole three picketed horses from under

the noses of two guards. A detachment of eight men took up the raiders' trail, which headed northeast.

After an eighteen-mile pursuit, the Riflemen entered a pretty rolling valley containing a water hole known as Charco Largo, about forty-four miles southeast of Fort McIntosh. The valley contained good grass and several small ponds of pure water amid small, chaparral-covered mounds. The Comanches had just finished resting and were mounting up when the soldiers galloped in. After a short, sharp fight, the Indians scattered. One Rifleman was severely wounded, and three Indians were killed. The soldiers recaptured the three stolen horses and rode away with about eight Indian ponies in the bargain.[191]

Ca. 14 April 1853
CLEAR FORK CROSSING *(Graham, Texas)*

In the spring of 1853, Capt. Henry H. Sibley commanded Fort Croghan on Hamilton Creek, fourteen miles above its junction with the Colorado River. In late March, raiding Indians stole nine of the best horses of Company I, Second Dragoons, right out of the post stables. Sibley took seventeen dragoons in pursuit. Although rain obliterated the trail, Sibley believed that the Indians were heading for villages on the upper Brazos River, 175 miles away.

At the Indian agency on the Clear Fork of the Brazos, Sibley conferred with agent Jesse Stem and learned that the horses had been taken by a party of Wichitas. Sibley sent the Indians a message demanding the return of his stock, then spent five days cooling his heels before the Wichitas showed up with a small herd of run-down horses. The Indians pitched their camp nearby, and Sibley met with Chief Koweaka, whom Sibley described as "insolent." With Stem interpreting, Koweaka said that "bad men of his tribe" had stolen the horses. Sibley, unwilling to accept the chief's story, seized him and all of his party but two, commanding the two to return with the right horses.

Koweaka, deathly afraid of becoming a captive, appealed to Sibley to let him go, promising to return with the horses. Sibley refused. That night, Koweaka begged Sibley to come to his lodge to talk. As Sibley was walking to the tipi in the moonlight, a Wichita warrior stepped up to an army sentinel and shot him through the heart. The camp exploded in gunfire. Rushing out of his lodge, Koweaka was shot and mortally wounded. All the Indians fled except one elderly woman. Inside the lodge, Sibley found Koweaka's wife and child both stabbed in the heart. The chief himself had killed them, preferring that they die rather than become captives. Sibley painted the scene as one of "devotion and self-sacrifice" on the part of the chief's wife. Sibley regretted the entire affair as a tragedy that James Fennimore Cooper couldn't imagine in a novel. Years later, he still felt sorrow at Koweaka's action, writing, "I cannot but die deploring it forever."[192]

18 June 1853
SAN YGNACIO *(San Ygnacio, Texas)*

Company F, Mounted Rifles, had been scouting around Charco Largo for some time when the soldiers received word on 17 June that Comanches had attacked a ranch about five miles away. The Indians had killed a man and two children and driven off several head of cattle and horses. The company divided in half, one squad searching in the vicinity of the ranch and the other heading downstream. The first group included brothers John and William Wright and Pvt. Gerald Russell.

The next day the Wright party struck a fresh trail that headed toward the Rio Grande. They rode west twenty-two miles until the trail disappeared in the chaparral about a mile from the village of San Ygnacio. Abandoning hope of finding the trail again, they decided to head to the

The Rio Grande at San Ygnacio, Texas

river to get water. Below the seventy-foot embankment they saw the other squad, who had trailed the Indians to the same point. The combined squads, under Lt. Gordon Granger, soon discovered a narrow trail leading down to the water. Twelve soldiers followed the trail to the river, where they found about thirty Comanches in the process of carrying across the goods they had just plundered from San Ygnacio.

Mutually surprised, both sides raised yells as the twelve riflemen charged into the Indians. In a fight of about five or six minutes, two soldiers were hit while three Indians fell. The Comanches then plunged into the river and swam to the Mexican shore. Granger ordered the detachment to dismount, holster their revolvers, and take aim with their rifles. The soldiers hit several more Indians in the water. After one warrior was hit on the bank and rolled twenty feet down to the river's edge, two of his companions went down to get him. Seeing this, William Wright ceased fire, considering the Indians' rescue attempt a noble endeavor.

The Indians left many animals as well as equipment on the far bank. The two Wright brothers, Russell, and one other soldier volunteered to swim across and recover what they could. Under cover of the other riflemen, the men succeeded in bringing back thirty horses, six mules, various stolen items, and some of the Indians' abandoned belongings. While swimming back with the last of the horses, John Wright was so exhausted that he was nearly carried away in the current, but his feet finally hit sand and he was able to crawl ashore.

William Wright was promoted to corporal for being the first volunteer, and Gen. Winfield Scott commended Granger for "destroying a party of fifteen Indians."[193]

17 July 1853
IVIE INCIDENT *(Springville, Utah)*
In July 1853, the Walker "War"—a series of raids and skirmishes led by Chief Wakara (Walker) and his band of Utes—began at a homestead near Springville, Utah. Tensions between the Utes and Mormon settlers had been building as the Mormons encroached on Ute lands and spread disease (measles). In addition, the church had recently passed a law prohibiting slave trading with Mexico, which had been the basis of Wakara's power and position. The spark that ignited the conflict started with a domestic spat.

On 17 July 1853, an Indian woman entered Mormon settler James Ivie's home, just northwest of Wakara's camp on Spring Creek, one mile north of present-day Springville. With her husband and another Indian outside, the woman asked to trade three trout for some flour. Ivie told his wife to give her three pints of flour for the fish. Flour was scarce, and the trade was fair, but the woman's husband, Shower-Ocats, was displeased with the exchange. He entered the cabin, venting his anger verbally at first, then he turned and began beating his wife. Ivie tried to intervene, and the situation deteriorated. Shower-Ocats tried to shoot Ivie, but Ivie fended him off and broke the rifle, then knocked the Indian senseless with the rifle barrel.

The other warrior then shot an arrow at Ivie that passed through his shirt. Ivie knocked him unconscious too. The woman then smashed a piece of firewood in Ivie's face. Still grasping the broken gun barrel, Ivie laid her out beside the other two.

Just then a neighbor, Joseph Kelly, passed by, and Ivie told him what had happened. They doused the Indians with water to revive them. The woman and her husband's companion regained consciousness, but Shower-Ocats remained still. The two Utes ran off to their village for help. Kelly instructed Ivie to take his wife and child to Springville for safety and to tell Bishop Aaron Johnson, the chief magistrate, what had happened.

Upon hearing the news, Bishop Johnson readied the community for a possible attack and placed the militia on alert. Capt. Stephen C. Perry took his company to Wakara's camp to see if the chief would accept a compensation payment of ponies, beef, flour, and blankets. Unfortunately, however, Shower-Ocats had died from Ivie's blow, and the Utes demanded that Ivie be turned over to them so they could try him in Indian fashion. The militia refused. Infuriated, Wakara's band decided to move to the Sanpete Valley, by way of Juab Valley and Salt Creek Canyon, apparently determined to exterminate all the whites they found along the way.[194]

July 1853–January 1854
WALKER WAR *(Central Utah)*

On 18 July 1853, the day after the Ivie Incident (see previous entry), Wakara's brother, Arapeen, killed militiaman Alexander Keele as he stood guard at the nearby settlement of Payson. In response, Col. Peter Conover left Provo with 150 men of the Nauvoo Legion and proceeded to Salt Creek Canyon. On 23 July, Conover sent a company to attack an encampment of twenty to thirty Utes on Pleasant Creek in the Sanpete Valley. Six Indians were killed in the skirmish. Soon afterward, Ute raids on the Mormons escalated, and the attacks would continue into the fall.

On 10 August 1853, Utes attacked Lt. R. Burns and ten men in his command while they were camped on Willow Creek near Mona, Juab County. Isaac Duffin was shot in the knee, two horses were killed, and one Indian was shot, possibly fatally.

With tensions rising, Gen. Daniel H. Wells of the Utah Territorial Militia alerted the smaller communities of the region to take refuge and not to work or travel alone, but not all settlers heeded this advice. On 17 August, Utes ambushed four men hauling lumber from a sawmill in Parleys Park, near present-day Snyderville. They killed two, John Quayle and John Dixon, and wounded John Hoagland. Hoagland and an uninjured John Knight escaped to Salt Lake City.

A month later, on 13 September, Pahvant Utes under Kanosh went to war as had Wakara's band. They killed William Hatton as he stood guard at Fillmore, then the territorial capital, in the Pahvant Valley. Next, in the early morning of 1 October, the Utes attacked four men—William Reed, James Nelson, William Luke, and Thomas Clark—who were camped at Uintah Springs, present-day Fountain Green, in Sanpete County. The Indians murdered all four of them and mutilated their bodies. Prominent Mormon settler Isaac Morley and his men discovered three of the bodies, but not Clark's. Later a posse of twenty men under James T. Guzman found Clark's severely mutilated body in his wagon. At Nephi on 2 October, Morley and his men fought a group of Indians who may have been trying to surrender. Morley and the townsfolk of Nephi killed eight Utes and took two boys and a woman prisoner.

Within days, the Utes struck again. On 4 October, John E. Warren and William Mills were out gathering wood near Warren's wheat mill, about one mile from Manti, when they were ambushed. The Utes killed both of them, badly mutilating Warren's face. Then, on 14 October about forty Utes led by Showan attacked several Mormons who were harvesting potatoes near Summit, now Santaquin, in Utah County. The Indians killed and scalped one, Fernee L. Tindel, but another, John Sheffield, escaped. The other farmers ran to Payson for help. Col. W. C. McClellan and forty men rode to the rescue, but the Utes took off after stealing some cattle.

More murders occurred in late October on the Sevier River, when Pahvant Utes under Kanosh attacked Capt. John W. Gunnison and his men, killing seven, in an incident known as the Gunnison Massacre.

In November, Indians burned Chase's sawmill in Sanpete County, and a few days later they burned six vacant houses near Payson. In January 1854, the settlement of Allred was burned to the ground.

That winter, Chief Wakara left the area and went to stay with the Navajos. When he returned in the spring, he met with Brigham Young to negotiate a peace with the Mormons. On 11 May 1854, Young sat down with Wakara and Kanosh at Chicken Creek in Juab County, where they finally agreed on a formal peace treaty. Using conservative estimates, about nineteen whites and twenty-two Indians were killed in the Walker War.[195]

— 1854 —

12 May 1854
ARROYO BALUARTE *(Falfurrias, Texas)*
After Lt. George B. Cosby and eleven men of Companies F and I, Mounted Rifles, fought Lipan Apaches in the 5 May 1854 Lake Trinidad Battle, Cpl. William Wright took over for the wounded Cosby. On 7 May Wright sent his brother, John, sixty miles north to Fort Merrill to get reinforcements and medical aid for the three wounded men. Racing to the fort, John Wright got there in seven hours but killed his horse in the process. He was assigned a small detachment of Company F and a hospital steward, and the party hurried back to the battle site. Near Agua Dulce Creek, they rode through a small camp of Indians but did not stop. The warriors chased them for a time before giving up. The detachment reached Lake Trinidad at daybreak the next morning.

William Wright took his new command, now numbering about twenty men, and followed the Indians' trail south until it came upon the Lipan camp along Arroyo Baluarte near where it flows into Laguna Salada, a few miles south of present-day Falfurrias, Texas.[196] As Wright barreled into the Indians, the scene became a jumble of shots, curses, and the swirling bright colors of caparisoned horses and Indians. Wright's horse, ominously named Death, was struck by a bullet and killed, throwing the corporal to the ground. An Indian rode up to dispatch him, but Wright shot the warrior as well as his horse.

After a few short minutes, the Lipans rode away into the chaparral, leaving behind four dead and taking with them about six wounded. Six soldiers were wounded, including one man who received a severe tomahawk blow to the head. Corporal Wright led his ragged detachment back to Fort Merrill. Both brothers' terms of enlistment ended in October 1855, and neither had any desire to renew their service in the army.[197]

July 1854
SAN PEDRO RIVER *(Benson, Arizona)*

Maj. Michael Erskine, a prominent landowner and stock grower in Guadalupe County, Texas, set out for California to test his cattle in the West Coast market. Accompanying him on the trip was his son-in-law, Judge Henry Maney, Capt. James H. Callahan, and thirty-five cowboys. Erskine paid Callahan $1,500 to secure enough men to drive the one thousand cattle and provide protection. Only twelve of the cowboys were on the payroll; the rest joined up to work their way to California. They left San Antonio on 25 April 1854.

Their long drive followed the Lower Military Road across south Texas, a land of deserts, mountains, and Indians. Only forty miles west of San Antonio, a thunderstorm blew in and the cattle stampeded. It took the cowboys a week to round them up, and forty head were lost. Then, on Limpia Creek in the Davis Mountains, Mescalero Apaches stole several head. Callahan, an old Indian fighter who had survived the Fannin Massacre in 1836, took ten men and trailed after the Apaches. They found them in a canyon ten miles away, but in too great a force to confront. Callahan had to abandon several of his horses as decoys to get out of the predicament.

Four more days on the waterless trail got Erskine and his drive to the Rio Grande, but not before some of the cattle died of thirst. From there the party went upriver to Fort Thorn, then west across southern New Mexico Territory to the Santa Cruz River near Tucson. At the Santa Cruz, Erskine met a man named Dunlap, who had left Texas before him with another herd of cattle. Dunlap said that Apaches had recently stolen a few hundred head of his stock, and he asked the cowboys for help in retrieving them. Eighteen of Erskine's men responded, including Callahan and Maney, plus twenty-five Mexicans from the Tucson garrison.

The Apaches' trail led upstream and east across the divide to the San Pedro River. When the Mexican scouts discovered the Indians' camp on the banks of the river, Callahan brought up the company, quickly readied them, and charged. About ten mounted Apaches splashed across the river and got away; the remaining two dozen put up a good fight. Only one Indian had a gun, which he fired at a Mexican soldier, shooting him dead from his horse. A Mexican officer, armed with only a saber, rode in among the Apaches, slashing and cutting his way through. One cowboy, J. T. French, was thrown from his mule and fell in a somersault, snapping off the stock of his shotgun. Nevertheless, he was able to fire first at an Indian about to shoot him.

Most of the Indians headed for the riverbank, running and rolling in the sand but discharging arrows all the way. Maney was the first across the river. He caught up to one Indian and was about to shoot when a Mexican lancer rode up to him, yelling "My Indian!" The Mexican meant he wanted to kill the warrior himself, and Maney let him. Another Mexican horseman threw his lariat over an Indian, jerked him from his feet, and dragged him through the cactus. A rider following behind finished the warrior off with a lance.

Meanwhile, Callahan was surprised by an Apache who sprang out from the bushes and ran at him with a lance. The captain tried to fire his pistol twice, but it failed to discharge. He narrowly deflected the lance's thrust with the bulk of the pistol, then fell backwards into the river and got away.

Suddenly, at about three in the afternoon, the firing stopped. Twenty-one Apaches lay dead on the ground, most of whom the Mexicans scalped, as the Mexican government offered bounties on Indian scalps. Callahan's side had lost only one dead and a few wounded. They recovered a captured Mexican boy, about fifteen years old, along with sixty-five cattle, ten horses, and a few mules. Carrying the dead Mexican soldier's body and the wounded men, they rode the rest of the day and all night, reaching the Santa Cruz River, forty-five miles away, the next morning. The rescued boy was returned to his parents in Tucson, and Callahan continued his drive with Erskine to California, with no more Indian encounters the rest of the trip.[198]

Ca. 20 August 1854
HOWARD'S WELL *(Pandale, Texas)*

While rivals Henry Skillman and David Wasson battled over who would win the government mail contract for the routes between San Antonio, El Paso, and Santa Fe, their drivers battled the Indians. In August 1854 Skillman's driver Louis Oge, a twenty-two-year-old Alsatian, captained a large caravan from El Paso to San Antonio. The seven-vehicle, thirteen-man outfit included a Philadelphia merchant with mule-drawn hacks carrying $300,000 in specie. The party moved without incident east of the Pecos River, and by the time they reached Howard's Well, the merchant had begun to relax.

But that water hole was no place to ease vigilance. While the caravan was halted at the wells, seventy-five Indians appeared. Oge quickly ordered the hacks and stages into a circle and positioned the men behind the vehicles, mules, and horses. Just as the wagoners were ready, the Indians charged. The defenders' first volley knocked several raiders off of their ponies. The Indians circled the defensive perimeter again and again, shooting, yelling, and drawing fire. They pressed the attack for four hours before they withdrew.

Guard James M. Adams believed that the Indians suffered "considerable loss" in the skirmish. No one from Oge's party was hit, but five of their mules were killed and several were injured. Nevertheless, Oge was able to put together enough mule teams to pull all the vehicles, and the caravan continued unmolested to San Antonio.[199]

15 November 1854
EL MUERTO SPRINGS *(Valentine, Texas)*
When David Wasson gave up his battle with Henry Skillman to control the San Antonio to El Paso mail routes (see previous entry), merchant George H. Giddings, who had a financial interest in Skillman's enterprise, agreed to pool his resources with Skillman. Their first mail and passenger coach headed for El Paso on 1 November, led by George Gidding's brother, Frank, and James Hunter. Skillman and merchant A. C. Rand, along with two Mexican guards, followed behind them one day later.

Heavy rain slowed both parties, but on the night of 14 November, Skillman caught up with Giddings at El Muerto Springs, near present-day Valentine, Texas. They breakfasted together the next morning. Skillman hit the road earlier, promising to wait for Giddings at Eagle Springs. Giddings began rolling soon after, but before he could catch up to Skillman, about fifty Mescalero Apaches caught up with him.

Hunter called out, "Stop, boys. We have got to fight these fellows. Sideline the mules."[200] The Indians reined up about 200 yards away and called out, "Amigos!" When their leader came forward, Hunter told guard Louis Dixon, who could speak Spanish, to warn them to stay back if they were really friends. The warriors pulled back and began circling. One of them waved a soldier's bloody jacket that had belonged to a dispatch rider they had killed a week earlier, west of Fort Clark. Instead of charging Giddings, however, the Apaches sped off after Skillman.

Reaching Skillman's coach, the Apaches tried their ruse of feigned friendship again, but like Hunter, Skillman was skeptical. When he waved them away, the warriors opened fire. Things began to get hot when Giddings's coach galloped up, broke through the circling warriors, and joined Skillman. "The prettiest part of the fight was now coming on, and the fun was not stopped 'till sundown," a coach passenger recalled.[201]

The fifteen straight-shooting Texans coolly met the circling Indians and held off their repeated charges. Some Mescaleros climbed a rise a few hundred yards away and began lobbing bullets into the Texans' position. Two passengers were wounded and several mules were hit, including Skillman's favorite. Giddings hitched up the teams to pull out of range while Skillman covered him.

Eyewitnesses said that Skillman was an excellent rifle shot, and he killed three Indians from 300 yards. Rand fired a dozen times with his Sharps. Eventually the Texans' sure, steady, fire drove the Indians out of range. The warriors continued the siege from a distance until nightfall, then they finally left. About five Indians were killed in the fight. When the expressmen reached El Paso and told their story, they were treated as heroes.[202]

— 1855 —

12 October 1855
LIVE OAK CREEK *(Iraan, Texas)*

Capt. Stephen Carpenter and the men of Companies H and K, First Infantry, established Camp Lancaster, near the junction of Live Oak Creek and the Pecos River, in August 1855. For the next several months, they were busy building quarters and making the post habitable. In October Carpenter, seeking a straight tall tree to make a flagpole, headed out to the head of Live Oak Creek. With him rode Pvts. Dennen and Beardall, both musicians of Company K; Pvt. Patrick McCulloch; civilian doctor J.D.B. Stillman; and a teamster driving the wagon. Carpenter brought along his two dogs, Cola and Quail, which Dr. Stillman credited with being the most effective sentries they had.

Near the head of the creek, about a dozen miles east of present-day Iraan, Texas, Carpenter's party found a grove of trees. As the soldiers cut poles, Stillman and Carpenter approached a smaller grove hoping to find some wild turkeys. Instead of turkeys, the dogs flushed out a band of Lipan Apaches, who were "well mounted, armed with shields, bows and arrows, lances, and a few with guns; they were painted and bedeviled for war," Stillman later wrote.[203]

The Indians charged. Stillman ran to save himself. He saw the Indians swarm over the teamster, who was also separated from the party. While the warriors concentrated on the teamster, Stillman got away and headed toward the post. Carpenter shouted to the remaining men to get back to the wagon. The Indians did not attack the wagon right away, so Carpenter moved his party cautiously in the direction of the post. When the Indians did charge, Carpenter was ready, and a steady fire held them back. An arrow whizzed past Beardall's head, and he took aim at a bush he had seen the Indian duck behind. He waited until the warrior rose again for another shot, fired, and hit him square.

The arrows flew fast. One hit McCulloch in the foot. Carpenter, too, was caught in the fire. One arrow hit his horse, another cut through his shoulder strap, a third lodged in his boot, yet another penetrated his coat, and a fifth struck his hand. Two warriors attacked Carpenter from different directions, but he held them off by pointing his pistol first at one, then the other; he did not fire, however, for he only had three bullets left. He aimed at one warrior, who raised his shield for protection, then he spun around and shot at the other, who was charging in with a lance. The bullet hit his attacker full in the chest. Carpenter turned back quickly to the other warrior, but he could not get a shot off. The Indian was about to strike the captain when a bullet from Deneen's rifle laid him low. With that, the attack ceased and the Indians pulled back.

In the meantime, Stillman had made it back to Camp Lancaster. Stumbling in, he reported that everyone in his party had probably been killed. A rescue party formed up and hurried out. They found Carpenter and the other survivors and escorted them back, reaching the post at nightfall.

One defender, the teamster, was killed in the raid, and two soldiers were wounded. At least three Indians were killed.[204] Stillman believed that the Apaches planned the ambush in great detail, and it "would have been successful in cutting off every man in the party, were it not that they wanted victory too cheap."[205]

24 October 1855
LOOKINGGLASS PRAIRIE *(Roseburg, Oregon)*

In early October of 1855, during the Rogue River war—a conflict that had been sporadically flaring up for years—several parties of armed Oregon

Volunteers attacked a village of Rogue River Indians along Little Butte Creek. Their actions, along with similar incidents, renewed the war that had sporadically flared up in southwest Oregon during the past few years. After the volunteers stirred up this hornet's nest in the Rogue Valley, some of them marched north along the South Fork of the Umpqua, vowing to wage war on any Indians they found.

On the morning of 24 October, a party of about twenty-five volunteers encountered a camp of Upper Umpqua Indians in the valley of Lookingglass Creek, about eight miles southwest of the village of Roseburg. Even though the Umpquas were friendly and known to be on good terms with the people of Roseburg, the volunteers attacked the camp of about thirty Indians, sweeping in at daybreak. The Indians owned only three guns, and after firing a few ineffective shots they tried to escape to the nearby mountains. About eight male Indians were killed and an old woman was wounded. The volunteers took no losses.[206]

8–9 November 1855
TWO BUTTES *(Yakima, Washington)*

In response to the September 1855 murder of Indian agent Andrew J. Bolon in Washington Territory, Capt. Granville O. Haller led an expedition against the Yakima Indians. The soldiers were defeated in the October battle at Toppenish Creek, after which they stumbled back to The Dalles. There, Maj. Gabriel J. Rains, Fourth U.S. Infantry, called for another expedition. Since Rains had so few troops, he asked for volunteers. Acting governor Charles H. Mason of Washington raised some

The Dalles, Oregon, 1860 —From authors' collection

troops, most of whom remained west of the Cascades. Oregon Territory governor George L. Curry raised a full regiment, called the Oregon Mounted Volunteers, commanded by Col. James W. Nesmith.

Rains gathered about 200 regulars of Companies G, H, I, and K, Fourth Infantry; Companies B, L, and M, Third Artillery; and a detachment of First Dragoons under Lt. Philip H. Sheridan. The soldiers left The Dalles on 31 October; later, a couple of companies of Washington Volunteers and Companies C, D, E, F, and G of the Oregon Volunteers joined the expedition, giving Rains and Nesmith a total of about 500 men. The soldiers marched northeast to the Yakima River, where the Palouse and Yakima Indians, who had greatly outnumbered Haller's forces in October, now faced a much more formidable foe. Seeing this, they wisely refused battle.

On 8 November, near the Yakima River, a small skirmish wounded two Oregon Volunteers. The Indians retreated. Rains and Nesmith moved up the river to a point where it was pinched between Ahtanum Ridge and the Rattlesnake Hills, a place called Union Gap, or Two Buttes, just south of present-day Yakima. While Rains maneuvered into position, two soldiers drowned in the river. The Indians at the gap made a brief stand. When Haller and Capt. Christopher C. Auger charged the Indians' position, the warriors fled. Only one, who was riding a slow horse, was killed; a few were possibly wounded.

The soldiers moved into Ahtanum Valley, and the next day, the Oregon Volunteers tried to surround the remaining Indians. After they failed to do so, Rains and Nesmith moved up Ahtanum Creek to the St. Joseph Mission. There soldiers found a buried keg of gunpowder and assumed, erroneously, that the Catholic missionaries had been supplying the Indians. They went wild, looting the abandoned mission and burning it to the ground. Meanwhile, Rains sent out scouts to find the Indians, but they were long gone. Nesmith took his men east to set up camp in the Walla Walla Valley, while Rains, amid complaints of incompetence, marched the regulars back to The Dalles.[207]

— 1856 —

26 January 1856
BATTLE OF SEATTLE *(Seattle, Washington)*
After fighting in southern Washington Territory erupted in the fall of 1855 (see previous entry), Indian troubles in the Puget Sound area increased.

It was nearly impossible to determine which factions of Nisquallies, Puy-allups, Snoqualmies, Snohomishes, Duwamishes, and other tribes were friends or enemies at any given moment. The small town of Seattle had been threatened on numerous occasions, and in early 1856 the Nisqually chief Leschi, the Puyallup chief Quilquilton, and the Yakima chief Owhi threatened to destroy the town. The Suquamish-Duwamish chief Seattle, who lived in the area, remained friendly.

A young Duwamish named Jim and another named Curley, who worked in Seattle at Henry Yesler's sawmill, learned of the planned assault and warned Yesler along with Capt. Guert Gansevoort of the sloop *Decatur* and Capt. C. C. Hewitt of the local volunteers. The hostile Indians, Jim and Curley said, hoped to capture the *Decatur* and take its cannons and powder.

Gansevoort went on high alert and Seattle's townsfolk prepared to defend themselves. Gansevoort pulled back from shore and, leaving only about thirty men on the sloop, sent ninety-six sailors, eighteen marines, and five officers ashore to assist the settlers. The townspeople and mili-tary men quickly built a defense line across the base of the settlement's peninsula, connecting a swamp on the southeast to a blockhouse on the northwest.

After nightfall on 25 January, the hostile leaders met at Curley's lodge and proposed an attack at two the next morning. Curley and Jim informed the chiefs that the *Decatur*'s crew was fully alerted and ready for them. The two advised them to wait until midmorning, when the tired shift would be going back to the ship to sleep. Leschi and Owhi agreed. Shortly afterward, Jim ran to town to reveal the attackers' plan.

About 10 a.m., Jim warned the settlers that there were many Kliki-tats approaching from the direction of a sand spit connected to the mainland east of the swamp. A Lieutenant Morris, whose division guarded that sector, fired a howitzer shell into the woods toward the point Jim had indicated. With that, about 800 Indians attacked. To the warriors' surprise, the townsfolk, reinforced by the sailors and marines, were ready for them. The two sides fired at each other along the defense line and from across the 200-yard-wide swamp, while the *Decatur*'s guns sent shells into the Indian lines. Lieutenant Phelps's division charged out to a hill east of Yesler's Mill and drove the Indi-ans back.

The warriors shifted their attack farther north toward the block-house, but they had no luck in that sector either. Many of them were shot down by guns or cannons, now aided by the bark *Bronte*, recently arrived in the bay. There were only a couple of casualties among the defenders. A lad named Milton Holgate was killed near the blockhouse, and in town a long-range bullet felled Christian White. The Indians did, however, capture some of the settlers' cattle.

The Indians suspended their fighting around noon and feasted on the stolen beef. After their break, they renewed the attack in the afternoon, but the results were about the same. Quilquilton attacked Phelps's division, but the latter's fourteen marines stood steadfast and halted them. Had the Indians pressed on into Phelps with their overwhelming numbers, they could have pierced the defense and poured into town. But they had faltered, so the attack was spent, and the battle now degenerated into long-range sniping.

Some warriors tried to close in and set fire to the settlement's buildings, but explosive shells from the *Decatur* scared them off. The Indians knew how a cannonball worked, but a shell was different: having a delayed fuse, a shell could hit the ground and sit there for a minute before "shooting again"—curious Indians who approached the shell could be killed without warning. The Indians believed its power to be supernatural. By morning the attackers had gone, carrying off their dead and wounded, estimated at between ten and fifty.[208]

22 February 1856
TINTIC CAMP INCIDENT *(Fairfield, Utah)*
Ute subchief Tintic's band of thirty warriors and their families in Cedar Valley, Utah, were reduced to beggary and theft after crickets destroyed their fall harvest of 1855 and an especially cold winter followed. In February 1856, after the Indians raided the Mormon settlements of Cedar Fort and South Fort (now Fairfield), federal judge W. W. Drummond issued writs of arrest for Tintic and several other Utes.

U.S. Deputy Marshal Thomas S. Johnson, who took the arrest warrants, recruited ten militiamen under Col. Peter Conover. While he led the posse to Cedar Valley, Johnson, unsure of how to approach the Indians, sent Conover to Salt Lake City to ask the advice of Brigham Young, Mormon Church president and ex officio superintendent of Indian affairs for Utah Territory. Young insisted that Tintic should be taken peacefully. Meanwhile, Johnson reached Cedar Fort, where he recruited more men. On 21 February he sent a detachment to South Fort to protect the settlers there, then he waited.

Johnson was now in a quandary. He had been ordered to serve the writs but warned not to start a war. Conover had not yet returned with Young's instructions. The marshal decided to send interpreter John Clark to Tintic's camp, near South Fort, and persuade the chief to come to Cedar Fort to talk. But in the meantime, Tintic and his band had seen the armed posse headed for South Fort and assumed they were after them. Before Clark had time to leave, Tintic's brother, Battest, rode to Cedar Fort to determine Johnson's intentions. Johnson asked Battest to bring Tintic in, but he refused, so Clark agreed to accompany Battest back to the Indians' camp, carrying two concealed pistols in his coat.

At the camp on 22 February, Tintic's warriors were preparing for battle. Clark approached Tintic's tent, went in, and sat down, followed by several Indians. Clark overheard Tintic whisper to his tribesmen, "Wait until he starts home, then we will kill him." Clark, trying to remain calm, told Tintic that Brigham Young wanted him to come to the fort to talk with Johnson, but Tintic refused. "I had to keep talking," Clark recalled, "as I dared not make a move to go."[209]

At the fort, Johnson, nervously awaiting Clark's return, decided to take action. He gathered a posse of thirty men and set out to rescue Clark and arrest Tintic. Clark, still in Tintic's tipi, heard Indian women call out that the Mormons were coming. Soon, Johnson and Deputy Sheriff George Parish entered the tent. Johnson seized Tintic by the hair, drew his revolver, and declared Tintic his prisoner. Tintic grabbed the gun, which discharged and sent a bullet through his own hand. He broke Johnson's grip and fled through the rear of the tent. The posse opened fire. The Indians inside the tent bolted for the exit, knocking Clark unconscious on the way. Battest fired his rifle at Parish but missed. A militiaman shot Battest through the head.

Most of the militiamen had only one shot in their guns, and the encounter was brief. The posse killed three warriors and a woman and wounded several other Indians. An Indian woman lanced one militiaman, George Carson, in the leg. The Indians fled to a cedar grove south of their camp. Having used up their ammunition, the posse did not pursue them. Woods Wilson picked up the badly wounded Carson and slung him over his horse. Carson died at the fort early the next morning.

Clark, meanwhile, was left unconscious in the tent. When he came to, he grabbed two nearby guns, mounted a horse, and galloped back to Cedar Fort.

The Indians later returned to their camp, packed up what they could, and fled, leaving one warrior and one woman dead on the field. Many of them went west to Rush Valley; others, including Tintic, moved east into Utah Valley, where they stole some cattle and drove them south into the Tintic Mountains, planning to stay there for the rest of the winter.[210]

23 and 26 February 1856
TINTIC WAR/UTAH LAKE RAIDS
(Utah County, Utah)

On 22 February Mormon settler Abraham Hunsaker, hearing of the recent Indian raids in Cedar Valley (see previous entry), headed out of the Salt Lake Valley with his son Lewis to the home of his second wife and their three children at Utah Lake, near Goshen, planning to escort them and their livestock back to Salt Lake. That evening, Hunsaker and his son spent the night at the ranch of Washington Carson and Henry Moran, in the Lake Mountains between Cedar and Goshen Valleys. At dawn the Hunsakers left for their own ranch, about twelve miles south in Goshen Valley. Shortly after their departure, several of Ute subchief Tintic's warriors attacked the Carson ranch and killed both men.

When Hunsaker reached his home about 10 a.m., some Indians suddenly appeared. Hunsaker sent his children into the house and watched as the warriors conferred some 200 yards away. After the Indians rode off, Hunsaker prepared to flee with his family. He sent Lewis out to fetch fresh horses and had two of his other sons, Allen and Lemuel, bring in the sheep and cattle. When the Indians saw Lewis leave, they assumed he was heading to Lehi for help and went after him. Seeing no sign of Lewis, Hunsaker and his family proceeded to leave, intending to look for him on the way out. They passed the spot where he should have been rounding up the horses, but he was nowhere to be seen.

Approaching Carson's ranch, the senior Hunsaker sent Allen ahead to alert Carson, but the boy found the place deserted and plundered. A short time later, 300 yards from the dwelling, the Hunsakers discovered Carson's mutilated body. The family raced for Solomon Wixom's house at Pelican Point, fearing an attack at any moment. They arrived at Wixom's at 1 a.m. on 24 February. Hunsaker left his family at Wixon's, and with another settler, David Sanders, hurried to Lehi for help. There, Lehi Militia leader Col. William S. Willis gathered twenty-five men and headed toward the Wixom and Carson ranches.

Near the Carson ranch, Hunsaker and Willis found Moran, dead, with two bullets through his back. His faithful dog sat between his legs, guarding him. Hunsaker and the militiamen spent the rest of the day searching for Lewis and rounding up cattle, and they continued the search the next morning. Near dusk that afternoon, 26 February, the men set up camp at Kimball Creek in Goshen Valley and enjoyed a good meal. One of them, Joseph Cousins, joked, "If the Indians kill me, I wish to die with a full stomach."[211]

After supper Hunsaker and his son Allen left camp to search again for Lewis. Cousins and Sylvanus Collet were gathering firewood when Collet spotted an Indian and shouted to Cousins to run, but Cousins seemed frozen to the spot. The Indians quickly killed and scalped him. They attacked the camp, killed another militiaman, wounded a third, George Winn, and drove off the cattle that the Lehi men had just recovered. When Hunsaker and his son returned to camp later that evening, they found Cousins's body, at first thinking it was Lewis's. Willis's militia almost shot the Hunsakers before realizing who they were. Willis vacated the camp that night, reaching Wixom's at two in the morning of 27 February. Winn died soon after.

Six Mormons died in "Tintic's War," including Lewis Hunsaker, who was presumed dead, though his remains were never found. The Mormons also lost about 250 cattle. In the original skirmish at Tintic's camp, Tintic himself was wounded, while Battest and three other Indians were killed; the Indians suffered no known casualties in the subsequent raids. Tintic spent the winter in the Tintic Mountains with his band. One Indian in Johnson's original arrest warrant, Squash, was eventually arrested. While in jail on 5 March 1856, he slit his own throat with a table knife. Tintic died around 1859, still hiding out in the mountains.[212]

15–16 July 1856
BURNT RIVER *(Hereford, Oregon)*

As part of Washington territorial governor Isaac Stevens's attempt to remove hostile Indians from settled areas, Lt. Col. Benjamin Shaw marched 400 volunteers to Oregon Territory. While Shaw and the main force left Fort Walla Walla to descend on the Grande Ronde Valley, one company of Washington Volunteers, under a Captain Goff, was detached to join a strike force of Oregon Rangers under Maj. Davis Layton to approach the valley from another direction.

Layton went west on the Emigrant Road, cut south in the vicinity of present-day Boardman, Oregon, and marched cross-country to the John Day River. From there he followed a band of Indians east up the John Day, across the Blue Mountains, and into the valley of the upper Burnt River, in the vicinity of present-day Hereford, Oregon. Layton's seventy-five Oregon Rangers and Goff's company of Washington Volunteers surprised several bands of Wascos, Deschutes, John Days, and Umatillas. Army officials described the two-day skirmish as "a substantial victory."

Layton continued on to the Snake River and swept north on the Emigrant Road. As a result of his operations, as well as those of Shaw, who destroyed the Indian village at Grande Ronde, about 900 Indians soon surrendered and were placed on Oregon's Warm Springs Reservation.[213]

Ca. 15 August 1856
MOUTH OF THE PECOS *(Comstock, Texas)*

In August 1856 Capt. James Oakes and Lt. James B. Witherell led thirty Second Cavalry troopers of Company C, nineteen First Infantrymen of Company B, and thirteen First Artillerymen of Company I, on patrol out of Fort Clark. They headed west toward the mouth of the Pecos River, searching for Comanches. They trailed through exceptionally rough ground where few white men had ever gone before, an area that perhaps gave the Indians a false sense of security.

Ten days into the mission, Oakes and Witherell reached the junction of the Pecos and the Rio Grande. The Indians' lax vigilance allowed Oakes to run roughshod along the banks, hitting three separate bands in one day. Even with surprise and numbers in their favor, the soldiers killed only four Indians and wounded four, in addition to capturing several horses and other property.[214]

Ca. 26 August and ca. 5 September 1856
BABBITT'S WAGON TRAIN
(Grand Island and Sutherland, Nebraska)

After the 26 August 1856 Grand Island Battle, in which Capt. George H. Steuart attacked a camp of Cheyennes along the Platte River, killing six and wounding ten, the angry Indians sought revenge. They found their first opportunity on the Council Bluffs Road about thirty-three miles northeast of Fort Kearny, where a small, four-wagon train carried emigrants headed to Utah. The party included Almon W. Babbitt, Secretary of Utah Territory and a delegate to Congress. The Cheyennes hit the camped wagons on the night of 25 August. They killed two men and one child, wounded a man, and carried off Mrs. Wilson, the mother of the slain child. When she was unable to ride fast enough to keep up with the raiders, she too was killed.

On 30 August, Cheyennes attacked another emigrant party at Cotton-wood Springs, eighty miles west of Fort Kearny. They killed Mrs. William Schvekendeck and captured her four-year-old boy. On 6 September, the Indians ambushed a Mormon train traveling east. This time they killed two men, a woman, and a child, and took one woman captive.

Despite his own recent experience with the Cheyennes, Secretary Babbitt brashly set out again across Nebraska. On 2 September, he and two other men left Fort Kearny in a carriage bound for Salt Lake City, ignoring Capt. Henry W. Wharton's advice to wait for an army escort. The Cheyennes spotted the party around 5 or 6 September and quickly killed all three of them. Their bodies were found on 26 September, on the north side of the Platte River near O'Fallon's Bluff. Following this attack, the raids abruptly ended. With fall approaching, the Indians called off the war to prepare for the coming winter.[215]

19–20 September 1856
YELLOWHAWK CREEK/STEVENS'S FIGHT
(Walla Walla, Washington)

The expedition that Washington territorial governor Isaac I. Stevens sent to Washington's Walla Walla Valley and Oregon's Grande Ronde to remove the Indians resulted in two victories for the volunteers in July 1856: the Burnt River battle (see Burnt River, 15–16 July 1856) and the Grande Ronde battle two days later. Most of the Indians had surrendered, so Stevens deemed it propitious to call for an Indian council to legalize white settlement in the Walla Walla Valley. Messengers went to notify the Indians, and Stevens asked Col. George Wright to provide him with an escort to the council site. Wright ordered Maj. Edward J. Steptoe, Ninth Infantry, to accompany Stevens's train with four companies of regulars and, once in the valley, to establish a post there.

Stevens left The Dalles on 19 August with 30 wagons, 80 oxen, 200 other animals, and his employees, escorted by Captain Goff's company of Washington Territory Volunteers. The rest of Steptoe's men followed behind with the supply train. At the meeting place near Waiilatpu, several Indian bands gradually assembled, most of them appearing sullen and unreceptive to Stevens. Stevens waited.

After a week, the Nez Perces arrived, and the council was set to begin. The Cayuse, Deschutes, and Tyigh bands in attendance were unfriendly toward Stevens. Some Palouses came to the council, but the Yakimas and Palouses under Kamiakin, Owhi, and Qualchin refused to attend, although they camped nearby. Stevens opened his talks with the Indians on 11 September, but after several days he had made no progress. The Cayuse Tumneh Howlish voiced the thoughts of many Indians when he said to Stevens, "I am equal to you. . . . I do not know why you are to tell me what to do."[216]

On 14 September, intimidated by the Indians' hostile attitude, Stevens moved his camp closer to Steptoe's soldiers, who were about four miles away. The move was fortuitous, as Kamiakin and 350 warriors had been planning to attack him that day. The council ended on 18 September, but the next day, as Stevens prepared to return to Fort Walla Walla, some Cayuse, Umatilla, and Tenino Indians set fire to the grass so Steptoe's horses would have no forage. Stevens's party headed out, with about fifty friendly Nez Perces riding along. The hostile Indians followed Stevens's train, harassing the governor and his small escort. On 19 September, near the junction of Yellowhawk and Cottonwood Creeks, the pursuing Indians began firing at them. Stevens and Goff corralled the wagons in a circle and prepared their defense.

Kamiakin, Qualchin, and the Sinkiuse Quiltenenock led the warriors in a long-range fight that lasted all day. The Indians did not charge up close, but neither did they let Stevens get away. Qualchin shouted to the Nez Perces with Stevens to abandon the fight, but they chose to stay. In the early hours of 20 September, Steptoe arrived in the darkness. The reinforcements appeared to discourage the warriors, but they kept firing until midmorning. When a bullet struck Quiltenenock in the hip, the attackers broke off the fight.

Two soldiers were killed in the skirmish, and several Indians were hit. Steptoe marched back to The Dalles with Stevens, arriving on 2 October.[217]

21 November 1856
PORT GAMBLE (Port Gamble, Washington)
The defeat of various tribes in the Puget Sound area at the Battle of Seattle (see Battle of Seattle, 26 February 1856) did not end hostilities in the region. On the contrary, it seemed to draw Indians from up and down the Pacific Northwest coast into the fighting. In early spring 1856,

U.S. gunboats repelled a band of Stikines from British Columbia and Alaska who had paddled their canoes for hundreds of miles. The *U.S.S. Massachusetts* arrived in February 1856, and the *John Hancock* appeared the next month, expelling sixty Indians from the Port Townsend area.

In October Stikines attacked a small schooner and killed a crew member. The *Massachusetts*, under Commander Samuel Swartwout, unsuccessfully pursued the culprits. Another band raided the Fort Steilacoom area, stealing crops and fighting with the reservation Nisquallies. On 20 November, Swartwout cornered the Stikines at Port Gamble, on the northern Kitsap Peninsula. He sent Lt. I. Young to meet with them and insist that they leave the sound, but with an offer to tow their canoes as far as Victoria Island. The Stikines answered with insolent words and gestures, challenging Young to bring his men ashore for a fight.

When Young reported the rebuff, Swartwout organized a stronger method of persuasion. He moved the *Massachusetts* in close to shore while sending a Lieutenant Forrest up the coast in the ship's launch to take a second position. He also directed the steamer *Traveler* to stand by, positioning the three vessels to rake the Stikine camp with gunfire.

The next morning, Lt. Alexander Semmes approached the Indians under a flag of truce to reiterate Swartwout's offer, while Forrest led a shore party of twenty-nine men farther down the coast with a small artillery piece. The Indians, about 117 in all, refused to leave. After seeming to take a defensive position, about sixty Indians blasted Semmes's men with their guns; nearly simultaneously, the batteries on the *Traveler* and the *Massachusetts* opened fire along with the onshore howitzer.

A Stikine chief fell with both legs broken. When two women ran out to pull him to cover, the Marines called for them to surrender. One did, but the other refused and she was shot down. Several of Semmes's and Forrest's men fired at the Indians while others destroyed their canoes and property. The onshore forces eventually returned to the boats, but the *Massachusetts* kept up its bombardment. By the next morning, the Stikines had had enough. Under a white flag, two of them went aboard the *Massachusetts* and surrendered.

The Indians suffered twenty-seven killed and twenty-one wounded. Swartwout lost one killed and one wounded. The fatality, Coxswain Gustave Englebrecht, had the dubious distinction of being the first navy man killed in action on the Pacific Coast. Swartwout boarded the surviving Stikines onto his ship, gave them bread and molasses, and took them to Victoria.[218]

— 1857 —

13 February 1857
KICKAPOO SPRINGS *(Vick, Texas)*

In February 1857 Comanches raided through Kerr County, Texas, stealing a number of horses from settlers near Center Point and Camp Verde. Camp Verde, established in 1855 on Verde Creek three miles north of Bandera Pass, had achieved minor notoriety as the "Camel Camp," or "Little Egypt," home of forty to seventy dromedaries that the army had brought in as experimental mounts. In charge at Verde was Capt. Innis R. Palmer of the Second Cavalry.

When the distressed settlers of the area complained to Palmer about the raids, he assigned Sgt. Walter McDonald and fourteen cavalrymen of Company D to catch the thieves. Mexican guide Jose "Polly" Rodriguez joined McDonald, along with civilians Dr. J. C. Nowlin and his nephew, Henry Moore. The troopers included Pvts. Fred Metzger and John Martin.

The night before the soldiers departed, Martin told Metzger about a vision he had in which his sister, who lived in Baltimore, had come to his tent and with outstretched hand told him to come home. Metzger said it was a bad omen and advised Martin to ask for a furlough. Martin thought he would do so after returning from the scout.

The company crossed the Guadalupe River near Dr. Nowlin's cabin and headed upstream, winding through some of the roughest country around. They saw evidence that the Indians had killed and eaten two of the captured horses along the way. For seven days, the guide Rodriguez kept on the Comanches' trail, which led to the headwaters of Kickapoo Creek, in the southeast corner of present-day Tom Green County.

Nowlin discovered the Indians first and called to McDonald, who brought the detachment in for the charge. Surprisingly, the Indians did not flee but countercharged them face-to-face. Nowlin fired first with his shotgun, badly wounding the lead warrior. Nowlin's second barrel misfired, however, and he dismounted to try to fix it. A Comanche rode up and shot at him, but the ball whizzed past his head and into his horse's neck. Then an arrow hit Nowlin in the leg. He lay on the ground with a jammed shotgun and an empty pistol.

The bugler, Jim Lafoyo (or Tafoyia), chased an Indian and tried to fire his six-shooter several times, but like Nowlin's weapon, the gun malfunctioned. The Indian hit Lafoyo in the back with an arrow, but the point penetrated only the layers of the trooper's rolled-up overcoat, barely scratching his skin. Metzger shot an Indian at close range, then went back to help Nowlin and McDonald, who were both defending themselves only with bluffs, pointing at the Indians with empty pistols. Not far away, Martin fell wounded.

Within a few minutes, the fight was over and the Comanches rode off. Several Indians had been hit, but they left no bodies on the battlefield. Two soldiers had been killed. The troopers recovered five horses, two mules, and five buffalo robes, but Nowlin recognized none of the brands on the animals. The soldiers' opponents in the battle had most likely been different warriors than the ones who had raided the settlements.

The badly wounded Martin was brought to Dr. Nowlin. The bullet had passed through both his lung and stomach, and he was bleeding from the mouth. McDonald called off the scout in order to take Martin to the nearest post, Fort McKavett, about thirty miles away. The company reached the fort the following day, but little could be done for the wounded man, and a short time later, Martin died.[219]

4 April 1857
NORTH BRANCH NUECES *(Rocksprings, Texas)*
In the spring of 1857, Company B, Second Cavalry, was based at Fort Inge, Texas. Scouts from there went out to all points of the compass hunting for raiding Indians. In late March, Lt. Walter H. Jenifer led a twelve-man detachment on a 300-mile scout to the north and west of the fort. Jenifer found a trail on the headwaters of the Nueces River and followed it until he came to terrain too rough for the horses. The lieutenant left five men with the mounts and took the other seven with him to pursue the trail on foot. After a four-mile hike, the soldiers suddenly discovered a camp of about 100 Lipan Apaches.[220]

With more bravado than good sense, Jenifer led his patrol to within 250 yards of the camp. What he planned to do remains unknown, but before he could do it, the Indians discovered the troopers and attacked. Jenifer's men fired as rapidly as possible to hold the Indians at bay. Luckily for the soldiers, the Indians' horses were out being watered, and night was approaching. Jenifer conducted a fighting retreat until darkness ended the pursuit. His men had killed two Lipans and wounded one, with no casualties of their own.

The next morning, displaying further lack of judgment, Jenifer led all his men back to the Indian camp. But again, luck was with the troopers, as the Lipans had pulled out during the night, probably believing that the previous day's small patrol was only an advance for a much larger force. Jenifer found no more Indians, but the men did run out of food on the ride back to Fort Inge. In spite of Jenifer's questionable leadership, headquarters cited the men's gallantry.[221]

19 July 1857
DEVIL'S RIVER *(Juno, Texas)*
On 19 July, William A. "Bigfoot" Wallace left San Antonio with a train of supplies and a herd of twenty-seven mules for the relay stations along the Lower Military Road mail route. His employer, Isaiah Churchill Woods, had instructed him to deliver nine mules to Fort Clark and eighteen to Fort Lancaster.

Wallace was driving a stage, with his passenger, William Clifford of New Orleans, seated next to him. About fifteen miles north of Camp Hudson, near the upper crossing of the Devil's River, war-painted Comanches sprang out of the bushes that lined the road and attacked the train. The war-whoops of the Indians frightened Wallace's team and the horses bolted, circling through a mesquite thicket. They hit a bump and the hitch broke. Wallace threw down the reins and dove off the stage, calling to Clifford to jump too. But the Indians blocked Clifford's retreat and lanced him as they rode by, headed for the valuable mules. The remuda was some distance ahead, but Wallace caught up and jumped onto a mule, commanding the herders to flee.

The defenders were greatly outnumbered, so to confront the Comanches would have been foolish. They turned and raced for Camp Hudson, hoping to outdistance their attackers. The Indians did not bother to chase them, instead turning their attention to the fine spoils the Texans had left behind. The raiders ransacked the coach and absconded with their booty, including most of the mules.

Wallace and his companions reached Camp Hudson about the same time as a Second Cavalry patrol from Fort Clark. The soldiers had Wallace lead them back to the site of the ambush in hopes of catching the Comanches, but they were too late. The men buried Clifford and dragged the remains of the coach back to Camp Hudson. The Indians had taken twenty-one mules, a box of mail, and various supplies. The cavalry later recovered the mules, but the animals were in such bad condition that they were worthless.[222]

24 and 26 July 1857
PECOS STATION *(Iraan, Texas)*

Regularly scheduled mail and passenger service between San Antonio, Texas, and San Diego, California, began in March 1857. First George H. Giddings, then James E. Birch received contracts to carry the mail. Both used the route called the Lower Military Road, which ran between Fort Lancaster and Fort Davis. The monthly express at this time consisted of an ambulance and a wagon, escorted by a detail from each of the two forts. From Fort Davis, Sgt. Ernest Schroeder led six men of the Eighth Infantry, and a Sergeant Libby headed a detail of six men of the First Infantry from Fort Lancaster.

On the evening of 24 July, the party was about twenty-five miles west of Lancaster, near Pecos Station, when about sixty Mescaleros appeared. The two sergeants ordered the teams to be unhitched and the men to take cover. Some Indians approached with a white flag, calling out in Spanish, but other warriors were hovering in a nearby arroyo. As Libby stepped forward, Schroeder warned him: "Look out, sergeant, for the

Ruins and parade ground, Fort Lancaster, Texas

sons of bitches—they will get the advantage of you if they can, and don't put yourself in danger."[223]

At that moment, a bullet tore into Schroeder's chest and killed him. Libby assumed command and ordered the party to retreat to Fort Lancaster, leaving Schroeder's body behind. The soldiers fired as they fell back, keeping the Indians at bay, but the going was slow and treacherous. At nightfall the Indians gave up the fight, and the tired men trudged on to the fort, finally stumbling in at three o'clock in the morning.

At Fort Lancaster, Lt. Alexander M. Haskell, First Infantry, quickly organized a punitive expedition. Lt. Edward Hartz, who happened to be at Lancaster with forty-six men of the Eighth Infantry, by seniority took command. All told, eighty men, including some from Companies H and K, First Infantry, and Companies C, D, F, and H, Eighth Infantry, climbed aboard several wagons. The canvas wagon covers were drawn closed to disguise the expedition as a provision train. This ruse was one of the few strategies the infantry could use to lure mounted Indians in close enough for foot soldiers to fire on them. The penurious U.S. Congress deemed cavalry too expensive to fully fund, so frontier officers had to make the best of a bad situation.

The expedition set out immediately. About forty-five miles west of Fort Lancaster, about forty warriors swooped in for an attack, but upon seeing a commotion inside the wagons, they quickly pulled back out of range. Hartz ordered half of the men out of the wagons to advance as skirmishers. But when the Apaches set the prairie grass on fire in an attempt to burn the wagons, Hartz recalled the soldiers and pulled his vehicles back to a bare depression. The advancing flames split and bypassed the dip on each side. After the fire passed, Hartz ordered his men forward, but by that time the Apaches were gone.

No soldiers were killed in the encounter; Hartz reported killing two Indians. In his report, the lieutenant decried the army's lack of mounted troops in the region, claiming that "the Indians are in virtual possession of the road."[224]

10 August 1857
WICHITA MOUNTAINS *(Lawton, Oklahoma)*

In late July 1857, Capt. Charles J. Whiting and Lt. James P. Major, with detachments of Companies C and K, Second Cavalry, out of Fort Clark, arrived on upper Devil's River, where several days earlier Lt. John B. Hood and seventeen soldiers had put up a valiant fight against a band of some fifty Comanches. Remarkably, all but two of Hood's men had survived. Whiting picked up the Indian trail from the battlefield and followed it north. The route was arid, with men and horses going without water for twenty-four hours at a stretch.

The trail led north all the way across the Red River into Indian Territory. Finally, in the southern reaches of the Wichita Mountains, the soldiers caught up with the band of Comanches they believed to be the ones who attacked Hood's men. Whiting's men cut the Indians off from their horses and drove them into a wooded ravine. Whiting killed two Indians in the chase and captured thirty-three horses, then decided to end the pursuit rather than get entangled in the thickets with an obscured enemy. Whiting suffered no losses in the skirmish.[225]

25 September 1857
SANTA CATARINA *(Santa Catarina, Texas)*

As a result of the army's new policy allowing soldiers to sell unclaimed captured stock, the soldiers in Capt. Charles J. Whiting's command divided $400 in proceeds from selling the horses they had recovered from Comanches in the Wichita Mountains in August 1857 (see previous entry). Now noncommissioned officers and enlisted men had extra incentive to round up stolen horses whenever they could.

In mid-September, Sgt. Charles Patrick, Second Cavalry, left Fort McIntosh and drove his twelve-man detachment of Company I through heavy rains during a seven-day pursuit of Comanches with stolen stock. After sixty hours and 160 muddy miles, they finally caught their quarry near Santa Catarina, in present-day Starr County, Texas. Patrick and his squad killed one Indian and wounded four in the chase, and they captured eleven horses. Though this was less than one animal apiece, each worth perhaps twelve to fifteen dollars (depending on its condition), that amount was approximately the same as an enlisted man's monthly army wages. In other words, each trooper had to sell only one horse to double his income for the month.[226]

— 1858 —

Ca. 15 January 1858
VAN HORN'S WELL *(Van Horn, Texas)*

Stage company employees at the isolated stations dotting the overland trails had one of the most dangerous jobs in the West. During the winter of 1858, Light S. Townsend was station chief at Van Horn's Well. The twenty-three-year-old Townsend was normally a driver for George H. Giddings's company, but he had injured his arm a few weeks earlier and was given station duty until he recovered. Three other employees, all Mexicans, worked in the station with him. One of them, Jose Lopez, was an experienced Indian fighter. Another was an unnamed man from Chihuahua who was half Indian, and there was something about him that Townsend mistrusted.

That evening, Townsend secured the hayricks, which contained seventy-five tons of feed, then he shut the mules in their stalls and locked the big gate at the corral entrance. The eastern stage was overdue. Townsend suspected Indian trouble, but all he could do was keep his men alert and prepare the weapons. The men stacked rifles and ammunition near the loopholes of the two-hut station, then they played cards and waited for the stage. At midnight, the stage still missing, Townsend had his assistants douse the lanterns and prepare for bed. He had just gotten his boots off when, in the darkness, he noticed yellow light coming through the loopholes and heard a crackling noise. The hay was on fire. He shouted to Lopez to go out and drive the stock to safety. But when Lopez swung open the door, several arrows whistled past him. "Los Indios!" yelled Lopez, slamming the door.

The four men each took a loophole and watched for one of the assailants to show himself in the darkness. Muzzle flashes lit up the night as balls slammed into the station like hail along with the flying arrows. Townsend tried to ignore the screams of the mules as flames spread from the hay to the roof of the stables. Smoke and the awful smell of burning animals filled the room.

The Indians, Mescalero Apaches, swarmed around the station. As a warrior tried to shoot through a rifle port, Townsend thrust the muzzle of his Sharps through the hole into the Indian's side and pulled the trigger. Then the station keepers heard warriors on the roof, trying to dig through the mud-and-wattle ceiling. Lopez stood beneath them with shotgun ready. A warrior poked through with a large stick, and when he put his eye to the hole, Lopez let him have a blast of buckshot, blowing him off the roof.

Townsend heard his Chihuahuan assistant call out to the Apaches several times, but he did not know what he was saying. He then saw the man pass something through a loophole to a warrior and told Lopez. The loyal Mexican knocked the man to the floor with the butt of his shotgun and said he would blow his head off if he got up. The mixed-blood never moved.

The fighting continued all night. Townsend estimated that they had killed one-third of their attackers by dawn, but ammunition was getting low. At daybreak, Townsend heard a voice call out in English, "Luz Lightie, come out; we are your friends and won't hurt you." Townsend was not about to fall for such an absurd ruse, but he kept the man talking while he and Lopez tried to locate his position. Townsend called out a question, and the Apache stepped into the open to reply. At that instant, Townsend and Lopez fired at the same time, "scattering his brains over the ground."[227]

With that, the station keepers, including the Chihuahuan, bolted out the door and ran to a nearby arroyo. Only a few Apaches pursued them; the others were probably discouraged by their losses and unwilling to face the sharp-shooting station keepers in the open. A short time later, the Apaches seemingly disappeared. Townsend elected not to go back to the station, however, in case the Indians had set up an ambush.

The four men headed east on the road to Fort Davis. Exhausted and thirsty, they would not have gotten far but for the fortuitous appearance of the long-overdue westbound stage. The bedraggled station keepers climbed aboard and returned to the station. There they found everything burned to the ground, the mules nothing but charred meat and bones. Already, wolves were edging in, attracted by the carnage. Townsend was just thankful to have survived.[228]

18 April 1858
GERTRUDE MASSACRE *(Jermyn, Texas)*

In April 1858, about a year after Jack County, Texas, was organized, a band of Indians, joined by several white bandits, raided a settlement in the northwest section of the county, murdering several residents. The community, located a few miles north of present-day Jermyn, on the north end of Lost Valley, was then known as Gertrude. The creek flowing through the valley is now called Cameron Creek—also spelled Camberon, Cambren, and Cambern—after the Cambren family, the victims of the most vicious of the attacks.

On the morning of 18 April, James B. Cambren and his two oldest boys, Luther and James Jr., were working in the field. The boys' mother, Mary, had just called her family in to dinner when they noticed Indians approaching, but they thought little of it, as friendly Indians lived nearby on the Lower Brazos Reservation. Without warning, the Indians attacked, sending an arrow through the senior James's torso, bringing down Luther with a bullet, and shooting the younger James as he clambered over the fence. White bandits grabbed Mrs. Cambren and the children and restrained them while other raiders ransacked the cabin. One of the leaders, a red-haired half-Indian, sent half a dozen raiders over to the Tom Mason homestead, about a mile away, where the Masons were eating dinner. The raiders killed Tom Mason and his wife, Mary, leaving Tobe, age three, and Milton, age ten months, alone.

The raiders stole the Cambrens' money box and other items, then, kidnapping Mary Cambren and her four youngest children, headed to a hill a few miles away. When the raiders stopped to tie one boy, Thomas, onto a mule, Mary and her youngest boy began crying and screaming. At this disturbance, the bandits shot Mary several times and ran a spear down the child's throat. The younger Mary Cambren, age seven, and her five-year-old brother, Dewitt, were left behind with their dead mother as the raiders rode off with Thomas. Mary later reported that she and DeWitt stayed by their dead mother until nearly sundown, at which point she led her little brother back to the house.

As the raiders were making their getaway with Thomas, they were spotted by some mounted men who were riding with an emigrant train on the Marcy-California Trail. When the men rode over to investigate, the bandits pushed Thomas off the mule and raced away.

The next morning, Isaac Lynn, father of Mary Mason, rode to the Mason homestead to visit his daughter. He was horrified to find her and her husband dead and their little son, Milton, crawling in his mother's blood. Lynn then hurried to the neighboring Cambren house, where he discovered a similar scene. "Is there anyone alive here?" he called out, and Mary Cambren answered, "Me and Dewitt are here."[229]

Lynn took the two Cambren children and his own two grandchildren back to his home on Lynn Creek, then rode to Jacksboro with the news. A posse formed up and sped out, but the men were much too late to do anything but bury the bodies. Nevertheless, they got a remarkably detailed description of the raiders from young Mary, and based on this, the posse members thought they knew who the culprits were.

While the Comanche raiders were long gone to Indian Territory, it was believed that the white bandits had headed south. The posse, which included W. L. Lasater, William Kutch, John Taylor, Bryant Herrington, and Oliver Loving, followed a trail through Palo Pinto County to Comanche County. Locals reported seeing four white men riding through, and the chase continued. The Texans caught up with their targets in Lampasas County, and brought them back to Jacksboro for trial. When Mary Cambren saw them, she exclaimed, "There is the man who killed Ma and took Pa's money from the trunk!"[230]

Incredibly, in Jacksboro, the defendants were released on some technicality, but their luck did not last. As one account explained: "Judge Lynch's court settled the affair near Austin, Texas."[231]

13 June 1858
GUADALUPE MOUNTAINS *(Whites City, New Mexico)*

On the last day of May 1858, Mescalero Apaches, identified as being from the bands of Marco and Gomez, stole some mules from a government mail party north of the Davis Mountains in West Texas. Following the incident, Lt. Col. Washington Sewell, Eighth Infantry, in command at Fort Davis, ordered 2nd Lt. William B. Hazen to "overtake and chasten" the culprits.

Hazen left the fort on 4 June with two Mexican guides, eleven mounted men, and nineteen infantrymen drawn from Companies C, D, F, and H of the Eighth Infantry. Most of the soldiers were quite green, and Hazen would later blame the disastrous expedition on the men's inexperience. The party followed the Indians' trail north across nearly waterless terrain between the Sierra Diablo and the Delaware Mountains to the southern end of the Guadalupe Mountains, then followed the mountain edge northeast into New Mexico Territory. Finally, on 13 June, Hazen's guides discovered an Indian camp cut into an escarpment in a canyon.

Hazen planned to surround the camp, which contained about fifteen lodges and about 100 Indians, during the night. The guides, however, overestimated the distance to the camp, and the soldiers found themselves standing just above the camp before sundown. Taking a chance, Hazen decided to attack at once, but the Indians saw them coming and fled up the canyon. Only one Mescalero warrior was killed and one woman was captured before nightfall ended the fight.

The next morning, Hazen rounded up twenty-nine government horses and mules and burned the abandoned camp. The soldiers found fifty white scalps—evidence that this band had been killing settlers. Hazen scouted for the Mescaleros through the rugged Guadalupes for a day and a half before calling it quits.

The return march was an ordeal. The soldiers suffered from lack of water and food, and the grain-fed horses were so broken down that the men had to dismount and walk. On the way to the Salt Springs, it got so hot that the men could not touch the metal parts of their rifles, and the little water they had left in their canteens was almost too hot to drink. Soon, even that was gone. Hazen reported that several men drank their own urine, which only increased their thirst.

The expedition camped at Salt Springs on 16 June. That evening, Pvt. Michael Kellett, Company D, went outside the perimeter to sleep. When he stumbled back about 4 a.m., the nervous sentry, issuing no verbal challenge, shot him dead. The sentry then yelled, "Indians!" startling the entire camp and causing another sentry, Pvt. Michael Heyers of Company C, to panic. When Heyers came running into camp screaming, the men mistook him for a charging Indian and blasted away at him, knocking him dead in his tracks. Stray bullets hit several horses, and pandemonium ensued. Not until dawn did everything calm down enough for Hazen to piece together what had happened.

The soldiers buried Kellett and Heyers in the desert and proceeded sadly home. They reached Fort Davis on 20 June.[232] Hazen later praised his scouts and a few of the soldiers, but of the remainder he wrote: "I never saw so worthless a set of men thrown together before in my life."[233]

Ca. 15 July 1858
GROUSE CREEK (Hyampom, California)

The so-called Wintoon (Wintun) War, a half-year conflict between the Wintun Indians and area settlers, arose from seemingly trivial causes. The Wintuns lived at the headwaters of Redwood Creek and along the Mad and Eel Rivers. Because they relied heavily on hunting game, the Wintuns were unusually proficient in the use of firearms.

In February 1858, a fight erupted between a mean-spirited man named Leroy and his Wintun wife. The couple lived near Angel's Ranch, about fifteen miles east of Arcata, California. The pair often fought, but a particularly severe beating by Leroy prompted the woman's relatives to seek revenge. Two Indians confronted Leroy and a fight ensued; Leroy was badly wounded by a hatchet blow, but he killed both Wintuns with his knife, then stumbled to Angel's Ranch to report what had happened. A party of settlers rode to Leroy's place to investigate and found that Leroy's wife was gone, along with all the couple's possessions.

A few days later, on the Trinity Trail, settlers caught an Indian who was thought to be one of Leroy's wife's band. The settlers bound him to a tree and made him "confess." The Wintun told his inquisitors what they wanted to hear and added that warriors of his band had killed two white trappers, Granger and Cook, who had disappeared in the vicinity the year before.

The two incidents inflamed the Wintuns to a war fever. On 23 June, packers Henry Allen and William E. Ross, along with two young Indian employees, were on the Trinity Trail near Grouse Creek when Wintuns attacked, badly wounding Ross. Allen hid in the woods while one of his Indian companions rode to A. L. Pardee's nearby ranch for help. After informing the ranch's inhabitants of what happened, the Indian boy rode thirty-seven miles along the twisting trail into Eureka to spread the word. A relief party rescued the packers.

In July a party of volunteers under John Bell rode out to punish the Wintuns. They began their search at Pardee's ranch, then continued along the trail near Grouse Creek. Several miles west of Hyampom Valley, the posse found a Wintun rancheria and attacked. Bell's men killed several Wintun warriors, and the Indians shot and killed one volunteer, Orrin Stevens. Bell also lost his provisions and ten mules. When more warriors appeared, Bell, realizing he was outnumbered and undersupplied, retreated back to Pardee's. But the "Wintoon War" was on.[234]

29 August 1858
OJO DEL OSO *(Fort Wingate, New Mexico)*
In August 1858 an advance party of an expedition to fight the Navajos gathered in Albuquerque. Capt. George McLane, son of statesman Louis McLane, was in command of the party. With twelve men of Company I, Mounted Rifles, as an escort for the wagons, and the temporary Navajo agent, Sam Yost, McLane rode west toward Fort Defiance. Twenty-two New Mexican irregulars under Blas Lucero joined McLane at Cubero. From there they picked up the pace, making about fifty miles per day, to the water hole at Ojo del Oso (Bear Springs).

Ojo del Oso was an established Navajo camping spot, and McLane knew he would encounter Indians there. He also knew that there had been last-minute peace talks at Fort Defiance, but he assumed they had failed. So when he discovered about 300 Navajos in scattered hogans about half a mile above the springs, he felt obliged to attack. Leaving half

Fort Wingate, New Mexico

his command with the wagons, McLane galloped up the rocky slope with only twenty-two of Lucero's men and four of his own, plus Yost.

The Navajos fired only a few shots before retreating uphill, where piñon and juniper gave them more cover. As they fanned out, seeming to threaten McLane's flanks, the captain dismounted and ordered his men to fire at a range of about 400 yards. Rather than firing, however, Lucero's men continued the pursuit. Yost figured they were "anxious for the fight and equally anxious for booty."[235] As McLane advanced, musket fire rang out from a concealed position on the left only 150 yards away. A ball smashed into McLane's chest, glanced off a rib, and exited, leaving a hole in his coat. Yost reported, "The shock was so great that he staggered some 10 paces, became very pale and sick at the stomach, and in fact gave every outward indication of a speedy death."[236]

The fight lasted only about fifteen minutes. McLane was taken to the wagons, which immediately left for Fort Defiance. Lucero and his irregulars continued the chase and the next day captured twenty horses. The army claimed ten Navajos dead, four wounded, and four captured; Yost said only six Indians were killed, however, and Lucero estimated only two. The wounded McLane healed quickly and was back in the saddle the following month.[237]

30 August 1858
ROSE-BALEY WAGON TRAIN *(Fort Mojave, Arizona)*

The families in the Rose-Baley emigrant train came from southern Iowa and northern Missouri. Most of them had made their separate ways to eastern Kansas, where they joined together for convenience and safety. Trouble with the Mormons had been reported along the central route to California, and the emigrants hoped to avoid this by taking the southern route. In addition to the Roses and Baleys, the other families included the Browns, Bentners, Udells, Daleys, Hollands, Hedgpeths, and Joneses, plus a number of employees. All told, the company comprised about ninety-two people, including thirty-four adult males. The train set out on the Santa Fe Trail in mid-May 1858.

Reaching Albuquerque in late June, the company learned of a new, supposedly safer and shorter route, Beale's Wagon Road. Although touted by the army and the citizens of Albuquerque, the road was unproven, and the families would have no other trains in advance of them that they might follow or from whom they might seek help. In spite of the risk, only the Udells voted against taking the shortcut. The emigrants hired a guide, Jose M. Savedra, who had guided several expeditions through the territory, including Edward F. Beale's earlier in the year, and the train pulled out on 26 June.

Despite Savedra's credentials, he had little luck in finding water holes along the arid route. By the time the emigrants reached what is now western Arizona, they were traveling at night and with the wagons strung out along the trail so as not to overtax the scarce water sources. On 27 August, they reached the rough terrain of Sitgreaves Pass in the Black Mountains. They had seen little Indian trouble thus far—only a bothersome band of Hualapais, who shot a few arrows at them and stole some cattle. They had heard that the Mojaves, whose lands they were now entering, were friendly. While most of the families rested at the pass, a few of the more persevering travelers, including the Rose, Baley, and Brown families, continued west, heading to the Colorado River.

Near the river, some Mojaves confronted the emigrants and demanded to know their intentions. Were they passing through, or did they plan to stay and settle? Although assured that the families were not staying, the Indians did not trust them and became agitated. One warrior grabbed Mrs. Leonard Rose's breast and she ran screaming back to the wagon. Her husband, hesitant to start a fight, held his anger in check. Other Mojaves approached the Alpha Brown wagon. Mrs. Brown asked them for some water, to which they replied that they'd give her some if she gave them her dress. Some of the other warriors indicated that they would like to take her boy. Mr. Brown was able to chase them off, but the incident bode ill.

Over the next few days, more members of the train rode down from Sitgreaves Pass, and the Mojaves began to appear in greater numbers. When the emigrants began to chop down cottonwoods to make rafts, the Indians may have thought they were going to build cabins. About 2 p.m. on 30 August, the Mojaves struck. Sallie Fox, the thirteen-year-old stepdaughter of Alpha Brown, was playing when she noticed some Indians creeping through the nearby underbrush. She cried out, "The Indians are coming, and they will kill us all!"[238]

The warning came just in time. The men of the train, who were taking a short siesta, jumped up, grabbed their weapons, and met the Indian charge head-on. Robbed of a total surprise, the Mojaves made a half-hearted attack, then pulled back to find easier targets. They caught Alpha Brown, Ed Akey, and Lee Griffin working on a raft near the river. Akey and Griffin made a run for the camp. Akey had his pistol out and shot two Indians, while Griffin took two arrows in the arm. Brown mounted his horse and tried to ride for the wagons, but a volley of arrows struck him. His horse carried him to the camp, where he dropped to the ground, dead. Akey, almost reaching the wagons, caught an arrow just below the left collarbone.

The wagon corral had about twenty-five men to fight off about 300 warriors. Luckily for them, the Indians, armed only with bows and arrows, did not make a concentrated attack. Instead they worked their way around the perimeter and fired wherever a target presented itself, wounding about a dozen emigrants, including Sallie Fox, Elizabeth Jones, William R. Baley, Tom Hedgpeth, and L. J. Rose. The fight ended when Gillum Baley, who had been in the Illinois Militia during the Black Hawk War in 1832, carefully aimed his rifle at a Mojave who appeared to be the chief. His shot hit the mark, and the chief, possibly Jose, crumpled dead to the ground. The Mojaves then backed off, but they ran off most of the emigrants' livestock before retreating. The Indians had lost about seventeen warriors in the fight.

Meanwhile, however, the Bentner family, who had left the camp the night before against the protests of some of the others, were caught alone. The Indians killed Mr. and Mrs. Bentner and all five of their children.

The body of the eldest girl, eighteen years old, was later found stripped with her face badly mutilated; the other bodies were never found. Back at the wagons, the emigrants saw the Mojaves ride by waving the fresh scalps from a pole.

The emigrants, shaken from the day's events, took a vote on what to do next. They elected to retrace their steps all the way back to Albuquerque. Having lost most of their draft animals, they had to abandon many of their wagons along with most of their possessions. The trip was long and hard. The few water holes they had found on their way out seemed to have since dried up, and the game had also disappeared. Only by running into some other wagon parties did the remnants of the Rose-Baley train survive. Upon hearing the families' harrowing story, the emigrants who had been following in their wake agreed to turn back to Albuquerque with them. The last of the original emigrants straggled into Albuquerque on 13 November, two and a half months after the attack. Emigrants seldom used the Beale Road after that.[239]

26 October 1858
PARDEE'S RANCH *(Eureka, California)*

Northern California's "Wintoon War," which began in July 1858 (see Grouse Creek, 15 July 1858), continued into the fall. While area settlers were still calling for the formation of new militias, on 14 September Wintuns murdered Paul Boynton on the Trinity Trail. The next morning, the Indians appeared at A. L. Pardee's ranch, near Redwood Creek, about twenty miles east of Eureka. They would have surprised the inhabitants had not Pardee's dogs begun barking. Warriors fired at Pardee and his partner, a man named Barney, but the settlers were not hit. That night, Pardee and his family headed to the coast. Later, a trader named Chauncey Miller was killed in the same area. The Trinity Trail was effectively blocked.

Residents of the coastal towns of Eureka and Union finally pulled together several volunteer companies. On 2 October a Captain Underwood, with thirty-six men, became the first to take a scout into the vicinity of Pardee's Ranch. A short time later, Capt. J. G. Messec organized an eighty-man company called the Trinity Rangers and proceeded to Pardee's behind Underwood. Messec's rangers became the first company to engage the Wintuns when they found an Indian camp on 26 October.

Messec planned to get his men in close and attack at dawn, but they were not quite in position when daybreak exposed them. The Wintuns took to the bushes and engaged Messec in a running fight, dodging and shooting from behind rocks and trees. Volunteer John Harpst was severely wounded by a bullet in the shoulder, but he was the militia's only casualty. The volunteers killed four warriors and captured six women and children.

Several more fights and a severe winter in 1859 brought the Wintuns' defeat. The Trinity Rangers mustered out in March 1859. Most of the Wintuns were sent to the Mendocino Reservation.[240]

27 December 1858
GARLAND'S MASSACRE *(Graford, Texas)*

In 1854 Congress created two Indian reservations in Texas. The one for the Comanches was on the Clear Fork of the Brazos River, near Camp Cooper, and the other, for the Wacos, Tonkawas, Caddos, and Anadarkos, was on the Brazos about twenty miles downstream from Fort Belknap. Area settlers complained long and loud about the reservations, and many called for the removal of the Indians from Texas altogether. These detractors claimed that, time and again, the Indians had stolen their stock and taken the animals back to the reservations. While the Indians had their defenders, including Superintendent Robert S. Neighbors, they had many more enemies, such as John R. Baylor.

During the Christmas season, when Neighbors was away in San Antonio, an armed band of locals decided to eliminate some Indians on their own. The men, under Peter Garland, made their plans known to the other settlers, and although some of them disapproved, they did nothing to stop them. The targets would turn out to be a peaceful band of Caddos and Anadarkos, led by an Indian known as Choctaw Tom. Tom's band had received permission to leave the reservation and camp where there was better grazing. Among the group were two warriors who had recently campaigned with Earl Van Dorn and his Second Cavalrymen, fighting Comanches at the Wichita villages.

Two days after Christmas, Garland's men rode in on the unsuspecting Indians as they were camped near the junction of Keechi Creek and the Brazos River. One local, James "Buck" Barry, claimed that Garland mistook Choctaw Tom's band for hostile Caddos. The Texans tore through the sleeping camp, killing four men and three women, and wounding three children. Two of Garland's men, named Stephens and Barnes, were also killed. One of the first people on the scene after the attack recalled: "A more horrible sight I never expect to see. There, on their beds, lay the bodies of seven of the best and most inoffensive Indians on the reserve, their bodies pierced by buckshot and rifle balls."[241]

When the guilty men were identified, the court ordered the Texas Rangers, under John S. "Rip" Ford, to arrest them. Ford refused, however, arguing that as a military officer, he could not enforce the orders of a civil court. The culprits were never brought to trial. Superintendent Neighbors was enraged at Ford, but public sympathies were not on Neighbors's side. The following year, after the Indians were removed from Texas, a man shot the "Indian lover" Robert Neighbors in the back at Fort Belknap. Rangers caught the killer, Ed Cornett, and hanged him without a trial.[242]

— 1859 —

13 February 1859
POSTOAK WATERHOLE *(Leakey, Texas)*
In mid-February 1859, Comanche raiders stole about eighty horses from stockman I. C. Isbel, who lived on the Frio River at the foot of the Balcones Escarpment. The alarm went out, and soon, fifteen local settlers had gathered at Isbel's place. From Fort Inge, a Sergeant Maloney and five soldiers from Company F, Eighth Infantry, joined them. The combined force, under Capt. Henry Robinson, took up the Indians' trail.

The raiders' tracks led north up the East Fork of the Frio River to the divide that ran between it and the Sabinal River, in hilly country covered with post oak and blackjack. At that point Robinson, following a hunch about where the Indians were heading, led his men off the trail, circling back to a point between Postoak and Frio Waterholes, about thirteen miles north of present-day Leakey, Texas.

The Indians were right where he guessed, and Robinson ordered a charge. The Texans outnumbered the Comanches, but they made the mistake of firing all their guns at once. Realizing this, the Indians countercharged. The soldiers and settlers, of whom only John Leakey and two others had repeating firearms, turned to run to the shelter of some trees where they could reload. Leakey and the other two kept the Indians at bay with their six-shooters for the critical first few minutes. Two warriors went down, then an arrow pierced John Cook's leg and pinned him to his saddle. A wounded warrior sitting on the ground sent a shower of arrows at the Texans until a soldier shot him through the head with a musket. At one point, Richard Ware had an Indian in his sights and was about to pull the trigger when a white man's head popped up in front of him. He pulled the rifle up just in time.

One mounted warrior, whom Leakey thought he had hit about six times, kept fighting. Henry Courtney, on horseback, chased the warrior down and blasted him with his shotgun, but he still kept going. Next, John Daugherty went after him, but the warrior's arrows forced Daugherty off his horse. The Indian dismounted and ran up to fight Daugherty, who had taken cover behind his horse. The two battled from opposite sides of the horse until Daugherty's pistol was empty. When Daugherty ran to a tree, the Indian mounted his horse and rode away.

The Indians finally got away, but at least three were killed and several were wounded. The Texans recovered about forty-nine stolen horses.[243]

20 May 1859
WEST NUECES *(Rocksprings, Texas)*
Soldiers stationed at the scattered outposts along the Texas frontier were constantly kept busy responding to reports of Indian depredations, thefts, and murders. In May, Kickapoos raiding from their home base in Mexico stole a small herd of horses near the ford of the Nueces

Lt. William B. Hazen
—From authors' collection

River in the vicinity of Fort Inge. Fort commander Capt. R. P. Maclay ordered 2nd Lt. William B. Hazen, Eighth Infantry, to lead a detachment in pursuit.

On 16 May Hazen led ten mounted men of Company F, two scouts, and four civilians to find the raiders. The trail led north along the Nueces. After three days and some seventy-five miles, Hazen's scouts discovered about twelve Kickapoos in camp near a spring on the West Nueces, southwest of present-day Rocksprings. Moving his command to the valley floor, Hazen charged, completely surprising the Indians. The Texans killed four Kickapoos and wounded the rest. They recovered seven stolen horses and other property.

In the camp Hazen found "safe conduct" certificates dating back to 1845. Hazen figured that either the letters were no longer valid or the Indians who carried them should have been more careful about their company. Upon his return to Fort Inge, Hazen was brevetted a first lieutenant for this action and one the year before (see Guadalupe Mountains, 13 June 1858).[244]

23 May 1859
RESERVATION WAR *(Graham, Texas)*

With thefts and killings occurring around the northern Texas reservations, such as Garland's Massacre on 27 December 1858 (see Garland's Massacre), it did not take much for local demagogues to stir up a mob. John R. Baylor publicly circulated charges that the Comanches of the Clear Fork Reservation had committed the murders. In late May, about 500 men gathered in Jacksboro, under the command of Baylor, Peter Garland, and Allison Nelson. They planned to first attack Camp Cooper and capture its artillery, then go after the Indians, killing them or driving them out of Texas.

Although their prime target was the upper (Clear Fork) agency, the volunteers had not gotten beyond the lower (Brazos) agency when they were confronted. Capt. Innis N. Palmer of the Second Cavalry informed them that it was his duty to defend the Indians on the reserve. Reluctant to take on federal forces, Baylor's men began to move on, but not before capturing one old Indian, whom they dragged away with a rope, then killed and scalped him.

The incident spurred an attack by fifty or sixty Indians who had been watching the Texans. Soon more warriors joined them, and a running fight exploded. Participant James "Buck" Barry wrote that the battle was "carried on in regular savage style by both parties, each putting to death all the prisoners taken."[245] The fight lasted until dark. About five Texans were killed, while the Indians lost one or two. The old Tonkawa chief Placedo lamented that it was the first time he had ever fought the whites. Many took the battle as proof that there could be no peaceful coexistence between Indians and Texans on the frontier.[246]

5 August 1859
FORT MOJAVE *(Topock, Arizona)*

Indian attacks on emigrants along the Arizona-California border (see Rose-Baley Wagon Train, 30 August 1858) prompted the establishment of Fort Mojave, Arizona, in April 1859. On 5 August, Capt. Lewis A. Armistead, Sixth Infantry, who would later die as a Confederate general at Gettysburg, encountered about 200 Mojave warriors twelve miles south of the fort. Armistead engaged them with only twenty-five men from Companies F and I, Sixth Infantry. Within thirty minutes, his remaining twenty-five men arrived on the scene, and the skirmish developed into a pitched battle. Both sides persisted, pushing back and forth across the valley near the Colorado River for many hours, but in the end the soldiers' superior weaponry proved the deciding factor.

Armistead's men lost three killed and a few wounded; the Mojaves lost twenty-three killed and "many" wounded, according to the army report. Three weeks later, the Indians sent a messenger to the fort to ask for peace.[247]

3 November 1859
NORTH LLANO *(Sonora, Texas)*

A war party of Comanches raided several homesteads along the Sabinal River in present-day Uvalde County, Texas, in October 1859. On 28 October the raiders killed two settlers: one, John Davenport, was struck down between the Sabinal and Rancheros Creek, and the other, John Bowles, was killed near the Patterson Settlement, south of present-day Sabinal, Texas. John Bowles's son, W. B. "Doke" Bowles, joined a party of twelve men who were already in the process of hunting down the marauding Comanches. At John Kennedy's store on the Sabinal, the men bought supplies and sent a messenger to Fort Inge to ask for help, arranging to meet the soldiers at the mouth of Frio Canyon. On the way to the canyon, along the Blanco River near the foot of the mountains, the party discovered a pair of bloody shoes, which Doke identified as his father's.

At Fort Inge, Capt. R. P. Maclay sent out his best Indian fighter, Lt. William B. Hazen, to assist the civilians. Hazen left on 30 October with nine mounted soldiers of Company F, Eighth Infantry. He reached Frio Canyon to find about thirty-two armed civilians waiting for him, including Doke Bowles and Clabe Davenport, the son of the other murdered man, John Davenport. The volunteers were organized under the command of John Q. Daugherty. The combined party rode out right away.

The trail, which indicated a small party of Indians driving about fifty horses, led up the canyon and headed northeast toward the North Fork of the Guadalupe, then turned northwest toward the Llano River. Bowles and a man named Williams were in the lead when the party caught up with the Indians on the North Llano, in the vicinity of old Fort Terrett. They found the Indians, about eight Comanches, breaking camp on the morning of 3 November, and Hazen hurriedly ordered a charge. When the disorganized soldiers and civilians came barreling in, the Indians scattered, trying to take their stolen horses with them.

A running fight ensued, with the Indians leading the Texans on several tangents. A settler named Arnette, knowing how badly Bowles wanted to avenge his father's death, offered to exchange his own faster horse for Bowles's. Bowles, taking the trade, soon caught up to Hazen in the lead. The Texans were gaining on one Indian when he turned on Hazen, and they both fired simultaneously. The ball from the Indian's pistol hit Hazen's right hand, went into his chest, and lodged in his back, and his horse threw him to the ground. The warrior was also hit but rode away. Bowles went to the fallen lieutenant, saw the wound, and felt the bullet protruding from his back. "There is one dead man, sure," Bowles murmured.[248]

The warrior Hazen had wounded still had plenty of fight left. A civilian named Everette confronted him, and the two men's pistols almost touched as they both fired. The Indian's bullet bounced off Everette's pistol, tore through his hand, knocked some of his teeth out, and lodged in his temple. Bowles assumed Everette, too, was dead as the warrior took off.

The other Texans had slightly better luck. They caught and killed one fleeing warrior and wounded another with a shotgun, but a civilian named Pulliam took an arrow in the back. On the dead Comanche the Texans found John Davenport's gun belt and John Bowles's scalp.

The Indian who had shot Hazen and Everette, armed with three pistols, kept the Texans at bay for several minutes. He was hit probably half a dozen times, yet he still managed to get away. The last few warriors jumped with their horses down a fourteen-foot embankment. Bowles, Williams, and two others chased after them on the fastest remaining horses. After several miles, only Bowles and Williams were able to keep up with the Comanches. Bowles hit one of them with the last load from his shotgun. The wounded warrior dismounted and ran at the two Texans. When Williams dismounted to fire at him, the Comanche, now out of bullets, shot an arrow into his breast. Williams cried, "I'm killed, Doke," and fell.

Bowles shot the Indian with his pistol's last bullet. Still the Comanche loosed several more arrows at Bowles, all of which missed, before catching Williams's horse and riding away. Bowles had counted nine wounds on this unstoppable Comanche, plus about fourteen on his horse. A short time later, Bowles saw the three last Indians on a distant hilltop and watched as two of them collapsed and slid from their horses to the ground. Seven out of the eight Comanches had been killed or mortally wounded.

Bowles put the still breathing Williams on a horse and rode back nearly twenty miles to the site of the first attack, passing dead Indians and wounded white men along the way. The soldiers had stopped where Hazen went down. A civilian named McCormick and about five soldiers rode the eighty miles to Fort Clark to get medical assistance. Although grievously wounded, Williams, Everette, and Pulliam all survived.

After waiting three days for help, Hazen, remarkably still conscious, ordered his little contingent to begin moving toward Fort Inge. Two days later, the party reached an old mission station on the Nueces, where another messenger was sent to Inge. An ambulance finally arrived, and the bloodied detachment reached the fort on 10 November. Hazen was sent to a hospital in San Antonio, where he recovered, though the bullet was never removed. Hazen was later granted a yearlong extended leave.[249]

— 1860 —

16 January 1860
PECAN BAYOU *(Baird, Texas)*
After the 1859 campaigns in Indian Territory, elements of the Second Cavalry pulled back to various posts in Texas. Capt. Kirby Smith, with about 60 men and 150 horses, went to Camp Colorado, on Jim Ned Creek in present-day Coleman County. There they found comfortable

quarters along with water and good grass for the horses. At midnight on 14 January 1860, a settler rode into the post to report that Comanches were stealing horses and mules about sixteen miles away. Lt. Fitzhugh Lee, recently arrived from Austin, volunteered to take a patrol out in pursuit. With twenty-two men of Smith's Company B, Lee rode out into the night against a howling norther.

At daybreak the soldiers arrived at the ranch where the stock had been stolen. Lee found the Indians' trail, which headed north, and was able to follow it despite the drifting snow. The cavalrymen doggedly kept riding, spending the night without campfires, eating hardtack and frozen pork. By dawn, some of the troopers were so stiff with cold that their comrades had to lift them up onto their horses. During the day, the sun appeared, raising the temperature and melting some of the snow. In the midafternoon of 16 January, the patrol caught up with the Indians, who were herding the stolen stock up Pecan Bayou, south of present-day Baird. Lee ordered his men to draw their pistols and charge.

The surprised Comanches scattered into the trees. The two slowest ones were spotted at the rear of the herd. A trooper shot one, while the other loosed arrows at Lee and his bugler, Jack Hayes, then rode off. Lee chased the warrior as he dodged among the trees. The Comanche dashed into some thicker cedars and dismounted, sending his horse in

Fitzhugh Lee —From authors' collection

one direction and running off in another. Unfooled, Lee and five other troopers tracked the warrior for a few miles through the snow-covered, wooded hills. The Indian then tried another ruse, laying his red blanket out where his pursuers would see it and concealing himself above a rock ledge several yards away.

Lee found the blanket, but, wise to battlefield tricks, he immediately spotted the Indian and leapt over the ledge to face his opponent. The Comanche shot an arrow that struck the stock of Lee's carbine. Lee dropped the weapon, and the two began wrestling. While the warrior jabbed his knife into the lieutenant's thick overcoat, Lee hit the Indian with his revolver. Both men eventually lost their weapons. Finally, Lee was able to pin his adversary tight against the ground. "Here was I on top," he recalled, "holding down, breast to breast, a live Camanche, and a very slippery one, with nothing to kill him!"[250]

Just then, the bugler Hayes arrived and helped restrain the warrior while Lee grabbed Hayes's revolver and shot the Indian twice. When he checked himself for wounds, Lee found his outer garments slashed to ribbons but he was otherwise unharmed. He gathered up the warrior's shield, headdress, and weapons, which he later displayed with great pride. The soldiers had killed two Comanches and recovered twenty-five horses.[251]

18 April 1860
BITTER SPRING *(Baker, California)*

For decades, Indians from as far away as Nevada and Utah would travel to California, cross Cajon Pass, and steal stock from grazing herds near Los Angeles. Paiutes from Nevada were accused of attacking travelers and stealing animals all along the Old Spanish Trail between Los Angeles and Salt Lake City, even though several tribes lived in the Los Angeles area, including Southern Paiutes of the Nuwa and Vanyume bands, as well as Mojaves and Chemehuevis. Mormons were rumored to have been encouraging the Paiutes to attack travelers and settlers, as they were said to have done in September 1857 with the Mountain Meadows Massacre.

In January 1860, after a cattleman was killed at Bitter Spring, a water hole in the Mojave Desert, and two teamsters were killed near the same place a few months later, a number of businessmen from Los Angeles petitioned the government to make the Spanish Trail safer for commerce. In response, Brig. Gen. Newman Clarke ordered Capt. James H. Carleton to go to Bitter Spring and punish any Indians in the vicinity. Carleton left Fort Tejon with three officers and eighty-one enlisted men of Companies B and K, First Dragoons, along with an interpreter, several civilian guides, and four army wagons. A week's march of 170 miles brought them to the junction of the Mojave River and Salt Lake Road. At this spot, where the usually dry Mojave River trickled with water, Carleton built Camp Cady, near the future town of Harvard, California. From there, he sent out several scouts to look for Indians.

On 18 April, Lt. Benjamin F. Davis and a portion of K Troop found two Indians hunting on the Mojave River about twelve miles southwest of Camp Cady. Davis charged after them, but the Indians stood fast and loosed several arrows, striking two dragoons. As the troopers fired back, a soldier accidentally wounded one of his comrades. The dragoons eventually killed both warriors and took their bodies back to Camp Cady. A few days later, soldiers took the bodies to Bitter Spring and hung them from an improvised scaffold as a warning.

At about the same time as Davis's encounter, Lt. Milton Carr was also scouting for Indians with a dragoon detachment. The men found and attacked another band of hunters, killing two. One soldier was wounded. On 2 May Carr and sixteen dragoons encountered a band of seven Paiutes at the base of Old Dad Mountain. The lieutenant sent a five-man detachment to cut off their retreat while ordering the rest of the men forward. The Indians shot arrows at them, but a high wind interfered with their aim. Carr killed three Indians, wounded one, and captured an elderly woman, taking no casualties of his own. Carr decapitated the three dead warriors and put their heads in a sack. A few days later, these grisly trophies were also mounted for display at Bitter Creek.

At the post, Carleton released the captive woman and told her to warn her people that they would all be hunted down unless they ceased hostilities. Still wanting to fight, however, Carleton tried to lure the Paiutes in with a decoy of three supply wagons with dragoons hidden inside, but nothing happened. Most of the Paiutes had probably fled the area. Carleton spent another month searching for Indians to the north and east. One of these scouts was a near fatal, waterless march into Death Valley.

When General Clarke read Carleton's dispatches, he chastised the captain for mutilating the dead and firmly instructed him to remove the corpses and body parts from public gaze. Nevertheless, Carleton was certain he had accomplished his purpose. Just before he left to return to Fort Tejon, an Indian delegation visited Camp Cady and promised him they would remain at peace. Carleton left for Tejon on 3 July.[252]

29 May 1860
SANTA RITA DEL COBRE *(Hanover, New Mexico)*

On 20 May 1860, Apaches attacked a mule train near the mines at Santa Rita del Cobre, killing five Mexican herders and stealing twenty-four mules. About a week later, they returned and stole nine mules from near the Mimbres River. The miners and settlers in the area sent their women and children to the relative safety of the Rio Grande settlements.

The move came just in time, for on the morning of 29 May, thirty Mexican and American inhabitants of Santa Rita Del Cobre were attacked just as they were rising. A very large band of Apaches, estimated at 400 by Confederate-captain-to-be Sherod Hunter, swarmed upon the settlement to do battle. The defenders fought courageously and eventually drove the Indians off. Eleven defenders were killed and eight wounded; Hunter believed they had killed or wounded twenty to thirty Indians.

During the battle, a messenger went for help, taking two arrows on the way out but making it to the stage station in Cooke's Canyon. From there, another rider carried the alarm to Mesilla. Samuel S. Jones and fifteen men rode out to the rescue, but the battle was over long before they arrived.[253]

20 June 1860
PAINTERS CREEK *(Ravendale, California)*

Several bloody fights between the whites and the Paiutes around Pyramid Lake in May and June of 1860 instilled near panic in the settlers around Honey Lake and Susanville, California, about seventy miles northwest of the action, and many were moving out. Indians, too, left the area, only to continue raiding elsewhere. Paiutes under Chief Numaga (Young Winnemucca) moved to the Smoke Creek Desert and to the mountains west of it. From there, they raided in the Honey Lake region, stealing stock, burning ranches, and killing settlers.

Frederick W. Lander, an engineer in the Department of the Interior, was in the Honey Lake region at the time of the trouble, working on a shorter overland route across the northern Great Basin. Lander agreed to help defend the settlers but asked that the able-bodied men in the area join him and his men. Capt. William Weatherlow and his Honey Lake Rangers were happy to help, and the two groups, about 100 men total, left on 19 June, heading northeast to look for Chief Numaga's Paiutes.

The party traveled north to the edge of the Madeline Plains, where they found tracks and caught sight of two mounted Paiutes watching them. At dawn on 20 June, Weatherlow rode east into the mountains with a small detachment to search for the Paiute camp, leaving Lt. U. J. Tutt in command. In the captain's absence, Tutt told Lander that Weatherlow had given him orders to move the command through a nearby canyon. Lander did not like the looks of it, but he reluctantly agreed to follow. In reality, Tutt had misunderstood Weatherlow's order *not* to go through the canyon. As the men rode up the narrow gap, about fifteen miles east of present-day Ravendale, Weatherlow's rear guard caught up to the captain and told him what was happening. Weatherlow hurried back, but he did not reach Tutt and Lander until most of the column was already in the canyon.

It was too late to berate Tutt, for the Paiutes now had the volunteers in a box, and gunfire erupted from the rock walls around them. Alexander Painter took a bullet and fell. His brother Ben rushed to him, but Alex, hit near the heart, realized he was a goner and told them to go on without him. Lander tried to organize his men to attack some warriors on a low hill to his right, while others charged the Indians standing in front of them. By the time Lander's men climbed the hill, the Paiutes had already fled. Lander and the rangers pulled back, then Lander grabbed a white flag and took a few men back in to try for a parley. The Paiutes ignored the flag and shot at him.

Riding back into the valley, Lander and Weatherlow agreed to attempt a mounted charge to break through to the Paiute camp, which they assumed must be farther up the canyon. The charge brought them a little farther down the canyon, where the Paiutes pinned them down for five hours. When the sun set, the Indians pulled out and Weatherlow and Lander retreated to the valley, carrying the body of Alex Painter. They buried him in the basin that came to be called Painters Flat.

Lander, guessing that Numaga had taken his people east to the Smoke Creek Desert, went there. He found a fortified Indian position at Wall Springs, on the western edge of the desert, but it was abandoned, and he saw no tracks. Lander and Weatherlow finally gave up the expedition and headed back to Susanville.[254]

9 September 1860
PEACOCK MASSACRE *(Great Bend, Kansas)*

When William Allison died in the spring of 1859, George Peacock took over his ranch and store at Walnut Creek Crossing, near the mouth of Walnut Creek at the Great Bend of the Arkansas River. Indians had always been a problem in the area, and the situation deteriorated after an incident on 21 September 1859. It started when two Kiowas, Satank and Pawnee, both reportedly drunk, entered Peacock's store and demanded goods. When clerks Rickman and Flournoy refused them, the Indians stormed out. Once outside, the furious Satank grabbed a sheep, slit its throat, and took a mouthful of the gushing blood, then walked back into the store and spit the blood in Rickman's face. Still in a rage, Satank then climbed onto the roof and ripped off the sod, vowing to return and destroy the place.

In response, Capt. William S. Walker, with Companies G and K, First Cavalry, who were patrolling the Santa Fe Trail, came to the ranch and waited for the Kiowas to return. When Pawnee rode in, alone and sober, Walker arrested him. But the Indian tried to escape, and Lt. George Bayard shot and killed him. This incident put Peacock in a dangerous position, but it was an indiscretion in the spring of 1860 that sealed his fate.

Satank, who apparently had made amends with Peacock, asked the ranch owner to write a letter for him that attested to his good character. Peacock wrote the note, but it said that the bearer was treacherous and dangerous to whites. After Satank had a Mexican translate it for him, he vowed vengeance.

That summer, violence in the area heated up. On 9 July, Kiowas killed two white men near Ash Creek Crossing, twenty-two miles west of Peacock's place. In mid-July, Hall and Porter's mail station was destroyed, and on 30 July the Leavenworth *Daily Times* reported that a white family of four was killed near Walnut Creek. Another report claimed that Indians had killed five emigrants on the trail to Pike's Peak.

Peacock's turn came on 9 September. Satank and about ten other Kiowas were at Peacock's store drinking whiskey when Satank told Peacock that soldiers were approaching. Since supplying whiskey to the Indians was illegal, Peacock was concerned. Taking his field glasses, he went out to climb a lookout tower he had built on the property. Once Peacock was on the ladder, Satank shot him through the head. The Kiowas then went on a murder spree. They killed the clerk, Myers, and four others. They also ransacked the store.

The Indians had killed everyone they found at Peacock's except a sick, wounded man who was recovering in one of the rooms from a buffalo goring. The store was abandoned for a few weeks until a man named Charles Rath salvaged what he could of the merchandise and took over operations.[255]

— 1861 —

Ca. 5 May 1861

BARILLA SPRINGS STATION *(Balmorhea, Texas)*

After taking care of some company business at Fort Stockton, George H. Giddings boarded one of his own coaches and, with Parker Burnham at the reins, headed west for El Paso. About three miles east of Barilla Springs (sometimes spelled Varela Springs) Station, midway between Forts Stockton and Davis, an Apache war party swept down on them. Arrows and musket balls peppered the coach while Burnham lashed the mules into a run. Guard Jim Spears, on top of the coach, and Giddings and the other passengers inside opened fire on the charging warriors.

Burnham recognized the Indians as Mescaleros from Chief Nicolas's band, having seen the chief once at Fort Davis. As Burnham whipped the mules to go faster, an arrow stabbed his hip and another sliced into his neck. He handed Spears the reins and collapsed into the storage boot beneath the driver's seat. The mules thundered along, nearly upending the coach as it took the curve on the upslope to Barilla Springs. Three mules were hit with arrows and the team slowed, but the stage's occupants were good shots too, and they knocked at least four of the pursuing warriors off their ponies.

When the coach pulled into Barilla Springs Station, the keepers swung the gate closed behind it. The passengers and station hands battled the Indians from behind the corral walls. Facing fortified walls, the Mescaleros soon gave up.

Burnham's companions held him down and extracted the two arrows. He soon recovered, but he left Giddings's employ a short time later for what he figured was safer service in the Confederate cavalry.[256]

27 August 1861

COOKE'S CANYON/AKE'S FIGHT

(Deming, New Mexico)

At the start of the Civil War, when U.S. troops pulled out of New Mexico Territory to fight back East, many settlers abandoned their homes. A number of ranchers and farmers from the Tubac, Sonoita, and Tucson areas gathered together to return to the States behind the soldiers. Felix Grundy Ake and William Wadsworth led the largest group of wagons. Moses Carson, Kit Carson's half-brother, joined the train in Tucson. The party of twenty-four men, sixteen women, and seven children moved

Cooke's Canyon, New Mexico

out in mid-August with six double wagons, two buggies, and a single wagon and driving hundreds of cattle, sheep, goats, and horses.

On the night of 26 August, as the travelers camped on the banks of the Mimbres River, a man named Eugene Zimmer rode into the camp, agitated.[257] Zimmer said he had been driving cattle through Cooke's Canyon the day before when Indians killed two of his Mexican herders and stole all his stock. Somehow, however, the travelers found Zimmer, with his nervous manner and thick German accent, suspicious and did not believe his story.

The next morning, the wagon party arrived at the edge of Cooke's Canyon, unaware that Apache chiefs Cochise and Mangas Coloradas were waiting for them with nearly two hundred warriors. The livestock entered the pass first, followed by the mounted men, then the vehicles. Near the far end of the pass, the trail became too narrow for two wagons to move abreast. As the train adjusted, one of the men spotted the nude corpses of the Mexican herders Zimmer had spoken of. The word spread down the line, and several riders at the rear of the column, including Sam Houston, nephew of the famous Texan, turned and fled back to the Mimbres. This left only about seventeen men to fight the Indians.

At first, nothing more happened, and the wagons moved cautiously forward. When the train reached the narrowest part of the canyon, however, the hillsides exploded with the noise of more than fifty Apache rifles. In front, John St. Clair and James May were killed, and several horses went down, blocking the train's path. William Redding and a few mounted men charged the Indians to divert their attention while Jack Pennington tried to turn the wagons around. A bullet broke Redding's leg, but he stayed in the saddle until several more shots killed him.

Robert and America Phillips grabbed their son and ran back to a defensive triangle Ake had formed with his wagons. From their little fort, Ake, Carson, Wadsworth, Nathaniel Sharp, and others fought back with determination. Sharp caught an arrow in the neck and ear, but he pulled the barb clean through and kept fighting.

The Apaches were primarily concerned with rounding up as much livestock as possible; otherwise they would surely have overrun the travelers. As the Indians herded the animals away, Ake and Wadsworth left the improvised fort and climbed a nearby hill for a better shot. As they did so, Chiricahua snipers pumped two bullets into Wadsworth, mortally wounding him. Tom Farrell ran out to help the two get back, shooting one Apache but taking a bullet in the back.

The battle dwindled to long-range sniping. Cochise and Mangas saw no need to rush the wagon fort, as they had already killed a few of the Americans and taken the livestock. Teamster Mariano Madrid killed one more Apache before the Indians finally withdrew, having captured perhaps 400 cattle and 900 sheep. The Apaches lost about five killed in the fight, and the wagon train lost four killed and about eight wounded.[258]

28 August 1861
MASTIN'S FIGHT *(Deming, New Mexico)*
When they arrived at the Mimbres stage station, the men who had deserted the Ake-Wadsworth train when the Apaches showed up in Cooke's Canyon (see previous entry) sent a messenger to Pinos Altos. En route the messenger ran into a company of Arizona Guards under Capt. Thomas J. Mastin, heading south in response to news of the attack on Zimmer's train the day before. Although Mastin's company was mustered into the Confederate service, their assignment was to fight Apaches.

When Mastin met the survivors of the Ake-Wadsworth fight, he enlisted the help of Nathaniel Sharp and a few others, then rode on to pursue the raiders. With his company of about thirty-five Guards, including Lts. Thomas Helm and Jack Swilling and Pvts. Hank Smith and William Fisher Scott, Mastin decided to detour around Cooke's Canyon and head south. He believed that the Chiricahuas would be heading directly for Mexico with the stolen livestock, and he hoped to make "a straight shoot" for the Florida Mountains to get ahead of them.

Mastin and his men rode all night to reach the barren mountains before dawn. There they set up an ambush. At daybreak, hidden in a dry wash, the Guards could see the Apaches coming right toward them. Scott later noted that the Indians "had a big surprise, not thinking there were a lot of gringos in there and not thinking that they would come and take them unawares."[259] When the Indians were almost upon them, Mastin's men charged out of the arroyo. The startled Indians, estimated at about eighty in number, held their ground briefly then scattered, leaving some of the livestock behind.

Private Smith believed they had killed eight warriors in the ambush. As Mastin's men drove the recovered cattle back to Cooke's Spring, they repelled an Indian counterattack. Back in the canyon, beyond the debris and bodies from the recent fight, Scott spotted a small flock of Ake's sheep, still guarded by his faithful dog. The soldiers buried the dead and returned the stock they'd found to the Ake and Wadsworth families.[260]

28 August 1861
EIGHTEEN MILE HOLE *(Sierra Blanca, Texas)*
With troops withdrawn from the frontier to fight in the Civil War, travel through south and west Texas grew more hazardous. In August 1861 James E. Terry and four companions attempted to take mail from El Paso to San Antonio. Due to increased reports of Indian attacks along the road, Terry chose to pack the mail on mules and try to make a fast ride to Fort Davis. After passing Fort Quitman without trouble, the riders negotiated Canon de Los Lementos (Quitman Canyon), a rough shortcut through the 6,000-foot Quitman Mountains, then turned southeast down the dry valley between the Quitman Mountains and Devil's Ridge.

The next water supply was at the heel of Devil's Ridge at Eighteen Mile Hole, or Tinaja de Las Palmas. The five riders were almost there when fifteen mounted Apaches charged them from out of the brush, while a larger party of warriors on foot came at them from another direction. Terry and his men cut the mules loose and ran for a rocky hill above the water hole. Reaching high ground, they whirled around

Quitman Canyon, Texas

and blasted the Indians with all the weapons they had. One warrior died instantly, and several others went down wounded.

Through the day and into the night, the Texans kept the Apaches at a distance with their Sharps rifles. They took turns shooting, maintaining a moderate fire while keeping the other weapons fully loaded and ready to repel a charge. By daylight the Apaches had collected their dead and wounded and disappeared. The Texans edged down the hill and wearily walked to the next station, at Eagle Springs. Terry later wrote that it was well the Mescaleros let them alone, "for [we] were in a humor to make a wicked fight, and many a warrior would have been laid out before the stage guard would have been destroyed."[261]

27 September 1861
PINOS ALTOS *(Pinos Altos, New Mexico)*

Their casualties in the fights in Cooke's Canyon and the Florida Mountains (see Cooke's Canyon/Ake's Fight, 27 August 1861, and Mastin's Fight, 28 August 1861) left the Apaches with a desire for revenge. Mangas Coloradas and Cochise gathered several bands of Chiricahuas, perhaps more than 300 warriors, to attack the settlement at Pinos Altos and the surrounding mining camps. At dawn on 27 September, warriors struck several locations simultaneously. The attacks trapped many miners at their diggings, though others were able to fight from inside barricaded cabins.

Fortunately for the settlers, Capt. Thomas J. Mastin and fifteen Arizona Guards had arrived in town the night before. Pvt. Hank Smith reached Whiskey Gulch in time to help drive the Indians off, then he sped off to Pinos Altos, where he found Indians and settlers in hand-to-hand fights. By noon, the battle had centered near two supply stores in the middle of town, Bean's and Roman's. At Bean's, Mastin was mortally wounded by a bullet that severed an artery in his arm, and two other men were killed at Roman's. Finally, six women at Bean's hauled out a small howitzer and, with the help of one man, loaded it with nails and buckshot and fired it at the Indians. Many witnesses agreed that the blasts of the howitzer saved the day. After that, a rally by the miners drove the Indians out of town.

Although the Apaches had pulled back, they kept Pinos Altos under siege from a distance. When a messenger tried to leave, his horse was killed before he was a mile away. The man made it back, however, and he remounted and rode off. This time he made it to Mesilla, reaching that settlement on 8 October. There, Confederate colonel John R. Baylor dispatched 100 soldiers to break the siege. The resulting fight was one of the largest and hardest-fought battles ever to occur between Apaches and whites.

Killed were Mastin and J. B. Corwin of the Guards and three other civilians; seven whites were wounded. Pvt. Smith reported that the Indians left ten dead on the battlefield and carried off about twenty dead and wounded. Among those killed may have been several chiefs, possibly including Chihenne leaders Chabnocito and Delgadito and the Chokonen Esquinaline.[262]

17 November 1861
THIEF CAMP *(Eureka, California)*

Conflicts between Indians and settlers in northwestern California flared off and on for years. Pardee's Ranch, near Eureka, was the target of several raids during the "Wintoon War" of 1858 (see Pardee's Ranch, 26 October 1858). Tensions increased after many Eel River Indians were killed in the Humboldt Bay Massacre of 25–26 February 1860, on the coast near Eureka. When a drunken white civilian murdered a Hoopa Indian boy, that tribe also joined in the conflict. On 7 November 1861, the Indians raided Brehmer's Ranch on the Mad River, killing three men.

Throughout this time of strife, volunteer companies repeatedly combed the wooded mountains for Indians. One of these companies, the Humboldt Home Guards, were hampered in their search during the summer and fall of 1861 by frequent forest fires. But on 17 November, the Guards, under Lt. J. P. Warren, had a chance to distinguish themselves. The day before, Warren and sixteen men stopped at Thief Camp, a rest stop on high ground at the headwaters of Redwood, Maple, and Boulder Creeks, about twenty miles east of Eureka. Warren, looking for Indians who had recently killed cattle in the area, spotted fires from a rancheria not far from Pardee's Ranch. He prepared his men for an attack the next morning.

At 7:30 a.m., the Guards charged into the rancheria. Warren soon realized he had made a mistake, for he faced an estimated 100 warriors protected by a substantial log stockade. The Indians did not flee, but instead pinned Warren's men down with their own heavy fire. The shooting continued for an hour, with the Guards fighting from behind trees against the well-fortified Indians. Things got worse for Warren when more warriors from a nearby rancheria joined the defenders. Warren's guide, Charles Huestis, was shot in the heart as he directed the Guards to better cover.

The fighting continued for two more hours, with the Guards probably taking the worst of it. Six of Warren's men were wounded, including Warren himself. Warren estimated that the Guards had killed twenty Indians, but that number is unlikely. Finally Warren broke off contact and hurried back to Thief Camp, sending messengers to Lieutenant Wilkinson's camp in the Larrabee Valley to ask for reinforcements.

Wilkinson arrived with eleven men, and the combined force went out to have another go at the Indians. By then, however, the rancheria was deserted. Wilkinson and his men found Huestis's body nearly buried in the snow, and a detachment carried it down to the village of Union for burial.[263]

19 November 1861
ROUND MOUNTAIN *(Yale, Oklahoma)*

The American Civil War affected the loyalties of many Indian tribes living along the Union and Confederate borders. Bitter divisions formed as Indians chose—or were forced to choose—sides. Opothleyahola, a revered Creek leader, attempted to remain loyal to the Union, assembling about 6,000 Union sympathizers among the Creeks and Seminoles in eastern Oklahoma. The Confederates, meanwhile, organized four Indian regiments. Commander of the Confederate Indian Department,

Col. Douglas H. Cooper, commanded the Choctaw-Chickasaw regiment, and Col. Daniel McIntosh commanded the Creek regiment. In November 1861, Cooper was determined either to turn Opothleyahola against the Union or force him out of the territory. Reinforced by about 500 men of the Ninth Texas Cavalry, Cooper and McIntosh had a total of 1,400 men for the expedition.

Opothleyahola, contending with dwindling supplies and deteriorating weather, slowly moved his people north toward Kansas, where he hoped the Union Army would succor him. Cooper was headed toward the Cimarron River when he learned from a captured prisoner that Opothleyahola was said to be constructing a fort somewhere in the region. Cooper found the Creek camp, but the Indians were gone. The colonel spotted some stragglers, however, and followed them to their new camp, in the vicinity of present-day Yale, Oklahoma.

The Confederates' advance reached Opothleyahola's camp near sundown on 19 November. Right away, about 150 men of Cooper's regiment dismounted and approached the outer camp. As the troopers made their way across a twisting creek and swamp, about 250 warriors confronted them. The Creeks fired on the soldiers, killing Pvt. John H. Crow and hitting several horses, then set fire to the prairie on the Confederates' right. Capt. R. A. Young, seeing Indians advancing on his flank in the darkness, pulled his command back. The Creeks followed for a time, then broke off the action. Young estimated the whole fight lasted only about fifteen minutes.

Cooper set out to attack Opothleyahola's camp again the next morning, but the Creeks were gone. The brief engagement was the first fight to take place in Indian Territory during the Civil War.[264]

9 December 1861
BIRD CREEK/CHUSTO-TALASAH
(Tulsa, Oklahoma)
After the fight at Round Mountain (see previous entry), Confederate colonel Douglas Cooper hoped to pursue Opothleyahola's Creeks right away, but he was detoured by the threat of Union forces advancing south through Missouri. The progressing winter soon convinced Federal forces to pull back, however, and Cooper was again free to chase Opothleyahola.

Cooper, reinforced by Col. John Drew's Cherokee Regiment and some Texas cavalrymen, caught up with about 2,500 Creeks at the Horseshoe

Bend of Bird Creek, just north of present-day Tulsa. The Indian camp was in a strong position. Opothleyahola's men advanced first, attempting to draw Cooper toward their lines. Cooper moved in about 2 p.m., crossing an open prairie that was within firing range of Creek snipers hidden in the trees. Col. Daniel McIntosh's regiment of Confederate Creeks charged from one side, Cooper's men from the other, and the Texans took the center. Cooper soon found out that Drew's Cherokees were not all willing to fight against their neighbors. Scores of Indian soldiers suddenly defected to Opothleyahola's camp, leaving Cooper with only about 1,300 effective men.

The battle ebbed and flowed for four hours. The Creeks pressed the Confederates back in a few instances, but Cooper stabilized the situation with counterattacks. Col. W. B. Sims took the Texans up Bird Creek about a mile to the Creeks' flank and maneuvered them out of their position. Although outnumbered, the Confederates finally forced the Creeks from their river position around dusk.

The Confederates lost 15 killed and 37 wounded. They counted 27 dead Creeks on the battlefield, and McIntosh estimated they had wounded 200. Opothleyahola escaped, but Cooper, short of ammunition, did not pursue him, retiring to Fort Gibson instead.[265]

26 December 1861
CHUSTENAHLAH *(Skiatook, Oklahoma)*

After the Bird Creek battle (see previous entry), Col. Douglas Cooper requested assistance in driving Opothleyahola's Creeks and Seminoles out of Indian Territory. Col. James I. McIntosh (no relation to Col. Daniel McIntosh) responded by taking about 1,380 men of the Sixth and Eleventh Texas Cavalry, the South Kansas-Texas Regiment, and the Second Arkansas Mounted Rifles into Indian Territory. McIntosh found Opothleyahola and about 1,700 warriors in a well-protected cove on Battle Creek, just west of present-day Skiatook, Oklahoma, and not far from the Bird Creek battle site. He approached Opothleyahola's position with the Eleventh Texas on the left, the Sixth Texas on the right, and the remaining units in the center. McIntosh described the opening move:

> *The charge was sounded, one wild yell from a thousand throats burst upon the air, and the living mass hurled itself upon the foe. The sharp report of the rifle came from every tree and rock, but on our brave men rushed, nor stopped until the summit of the hill was gained and we were mingled with the enemy.*[266]

The fight began around noon and lasted four hours, at some points becoming hand-to-hand. The defenders were driven from hilltop positions into the woods and ravines to their rear. As the Confederates rushed through the Creeks' camps, the women and children panicked and fled. McIntosh's riders cut down many fleeing Indians. Opothleyahola's men fought hard, but they were no match for the battle-hardened Texans and Arkansans. To make matters worse for Opothleyahola, the Cherokee Stand Watie and his regiment of 300 Confederate warriors arrived to join in, killing and capturing many Creeks.

The Confederates lost 9 killed and 40 wounded, while Opothleyahola lost 250 killed, an unknown number of wounded, and 160 captured. McIntosh rounded up 30 wagons, 70 oxen, 500 horses, 100 sheep, and several hundred cattle. The defeated Creeks and Seminoles fled north to Kansas, suffering through the severe winter with little food and few supplies.[267]

— 1862 —

6 April 1862
MAYFIELD'S FIGHT *(Paradise Camp, California)*
During the severe winter of 1861–62 in California, hungry Indians in the Owens Valley poached some settlers' cattle. The cattle owners retaliated, killing several Indians, and a small war was on. After the Indians killed four settlers, named Talman, Hanson, Taylor, and Crosen, the ranchers congregated about thirty miles above Owens Lake to organize a militia, sending requests for help to Visalia, California, and Aurora, Nevada. In late March 1862, after about eighteen miners from Aurora arrived, the combined force of about sixty men under a "Colonel" Mayfield moved up the valley to the vicinity of present-day Paradise Camp.

On 6 April, bands of Paiutes, Tulares, and Owens River Indians appeared near the mountains southwest of Mayfield's camp. The militia moved to meet them in two divisions, but they lacked coordination and fighting prowess. The Indians shot and killed miner C. J. Pleasants from Aurora, and Mayfield retreated.

Back near camp, Mayfield and his men took cover in an Indian-built irrigation ditch. Shots were exchanged until nightfall. Sheriff Scott of Mono, California, was killed by a bullet to the head, while a man named Morrison, from Visalia, was shot in the stomach and died the next day.

One Indian was killed. When the moon set and full darkness enveloped the scene, Mayfield pulled out and retreated, leaving behind the dead, eighteen horses, and considerable ammunition.

On their way down the valley the next morning, Mayfield and his men met and joined forces with Lt. Col. George S. Evans, Second California Cavalry. The combined units would fight the Indians two days later in the Bishop's Creek Battle of 9 April 1962, but with no more success. Mayfield himself was killed in that fight.[268]

5 May 1862
DRAGOON SPRINGS *(Dragoon, Arizona)*
The Tucson area was the farthest western point reached by Confederate forces during the Civil War. When Union reinforcements approached from California in the spring of 1862, the badly outnumbered Confederates had to retreat east. Capt. Sherod Hunter and his Confederate Company A, Arizona Rangers, abandoned Tucson on 4 May. Moving east ahead of the main company was a party of rangers seeking to gather stray cattle near the abandoned Butterfield Overland station at Dragoon Springs, on the north slope of the Dragoon Mountains, about sixteen miles east of present-day Benson, Arizona.

A band of about 100 Apaches under Cochise and Francisco had spotted the detachment and waited for them at the springs. As the party entered a narrow box canyon nearby, the Apaches attacked. The rangers offered little resistance. Four of them were killed: Sgt. Sam Ford; a private called Richardo; another private, possibly John Donaldson; and one unknown private. The rest escaped, leaving behind twenty-five horses and thirty mules. The fatalities were the most westerly Confederate battle deaths in the Civil War and the only ones to occur within the modern-day boundaries of Arizona.[269]

18 June 1862
JONES'S FIGHT *(Apache Pass, Arizona)*
Union Brig. Gen. James H. Carleton slowly moved his California Column east in an attempt to meet up with Brig. Gen. Edward R. S. Canby at the Rio Grande, where the two forces planned to organize a cooperative effort to capture the Confederate brigade of Brig. Gen. Henry H. Sibley. En route, Carleton needed to send a message to Canby, and while the two forces were still more than 200 miles apart, he ordered couriers out from Tucson.

Civilian expressman John Jones; Sgt. William Wheeling, Company F, First California Infantry; and a Mexican guide named Chavez left with the dispatches on 15 June. They preferred travel by night and rest by day, but circumstances sometimes forced them to make adjustments to their schedule. On 18 June the party stayed over in a canyon about seven miles west of Apache Pass until 3:30 in the afternoon, when they set out to cross the plain, hoping to reach the pass and get through the mountains before dark. Two miles west of the pass, the couriers saw Apache smoke signals, but they decided to keep going. The three made it through the mountains to the San Simon Valley, but by then their horses were exhausted.

Suddenly, Apaches sprang out of the brush and fired at the party. As the messengers dismounted to return fire, the Indians mounted up and charged. Three of the couriers' spare horses broke free, and some warriors rode after them. Chavez fired just once before he dropped all his percussion caps in the sand. After taking a bullet in the hip, Chavez and his companions decided to mount and make a run for it. But when Wheeling was thrown off his mule, they changed their minds, choosing instead to stand and fight.

When the Indians who had chased the horses returned, however, the odds turned against the three defenders. As the Apaches crawled up close, Jones told Wheeling they should run. The wounded Chavez begged the other two not to leave him, but Jones told him that they had no chance if they tried to fight, and he took off. Wheeling, however, did not make it out.

The Indians taunted Jones as he fled. "They followed after me on horseback yelling, saying, 'Now let's have a race. Mucho buena mula. Mucho bravo Americano.'"[270] As the Apaches closed in, Jones shot one in the side and another in the shoulder. Six Indians pursued him until sundown, but they failed to catch him. Jones escaped the Indians only to be captured by the Confederates on the Rio Grande, six miles above Mesilla. His dispatches were taken from him and he was thrown in jail. Nevertheless, Canby did get word of Carleton's approach.[271]

Ca. 20 June 1862
CHACON CREEK *(Devine, Texas)*
Early one morning in June 1862, Hondo Valley, Texas, settler Jerry Bailey went to see his neighbor, Rube Smith, about some business. Smith's wife told Bailey that Rube had gone out to get his horse and would be back shortly. After a long wait, Bailey went out to look for him. On his way

out he saw another neighbor, Manuel Wydick, running toward him. Wydick told him that Smith had been caught and killed by Indians. The Indians, probably Kickapoos or Lipans, were raiding down Hondo Creek and attacking homesteads in the Hondo Valley.

Bailey and Wydick rushed to where Smith had last been seen. They found fresh horse tracks, footprints, and evidence that a man had been tied up and dragged behind a horse. Investigating further they found Smith's body in the bushes, lanced and mutilated. Nearby lay the body of a dog belonging to another neighbor, James McCombs.

All the families living in the area gathered at Smith's house, and the men prepared to pursue the Indians. Nine men joined the posse: Bailey, Wydick, William Mullins, Nathan Davis, West McCombs, Lewis McCombs, Sam McCombs, Monroe Watkins, and John Brown. They followed a trail leading south. On the second day, the posse caught sight of about forty Indians, but they could not catch up with them. They were too outnumbered to take the Indians on, anyway, so Lewis McCombs and John Brown rode off for San Antonio to try to enlist the help of a ranger company there.

When the Indians slowed down, the remaining members of the posse caught up with them. The seven decided to fight, regardless of the odds. The Indians, seeing the small number of pursuers, holed up in a small grove of timber on Chacon Creek, just above its junction with the San Miguel River. Bailey led the charge, but he was the only one to rush into the trees—his men veered off to shoot from a cover of boulders. Bailey blasted away with his shotgun, to little effect. As the Indians moved closer, Bailey called to Wydick to help him, but Wydick refused.

Finally, Nathan Davis convinced the men to follow him across the open ground to Bailey. Several horses were hit in the charge, but the men reached Bailey unscathed. Both sides fired steadily, from about sixty yards apart. An arrow pierced Davis's shoulder and came out his back. Mullins came to his aid, cutting off the arrowhead and pulling the shaft through. The posse's remaining horses were all hit in the fighting. Mullins eventually got a good look at the Indian they believed to be the chief. Mullins's well-aimed shot got the chief through the heart, and when their leader dropped, the other Indians appeared to lose their nerve. The Texans charged, and the Indians broke and fled, unable to take their dead chief with them. The posse scalped the chief and waved the bloody trophy at the Indians, then placed Rube Smith's hat on a stick and held it up where all could see it.

In searching the timber, the posse found several more dead warriors, and they considered their vengeance taken. It was a victory against tough odds, though it ended in a long walk home.[272]

25 June 1862
APACHE PASS/EYRE'S SCOUT *(Apache Pass, Arizona)*

On 17 June Brig. Gen. James H. Carleton ordered Lt. Col. Edward E. Eyre out from Tucson to patrol the road between Tucson and Mesilla. Eyre had 140 men of Companies B and C, First California Cavalry, with three six-mule teams and supplies for thirty days. They left Ewell's Station at 1 a.m. on 25 June, and at 6 a.m. they reached the abandoned Butterfield Overland station just west of Apache Springs. Although they saw signs of Indians, the soldiers felt safe being in such large numbers and let down their guard. Horses were set free to graze, and some of the soldiers wandered away from the camp to meander.

Around noon, four shots rang out near the springs, and Indians appeared on a hill to the east. The soldiers prepared to fight, but Eyre had been ordered to avoid an engagement if possible. When the Indians waved a white flag, Eyre returned the signal to attempt a peace talk.

Gen. James H. Carleton
—From authors' collection

Cochise and seventy-five warriors showed themselves, but it took an hour for the chief and twelve of his men to come close enough to parley.

Eyre told Cochise he was a friend of the Apaches and insisted he only wanted to pass through. He handed out tobacco and pemmican, which the Indians accepted. Eyre told them that a larger group of soldiers were coming and that "a great captain" (Carleton) wished to make peace with the Apaches and give them presents. According to Eyre, Cochise assured him that neither his men nor the animals would be molested. Thus concluded the so-called "Pemmican Treaty," but in truth Cochise had no intention of letting the white soldiers peacefully cross his land.

After the parley was over, soldiers discovered the bodies of troopers John Maloney, Albert Schmidt, and James Keith nearby. They had been shot, stripped, and lanced through the necks. A furious Eyre sent patrols out into the surrounding hills, but the Apaches stayed just out of reach. Eyre pulled out and crossed Apache Pass before nightfall. The soldiers made camp a few miles east of the pass, near where Jones had been ambushed one week earlier. That night, Indians fired into the bivouac, wounding Acting Assistant Surgeon Kittredge in the head and killing a horse. Eyre left for the Rio Grande the next morning.

Eyre had lost men and supplies, and in the end his efforts served only to warn Cochise that more soldiers were coming.[273]

September 1862
GRAVELLY FORD MASSACRE *(Beowawe, Nevada)*
Indian attacks in the 1850s and 1860s made the trails across Nevada very dangerous. By 1860, several massacres had already occurred in the region, including the Humboldt Wells and Egan Canyon battles of 13 August 1857 and 11 August 1860, respectively. Another took place in early September 1862, when an emigrant party of four families attempted to cross Nevada to reach California.

The emigrant train camped for three weeks at Charles Stebbins's trading post in Ruby Valley to rest up for the final hard push across the desert and mountains. The party numbered between thirteen and twenty-three, depending on the source, and included five children. One of the children, a girl of ten, became attached to Mr. and Mrs. Stebbins, as well as to a Paiute woman named Maggie who worked for Stebbins. Stebbins and his wife tried to persuade the girl's family to leave her with them, but the family said no. When the wagon train left, however, Maggie followed behind, suspecting an attack.

Several days after the emigrants left the Stebbins place, near Palisades Canyon east of Gravelly Ford, Paiutes or Shoshones attacked them. The entire party was killed, except for the young girl. Maggie had rushed in during the chaos, snatched the girl away, and escaped. On their way back to Ruby Valley, however, some warriors caught up with Maggie and the girl. They beat Maggie senseless and took the child. They tied the girl to a stake in the ground, committed "a nameless outrage upon her," and stabbed her to death.[274] When Maggie regained consciousness, she made her way back to Stebbins's store with the news.

Stebbins sent word to the military, then with several other men, he set out to search for the girl's body. The men found her remains and buried them. When Nevada governor James W. Nye received word, he asked Gen. George Wright, in a 15 September communication, for troops to be stationed from the Humboldt River to Ruby Valley. "There has been some bloody work there within a few days," he wrote.[275]

Nye also wanted some of Col. Patrick E. Connor's California soldiers, who were being sent to Salt Lake City, to remain in the Gravelly Ford area until the end of the emigration season. Connor, who arrived in Ruby Valley in late September, heard the news and ordered Maj. Edward McGarry to take two companies of the Second California Cavalry to search Gravelly Ford and track down the attackers. During the October Humboldt Expedition, McGarry killed twenty-four Indians and captured some others, whom they released to warn their tribesmen to stop killing emigrants.[276]

— 1863 —

February 1863
HEAD OF PEDERNALES *(Harper, Texas)*

Judge James M. Hunter, who came to Texas from North Carolina in 1851, had several scrapes with the Indians, including one while working as a mail conductor (see El Muerto Springs, 15 November 1854). He quit the mail service in 1856 and worked as a surveyor until the Civil War, when Governor Francis R. Lubbock appointed him captain of a ranger company.

In February 1863 Hunter's Rangers, many of whom were from the Guadalupe Valley, got word of Indian marauders in the area. Hunter led eleven rangers out of Camp Davis, near White Oak Creek and the Pedernales River, to find them. They picked up a trail on the Llano River and traced it up the James River to its source, then went east toward the headwaters of the Pedernales, west of present-day Harper, Texas. Here, Hunter suddenly came upon eleven Comanches, but with only two horses among them—evidently they were just entering horse country in search of ponies to steal.

Hunter charged. The Comanches stood their ground until about half of them were hit and a warrior who appeared to be the leader was killed. The Indians then fled in all directions. The Comanches stopped for a moment to fight, but they took off again when the rangers paused to reload their guns. During the fight, ranger John Benson took an arrow in the hip, and the spike curled around the bone like a fishhook—a doctor later extracted it with much difficulty.

Hunter reported six Indians killed in the skirmish. He believed that the rangers could have killed all of them but for the fact that the rangers were using what Hunter called "Confederate powder," a substance made in the South from salvaged components and apparently too coarse and dirty to produce good results.[277]

22 March 1863
EIGHT MILE STATION *(Tippett, Nevada)*

After an intense battle at Bear River near the present-day Utah-Nevada border in January 1863, in which the Shoshone Indians suffered severe losses, peace talks ensued between the U.S. Army and the Shoshones. Farther west, however, the Goshutes had not yet engaged in a major battle with soldiers. Continued incursions by white emigrants and their infringement on the Indians' scarce resources eventually prompted retaliation.

The first shots in what would become known as the "Goshute War" were fired at the Eight Mile stage station, where Goshute raiders killed the station workers and ran off the stock. Just as the Indians were about to set fire to the buildings, they saw rising dust from an approaching stagecoach. They quickly set up an ambush.

The stage, headed to Utah from California on the Overland Trail, had nearly crossed the width of present-day Nevada without incident. As they neared Eight Mile Station, the driver, "Happy Harry" Harper, and his passengers, Judge G. N. Mott and an elderly man with his two sons, were unaware that Goshutes had just attacked the station and were now laying in wait for them.

As the stage slowed to enter the station, the Indians blasted it with bullets and arrows. One arrow hit Harper with such force that it nearly knocked him to the bottom of the coach's boot, but he held the reins as the frightened horses galloped off. A few of the Indians mounted up and gave chase, but Harper kept urging his team forward until his wound caused him to lose consciousness. Before he fainted, he called out for help. Judge Mott climbed out of the window of the careening coach and made it to the driver's seat just in time to take the reins.

Mott drove the exhausted horses another nine miles to Deep Creek Station. The pursuing Indians dropped back, and the passengers were safe. Harper's wound, however, would prove fatal. With a fresh team, the stage continued to Salt Lake City, and once there, the passengers spread the word of the attack. Capt. Samuel P. Smith and his California Cavalry immediately left Camp Douglas to search for the raiding Indians. Smith reached Fort Ruby in April, without having made contact with the Goshutes.[278]

April 1863
STANDIFER'S FIGHT *(Malheur River, Oregon)*

The first organized mining parties entered the Boise Basin, northeast of present-day Boise, Idaho, in the spring of 1862. That summer, a party under Tom Turner met up with a party under George Grimes, and the miners fanned out into the hills. Shortly after the prospectors made a major discovery in August, however, Indian raiders killed Grimes, and the miners retreated to the Walla Walla Valley. Despite the attack, when news of the lode spread, miners flocked to the area. By fall, prospecting parties under Relf Bledsoe, Jefferson Standifer, J. Marion Moore, William Tichenor, and Daniel Moffat were scouring the area. Camps such as Bannack City (Idaho City), Placerville, Pioneer City, and Centerville sprang up, and by January 1863, nearly 3,000 fortune-seekers had gathered, waiting for the first thaw so they could begin digging.

As the miners passed the time, they discussed Grimes's murder and other depredations that had taken place during the preceding months. The previous summer, several emigrants had been killed in the Massacre Rocks attack near Fort Hall. Later that autumn, five more people were killed on the road to Salmon River. Two prospectors were killed at Olds' Ferry on the Snake River, and others were attacked on the Malheur River in Oregon. The miners in the Boise Basin came to believe that the Indians must have a hideout somewhere in the mountains beyond the Malheur River, and they felt they would not be safe until it was cleaned out.

In March 1863, a group of Boise miners banded together as "independent rangers" under the tall, black-haired and black-eyed Capt. Jefferson Standifer. The men followed an Indian trail south to Salmon Falls, where they found a Shoshone fortification and attacked, killing fifteen Indians and wounding many more. In April Standifer raised a company of 200 miners, who scouted down the Payette River to the Snake, then headed west into Oregon. Trailing up the Malheur River, the party discovered a hilltop fortification with rifle pits. Standifer had his men surround the place, taking a full day to maneuver the miners into position. On the second day, the miners unleashed their rifles, hitting several Indians. Standifer had his men construct moveable shields made of willow rods, grass, and mud, and slowly rolled them closer to the Indians' fort. Before long, the Indians sent a woman out to ask for a parley.

When Standifer entered the fort, the Indians agreed to surrender all the property they had stolen. The miners, however, were in no mood to let the Indians off so easily. They poured into the fort and shot down everyone in sight, including women and children. The number of dead was not recorded. Only three Indian boys escaped. One four-year-old boy was taken and adopted by John Kelly, who taught him to play the violin; the boy became an accomplished musician.

After the bloody episode, the miners returned to the Boise Basin, satisfied that they had chastised the Indians. The U.S. Army and the territorial militia, however, did not approve of the civilians' exploit. Brig. Gen. Benjamin Alvord ordered Maj. Pinkney Lugenbeel, Nineteenth Infantry, to disperse Standifer's "independent rangers" and prevent any future unauthorized actions. In July, the army established Fort Boise near the mining district to protect emigrants and local residents.[279]

19 April 1863
KERN RIVER *(Kernville, California)*
On 10 April 1863, Capt. Moses A. McLaughlin, Company D, Second California Cavalry, was ordered to proceed from Camp Babbitt, near Visalia, California, to Camp Independence in the Owens Valley, where Indians troubles had flared up again. McLaughlin took twenty-four men of Company D and eighteen men of Company E, under Lts. George D. French and Robert Daily, respectively, supplied with one howitzer and four six-mule government teams.

Ordered to inspect reports of Indian troubles on the Kern River, McLaughlin stopped at Keysville to talk to the local settlers. They told him that Indians had recently murdered one man and stolen 150 head of stock. The raiders, they said, were Tehachapi (Kawaiisu) and Owens Valley (Paiute) Indians who had moved into the area to escape the military. They also said that Jose Chico, a friendly Paiute, was camped nearby. McLaughlin sent for Jose, who confirmed the locals' account.

With Jose as a guide, McLaughlin took Daily and twenty men ten miles up the Kern River to the Indian encampment near present-day Kernville. The soldiers surrounded the camp, and the Indians surrendered. Jose and several settlers separated the Indians they believed to be guilty of depredations from those they deemed innocent.

McLaughlin was in no mood to show mercy. After sending the women, old men, and children back to the camp, he told the thirty-five "guilty" Indians to prepare to fight or die. Those Indians "for whom no one could vouch" were either shot or sabered. According to McLaughlin, "Their only chance for life [was] their fleetness, but none escaped, though many of them fought well with knives, sticks, stones, and clubs." Explaining his decision, the captain wrote, "This extreme punishment, though I regret it, was necessary, and I feel certain that a few such examples will soon crush the Indians and finish the war in this and adjacent valleys."

After the episode, McLaughlin and his Californians continued to Camp Independence, arriving on 24 April after a march of about 250 miles.[280]

4 May 1863
DUCK CREEK *(McGill, Nevada)*

In the continuing Goshute War (see Eight Mile Station, 22 March 1863), Goshute Indians raided whites along the Overland Trail in the spring of 1863. Capt. Samuel P. Smith, hoping to stop them, left Fort Ruby on 1 May with most of Company K, Second California Cavalry, heading southeast toward the Goshutes' reported hideouts in the Schell Creek Mountains. Moving quickly, Smith reached Schell Creek Station the next day and concealed his men in the canyon to wait for passing raiders. Later that day, Lt. John Quinn brought a detachment to join Smith.

That evening, the soldiers slipped out of the canyon and moved down Steptoe Valley along the western slopes of the Schell Creek Mountains. At daybreak, Smith again took his men into a mountain canyon to hide. They were about ten miles north of the spot where, according to the Shoshone scouts, the Goshutes were camped on Duck Creek.

Before daylight the following morning, 4 May, Smith sent half his force ahead to move south of Duck Creek, about sixteen miles north of present-day Ely, Nevada. He took the other half to the north side, then both units moved upstream. The troopers dismounted and successfully gained positions around the sleeping Goshutes. At dawn the signal was given, and the soldiers and Shoshone scouts charged the camp, taking the Goshutes completely by surprise. Only two Indians escaped, while twenty-four were left dead on the battlefield. Pvt. John L. Cree was slightly wounded by an arrow in the back.

Smith waited at the site and established pickets along the perimeter, anticipating that more Goshutes would be coming. That afternoon, five unwary warriors rode in, and Smith ordered a charge. All five Goshutes were killed in the quick fight, while one trooper suffered a slight wound. The next day, Smith moved out toward the Schell Creek Range to continue his pursuit.[281]

6 May 1863
CEDAR SWAMP *(McGill, Nevada)*

After Capt. Samuel P. Smith drove the Goshutes out of their camp on Duck Creek on 4 May (see previous entry), he and Company K, Second California Cavalry, continued east over the Schell Creek Range and into Spring Valley. Moving at night, Smith marched his men south to a boggy area called Cedar Swamp, about fifty miles south of the Spring Creek stage station, where a band of Goshutes were camped. At daybreak on 6 May, he attacked. The marshy ground slowed the charge, enabling many Indians to get away, but the troopers nevertheless killed twenty-three Goshutes, with only one of their own men wounded.

After this success, Smith circled north, scouting for Indians all the way. He returned to Fort Ruby on 10 May, after a march of 250 miles.[282]

15 May 1863
VERDIGRIS RIVER *(Independence, Kansas)*

During the Civil War, the threat of Confederate guerrilla attacks on U.S. soldiers and civilians in the West was real, but the Union sometimes found help from unexpected sources. Government authorities in Colorado and Kansas feared a Confederate-inspired Indian invasion. Early in the war, Southern sympathizers W. Park McClure and Charles Harrison had been run out of Colorado because of their rabblerousing. The pair joined the Confederate Fourth Missouri and told Gen. Sterling Price that they could go back to Colorado and raise a Confederate regiment. Price gave them his permission.

In May 1863 Capt. McClure, Harrison, and twenty-one other men, enough for a full complement of regimental officers, rode west from southern Missouri, traveling across the Osage Reservation in southeastern Kansas toward Colorado. Federal authorities had asked the Osages to report any strangers who crossed their lands. The Indians did more than that. About 150 Osages discovered the Rebels on 15 May, shots were fired, and a running fight of more than eight miles ensued.

When the Confederates' horses gave out, they pulled up in a small streambed, where the Indians surrounded them. McClure's men suffered several casualties, but with their horses rested, they broke out. As he climbed up the bank, McClure's saddle broke and he fell off his horse, whereupon the Osages captured and killed him. The remaining Rebels rode two miles farther to the Verdigris River, a few miles northeast of present-day Independence, Kansas. The far bank was too steep to climb, so they hid on a sandbar. The Indians found the trapped Confederates and killed nineteen of them. Only two, Warner Lewis and John Rafferty, escaped, making their way along the weed-choked riverbank and across the plains back to Missouri. The Osages beheaded the dead Confederates, held a war dance, and took the heads back to the Union troops as proof that they obeyed orders.[283]

6 July 1863
EGAN CANYON STATION *(Schellbourne, Nevada)*
After California soldiers killed the wife and child of Goshute chief Peahnamp and others in June 1863, the chief and his warriors took partial revenge by attacking Egan Canyon stage station, near present-day Schellbourne, Nevada, a few days later. Peahnamp killed a few of the station's defenders during the 23 June attack, but others survived, so he returned on 6 July to finish the job.[284]

At the station that day were William "Deaf Bill" Riley, his assistant, and four soldiers of the Third California Infantry: Pvts. Thomas Grimshaw, Michael McNamara, Anthony Meyers, and Lewis Pratt. At sunrise, Riley was currying a horse in front of the barn when a Goshute in hiding shot him dead. When his assistant ran out of the barn, he was also shot and killed. Then Grimshaw rushed out of the sod dugout the soldiers were staying in, and he too was shot down.

The three remaining privates quickly assessed the situation and concluded that their only hope was to get to the horses in the nearby barn. As they burst out and ran through the open yard, McNamara was hit and crumpled dead in the dirt. Meyers and Pratt reached the barn, barricaded the openings with grain sacks, and fired back for an hour. The Indians finally set fire to a haystack next to the barn. When the flames reached the structure, Meyers and Pratt had no choice but to make a run for it. One of the horses was known to be a fleet runner, and the two drew straws for it. Pratt won. The two men shook hands, mounted up, and dashed out.

Bullets kicked up dust and whizzed by their heads as they headed for Willow Springs Station, the next stage stop to the east. On the good horse, Pratt outdistanced his comrade. The Goshutes caught up to Meyers and put a bullet in his back, and he tumbled from his horse. Pratt rode on, and it seemed as if he would get away, but either his horse tired or the Indians had faster mounts, and they eventually caught up to him. Pratt had ridden about fifty miles and had nearly reached Willow Springs. An emigrant party later found Pratt's dead horse with its mortally wounded rider lying nearby. They took Pratt to the station, where he died shortly afterward.[285]

Ca. 15 August 1863
STEPTOE VALLEY *(Currie, Nevada)*

The Cherry Creek Mountains of northwestern Nevada contained numerous streams, game, pine nuts, and other resources hard to come by in the region. As such, they were a prime location for the hunting-gathering Goshutes. When fighting broke out between the Indians and whites in the area, the Cherry Creek Range became a target for Indian-hunting soldiers.

In August, Lt. Josiah Hosmer, who had been commissioned from private in the Third California Infantry, led Company E in search of the raiding Goshutes. Operating out of Camp Douglas, Utah, and Fort Ruby, Nevada, Hosmer marched his footsore soldiers all through the region's ranges and basins. He finally found a Goshute camp in the Steptoe Valley, on the east side of the Cherry Creek Range, about twenty-five miles north of the Egan Canyon stage station. Hosmer attacked, killing five Indians with no losses of his own.[286]

After this incident, the Goshute War subsided. The conflict ended with a treaty signed in Tuilla Valley, Utah Territory, in October 1863.

8 September 1863
MIMBRES RIVER *(Dwyer, New Mexico)*

Capt. James H. Whitlock raised his Company F, Fifth California Infantry, in Plumas County, California, but the unit spent much of its service in Arizona and New Mexico Territory. After serving at Fort Yuma, Tucson, and Las Cruces, the company moved to Camp Mimbres, near present-day Dwyer, New Mexico, in August 1863. Mimbres was not a permanent camp, so the troops may have moved around to different spots for better water and grass.

On 4 September, Whitlock took a detachment out to scout for Apaches. The soldiers found an Indian camp the next day, but the warriors fled. Without a fight, Whitlock captured two mules, a Sharps carbine, an army blanket, and 1,000 pounds of mescal, then he burned the camp. On 8 September, Whitlock surprised another Apache camp and engaged the Indians in "a spirited fight" for fifteen minutes.

The warriors took away their wounded, so the Indian losses were unknown, but Whitlock suffered one soldier and one civilian guide seriously wounded. After another short stint at Camp Mimbres, Whitlock moved his command to Fort West, on the Gila River.[287]

25–26 December 1863
CHRISTMAS PRAIRIE *(Arcata, California)*

Discontentment among Indian bands in northwestern California kept detachments from the area's many small forts constantly on the march. In December 1863, a friendly Indian brought word to Lt. Col. Stephen G. Whipple, commander at Fort Gaston, on the Trinity River, that hostile Indians had built a fortification to use as a base for conducting raids. Whipple sent Lt. Thomas Middleton of Company C, First Battalion California Mountaineers, with thirty men and a few Indian guides to the location.

Middleton reached the Indians' fort, on a small prairie south of Bald Mountain, about twelve miles east of present-day Arcata, California, on Christmas Day. The fortress, which comprised five log structures with firing loopholes, all connected by covered passages, could command approaches from all directions, so Middleton was hesitant to make a direct assault. When he sent Pvt. Philip Leonard on reconnaissance, the soldier was shot. The troopers immediately shot down the assailant, and sporadic fire commenced. Unwilling to risk his men in a charge, Middleton pulled back and sent for help.

In response, Capt. George W. Ousley arrived from Fort Gaston, twenty-three miles away, with portions of Companies A and B of the Mountaineers. Ousley, who had been wounded in the leg in a fight the previous month, nevertheless accompanied the reinforcements, bringing a mountain howitzer along for good measure. On 26 December the soldiers set up the howitzer and began blasting the fortress, but the Indians were not shaken. Some structures were damaged, but the defense remained secure. During the fight, Pvt. Charles Smith was wounded in the arm. By the day's end, Ousley was still not sure if he could take the fort. Now out of howitzer ammunition, he sent Middleton to Fort Gaston for more shells. When the lieutenant arrived, Whipple decided to send more men as well.

Whipple himself accompanied the next reinforcement party, but when he got to the scene on 27 December, the Indians were gone. Ousley had surrounded the fort during the night, but the Indians managed to slip away in the snow-blown darkness. The soldiers found two dead Indians in the fort, which was in shambles, and they assumed others had been killed and wounded. Four horses and mules, several guns and saddles, and a large amount of provisions were recovered, but more than 200 Indians had escaped.

Whipple was dissatisfied with the outcome of the effort, but he conceded that "after observing the situation of the ground and taking into consideration the continued exposure of the men in the storms and their consequent fatigue, with other adverse circumstances, no other result could hardly be expected." He also saw an upside: "One important result," he wrote, "is that the savages are now convinced that they are not safe in any fortifications which they can construct."[288] Discouraged or not, the Indians who escaped continued their raiding.[289]

29 December 1863
BUTTERWORTH'S FIGHT *(Patagonia, Arizona)*

During the Civil War, Apaches raided with abandon along the United States-Mexico border. On 29 December 1863, prospectors J. B. Mills Jr. and Edwin C. Stevens were murdered along the trail from Santa Cruz, Sonora, to the Patagonia, or Mowry, Mines, about ten miles north of the border. The canyon south of the mines, Patagonia Canyon, or San Antonio Canyon, already contained the graves of seventeen white men, fifteen of whom were victims of Indian violence.

Only six hours after Mills and Stevens were killed, Arizona Mining Company president Samuel F. Butterworth, inspecting mining prospects in the territory, approached the same canyon. He was accompanied by a Mr. Janin, five Mexicans, and an American wagon driver. Suddenly about twenty-five Apaches, two of them armed with the murdered miners' weapons, fired from the brush along the Santa Cruz River. Butterworth and the others drove their wagons to a mesquite tree on the roadside. Butterworth tried to rally his companions behind the wagons and fight, but there was no time. The Indians set the dry grass on fire, and the flames swept up to the wagons so rapidly that the men abandoned their position and drove one wagon to a rise about 200 yards away.

Again the Indians fired the grass, and this time the five Mexicans and the American driver fled the scene, leaving Butterworth, with his double-barreled shotgun, and Janin, with his Henry rifle, behind. Though Janin had the better weapon, he had poor eyesight. He asked Butterworth to lend him his glasses, but Butterworth declined, telling Janin to make a run for it and save himself. But by then the smoke was very heavy, so they both ran. Janin made it into a ravine while Butterworth stopped behind another mesquite tree to continue shooting. The encroaching grass fire drove him up the tree, burning his pant legs as the flames swept by. When the blaze passed, Butterworth climbed down and ran again. Rather than chasing him down, the Indians turned back to plunder the wagons before the flames claimed them.

After looking for Butterworth, who was nowhere to be found, Janin met up with one of the Mexicans, and they both made it back to Santa Cruz. There, a party of Mexicans went out in search of Butterworth. Two days later, a searcher named Commodoran came across a disheveled man, who held up his shotgun and shouted, "Vamos!" Commodoran shouted, "Yo Amigo. Patagonia! Patagonia!" as he held out a note from Janin. Butterworth took a look, realized he was rescued, and rode with Commodoran back to Santa Cruz.[290]

— 1864 —

23 May 1864
GROUSE CREEK (*Hyampom, California*)
The six companies of the First Battalion California Mountaineers, organized in 1863, were constantly on the move, hunting small, elusive bands of Pomo, Yuki, Hoopa, and Wiyot Indians in northwestern California. They had a number of skirmishes in the spring of 1864, including the Kneeland's Prairie, Thomas's Ranch, and Big Flat Battles.

Company E, organized by Capt. John P. Simpson, was based at Camp Grant, on the Eel River just above its junction with the South Fork. One particularly long and exhausting scout began on 13 April. Sgt. Richard B. Harris and six men of Company E marched from Camp Grant to the Van Duzen River, where they picked up two civilians. From there the party went upstream and continued across to the Mad River. Near the Hettenshaw Valley, they picked up an Indian trail and tracked it until they reached the Hay Fork of the Trinity River. When the company arrived at Hay Fork settlement, they stopped at the house of a Mr. Rodgers, whom, they learned, Indians had just robbed. Harris's men rested at the settlement, where more civilians joined them, bringing their number to seventeen. In late April, a report of Indians killing a settler sent them searching up and down the Hay Fork for the culprits.

After another short rest, Harris's group scouted on the South Fork of the Trinity, where they captured an old Indian woman. She told them that the Indians they sought were well-armed but said nothing else, and they let her go. The party recrossed the mountains and spent a few days scouting up and down South Fork Mountain. In between rainstorms, they struck a trail and followed it all the way back to the Van Duzen River. On 14 May four friendly Indians joined the party, and the searchers kept up their scout until they reached Pilot Creek. On 20 May, with Harris now out of provisions, two civilians and three Indians left. Harris led the remaining men to Camp Iaqua on Yeager Creek, where he got fifteen days' rations and continued on.

Back at Pilot Creek, Harris picked up another trail, which led to the dividing ridge between Pilot Creek and Grouse Creek. There the scouts spotted campfire smoke some miles in the distance, and Harris moved closer, marching in the darkness until about 1 a.m. on 23 May. Finally, at sunrise, the company crept up to a small rancheria near Grouse Creek, about twelve miles west of present-day Hyampom, California. Harris noticed someone who may have been a white man among the Indians. The man spotted Harris and raised the alarm. Harris ordered a charge, and his force was "amongst them before they could get out."[291] The company killed nine Indians, wounded several others, and captured two women, two children, three rifles, a horse, and all the camp equipment.

Harris left for Camp Grant the next day, catching two deserters from the Sixth California Infantry on the way. They arrived at the post on 30 May, having been out forty-seven days and having marched 600 miles. Harris turned in his report, but rather than praise, it elicited complaints from Lt. Jacob P. Hackett, Sixth California Infantry, and Lt. Knyphausen Geer, First California Mountaineers. The lieutenants felt that Harris had personally accomplished little and noted that he had not turned over any deserters or any property other than one rifle. They expressed suspicion that the sergeant had exaggerated most of his report.[292]

3 June 1864
BATTLE FLAT *(Goodwin, Arizona)*

In May 1864, miners Stewart Wall, Frank Binkley, Frederic Henry, DeMorgan Scott, and Samuel Herron, departed Walnut Grove on the Hassayampa River for a prospecting trip. They went east into the Bradshaw Mountains, crossed the divide, and moved down Turkey Creek. The creek was generally rocky and narrow, but the miners found a level, open spot to camp on the night of 2 June. They picketed their horses and bedded down for the night without posting a sentinel. Experienced Indian fighters, the men were perhaps overconfident and therefore careless.

Watching the five miners were about fifty Indians, probably Yavapais. During the night, the Indians crept into the camp and stole a few of their horses, silently leading them away. The warriors also quietly constructed a series of rock breastworks all around the sleeping men. Just before daylight, as the Indians stealthily closed in, one of the miners rose up from his blanket. He instinctively grabbed his rifle and began to fire. The Indians blasted back, and within a minute all five miners were wounded.

The defenders took what little cover they could behind saddles and packs as Indians charged. The miners kept their attackers at bay with quick-firing revolvers. Another charge came within ten paces of them before they drove the Indians back. By now each of the white men had two or more wounds.

The siege lasted until 10 a.m., when the miners made a break for better defensive ground, up a chaparral-covered ridge nearby. They hobbled and limped their way up, two of them dragging a man with a broken leg, as bullets kicked up dirt all around them. Henry was shot in the chest, and a ball hit Binkley in the face and tore out one of his eyes. When they got to their new position, the plucky whites still managed to find humor in the situation. Binkley put his hand to his eye socket then held out the clotted mess to Henry. "Fred," he said, "look and see if that ain't my brains." "No, you fool," Henry replied, "you wouldn't be talking if that was your brains."[293]

Incredibly, Binkley took another arrow in the same eye but still kept fighting. Around 11 a.m. the Indians may have been running out of ammunition, for they began throwing rocks. Henry and Binkley, who still had use of their legs, decided to go for help. Of the remaining three men, one was unconscious. An Indian slipped up to the insentient man and lifted a huge rock to crush his head, but a blast from the shotgun of another wounded miner interfered, killing the assailant. After this, the Indians disappeared into the forest.

Meanwhile, Binkley and Henry struggled across the mountains to Walnut Grove, nearly twenty miles away. When they reached the settlement at eight o'clock the next morning, a rescue party of ten miners assembled under J. W. Swilling. The rescuers hurried to Turkey Creek and found the three men still alive, though two were unconscious. They also found the bodies of fourteen Indians. The wounded miners were transported to Walnut Grove, where Sam Herron succumbed to his wounds nine days later. The other four survived.[294]

26 June 1864
LITTLE CHEYENNE RIVER
(Gettysburg, South Dakota)

After the bloody Minnesota Sioux Uprising of 1862, the army was determined to punish the Sioux. Gen. Alfred Sully led a new campaign that began in September 1863 and immediately scored a tremendous success at Whitestone Hill. Taking up the campaign again the following summer, the general left Fort Sully on 26 June with about 3,000 soldiers. The expedition marched north, staying a dozen or more miles east of the Missouri River. Two days after Sully's departure, near the headwaters of the Little Cheyenne River, not far from present-day Gettysburg, South Dakota, some of the soldiers ran into trouble.

Capt. John Feilner, First Cavalry, was appointed to the expedition as Sully's topographical engineer, assigned to make meteorological observations and report on the region's geology, botany, fauna, and the like. On 28 June Feilner, along with two enlisted men he had trained to help him, rode ahead of the main column to examine a large rock on the Little Cheyenne. The boulder, of a type the Indians called a "medicine rock," was embedded with human footprints. Sully had warned Feilner about wandering off on his own and had offered him a larger escort, but the captain shrugged it off, saying he doubted that there were any Indians in the territory.

Feilner and his assistants picketed their horses and walked to the river with their canteens. At the water's edge, three Sioux jumped from out of the bushes and fired. A bullet hit Feilner in the chest, mortally wounding him. One of the assistants was also hit, but he and the other private managed to get away. The warriors went for the horses, but the animals pulled up their picket pins and ran off. The soldiers ran back to Sully's column and breathlessly reported the incident. Sully ordered Capt. Nelson Miner to take a dozen of his Dakota Cavalrymen and go after the Indians.

After an eight-mile chase through gullies and over hills, Miner cornered the three warriors on foot in a buffalo wallow. Miner's troopers made short work of them, shouting "Death to the murderers!" as they riddled them with bullets. Miner took the Indians' weapons as trophies, but Sully asked for more. Returning to the scene with Miner, Sgt. Benjamin Estes decapitated the warriors with a butcher knife, placed the heads in a gunny sack, and brought them back to Sully. The general ordered Sgt. Abner M. English "to hang the heads on poles on the highest hill as a warning to all Indians who might travel that way."[295]

The Powder River in Wyoming

As news of the mutilations traveled through Dakota Territory, it mostly served only to inflame Indian animosity toward whites. Some Indians in the area were intimidated and backed off, but many more gathered in the territory's northwestern badlands and resolved to fight.[296]

7 July 1864
TOWNSEND'S WAGON TRAIN *(Kaycee, Wyoming)*

Only four wagon trains are known to have taken the new Bozeman Trail to Montana (then Idaho Territory) in 1864, and among them only the third train was attacked. In subsequent years, however, Indian attacks on the "Bloody Bozeman" would become so frequent that a treaty was signed to shut down the road in 1868. The elected captain of the ill-fated third train was A. A. Townsend of Wisconsin, who started north from Richard's Bridge on the North Platte with some of the wagons on 28 June. On 3 July the rest of the train joined them at the head of Salt Creek.

Guides Rafael Gallegos and John Boyer led the full train of 150 wagons, 375 men, 36 women, and 56 children down the alkaline, nearly dry Salt Creek. They reached good water at the Powder River on 5 July, crossed to the north bank, and moved upstream three miles, where they rested one day. On the morning of 7 July they pulled out but went only two miles before stopping for breakfast. While the wagons were corralled, a man named Mills rode back toward the first camp to look for a stray cow, and another man, Frank Hudelmeyer, went out hunting. As the emigrants were preparing their meal, a dust cloud announced approaching Indians, and the guides rode out to see what they wanted. The Indians, mostly Cheyennes, said they were out searching for Crows, but they demanded that the emigrants feed them, then turn around and return to the North Platte. The travelers gave the Indians some food, but their "guests" nevertheless grew quite belligerent.

Suspicious of the Indians, six of the emigrants, including Dr. Henry N. Crepin, T. J. Brundage, E. Butterfield, and Asher Newby, rode out to look for Mills. They were about two miles east of the wagons when they heard a shot. As they turned back, they saw about forty warriors riding toward them. Crepin tried to veer off toward the river, but the warriors forced him back. Closing in, the Indians fired a volley but missed. The six emigrants halted to fire off a round, then they charged directly into the warriors, hoping to break through to the wagons. In the dash, Newby, who had served as a Confederate captain, was hit in the back with an arrow and fell from his horse. As Brundage rode back to get his wounded companion, men from the wagon train rushed out to fire at the Indians.

Now focused on the train, the Indians set fire to the surrounding prairie. The men of the party formed a ring around the corralled wagons, keeping the Indians at bay with long-range rifles, while the women and children helped dig a trench around the corral and hauled buckets to and from the river to wet down the area. Emigrant A. Warren was hit in the abdomen during the siege, which lasted until three in the afternoon. When the Indians finally gave up, the train crossed to the south side of the Powder River, moved two miles upstream, and camped for the night.

About twelve Indians were killed in the fight, and several were wounded. The emigrants suffered four mortalities. Warren's wound proved fatal, and he died the next morning. Mills, the man who had gone out looking for the cow, was confirmed dead when the next train through the area found his scalp and horse. Hudelmeyer was killed while out hunting; his body was found punctured with eleven arrows. One other emigrant was missing and presumed dead. The seriously wounded Newby, however, recovered.[297]

19 July 1864
BROWN'S SPRING *(Orpha, Wyoming)*

Attacks on emigrants, stage stations, and military posts along the Overland Trail increased during the summer of 1864. On 12 July, an attack on the Kelly-Larimer wagon train along Little Box Elder Creek, just beyond LaPrele Station, Wyoming, left four men dead and three wounded, along with two women and two children captured. Mrs. Larimer and her child were able to escape their captors soon afterward, but another captive, Fanny Kelly's daughter, was found dead along the trail. At Fort Laramie, Col. William O. Collins, Eleventh Ohio Cavalry, ordered an expedition be organized to pursue the attackers and rescue Fanny Kelly.

All of Company H, thirty men of Company G, and detachments of companies E, I, and K, Eleventh Ohio assembled at Deer Creek Station. The expedition, under Capts. Jacob S. Shuman, Company H, and Levi G. Marshall, Company E, set out at 1 a.m. on 19 July with about 160 men and two howitzers. After crossing the North Platte River, the command divided, with half moving north and half northeast. The northeastern command, under Marshall, followed the tracks of a large horse herd to a small stream about four miles south of the Dry Fork of the Cheyenne River, where they camped for the evening.

Scouting ahead, Lt. John R. Brown, Company E, accompanied by Fanny Kelly's husband, Josiah, and about a dozen troopers encountered a band of about forty warriors. Several skittish soldiers broke for the rear, but Brown raised his arm and called out to them. The Indians, probably Oglalas, sent an arrow into Brown's back, knocking him off his horse. Josiah Kelly and the rest of the troopers sped away.

Back at Marshall's camp, the main command were stacking their arms and settling in for supper when they heard screams. The sounds came from a teenage boy, who was out herding horses east of the trail when he was attacked, killed, and scalped. Just then, Brown's returning men rode into camp and reported their own confrontation. A large pursuit was quickly mounted, but the Indians escaped in the gathering darkness.

The next morning, an ambulance went out to retrieve the body of Brown, who was presumed dead, but to the crew's surprise, he was still alive. One of the soldiers reported that Brown had one arrow in his back and another in his neck, and he had been stripped of his clothing except for his shirt and boots. The arrow in his neck was snipped off and pulled through, but when the medics tried to remove the arrow in his back, the barb broke off and it had to be dug out.

Brown died of his wounds the following morning. The soldiers buried him in a shallow grave and the command moved on, but the expedition later turned back. On their return, the troopers retrieved Brown's body and brought it to Deer Creek Station, where the lieutenant was buried with full military honors. The site where he was fatally wounded became known as Brown's Spring.[298]

20–22 July 1864
COW CREEK *(Lyons, Kansas)*

In the summer of 1864, Indian troubles in central Kansas became so serious that Maj. Gen. Samuel H. Curtis personally led a column of soldiers into the area. Curtis moved from Fort Leavenworth to Fort Riley, where he gathered a battalion of Kansas militia and U.S. volunteers, then headed out for Fort Larned.

Meanwhile, four government trains, loaded mostly with ordnance and driving hundreds of cattle, banded together in Council Grove for a trip west. On 20 July at Cow Creek Station, near the bridge crossing, an estimated 500 Indians surrounded the trains. The Indian force included some Comanches, Kiowas under Kicking Bird, and Big Mouth's Arapahos. After a two-day siege, a messenger rode the 100 miles back to Council Grove to report that unless the wagoners got help, they would have to abandon the trains. In response, Capt. James H. Dodge raised 100 Kansas militia and, along with a section of his Ninth Wisconsin Battery, hurried to the wagoners' aid on 24 July.

At Cow Creek, the wagoners had kept the Indians at bay, losing only two men, but they'd lost nearly 300 head of stock. Before Dodge's men had time to arrive, however, William "Buffalo Bill" Mathewson, the operator of Cow Creek Station, came to the wagoners' rescue. Mathewson, who had made defensive preparations at his station when the Indian troubles first flared up in Kansas, had a remarkable store of weapons, including a two-pound artillery piece. When the plucky frontiersman fired the small cannon at a band of warriors near the bridge, the resulting carnage was great enough to break the siege. One man at the station, Charles Christy, estimated that the artillery killed twenty Indians, and ten more were killed by the defenders' carbines.

The trains crawled forward, meeting up with General Curtis's column at Camp Dunlap, which later became Fort Zarah, near the mouth of Walnut Creek. Curtis wrote to Maj. Gen. Henry W. Halleck on 28 July that the trains were safe with him, and that he and his men would proceed to Fort Larned the next day.[299]

1 August 1864
WAGON BED SPRING *(Ulysses, Kansas)*

After killing a sentry at Fort Larned and stealing horses from the fort's herd on 17 July, Kiowas under Satank and Satanta moved west, striking at any convenient targets along the way. At the Cimarron Crossing of the Arkansas River in late July, they attacked a stage and killed two men. Then, on 1 August, about seventy Comanches and Kiowas approached a small wagon train camped at Lower Cimarron Springs (also called Wagon Bed Spring, where mountain man Jedediah Smith had been killed by Comanches in 1831), about ten miles south of present-day Ulysses, Kansas. The Indians approached the train, owned by a Mr. Allison, in a friendly manner and asked for food. Then, without warning, they attacked.

The Indians killed Allison and the four other Americans in the party, but they spared the lives of the Mexican teamsters, saying they had no quarrel with them. They left the Mexicans one wagon and a yoke of oxen and told them to leave the area. Thankful for their lives, the Mexicans hurried west on the Santa Fe Trail. Near the Canadian River, Capt. Nicholas S. Davis of the First California Infantry encountered the Mexican teamsters, who told him what had happened. They said that the Indians warned "they would kill every white man that came on the road."[300] Davis proceeded to Wagon Bed Spring and buried the bodies of the five Americans.[301]

6 August 1864
MOFFITT MASSACRE *(Lincoln, Kansas)*

Among the first settlers in Lincoln County, Kansas, were brothers John L. and Thomas Moffitt, John W. Houston, and James Tyler. The partners' place was located on the north bank of the Saline River, across from the mouth of Elkhorn Creek. The Moffitts had emigrated from Illinois, where their parents and sister still lived. On 30 June Thomas wrote in a letter to his sister that he didn't like Kansas, but since he and Jack had just bought fifty cows, he would stay for a while. He also said that hostile Indians prevented him from venturing far from the house, noting that he had to carry his revolver even to go out to the stables. Nevertheless, he said he did not expect an Indian attack at the ranch.

On 6 August, Houston's relatives visited the ranch, and having extra mouths to feed, the ranchers decided to go on a buffalo hunt. That morning, the four partners saddled up and headed up Beaver Creek, which flowed into the Saline just west of their spread. They didn't get far. Less than a mile from home, about fifty Indians jumped them. The ranchers turned around and ran for a ledge of rock above the creek. Judging from the number of bullets and arrows later found at the site, the four must have put up a good defense, but they were eventually overwhelmed.

The attackers then approached the ranch house and tried to entice Houston's guests outside. One Indian, apparently speaking English, declared that they were good Indians and would not hurt them. Unconvinced, the occupants refused to come out, and the Indians left, but they returned the next morning to plunder the ranch. Old Mr. Houston dislodged a chink in a wall of the house and shot at the intruders, hitting one, and the rest of them fled.

About four days later, twelve settlers and a few soldiers of Company H, Seventh Iowa Cavalry, visited the scene of the attack on Beaver Creek. They found the horses dead and the wagon burned. Numerous bullet scars on the ledge above the creek and dozens of arrows on the ground showed a hard fight. The four men were buried side by side where they had fought. In September another Moffitt brother, Robert, went to the site to disinter his brothers and ship their bodies back to Illinois. Houston and Tyler were left where they were.[302]

21 August 1864
CIMARRON CROSSING *(Cimarron, Kansas)*

From camps in western Kansas, Cheyennes continued to send out war parties to the Arkansas River throughout the summer of 1864. Only large and well-armed wagon trains were allowed to travel past Fort Larned. In August, a caravan that included a Mexican wagon train, another train of fourteen wagons under Andrew Blanchard, and a Stuart, Slemmons & Company train under Charles P. McRae and John Sage passed Fort Larned with 95 wagons and more than 100 armed men. They approached the Middle Cimarron Crossing of the Arkansas on 21 August with McRae leading, followed by Sage, the Mexican train, and Blanchard. As they stopped to rest, the first three trains formed up in a circle, leaving an opening for Blanchard, but inexplicably he moved on and corralled half a mile beyond the others.

Fort Larned, Kansas

The party camped early in the day, trying to rest up for the long, dry journey ahead, and most of the men were asleep when the Indians appeared around 1 p.m. Three men from McRae's train were outside the wagon corral shooting prairie dogs when one of them shouted, "Indians!" About forty Cheyenne warriors under Little Robe charged in from the north, trying to cut the three hunters off from the wagons. Before the other teamsters had even awakened, six mess cooks grabbed rifles and rushed to the edge of the circle, covering the three hunters as they ran to safety.

Five Indians led by Bear Man cut in between McRae's and Blanchard's trains. Blanchard, in a foolhardy move, drew his pistol and rode out after the five, evidently not noticing the other Indians circling around his wagons nor the mounted Indians still waiting on the bluffs. He was 200 yards from the camp before he realized his mistake. While most of the Cheyennes drove off his cattle, several warriors rode up to Blanchard, knocked him off his horse, and captured him.

About fifteen of Blanchard's teamsters grabbed their weapons and rushed out to help him, firing as they ran. As the teamsters closed in, the warriors were forced to drop their prisoner. Upon reaching Blanchard, however, the teamsters discovered he had been wounded several times, with multiple gunshot wounds, an arrow protruding from his stomach, and a lance gash through his shoulder. They carried him back to the corral, but he died within the hour. They buried him beside the road. Ten other train members were also killed in the attack.

The Cheyennes drove off 130 mules, about one-third of McRae's and Sage's herds. Of Blanchard's stock, all but two oxen were taken. The Indians took their plunder south of the river and ultimately escaped. Another wagon train with a cavalry detachment from Fort Larned eventually reached the stranded caravan. Thus fortified, the wagoners continued their journey.[303]

13 and 16 September 1864
THREE ISLAND CROSSING *(Glenns Ferry, Idaho)*

Lt. Charles Hobart, with twenty-one men of Company A, First Oregon Cavalry, and Lt. Charles F. West, with twenty-eight men of Companies D and I, First Washington Territory Infantry, left Fort Boise on 27 August 1864, heading for the Salmon Falls of the Snake River to hunt for hostile Indians. Hobart, in charge of the expedition, had one mountain howitzer, a hundred rounds of ammunition for each man, and forty days' rations. While en route to the falls, Hobart met Zachias Van Ornum and his young nephew Reuben. The boy had been captured in 1860 by Bannocks in the vicinity; his uncle recovered him two years later. Because they were familiar with the surrounding country, and perhaps hoping for some revenge, Zachias and Reuben offered to scout for Hobart.

On 7 September, the contingent arrived at the mouth of Salmon Falls Creek, where Hobart learned of several recent stock raids in the area. Only the night before, Indians had stolen fifteen mules from a man named McFarland. Hobart sent out a party under Sergeant Wood, Company A, First Oregon Cavalry, to pursue the culprits. Following the trail of the missing stock, Wood found the Indians on the north side of the Snake River about twenty-five miles above Salmon Falls. He killed three warriors, one of whom, Hobart later learned, was an Owyhee medicine man named Ebigon. Wood recovered a mule, a horse, and an ox.

Upon Wood's return, on 13 September Hobart sent some men on a scout to Shoshone Falls and Rock Creek, while he himself took eighteen cavalry, four infantrymen mounted on mules, and his howitzer down the Snake River. At dawn, below Salmon Falls, Hobart surprised another group of Indians he believed to be from Ebigon's band. In the ensuing running fight, Hobart killed six Indians and wounded a few as they escaped across the river. The next day, he and his men continued downriver, where they had two slight skirmishes, killing one Indian and wounding another.

Hobart's troops camped that night at Three Island Crossing, a frequently used ford of the Snake, at present-day Glenns Ferry, Idaho. Early the next morning, Indians began firing on them from the opposite bank. Hobart sent parties up both sides of the river to capture the aggressors, but the attempt failed. Hobart left the crossing at 1 a.m. on 16 September, heading for an island about ten miles downriver, where he believed another Indian band was encamped.

At daylight, Hobart spied a band of about thirty to forty Indians on the island. He sent men along both banks to trap the Indians, then fired a howitzer shell into the middle of the island to signal the attack. As the startled Indians fled toward both banks, Hobart's men killed eight of them. "I had them surrounded," he reported, "and had it not been for the haste and excitement of the men sent on the east side of the river would have killed the whole party."[304]

Hobart destroyed the Indian camp and returned to Three Island Crossing. After a quick scout to the Bruneau River, which turned up nothing, he returned to Fort Boise on 5 October.[305]

Ca. 17 October 1864
PAULINA CREEK *(LaPine, Oregon)*

On 14 October 1864 Oregon Indian superintendent J. W. Perit Hunting-ton and the U.S. Indian agent for Oregon, William Logan, concluded a treaty at Klamath Lake, Oregon, with the Klamaths, Modocs, and the Yahooskin band of Snakes ("Snake" being a name used for any of several bands of Paiutes and other tribes, erroneously grouped together). Huntington distributed presents and deposited 16,000 pounds of flour at Fort Klamath, to be issued to the Indians who remained in the area through the winter. Conspicuously absent from the accords were the Paiutes under Chief Paunina (also spelled Paulina or Po-li-ni), who had been at war with the whites for the past two years.

With the treaty made, Huntington and Logan returned to The Dalles, traveling the same route they had come by, along the eastern edge of the Cascade Mountains. They were escorted by a detachment of First Washington Territory Infantry under Lt. J. Halloran, who commanded the Warm Springs Reservation, and a party of Warm Springs Indians led by the mixed-blood William C. McKay. A few days into their jour-ney, near the headwaters of the Deschutes River, Halloran surprised and captured two Paiutes. When he learned from them that Chief Paunina was camped nearby, he sent out soldiers to find him. A search of several hours revealed a band of Indians camped on Paulina Creek, a tributary of the Little Deschutes. Halloran captured them all: three men, three women, and two children. Among the captured were Paunina's wife, Falling Star, and their child.

Back at camp, Huntington questioned some of the captives as to the whereabouts of Paunina, hoping he could find the chief and convince him to surrender. The five warriors, however, suddenly seized a number of guns from the soldiers and fled. The infantrymen chased them down, killing four. The fifth warrior was wounded but managed to escape to Paunina's camp and tell the chief what happened.

Huntington brought the five remaining captives, all women and children, to Fort Vancouver on 27 October. On 8 November Paunina came to Fort Klamath and told Capt. William Kelly, First Oregon Cav-alry, that he was tired of war. He said he would promise peace if he could be protected from his enemies on the Warm Springs Reservation. Hun-tington sent word that he would meet Paunina the following summer to negotiate a treaty.[306] Paunina got his family back in August 1865, after the treaty, but he went back on the warpath in 1866.

— 1865 —

17 February 1865
FORT BUCHANAN *(Sonoita, Arizona)*

Cochise and his Chiricahua Apaches had been marauding almost without letup since the bloody Bascom Affair of February 1861. In January 1865 they attacked cavalry couriers on the San Pedro River and later killed one man and wounded another riding in a wagon near Tubac, Arizona. On 17 February, they attacked a ranch near the Santa Rita mines, chasing William Wrightson and Gilbert W. Hopkins about a dozen miles to old Fort Buchanan before catching and murdering them. Afterward the Apaches approached the dilapidated fort, evacuated in 1861 but occasionally occupied since then as a cavalry vedette station.

Six men of Company L, First California Cavalry, under Cpl. Michael Buckley, were stationed at the post at the time, but only three men were inside when the Indians attacked. One private was out hunting, and two were cutting hay. "I was sitting at the door of the house when an Indian shot me through the thigh," Buckley recalled. "This was the first knowledge we had that the Indians were around. I drew my pistol and shot the Indian, at the same time Private [Joseph] Berry shot another."[307]

About seventy Indians closed in on the post, and within minutes, they had set the building on fire. Buckley and the two privates kept shooting until the roof began to collapse on them. The three broke from the house "amidst a shower of arrows." They reached the cover of the riverside brush, turning to fire at the Apaches whenever they got close. Hearing the shots, the two privates who were cutting hay also fled. Five of the six soldiers finally made their way to safety at the Santa Rita mining camp, but the Apaches caught the soldier who was out hunting and killed him.

Upon receiving news of the attack, Capt. John L. Merriam, First California Cavalry, left the post at Tubac with twenty-four men, reaching Fort Buchanan the following afternoon. The men found the place burned to the ground and discovered that the Indians had captured six horses and all the equipment, supplies, and ammunition. Merriam ordered that Fort Buchanan be abandoned.[308]

Ca. 15 March 1865
GRANITE CREEK STATION *(Gerlach, Nevada)*

Granite Creek Station was on the Noble's Cutoff, or Honey Lake Road, at the mouth of Bowen Canyon in the Granite Range, about five miles north of present-day Gerlach, Nevada. A stage and freight station, it consisted of a storehouse, a stone corral, and a sod house. It was the first westbound stop for fresh water after crossing the Black Rock Desert, between the Humboldt River and California. Granite Creek irrigated the meadow surrounding the station, providing forage for stock and making it a rather pleasant spot in the otherwise bleak Nevada landscape.

In late February 1865 a local named "Puck" Walden murdered a Paiute Indian without provocation, a foolish act for which others would pay. In mid-March Paiutes set on revenge converged on Granite Creek Station. They took positions in the stone corral and began shooting. The station employees, A. J. Curry, Cyrus Creel, and Al Simmons, took cover in the sod house and returned fire through the rifle ports in the walls. Using the storehouse as cover, the Indians got to a blind side of the "soddy" and set fire to its roof. The defenders held out as long as they could, then two of them burst out. Curry waited too long and was trapped inside to die.

Simmons and Creel took off on foot, running in opposite directions. Creel went south across the playa toward Trego Hot Springs, and Simmons ran west toward Deep Hole Station. Simmons didn't get far before the Indians caught and shot him. His body was dragged across the rocky ground and severely mutilated. Creel was even less fortunate. Three mounted Paiutes caught him at the dry lakebed. They brought him back to the station, tied him to the ground, and burned him alive. In a rage, the Indians smashed, hacked, or burned everything in the house. Even the station's mongrel dog was killed, skinned, and staked out.

After the incident, a new wave of panic swept through the region's settlers. In response, the army established several temporary military camps along southwestern travel routes.[309]

6 April 1865
COTTONWOOD CREEK *(Paradise Valley, Nevada)*

After the killings at Granite Creek Station (see previous entry), violence spread across northwestern Nevada. On 5 April Paiutes attacked a cabin near Cottonwood Creek in the Paradise Valley. The Indians killed two settlers, Christopher Fearbourne and a Mr. Collins, by burning them alive. A Mr. Barber escaped the attack and went to neighbors for help, but by the time he returned with them, an overwhelming number of Indians had gathered at the cabin. Led by a Mr. Denio, the settlers forted up in the corral of a Mr. Hamblin. The Indians surrounded the group of about eighteen men, women, and children.

One of the settlers, Thomas Byrnes, volunteered to ride twenty miles south to Willow Point, a camping ground on the Little Humboldt River that was frequently used by military units in the area. Galloping through the Indian lines, Byrnes made it out to Willow Point, where he found Lt. Joseph Wolverton and twenty-five men of Company D, First Nevada Cavalry. Wolverton immediately rode out. At Cottonwood Creek, the Paiutes had gone but Wolverton found their trail still fresh. The tracks led north and east, to a spur of the Santa Rosa Mountains that juts out into the Paradise Valley, about twelve miles northeast of the present-day village of Paradise Valley, Nevada.

Either the Indians' ponies were in poor shape or the raiders did not expect a quick pursuit, for they did not get very far, and Wolverton caught up to them the next day. In a quick charge, Wolverton cut through the Paiute camp and killed ten warriors. The fleeing Indians hurried up Martin Creek into the mountains, but Wolverton doggedly followed. Before the day was over, his men had killed two more Indians near Martin Creek Gap, losing only one cavalry horse in the daylong affair. Wolverton returned to the burned cabin on Cottonwood Creek, where he buried Fearbourne and Collins before heading back to Willow Point.[310]

26 May 1865
FORT RICE *(Fort Rice, North Dakota)*
Col. Charles A. R. Dimon and his First U.S. Volunteers, a "Galvanized Yankee" regiment of ex-Confederate soldiers, had been garrisoned at Fort Rice since October 1864. The post, in the middle of the Lakota hunting range, was a target of many raids in 1864 and 1865. A small band of friendly Hunkpapas under young Bear Ribs camped close by the fort, but their presence did not deter the many hostile bands of Hunkpapas, Brules, Minneconjous, Sans Arcs, and Two Kettle Lakotas who roamed the area.

On 19 May a band of Indians wounded a member of a fatigue party, Pvt. John Cumby. One week later, two war parties simultaneously attacked herding and logging details near the fort's north and south walls. The raiders wounded Lt. Benjamin Wilson, who had been wounded three times in the Civil War back East. Wilson was riding out to check on the logging detail when about twenty-five Lakota warriors dashed out from a ravine and hit him with arrows in his shoulder, thigh, and chest. He fell from his horse, breaking his left hip. Eagle Woman, wife of

Site of Fort Rice, North Dakota, on the Missouri River

trader Charles E. Galpin and daughter of the Two Kettle chief Two Lance, witnessed the attack. She rushed from the fort and threw herself over Wilson as a shield. When the warriors rode up to scalp him, she scolded them harshly: "This man belongs to me now! You can not mutilate him or touch him! Be gone, every one of you!"[311]

The attackers turned away but continued their sweep, trying to cut off a small party of soldiers near the fort. Seeing this, Colonel Dimon immediately rode out with a few soldiers and some of Bear Ribs's warriors. They chased the Lakotas away, killing two of them in a running skirmish but losing one of the army's horses in the process. Wilson was taken into the fort, where post surgeon Herrick tried his best to treat the wounds. Wilson had complicated his condition by trying to extract the arrows himself, succeeding only in breaking off two of them and making it harder for the doctor to remove them.

The besieged soldiers suffered another fatality on 30 May, when a sentry was shot on duty. Meanwhile, Wilson's condition deteriorated. After a few days he died, holding Mrs. Galpin's hand. He was buried on 2 June in the post's expanding cemetery.[312]

12 June 1865
FORT DODGE *(Dodge City, Kansas)*
During the late spring of 1865, Fort Dodge was manned by elements of the Second U.S. Volunteers, known as "Galvanized Yankees," and commanded by Maj. William F. Armstrong. Garrisoning the post were Capt.

William Hayward's Company F and Capt. Thomas Maloney's Company G, along with some Eleventh Kansas Cavalry. The fort was originally little more than a collection of sod dugouts and shoddy tents overlooking a lower crossing of the Arkansas River. Armstrong kept the men busy constructing more substantial buildings, complete with cellars. Lacking any stores of grain, Armstrong had no choice but to take the fort's herd of about seventy horses and mules out daily to graze. As the weeks passed, the herders had to move the animals farther from the fort.

On 8 June, at about 3 p.m., the herders were walking the stock to water at the Arkansas River when a line of blue-uniformed riders appeared out of a ravine and rode toward them. Assuming the riders were men of Company H coming from Fort Larned, the herders continued on to the river. Suddenly the riders, who were actually Kiowas dressed in stolen uniforms, charged the loose animals and began driving them off. The herders were able to cut off about ten horses, but the Indians got the rest. Armstrong sent Maloney in pursuit, and by nightfall, the captain had recovered about twenty horses and mules.

Armstrong, vowing not to lose any more stock, doubled his pickets. But on 12 June, about 300 Kiowas crossed the Arkansas River about eight miles downstream of the fort and crept up in a thick morning fog. As the sun burned away the mists, the Indians stormed out between the stock and the post, cutting off the animals. The Galvanized Yankees put up a good defense, but they were badly outnumbered. While some of the warriors drove the stock away, others rode down the guards. They wounded three soldiers and carried off two, whose bodies were never found. The Kiowas took their plunder northwest a few miles before recrossing the Arkansas. As the fog cleared, the soldiers saw another 200 Indians watching them from across the river.[313]

Armstrong wrote to Col. James H. Ford, commander of the District of the Upper Arkansas, requesting more men, more horses, and a couple of howitzers. "Having no mounted men or transportation at present here, and rations rather short," he stated, "I think the post is in rather a dangerous situation."[314]

21 June 1865
SWEETWATER STATION *(Alcova, Wyoming)*
During the spring and summer of 1865, the overland trails through Wyoming were dangerous places. Soldiers stationed at isolated posts escorted emigrant trains and freight wagons, carried mail, and guarded

the telegraph lines. Sweetwater Station, or Sweetwater Bridge, was a sizable fort north of the Sweetwater River and south of the Emigrant Road, about twenty miles west of present-day Alcova, Wyoming. It consisted of a telegraph office, storeroom, squad room, orderly room, doctor's office, commanding officer's room, commissary, stables, sinks, sentinel box, and parade ground. Housed at Sweetwater were members of the Third U.S. Volunteers ("Galvanized Yankees") and of Company E, Eleventh Ohio Cavalry.

As the season advanced, Indian activity increased, and several stations along the same route as Sweetwater were attacked. On 26 and 30 May, Indians ran off some of Sweetwater Station's horses. During the raids, soldiers killed one warrior and wounded another. Afterward, warriors cut the telegraph line about 1,000 yards east of the station and carried off 100 yards of wire.

On 21 June, about forty or fifty Arapahos cut the wire about nine miles east of Sweetwater Station, near Horse Creek, formerly a Pony Express relay station. Perhaps thinking it was just a routine repair job, Pvt. Edgar M. Gwynn of the Eleventh Ohio, who served as the station's telegraph operator, headed out to find the break with only a ten-man escort. The Indians may have cut the line far away from the post in order to lure out a repair crew.

While the men worked, the Arapahos attacked. Gwynn caught a slug directly in his heart and died almost instantly. A warrior shot Jim Patton of Company E in the collarbone. The Arapahos, outnumbering the soldiers five-to-one, pinned the troopers down and peppered them with arrows and bullets. Nevertheless, the soldiers hung on all day, and their effective fire eventually drove the Indians off. Three troopers were killed and several were wounded; all their horses were also hit. Despite the trouble, the soldiers repaired the line, and telegraph service to Salt Lake City was restored by the next day.[315]

1 July 1865
SAN ANDREAS PASS *(Organ, New Mexico)*

Lt. James J. Billings, after being promoted from sergeant in the Second California Cavalry, was posted to Company H, First California Cavalry, at Fort Craig, along the Jornada del Muerto in New Mexico Territory. In June Capt. Lewis F. Samburn directed Billings to lead a nine-man detachment on an Indian scout. The determined second lieutenant marched from Fort Craig into the San Andres Mountains. On 1 July, near San Andreas Pass, about twenty miles north of present-day Organ, New Mexico, Billings discovered and attacked an Apache camp. Pvt. Abner H. Lull was severely wounded in the groin, and one army horse was killed, but Billings reported killing ten Indians. The patrol returned to Fort Craig after a march of nearly 600 miles.[316]

4 July 1865
MARTIN'S SETTLEMENT (Dilley, Texas)

Martin's Settlement was an isolated community of scattered ranches on Todos Santos Creek, near its junction with the Leona River, about a dozen miles northwest of present-day Dilley, Texas. Settlers in the vicinity included the Martin, English, Burleson, Williams, and Berry families.

On the morning of 4 July, 1865, Ed Burleson, Jr., was driving in some horses when two Indians appeared and came after him, coming within a few yards of catching him before he reached his house. A number of neighbors were there at his ranch, preparing to celebrate the Fourth. Instead, the men of the group hastily fetched their weapons and horses and formed a posse. Eleven joined the pursuit: Levi English, Bud English, L. A. Franks, G. W. Daugherty, W. C. Bell, Frank Williams, Dan Williams, Dean Oden, John Berry, Ed Burleson, Jr., and a man named Aikens. The eldest man present, Levi English, was named captain.

The posse trailed the Indians down the Leona River and crossed a stream near Bennet's Ranch, about four miles from Burleson's place. About ten miles farther on, near Martin's Ranch, just above the junction of the Leona and the Frio, the settlers spotted the Indians about two miles off. The posse advanced, dipping into a valley, and when they emerged they were only 200 yards away from thirty-six Comanches, mounted two to a horse. The warriors kept riding, and the impetuous settlers dashed after them, firing their weapons to no effect. After a mile, the Indians stopped, correctly figuring their pursuers had used up their shots. One warrior from each horse dismounted and charged the settlers while the mounted Indians circled to the left and right.

Captain English tried to pull his boys out of the circle, but within a minute the settlers were nearly surrounded, frantically reloading their guns. The warriors charged in at close quarters, and Dan Williams was shot from his horse. As the warriors tried to seize him, English mounted a countercharge to rescue him. Doing so, however, exhausted the posse's last loads of ammunition. The Indians charged in again. Frank Williams tried to get his brother on a horse, but Dan handed him his pistol, saying, "Take this and do the best you can. I am killed—cannot live ten minutes. Save yourself."[317]

Dean Oden was hit next, and his horse pitched him off. As he tried to remount, he was hit six more times, and the Indians fell upon him. Bud English went down with a bullet in the chest. His father tried to stay with him, but with the last of his men retreating, he had to leave his boy behind. The Indians pursued the fleeing posse in a moving fight. An arrow struck Levi English in the side, another struck Daugherty in the leg, and yet another hit Burleson in the leg. Bell took an arrow in his side and Aikens was hit in the chest. The five wounded and three unscathed settlers made it back to Burleson's Ranch, however, and the warriors gave up the chase.

The women and children waiting at the ranch, only hours before ready to celebrate the holiday, instead collapsed into mourning for the three fallen men. The next day, a party returned to recover the mutilated bodies. Dean Oden and Dan Williams, brothers-in-law, were buried in the same coffin. Later that year, Levi English moved his family to Carrizo Springs in Dimmit County.[318]

22 July 1865
HUACHUCA MOUNTAINS *(Sierra Vista, Arizona)*

After Brig. Gen. John S. Mason took command of the District of Arizona in January 1865, the army authorized increased forces to protect the settlers in the district. Among the additional troops were ten companies of the Seventh California Infantry, under Col. Charles W. Lewis; a company of First California Cavalry; and a four-company battalion of Native California Cavalry. In June Lewis moved his command from Tubac to Calabasas, later named Fort Mason, eight miles north of the Mexican border, where his men could guard the roads from Sonora to Tucson. At first, Lewis had only Companies D, E, and G, Seventh California Infantry, to protect this region. To cover more territory, he reestablished a temporary outpost at Tubac, putting Capt. Hiram A. Messenger in command. On 13 July Messenger took thirty men from Company E on a scout to the east. During the scout, Messenger split his party in half, probably to cover more ground. On 22 July in the Huachuca Mountains, the captain and his fifteen men were attacked by a large number of Apaches—the troopers estimated that there were more than 100 of them.

Although surrounded, Messenger organized a tight defense and stubbornly fought the Indians for more than an hour. At sunset, a heavy rain began to fall, and the warriors took off. Sgt. William D. Kelly and Pvt. John Henry had been killed in the fight, and Pvt. Abel Roe was wounded in the knee. Messenger's bloodied party stumbled back to Tubac on 4 August.[319]

26 July 1865
WILLOW POINT *(Willow Point, Nevada)*

Willow Point, a watered, grassy area along the Little Humboldt River, frequently served as a campground for military units. When area rancher R. H. Scott requested military protection from raiding Indians, Sgt. David Thomas and ten men from Company D, First Nevada Cavalry, joined forces with twenty-one men from Company I, Second California Cavalry, under Sgt. James F. Stephens and Corp. Charles S. Rugg, and the soldiers set up camp at Willow Point.

On 26 July, Rugg and six California troopers were helping Scott gather hay in his field, about four miles from the soldiers' camp. Suddenly, a band of about twenty-five Paiutes appeared from the Hot Springs Range to the east. Rugg raised a white flag to signal a parley, while Scott rode back to camp to rouse the rest of the force. There, Thomas rounded up eight Nevada Cavalrymen who were tending livestock; several California troopers joined him, as did five or six civilians. The ad hoc force rode east and south to try to cut off the Indians' escape route into the mountains.

With Thomas's arrival, the numbers on each opposing side became about even. Someone fired a shot and the Paiutes broke for a swampy area along the Little Humboldt. Five warriors took shelter in an empty cabin, but the soldiers torched it and shot the warriors as they ran outside. A running battle followed, covering several miles and lasting from about 2 p.m. until dark. Twenty-one Paiutes were killed, but they exacted a toll on their pursuers. Three casualties were from the Second California: Pvt. Augustus Herford was killed, and Pvts. Thomas J. Rehill and Joshua C. Murphy were wounded. Three others were civilians: Joseph Warfield was killed, and civilians named Travis and Haviland were wounded. After the fight, Stephens took the Californians north to Camp McDermit.[320]

31 July 1865
COTTONWOOD CANYON *(Carlin, Nevada)*

Troubles with the Paiutes continued throughout the summer of 1865. During that time, Lt. William B. Seamonds led a scout of twenty mounted soldiers of Company B, First Nevada Infantry, southeast of Gravelly Ford on the Humboldt River. On 25 July, after replenishing supplies at Camp Ruby, Seamonds, with only fifteen mounted men and an Indian guide, headed out to scout north of the Humboldt.

At a site recorded as Cottonwood Canyon, Seamonds came upon Chief Zeluawick and his band on 31 July. In the ensuing fight, the Nevadans killed Zeluawick and eleven of his warriors. Among the soldiers, Sgt. Edwin D. Sherrill was seriously wounded in the neck by a barbed arrow, but he survived.[321]

1 September 1865
SAWYERS'S WAGON TRAIN *(Ranchester, Wyoming)*

In the summer of 1865, James Sawyers led a road-building and freighting expedition, consisting of fifty-five wagons, across present-day Wyoming. Leaving from the mouth of the Niobrara River in Nebraska, the party was headed to Virginia City, Montana. The expedition remained unmolested until mid-August, when they faced a run-in with Lakotas and Cheyennes at Bone Pile Creek, near today's Gillette, Wyoming. After the fight, Sawyers turned the train south to Fort Connor, where he picked up a company of Sixth Michigan Cavalrymen to assist his original escort, a company of First Dakota Cavalry. The expedition then continued north along the base of the Bighorn Mountains.

As the train approached the Tongue River on 31 August, Capt. Osmer F. Cole of the Sixth Michigan, riding ahead, was caught and killed by a party of Arapahos. The following morning, while the wagons were fording the river, Arapahos attacked the cattle herd at the rear of the train and captured several animals. The long train was caught strung out along the valley, and the Indians began shooting at it. Sawyers corralled the train while the soldiers pulled out a howitzer to shell the Arapahos. The artillery fire killed war leader Heavy Horn and dispersed the rest of the attackers.

With the warriors seemingly gone, the train moved north to the bluffs, where they discovered more Indians, who began firing from the shelter of the hills. Sawyers headed the wagons back toward the river and followed it east, only to face more Arapaho fire along the riverbank. He turned the train around again and headed back upstream. The wagons corralled a second time, but they were still too near the bluffs. Concealed Indians fired into the circle, mortally wounding teamster James Dilleland and emigrant E. G. Merrill. Still under fire, Sawyers moved the wagons north again, away from the river.

Late in the afternoon, the Arapahos came in under a flag of truce. The Indians declared that they believed they were firing at Gen. Patrick E. Connor's men, who had attacked their camp a few days earlier. Sawyers, meanwhile, hoped his messengers would soon reach Connor and bring back reinforcements. While they waited, the expedition members buried Cole, Dilleland, and Merrill inside the corral.

Sawyers was trapped in place for nearly two weeks, averting further bloodshed but unable to proceed. A near-mutiny by his disgruntled employees forced him to turn back on 13 September. That very evening, reinforcements from the Second California Cavalry under Capt. Albert E. Brown arrived. The weary men of the train, many of them disgusted with Sawyers's handling of the expedition, nevertheless made another about-face and continued their long-delayed trek to Montana.[323]

3 September 1865
TABLE MOUNTAIN *(Unionville, Nevada)*

The mixed Bannock-Paiute chief Mogoannoga was a major instigator in the Paiute War of 1860, which began when his band killed five white men at Williams Station in western Nevada. Mogoannoga escaped punishment for his part in the conflict, and in subsequent years he showed quite a turnabout. In April 1865 Mogoannoga, now known to the whites as Captain Soo, forged an agreement to cooperate with the military. According to its terms, part of the Paiute Nation would move from the Humboldt River to the Carson River, out of the path of military scouting operations. Few Indians, however, actually received word of the plan, which in effect declared open season on all Indians outside the Carson River drainage.

Troops operated out of Camp Dun Glen, in the mountains about ten miles northeast of present-day Mill City, Nevada. The camp was the headquarters and central supply depot for operations in the Humboldt, Quinn, and Owyhee River drainages. In August, responding to a request by an area rancher named Stafford, Lt. Henry C. Penwell took twenty soldiers from Company B, Second California Cavalry, from Dun Glen and rode southwest to Unionville. Stafford met him there with three more Indian guides and directed the party to a rancheria at the foot of Table Mountain, about thirty-five miles east of town. The camp reportedly contained renegade raiders led by the Paiutes known as Black Rock Tom and Buffalo Jim.

Penwell's party found the camp and attacked at dawn on 3 September, but it turned out to be overkill. The Indian camp contained only seven men and three women. The company dispatched the warriors quickly; the three women were also killed, reportedly by accident. Penwell had his men destroy "a large quantity" of ammunition and supplies, then the detachment returned to Dun Glen.[322]

13 September 1865
WILLOW CREEK *(Orovada, Nevada)*

A band of renegades from various tribes, led by the Paiute chief Black Rock Tom, had been raiding in the area for months when Capt. Robert Payne and soldiers from Company E, First Nevada Cavalry, went on a scout in the Quinn River valley, in present-day Humboldt County. Payne located an Indian camp on Willow Creek, which flows west out of the Santa Rosa Mountains to the Quinn River. In the predawn darkness, Payne crept up to one side of the camp with nine soldiers, while Lt. John Littlefield took another nine men to the other side.

With just enough daylight to see, Payne attacked. Most of the surprised Indians scattered, but enough others remained to put up a spirited resistance. One mounted warrior charged at Littlefield, trying to lance him where he stood. Littlefield held his ground and waited until the warrior was only a few yards away before shooting him from his horse.

The surprise attack turned into a three-hour running fight, with the Indians getting the worst of it. Only one trooper was wounded, while Payne reported killing thirty-one Indians. Payne would later put his knowledge of northern Nevada to dubious use, when he mustered out of military service and turned his attention to cattle rustling.[324]

17 September 1865
MIMBRES MOUNTAINS *(Kingston, New Mexico)*

The First Battalion of California Veteran Infantry was formed in December 1864 by consolidating the First California Infantry and the Fifth California Infantry. Commanded by Lt. Col. Edwin A. Rigg, the battalion's seven companies were scattered about various posts in New Mexico Territory. From February 1865 to February 1866, Company D was posted to Fort McRae, on the Rio Grande. In September 1865 Apaches raided the fort's stock, running off a number of horses. Lt. John Slater, with ten mounted men and twenty foot soldiers, left the post on 12 September in pursuit of the thieves.

The Indians' trail crossed the Rio Grande and headed into the mountains to the west. Slater followed the tracks along the length of the Black

Range and through the Mimbres Mountains. On 17 September the soldiers overtook the Apaches in a mountain canyon, but the Indians were not willing to give up their horses without a fight. The warriors were armed exclusively with rifles and pistols, and during a hot exchange, Slater and two privates, John Kelly and Richard B. Mason, were severely wounded. Nevertheless, Slater emerged the winner. He reported that he and his men killed several Apaches and wounded many others. In addition, they recovered most of the stolen stock and captured many Indian ponies and mules to boot. The troopers returned to Fort McRae on 20 September, after a march of 275 miles.[325]

5 November 1865
MESCAL CANYON *(Chiricahua, Arizona)*

With the approach of winter, Apache chief Cochise traveled to Fort Bowie in October 1865 to discuss peace. The commander there, Maj. James Gorman, First California Cavalry, was in the process of strengthening the post and making war plans. Cochise's arrival left him in a quandary; in Gorman's judgment, it was in the army's best interest to keep fighting. Gorman told Cochise that only his superior, Brig. Gen. John S. Mason, had the authority to make peace. He instructed the chief to leave the area and wait twelve days until Mason had given him an answer.

On 1 November, without instructions from the general, Gorman departed Fort Bowie with Lt. Alfred W. Norton and thirty-four men of Company L, First California Cavalry, to look for Cochise's camp. With most of the men hidden in two large wood wagons, the expedition headed south toward the pinery. Scout Merejildo Grijalva led the company by night along the west face of the Chiricahua Mountains, and the men hid during the day. Finding tracks near Turkey Creek, they headed southwest into the mountains.

On 4 November, Grijalva found the rancheria in what was then called Mescal Canyon, likely a part of today's Rucker Canyon. Gorman left eight men with the horses and took the rest on foot. Slipping past a sentinel, they had nearly entered the sleeping camp before an alarm was raised. The soldiers raced to catch the Apaches before they could flee into the cliffs. The soldiers halted at the canyon walls, targeting the Indians clambering up the rocks, killing seven and sustaining only one of their own wounded. Gorman confiscated a great quantity of supplies, equipment, horses, and cattle. Gorman learned of a second rancheria only half a mile away, but, he said, "the Birds had flown, leaving everything behind them."[326]

Gorman claimed to be the first man ever to surprise Cochise in one of his camps, but the achievement was tainted by the fact that Gorman had led the great chief to believe he was under a truce.[327]

17 November 1865
LEONARD CREEK *(Humboldt County, Nevada)*

The army's summer-long hunt for Paiute, Bannock, and Shoshone renegades in Nevada continued into the fall. Black Rock Tom's band, the focus of several expeditions, was thought to be camped near Paiute Creek, which flowed east from the Black Rock Range to the Quinn River. Lt. Henry C. Penwell left Camp Dun Glen, near present-day Mill City, Nevada, with twenty-six troopers of Company B, Second California Cavalry, and headed north. As he had done earlier that year, the Paiute-Bannock chief Captain Soo guided Penwell's party (see Table Mountain, 3 September 1865).

Soo's expertise, so helpful to Penwell before, failed him this time. Unseen eyes were watching the soldiers as they trailed up Paiute Creek into the mountains. On 9 November, Penwell's force reached a point where the canyon narrowed and the rock walls were steep. Suddenly the Indians attacked, pouring down a heavy fire on the surprised soldiers. With bullets seeming to come from every direction and the assailants almost invisible, Penwell ordered a withdrawal. The troopers retreated seven miles into the Black Rock Desert to regroup and camp for the night. In the morning, knowing he faced a large, alert, and well-armed force, Penwell returned to Camp Dun Glen for reinforcements.

On 13 November Lt. Richard A. Osmer, Company H, Second California Cavalry, led sixty men of Company B and a mountain howitzer back to the scene. Four troopers deserted on the way, but seven enlisted men on detached service, two civilians, and Captain Soo with ten Paiute warriors joined Osmer at Willow Creek. The Indians' trail led to the southern face of the Pine Forest Range, about twenty miles northeast of the site of Penwell's encounter. Captain Soo reportedly saw the smoke of Black Rock Tom's camp from nine miles away.

On the morning of 17 September, Osmer was within two miles of the camp when the troops were discovered. He yelled, "Come on, boys!" and the entire force charged forward for two miles and barreled into the camp. The Indians scattered, but the soldiers chased them into the rocks and ravines, killing a great many. Osmer placed the number of Indian mortalities at 120, of which 80 were warriors. Another report stated, more realistically, that 55 Indians were killed. In either case, it was probably the largest battle loss for the Indians in all the years of fighting in Nevada. Of Osmer's force, only Pvt. David W. O'Connell was killed, and two enlisted men were wounded.

Among the Indians killed were a substantial number of women and children. An army report later indicated that it had been very difficult to distinguish between males and females during the battle. The report further stated that unrestrained Paiute allies had committed most of the slaughter. The two civilians accompanying Osmer, however, were responsible for killing some of the noncombatants. After two soldiers captured a wounded woman and her child, they turned the captives over to the civilians. Moments after the soldiers left, the pair shot both captives.

After the fight, Osmer's men recovered plunder from the camp, including supplies from the wagon of a Mr. Bellew, who had been attacked near Willow Creek earlier in the month. The friendly Indians were given five captured horses and all the guns, ammunition, and supplies they could pack out. Whatever was left was burned. Osmer's troops returned to Dun Glen on 20 November, having marched 250 miles.

After all the time the army spent chasing Black Rock Tom, he finally surrendered to Captain Soo, who turned him over to Nevada authorities in late November 1865. They sentenced him to hang at Fort Churchill. Soldiers from Company K, Second California Cavalry, took custody of Tom on 21 December. Four days later, on the march to the fort, he was killed while attempting to escape.[328]

— 1866 —

12 January 1866
BATTLE CREEK *(Humboldt County, Nevada)*

After Black Rock Tom's defeat at Leonard Creek in November 1865 (see previous entry), the surviving Paiutes, Bannocks, and Shoshones moved farther north and joined with Captain John and his discontented Warner Lake Shoshones in northern Nevada. Captain John was thought to have ambushed and killed Lt. Col. Charles McDermit in August 1865. The Second California Cavalry were kept busy searching for Captain John and his group.

On 8 January 1866, Capt. George D. Conrad took thirty-seven men of Company B out from Camp Dun Glen on a scout. With them rode nine civilian volunteers and twelve friendly Paiutes under Captain Soo.

They traveled north to Cane Springs, at the north edge of Bloody Run Hills near present-day Amos, Nevada. Here Lt. Robert L. Duncan and twenty-five men of Company I joined Conrad, and the combined force headed west into the Quinn River valley. A heavy snow fell, which concealed the troops' movements but made the going miserable.

As the expedition members ascended each succeeding mountain range, they scoured the horizon for signs of smoke from campfires. On 11 January, from a hilltop near the Quinn River, they spotted smoke across the Black Rock Desert, perhaps a dozen miles southwest of the site of the Leonard Creek fight. The men prepared to move out by 11:30 p.m., having about twenty miles of desert to cross before dawn.

Despite the snow, fog, and darkness, the long, single-file column moved across the desert rapidly. By 3 a.m. they were as close to the Indian camp as they dared to move without revealing their position. To keep his men from freezing, Conrad had them dismount and run in circles for the few hours remaining before dawn. This extraordinary effort undoubtedly saved some men from frostbite and even death, though twenty soldiers still suffered frozen hands, feet, and faces.

When the eastern horizon finally turned gray, Conrad had the soldiers rest for a while before creeping closer to Captain John's camp. Duncan took Company I to the right flank while Sgt. Louis Korble took a detachment from Company B to the left flank and Conrad advanced in the center with the rest of the soldiers, the civilians, and the Indian scouts. The camp lay in a three-mile-wide basin in the foothills of the Black Rock Range, along a cattail-lined stream that would later be called Battle Creek. Numerous gullies and tall grasses provided excellent cover.

Despite all the soldiers' preparations, the Indians discovered them about a mile from the camp. Conrad charged, but the Indians had time to grab weapons and break off in defensive clusters along the creek banks. Conrad's surround was almost perfect, however, and he advanced in a tightening circle. Korble's men fired first, which distracted the Indians and allowed Conrad and Duncan to get in close. The trapped and outnumbered Indians fought with great desperation, and the fight lasted nearly three hours. Captain John himself fought to the end, making no attempt to escape. A volunteer named Rapley finally felled him with a bullet to the head.

After the fight, thirty-five Indian bodies were found in the camp, including those of two women. Three badly wounded warriors crawled

off into the gullies to die. Indian sources later said that only one warrior survived the fight and escaped. Conrad gave provisions to the
survivors—all women—and set them free. The army suffered no fatalities. Corporal Biswell and Private Allen of Company I and Privates
Duffield, Riley, and Schultz of Company B were wounded. One of the
Paiute scouts, Jim Dunne, was wounded in the back by an arrow. Conrad
and his men returned to Camp Dun Glen on 15 January, after a march
of 220 miles.[329]

17 January 1866
OAK GROVE *(Deming, New Mexico)*

From April 1865 to July 1866, Company G, First Battalion of California
Veteran Infantry, had the bad luck to be assigned to Fort Cummings, one
of the most dangerous posts in New Mexico Territory. It was even worse
luck for the six men who were out cutting wood on 17 January. The wood
detail, led by Sgt. Louis Weber, was camped at Oak Grove, in Cooke's
Range, about four and a half miles northwest of Fort Cummings. Four of
the privates, Thomas Daley, Charles Devine, Louis Hunter, and Thomas
Ronan, were close friends. They had enlisted together in Company G, Fifth
California Infantry, in October 1861, had served together for four years,
and had all volunteered for additional duty with the First Battalion.

On 16 January, Weber left the camp to get supplies at the fort. The
next morning, about forty Chiricahuas attacked the wood camp, almost
immediately killing Daley, Devine, Hunter, and Ronan. The four friends
who had been together for so long now died together at the hands of
Apaches.

Nathaniel B. Goldsberry was hit next, taking an arrow in the hip,
and he went down. The Indians would have killed him but for John
Matthews, who had once tried to desert the army but now rose to the
occasion. Matthews grabbed his weapon and fought like a demon, keeping the Apaches back and pulling Goldsberry to safety. The forty warriors
should have been able to overwhelm the lone soldier, but perhaps they
admired Matthews's courage and let him go.

The two men walked back to Fort Cummings with word of the attack,
and a relief party hurried to the scene, but the Indians were gone. Evidence indicated that one Indian had been killed and at least one other
wounded. The four dead privates had been stripped naked and mutilated.
A general order issued at Fort Cummings the same day said: "The troops
of this post will be paraded tomorrow at 8 p.m. to attend upon the last

sad rites of Privates Daley, Devine, Hunter, and Ronan." The four friends were buried together in a single grave on Cemetery Hill, about half a mile southeast of the fort. In 1892 the bodies of all soldiers buried on the hill were exhumed and reburied at Fort Leavenworth, Kansas.[330]

21 January 1866
COTTONWOOD SPRINGS *(Fort Grant, Arizona)*

The original Second California Infantry was mustered out in October 1865, but a number of veterans as well as new recruits were organized into a new regiment, with Thomas F. Wright as colonel. Camp Grant and Camp San Pedro, which were essentially two halves of the same post on opposite sides of the junction of Aravaipa Creek and the San Pedro River, were declared regimental headquarters. Companies B, C, E, G, and I spent time there in the fall of 1865 and winter of 1866.

During a scout in January 1866, Wright and Company C crossed paths with a band of Apaches near Cottonwood Springs (Cedar Springs), about thirty miles east of the forts and sixteen miles northwest of present-day Fort Grant. Wright's Californians killed thirteen Indians and captured six. This would be one of the only fights the new Second California Infantry had before its final mustering out in the spring of 1866.[331]

15 February 1866
GUANO VALLEY *(Washoe County, Nevada)*

The last battle of the Nevada Indian war that began in March 1865 (see Granite Creek Station, ca. 15 March 1865) took place in the most remote area of the region. In the late winter of 1866, bands of Paiutes, Shoshones, and Bannocks raided into Surprise Valley, California, stealing livestock and other property. Several columns of cavalry combed the area looking for the culprits. A nineteen-man detachment of Company F, Second California Cavalry, under Capt. Augustus W. Starr marched east from Fort Crook, California, and joined thirty-two men under Lt. George H. Robinson of Company D, Second California, out of Camp Smoke Creek, Nevada. The combined force comprised about fifty-three soldiers and thirty civilians under the command of Maj. Samuel P. Smith.

Heading northeast from Camp Smoke Creek, Smith marched for five days before discovering the raiders' camp in the valley below the high Guano Rim, just south of today's Oregon-Nevada border and about eighty miles east of Fort Bidwell, California. Smith attacked at 9:30 a.m., killing leader Smoke Creek Jim in the initial charge. The troops captured

Guano Valley, Nevada

nineteen women and children, while the remaining Indians fled up Rock Canyon. Smith's men followed the Indians into the rocks, killing many as they went. Isolated groups of warriors fought tenaciously, but without a leader they could not marshal an organized resistance.

The battle lasted six hours. Fifteen women and children were inadvertently killed in the fight, along with eighty-one warriors. About fifteen wounded warriors escaped. Smith himself was wounded during the fight, as were Pvts. Edward Resler, Henrich Ruhmann, and Frank Belto of Company D, and Pvts. Alexander Mills and Charles H. Smith of Company F. Pvt. Charles Austin of Company D was killed.

The next morning, the captured women and children were given provisions and allowed to leave. Major Smith recovered about seventy-five horses stolen from Surprise Valley settlers. He ordered the thirty-five Indian wickiups to be burned, along with equipage and supplies, including about three tons of dried beef. The battle was the final large-scale encounter between Civil War volunteers and Indians in Nevada.[332]

23 February 1866
DRY CREEK *(Malheur County, Oregon)*

The three battalions of the Fourteenth Infantry were among the first troops to arrive in the West following the Civil War, in late 1865. The

Second Battalion went to the Department of the Columbia, and by the winter of 1866, some of its companies were posted to the interior, including two companies under Capt. John H. Walker, who were stationed at Fort Boise. Prior to Walker's arrival in the area, several Indian depredations had occurred, part of the ongoing Snake War (see Three Island Crossing, 13 and 16 September 1864). A man was killed at the mouth of the Oywhee River, horses were stolen from Boise Ferry, and pack mules were stolen from Camp Alvord in Oregon.

Shortly after another incident, on 13 February, in which Indians killed a settler and stole fifty horses from his ranch near Ruby City, Walker and Lt. Thomas F. Tobey organized a scout. The party comprised thirty-nine men, including fifteen soldiers from Companies C and D, Fourteenth Infantry, and twelve men of the First Oregon Cavalry. Crossing the Snake River, the soldiers traveled up the Owyhee into Oregon.

On 23 February Walker trapped twenty-one "Snakes" (a generic term for any of several bands) in a steep canyon near Dry Creek.[333] The canyon made a clean getaway difficult, and the Indians could not flee without losing their plunder. They fought until nightfall ended the action. Eighteen Indians were killed, and three, including two wounded, escaped. One infantryman was killed and one was wounded.[334]

11 March 1866
BLACK HILLS *(Camp Verde, Arizona)*
Capt. Hiram S. Washburn commanded Camp Lincoln, at the junction of Clear Creek and the Verde River, garrisoned by Companies A and E of the Arizona Volunteers. He ran the post on a shoestring, sending out makeshift scouts with limited means, yet he won some minor victories. Supplies were scarce, and Washburn spent much of March and April 1866 trying to procure provisions and equipment from Fort Whipple, near Prescott.

On 11 April Washburn led twenty-seven men of Company E on a supply run to Fort Whipple. He decided to try a seldom-used route to the north of the usual one, hoping it would prove easier for getting wagons over the Black Hills and through the Verde Valley. At noon, a half day's march from Camp Lincoln, Washburn inadvertently discovered an Apache rancheria. While the element of surprise was mutual, Washburn's soldiers killed six Indians and took one prisoner. In addition to his serendipitous victory, Washburn was right about the route being better for wagons.[335]

22 March 1866
COTTONWOOD SPRINGS *(Oracle Junction, Arizona)*

Capt. James F. Millar, Fourteenth Infantry, led a seven-man detachment to escort Dr. Benjamin Tappan, assistant surgeon of volunteers, as the latter changed posts from Fort Yuma, California, to Camp Grant (old Fort Breckinridge), near the junction of Aravaipa Creek and the San Pedro River. The escort was entirely inadequate for the dangerous route they were to travel. Millar tried to allay the others' fears by declaring that no Indians lurked in the area. The party left Yuma on 7 March, and the next day the men were only twelve miles from their destination when Apaches ambushed them west of Cottonwood Springs, near the south end of the Tortilla Mountains. Millar, who had asserted so confidently that the route was safe, was one of the first men killed. He and Privates Richards, Powell, and Donnell were left dead on the field as the others fled. The bodies were mutilated soon afterward. Dr. Tappan was wounded twice in the torso and once in the foot, but he and the other four escaped.

The survivors wandered through the sun-parched hills and arroyos for more than two weeks. On 24 March Tappan gave his derringer to Cpl. John Berg, Company F, and sent him and teamster Stevens Sumner ahead to look for water. They found none, and upon returning could not find the other three men. They continued searching for water but came up dry. The two were saved when some men of the First California Cavalry happened by.

One of the Californians hurried to Tucson with news of the attack, and Maj. John S. Mason ordered all available troops from Tucson and Camp Grant to search for the missing men. Meanwhile Tappan, believing his own death to be imminent, told his two companions to leave him behind. The pair staggered south toward Tucson, and searchers found them en route, close to death.

The twenty-man search party from Tucson, under Capt. Jonathan B. Hager, Fourteenth Infantry, rode to Cottonwood Springs and found a party from Camp Grant already encamped there. Taking some men from that command, Hager moved west, where he found and buried the bodies of Millar and the three privates. Riding toward Picacho Peak, Hager discovered what appeared to be Tappan's trail—the surgeon had apparently removed the boot from his wounded foot. Hager rode almost thirty miles to Picacho Peak, nearly succumbing to heat and thirst, before giving up.

The searchers returned to their bases on 31 March. Years later, a human skeleton, thought to be Tappan's, was found in Canyon del Oro, in the Santa Catalina Mountains north of Tucson.[336]

25 March 1866
SALT RIVER *(Central Arizona)*

After the Civil War, the Arizona Volunteers were formed to replace the California Volunteers, who were heading home. It never became a full regiment, but it always had at least five companies. In January 1866 Companies A and E, under Capt. Hiram S. Washburn, moved to Camp Lincoln (later called Camp Verde). From there Washburn sent out a number of expeditions to "chastise" the Apaches.

On 20 March Lt. Primitivo Cervantes led twenty-six men of Company A on a scout toward the Salt River. Although lacking adequate supplies, weapons, and guides, Cervantes quickly found and attacked an Apache rancheria. Sustaining no losses of its own, Company A was officially given credit for killing twenty-two Indians, wounding seven, and taking two prisoners.[337]

Ca. 29 April 1866
ESCONDIDO SPRINGS *(Bakersfield, Texas)*

Following four years of interrupted mail and freight service in Texas during the Civil War, in 1866 Bethel Coopwood opened a new freight line from San Antonio to El Paso and Chihuahua. Coopwood's trains included pack mules and ambulances with space for passengers. With the first train, which departed 24 April, was an escort of forty mounted men under Capt. Theodore A. Wilson, and passenger James Magoffin, ex-consul to Mexico.

The large escort kept unfriendly Indians away until the train passed Fort Lancaster and crossed the Pecos River. Near the abandoned station at Escondido Springs, Mescalero chiefs Espejo and Jose Cigarito lay in wait with their many warriors. When the Indians started firing, Wilson led the caravan up a hill and placed a skirmish line around the coach, mules, and supply wagon. According to guard Robert M. Keating, the amount of fire from the riders' repeating carbines caused the Indians to fall back in confusion.

From a sheltered spot, Chief Espejo waved a white flag, but his call for a parley was answered by more fire, as the expressmen figured it was a ruse. Neither side was going to give up easily. The siege lasted two days.

Finally, the Mescaleros realized they could not drive the determined men out and rode away. The train reached El Paso on 6 May.[338]

18 May 1866
LITTLE CHEYENNE CREEK *(Jamestown, Kansas)*

By 1866 beaver trapper Lew Cassil could have been considered an anachronism. Around thirty years old, the big, rough-hewn man had ridden from Minnesota to Kansas on his black horse, Raven, and toting his blanket roll, long rifle, and beaver traps. By this time, buffalo hides were more lucrative than beaver pelts, but Cassil still worked the icy winter creeks of the middle West, making his living trapping and hunting. Over the years, he had a number of run-ins with Otoes and Cheyennes, whom he accused of tampering with his traps and stealing his catch.

In the spring of 1866, with beaver season over, Cassil joined a group of Kansas settlers for a buffalo hunt. The party—which included Walter Haynes, a Mr. Roberts, a Mr. Tallman, and two sons of William Collins—headed for Brown's Creek in Jewell County. They had reached the headwaters of Buffalo Creek when they were attacked by a band of Cheyennes. Though a few of them were wounded, the hunters were able to fight their way out and find a defensive spot near Buffalo Creek. The accuracy of the buffalo guns kept the Indians at a good distance, but the hunters were outnumbered, and reloading the weapons took time.

While the defenders made their stand, both sides took casualties. The hunters took off in a desperate running fight, trending east and south until they reached a grove of trees along Little Cheyenne Creek, just east of the Cloud County line. But the Cheyennes got ahead of them and set up an ambush. All six hunters were shot down in the grove. Several days later, a party under a Captain Brooks found their remains, scalped and horribly mutilated. Cassil still held an empty revolver. The Indians took only the horses, leaving the wagon and supplies, possibly indicating that they had suffered considerable losses themselves. Brooks transported the bodies to Clifton, in Washington County, where they were buried.[339]

27–28 May 1866
THREE FORKS *(Malheur County, Oregon)*

Miners moving into the Silver City and Boise regions of Idaho Territory in the 1860s caused an already volatile situation with the local Indians to flare up into what became known as the "Snake War," an ongoing conflict that began in the spring of 1864 (see also Three Island Crossing, 13 and 16 September 1864). Several small posts were built in the affected area. One of them, Camp Lyon, was established in June 1865 by Lt. Charles Hobart, First Oregon Cavalry, on Cow Creek, on the present-day Oregon-Idaho line, about twenty miles northwest of the Silver City mining district. Military forays out of Camp Lyon pursued many Indians but caught few.

Miners who organized Indian hunts also had little success. Their complaints forced Gen. Frederick Steele to send Maj. Louis H. Marshall, Fourteenth Infantry, in March 1866 to take command of the newly organized District of Boise and secure the area. On 11 May Marshall personally took charge of an expedition to find and punish the Snake Indians. He moved from Fort Boise to Camp Lyon with eighty-four men, including parts of Companies A and C, Second Battalion, Fourteenth Infantry, and Oregon Cavalrymen under Lt. Silas Pepoon. They marched down the Jordan River to the Owyhee, then going upriver, they circled back into Idaho Territory.

On 19 May Indians on lower Jordan Creek in Oregon wiped out two parties of Chinese miners on their way from California to Idaho, killing forty-nine out of fifty.[340] Marshall, not in the area at the time of the massacre, continued marching up the Owyhee River. At the Three Forks of the Owyhee, in a remote area of present-day Malheur County, Oregon, Marshall found more than he bargained for. Nearly 250 warriors were well positioned across the river, along the east bank.

The two sides blasted away at each other for almost four hours. The Indians were well armed with guns and ammunition, some of which may have been stolen from the murdered Chinese. Although outnumbered, the soldiers killed seven Indians and wounded twelve others. A chief, dressed in red and riding a white horse, pranced up and down the riverbank with impunity until Marshall directed his men to fire a volley at him. When the chief tumbled off his horse onto his head, the soldiers heard a great lamenting howl.

Marshall fired five howitzer shells into the wickiups beyond the bluffs, but to what effect he could not tell. Finally, he moved his men downstream to try to raft across the river and flank the Indians. The soldiers had just reached the east bank and climbed to a pass in the bluffs when the Indians attacked, killing a noncommissioned officer.

The soldiers went back to the raft and tried to return to the other shore, but the raft capsized and the howitzer sank to the bottom.

The Indians roped an Oregon cavalryman named Phillips and pulled him up the bluffs. Pepoon volunteered to take a detail to attempt a rescue, but Marshall denied his request, angering the other Oregonians. The men became even more incensed when Marshall abandoned four soldiers who had gotten trapped on the opposite bank when the raft sank.

Sorely pressed and depleted of ammunition, Marshall pulled out and marched back to Camp Lyon, arriving on 2 June. When General Steele visited Camp Lyon in September, he determined that conditions required a change of command. Lt. Col. George Crook, Twenty-third Infantry, was called in to take over in December.[341]

2–7 July 1866
JENNING'S FIGHT *(Silver City, Idaho)*

By the summer of 1866, miners had been in the Owyhee Mountains of southwestern Idaho for several years, but they had never been able to come to peaceful terms with the surrounding Shoshone, Bannock, and Paiute tribes, collectively known as Snakes. Even military expeditions into the area were less than successful. The miners periodically tried to take matters into their own hands by organizing Indian-hunting expeditions.

In June 1866 miners from the Owyhee District organized a company of about forty men under Capt. J. Jennings, who had gained some military experience in the Civil War. On 2 July on Boulder Creek, only about a dozen miles south of Silver City, Jennings and his company encountered an Indian band. The miners found their adversaries tougher than they expected. When Jenning's men attacked, they soon found themselves outnumbered and surrounded. As the miners formed up in a defensive position and dug entrenchments, a messenger rode to nearby Camp Lyon to request help.

Fighting from pits and rock breastworks, Jenning's men held the Indians off all that day and into the next. Thomas B. Cason, in an individual stone fortification, was reported to have shot fifteen Indians before he was killed. Surprisingly, no other miners were killed, and only two were wounded, Aaron Winters and Charles Webster. When assistance from the Fourteenth Infantry arrived on 7 July, the Indians pulled away. The miners reported killing thirty-five warriors, but that number is certainly exaggerated.[342]

7 July 1866
BARILLA SPRINGS *(Balmorhea, Texas)*

On 1 July 1866 conductor Tom Davis led one of Bethel Coopwood's east-bound stages out from El Paso with four passengers. Davis was relatively inexperienced in west Texas and was aided by only two Mexican guides—it was a recipe for trouble. Davis passed Fort Davis safely, but on 7 July, on his way down Limpia Canyon, he saw a white flag wave and foolishly stopped. It was Mescalero leader Espejo with about 100 warriors.

It took only a few seconds for Davis to realize his mistake. Bullets started flying, and Davis whipped his mules forward in a race to the next station, Barilla Springs. He knew the station was abandoned, but its walls offered defensive cover. If he and his companions could reach it, they might stand a chance. The bouncing stage careened for miles across the prairie. The coach had just reached the station when its pole snapped, bringing the outfit to a jolting halt. The men scrambled for the station just as the Indians galloped up the hill behind them. The defenders' fire was enough to drive the Indians away from the building, but not to end the battle. For the next twelve hours, the station remained under siege, during which time all the mules were killed or stolen and Davis was shot in the leg. When the sun went down, the fighting slackened.

With his mules gone and with no way to repair the coach, Davis told the rest of the party to slip away and make for Fort Stockton. He himself would stay behind and continue firing as a distraction. When it was completely dark, the others left Davis behind. The six walked to Comanche Springs, where Robert Keating, driving the westbound stage, found them and took them east to safety.

Keating and his companions continued their journey, expecting to have to fight their way through to Fort Davis. When they warily approached Barilla Springs Station, they found the Indians gone. Presumably, the Apaches discovered sometime during the night that only one man opposed them. Keating described what he found of Davis: "He had shot himself as the Indians were coming to scalp him. We found the top of his head and part of his body and buried it."[343]

The coach had been destroyed but the mail, surprisingly, was left intact. Keating retrieved the mail and transferred it to another east-bound stage. After the incident, Bethel Coopwood doubled the guards on his stages and hoped for the best.[344]

18 July 1866
RATTLESNAKE CREEK *(Harney, Oregon)*

During the Snake War of 1864 to 1868, numerous military scouts operated out of several posts in eastern Oregon and western Idaho. After arriving in California from the East in late 1865, elements of the First Cavalry operated out of Camp Watson, in Wheeler County, Oregon. Lt. Reuben F. Bernard was sent out on 4 July with forty-five men of Company I to pursue and "punish" the Indians who were hiding out in the wilds of south-central Oregon.

For two weeks, Bernard marched all through the region. In mid-July the expedition camped on the Malheur River in the vicinity of present-day Drewsey, Oregon. After returning from a scout of his own, on 18 July Bernard sent Sgt. Thomas W. Connor and nineteen troopers to scout to the south and west. That very morning Connor encountered a large camp of about 300 Paiutes under Chief Te-oh-ah, near the divide of the Malheur River and Harney Lake Valley, by the headwaters of Rattlesnake Creek.[345]

About eighty warriors protected the camp, but Connor barreled into them and drove them into the hills, killing thirteen, wounding many, and capturing four horses and mules. Only one soldier, Cpl. William B. Lord, was killed. After Connor returned to the Malheur camp and reported the incident to Bernard, the lieutenant saddled up the whole command and returned to the battle site. The soldiers were now accompanied by forty-seven civilians from the Powder River settlements, who were searching for the same Indians.

Bernard left the civilians to destroy the abandoned camp and continued hunting for the Paiutes. He found them only a mile from where Connor had fought them, fortified in a deep canyon. The Indians saw Bernard approaching and fled. He chased them west to the Silvies River, but he succeeded only in capturing two women and two children.

The cavalrymen marched back to Camp Watson, concluding a scout that had lasted twenty-six days and covered about 630 miles. The official report noted that the operation "furnishes an example well worthy of imitation." On 28 July Bernard received a captaincy.[346]

24 July 1866
FLOYD'S WAGON TRAIN *(Orpha, Wyoming)*

Eight solid days of raiding up and down the Bozeman Trail began on 17 July, with attacks on emigrant wagon trains in a number of locations. The most severe of these, in terms of casualties, occurred on 24 July.

Nathan Floyd, an Irishman who had arrived in Montana Territory in 1863 from the Colorado mines, set out for Fort Leavenworth, Kansas, in 1866 to buy merchandise to bring back to Virginia City. His train of about thirty-six wagons was between Brown Springs Creek and the Dry Fork of the Cheyenne River when the Indians struck.

Floyd was riding ahead of the wagons, looking for the next water source, when he was surprised and killed. Hearing the shooting, thirteen men, some armed with Spencer rifles, rushed ahead to help, but they ran into a hornet's nest. Indians surrounded them, and in a few minutes eight more of the men were dead or dying. The remaining five, two of them wounded, managed to escape. The wagons corralled for two days before going on.

The victims' bodies were later found and buried. Floyd had been beheaded. Charles Barton, nicknamed "Blowhard," had twenty arrows in him, a knife stuck in his side, and his whiskers scalped from his chin. The body of eighteen-year-old Zach Husted, like Barton's, was severely mangled. Also killed were William H. Dearborn, Hiram H. Campbell, John Little, Stephen Carson, William Bothwell, and John Sloss. Succeeding emigrants passing the site saw the graves and the dried blood and took it as an ominous sign. George W. Fox, who traveled by on 29 July, remarked, "This begins to make things look 'skaly.'"[347]

29 July 1866
CAMP CADY *(Harvard, California)*
Lt. James R. Hardenbergh, Ninth Infantry, was posted in the barren desert at Camp Cady, named for the former colonel of the Eighth Infantry, Albemarle Cady. The post, near present-day Harvard, California, afforded travelers some measure of protection from the bands of hostile Indians who wandered the Mojave Desert. But the day after Hardenbergh's promotion to first lieutenant on 28 July 1866, he and a detachment of Company D had trouble protecting themselves. A sharp fight with Indians, possibly Paiutes but probably Chemehuevis, erupted near the fort. Three enlisted men were killed and a civilian guide was wounded.[348]

13 August 1866
GRAPEVINE SPRING *(Skull Valley, Arizona)*
Lt. Oscar Hutton, commander of Company F of the Arizona Volunteers, was based at Skull Valley and Date Creek for half of 1866. His little company was constantly in the field escorting wagons, guarding ranches, or

scouting. On 12 August Hutton led eighteen of his Volunteers plus eighteen soldiers of Company B, Fourteenth Infantry, and thirteen civilians on a scout from Skull Valley.

The next day at Grapevine Spring, Hutton and a detachment of fourteen soldiers and all the civilians attacked a rancheria of Indians, probably Yavapais. The surprise attack killed twenty-three Indians, with a loss to Hutton of one soldier killed and one civilian wounded. The remainder of the scout was less eventful. Over the following weeks, Hutton traveled 300 miles north and east, skirmishing on the 17th and 24th. The Indian casualties of the two fights together were one killed, one wounded, and two children captured. The tired command returned to Skull Valley on 2 September.[349]

3 October 1866
CEDAR VALLEY *(Central Arizona)*
In May 1866 Capt. George B. Sanford, in command of Company E, First Cavalry, arrived at Camp McDowell, Arizona Territory, from Drum Barracks in Los Angeles. After a summer of negotiations with the Tonto Apaches, peace talks broke down, and Sanford was ordered to go after the Indians. On 27 September he led a scout of ninety-one men of Companies C and E, First Cavalry, and Companies B, D, and F, Fourteenth Infantry.

The expedition marched northeast across the Mazatzal Mountains and the Sierra Anchas. West of the Mogollon Rim, near Cedar Creek, in present-day Gila County, the soldiers found what they were looking for. Sanford and his troops charged into a Tonto rancheria, shooting down men, women, and children as they ripped through the camp. With no loss to his force, Sanford killed fifteen Indians and captured ten.

Sanford returned to Camp McDowell on 6 October. It was the first time the U.S. Army regulars had been successful against Indians in Arizona Territory. Having long contended that regulars were all but useless as Indian fighters, newspapers finally conceded that they could be as effective as the volunteers.[350]

26 October 1866
LAKE ABERT *(Valley Falls, Oregon)*
After the Civil War, the First Cavalry was transferred to the West, arriving in California in January 1866. Company A went first to Drum Barracks, then to Camp Bidwell, in northeast California. On 22 October Lt. John F. Small, with twenty-seven men of Company A, joined Lt. Harrison B.

Oatman, with twenty-one men of Company I, First Oregon Infantry, and five Klamath Indian scouts on an expedition to search out hostile Paiutes, Klamaths, Modocs, and other bands (often grouped as "Snake" Indians).

Guided by Klamath chief Blow, Small led the command north into Oregon, and on 26 October the men came upon Indians near Lake Abert, in the Chewaucan River valley. The Indians ran for the mountains, where they had chosen a good defensive position on Abert Rim. Small had to dismount and climb up the rocky slopes to attack. The fight began at noon and lasted almost three hours, during which time two soldiers were wounded. Small routed the Indians and destroyed their camp, killing fourteen warriors, wounding twenty-eight, and capturing three women and four children. The command returned to Camp Bidwell on 29 October.[351]

30 October 1866
O'BEIRNE'S FIGHT/MALHEUR COUNTRY
(Malheur County, Oregon)
Capt. Richard F. O'Beirne, originally with the Fourteenth Infantry, became a captain in the Thirty-second Infantry in September 1866, after the army's reorganization in July of that year. While much of his newly constituted regiment was serving in Arizona, O'Beirne remained in Idaho Territory. On 13 October he left Camp Three Forks with a mounted detachment of Company E, Twenty-third Infantry, in search of hostile Snake Indians.

The scout took him into what was called "the Malheur country" in present-day western Malheur County and eastern Harney County, Oregon. On 30 October the mounted infantrymen found and attacked an Indian camp, killing two, wounding eight, and capturing eight. They also captured thirty-eight horses, two mules, an ox, and a large amount of supplies and ammunition. O'Beirne sustained two men wounded, one severely.[352]

Ca. 8 November 1866
BIG BUG *(Prescott, Arizona)*
The mustering out of most state volunteers at the end of the Civil War, left many western territories with little protection. Companies of Arizona Volunteers did their best, but they were overburdened. When the volunteers disbanded in the fall of 1866, a meeting was called in Prescott to organize a ranger force.

In the meantime, local settlers had to take their chances. In November King S. Woolsey, who owned a ranch on the Agua Fria, sent four of his employees with a team of oxen to the Bully Bueno Mill on upper Turkey Creek, a dozen miles southeast of Prescott. Indians, probably Yavapais, watched the small party travel into the mountains, and just before the four men reached Big Bug Creek, the Indians attacked. Three of the cowboys, Leroy Jay, William Trahen, and L. M. Linton, were killed, but a fourth, Harvey Twaddle, escaped. The Indians made off with three of the four yoke of oxen.

A rescue party arrived to find the three bodies "cut to pieces"; even their mustaches were "picked with the lip and all," according to witness Daniel E. Conner. One body had seventeen arrows sticking in it. "They were otherwise mutilated in a manner too shocking to relate," reported Conner.[353]

Twaddle survived, but the following July, while hunting for lost mules near Walnut Grove, west of Big Bug Creek, he was again ambushed by Indians. He and a warrior fired at each other simultaneously; the Indian was killed and Twaddle took an arrow above his heart. As he pulled out the shaft he saw another warrior aiming at him. He killed that Indian and wounded a third. Holding the arrow that he had pulled from his chest, Twaddle drove the mules back to camp, where he related his story then laid down to die.[354]

Ca. 17 November 1866
FORT KLAMATH *(Fort Klamath, Oregon)*

In early October 1866, the Paiutes under Paunina had professed their friendship to agent Lindsay Applegate, but Applegate was not convinced. He told them they must come to the Klamath Lake Reservation, as they had agreed to do in a treaty in 1865 (see under Paulina Creek, 17 October 1864). The Paiutes came, but they did not stay there long; in November they threatened to attack the Klamath Indians at the reservation in revenge for Klamath scouts assisting soldiers in a battle the previous month (see Lake Abert, 26 October 1866). The Paiutes then left the reservation, stealing Klamath horses on the way.

Shortly afterward, Paunina invaded the Sprague River Valley, home of the Modoc leader Schonchin, who was friendly to the whites. The Paiutes stole some of Schonchin's horses, but the old Modoc and some of his warriors pursued the raiders. He did not kill any of them, but he did capture two of Paunina's women. Schonchin had learned from some of Paunina's warriors that the chief was concentrating his force at Goose Lake and was planning to attack the reservation and Fort Klamath itself. The Modoc reported this to Applegate, and the agent notified the fort commander, Capt. F. B. Sprague, First Oregon Infantry. Applegate had already commenced building fortifications around the agency and requisitioned four enlisted men from the fort to help defend it.

In the mid-November, Paunina's warriors advanced down the Sprague River. They were within a few miles of Fort Klamath when they confronted a force of Company I, First Oregon Infantry, under Lt. Harrison B. Oatman, accompanied by friendly Klamath and Modoc Indians. Paunina's men were no

Chief Paunina, ca. 1865
—From authors' collection

match for them. The Oregonians killed ten warriors, and their Indian allies killed three more. Together they captured about twenty Paiutes. Two enlisted men were wounded. Paunina himself escaped with the remnants of his band, retreating to eastern Oregon.[355]

17 November 1866
SIERRA ANCHA *(Punkin Center, Arizona)*

Camp McDowell provided a home base for many Apache expeditions in 1866. On 14 November Capt. George B. Sanford and Lt. Camillo C. C. Carr took forty-seven men of Company E, First Cavalry; a hospital steward of Company B, Fourteenth Infantry; guides Max Strobel and Thomas Ewing; and thirteen Pima and Maricopa Indians out from the camp at sunset. Camping during the day and traveling at night, the troops traveled light, carrying pinole (cornmeal), jerked beef, and coffee in their saddlebags. They took only four pack mules as emergency replacements for worn-out horses.

The expedition crossed the Rio Verde and moved northeast twenty-five miles to Sycamore Creek, then crossed the Mazatzals to Tonto Creek. Scouts brought news of Indians crossing the creek and heading east toward the Sierra Anchas. Sanford followed the Indians' trail, and by

10 p.m. on 16 November, the company had reached the summit of the Sierra Anchas. Clouds obscured the moon, and tracking over the rocky slope was difficult. At 1 a.m. Sanford halted to wait for sunrise.

At dawn, a half hour's travel brought the expedition to an Apache rancheria at the head of a canyon, surrounded on three sides by nearly perpendicular walls hundreds of feet high. Guide Ewing called it "the worst place to get into that [I] ever saw."[356] The soldiers and Indian auxiliaries immediately charged. Sanford later wrote that "leaping from their horses, [they] pursued the flying Apaches over the hills and across the canyons in the most gallant manner."[357]

Six Apaches were killed and five were taken prisoner. There were no casualties from Apache bullets, but several of Sanford's men took bad falls on the rocks. The troops found a large amount of winter stores, including seeds, acorns, and nuts, in the rancheria and destroyed them. They also found two government-issue canteens, mailbags, and a copy of the New Testament. After they burned the rancheria, the soldiers went looking for some cattle that an Apache prisoner claimed were in Green-back Valley, about five miles away. When the search proved fruitless, the company continued south toward the Salt River.

Later the scouts saw more Indians in the distance, but they were too far ahead, and the soldiers failed to catch them. Retracing their steps, Sanford's company got back to Camp McDowell on 19 November.[358]

18 November 1866
BELL'S CANYON *(Kirkland, Arizona)*

In November 1866 George W. Leihy, Superintendent of Indian Affairs in Arizona, was traveling from Prescott to La Paz along the Colorado River. Leihy, along with his clerk, H. C. Everts, two soldiers, and an Indian interpreter were on their way back from Fort Whipple, bringing a Yavapai captive back to the reservation. Unbeknownst to Leihy, Yavapais living in the region believed that the superintendent was responsible for the deaths of about thirty-five Indians who were killed the previous year, supposedly by soldiers at Fort Mojave. In truth, however, Leihy had been trying to stop settlers and soldiers from killing Indians on sight—he wanted them to be captured and returned to the reservations. Unaware of Leihy's efforts on their behalf, the Yavapais planned to ambush him.

Ten miles beyond Skull Valley, between Kirkland and Date Creek, the road passed through Bell's Canyon. There, the Yavapais confronted Leihy's little party. Leihy called out to the Indians not to harm them.

He announced who he was and said he was on his way to La Paz with one of their own people. The Indians were happy to hear this—now they knew they had the right person.

The Indians shot down the traveler's horses and rushed in. One Yavapai called out that all the warriors should take part in killing the agent, so no one could claim credit for himself. All the men in the party, except the captive, were quickly killed. Only fast talking by the Yavapai prisoner kept him from being killed too.

Three days later, the five bodies were discovered, all mutilated. Leihy's head had been crushed by a giant rock, while Everts's head was severed from his body and never found. The killers returned to the reservation to spread the news. The settlers of La Paz wondered why the Indians carried on two days of feasting and celebration.[359]

— 1867 —

6–7 January 1867
CROOKED RIVER *(Prineville, Oregon)*
As settlers and their military allies continued to fight with the loose confederation of Northern Paiutes, Northern Shoshones, and Bannocks collectively called "Snakes," many whites concluded that getting Indians to fight other Indians would help their cause. An act passed on 1 August

William McKay, 1875
—From authors' collection

1866 authorized the army to recruit Indians to act as "scouts" with the same pay and allowances as cavalry soldiers. The Adjutant General's Office allotted 100 scouts to the Department of Columbia.

When Oregon governor George L. Woods received official sanction, he enlisted two companies of Warm Springs Indians. "Warm Springs" was a designation for several bands of Plateau Culture Indians, including about 900 members of bands agent John Smith labeled Tyghs, Deschutes, and Wascos (Walla Wallas), who were traditionally hostile to the Paiutes and Shoshones of the Great Basin. Lts. William McKay and John Darragh commanded the Indian companies. Though they were referred to as lieutenants and later as captains, they were paid as interpreters.[360]

In early January 1867, McKay and Darragh were hunting hostiles in central Oregon. They built a camp on what is now McKay Creek, north of today's Prineville. On 6 January, while tracking footprints in the snow, the scouts discovered a small camp of Paiutes near the bend of the Crooked River, southeast of Prineville. They attacked the camp, killing three Paiutes and capturing three horses along with a great deal of ammunition.

After the fight, McKay kept searching. Later the same day, he discovered a larger camp, under Chief Paunina, on a nearby mountain. The scouts climbed 2,000 feet up a rocky slope and engaged the Paiutes for a few hours, "killing three Snake Indians in their hiding holes." One of McKay's men was wounded and three horses were killed. They pulled back to rest, then continued the assault at dusk, pursuing Paunina's band until one o'clock the next morning. McKay attacked again at dawn, in a snowstorm. This time the scouts killed twelve Paiutes and captured three children. A running fight culminated in an attack on another camp, where the scouts killed eight more Paiutes and captured several others. By then, the snow was about sixteen inches deep, and without forage and rest for his horses, McKay could no longer follow Paunina's trail.

In all, Darragh and McKay's Warm Springs scouts had killed twenty-eight Indians and captured eight, though they had been ordered by Gen. Frederick Steele to take no prisoners. McKay and Darragh, in their personal accounts of the campaign, admitted that their men had killed fourteen women and children, "against the wishes of the Indian scouts." Their reported reluctance, however, came less from humanitarian feelings than from their fear that the Snakes would retaliate by murdering the scouts' own wives and children. In any case, the Warm Springs scouts continued to be greatly helpful in gradually wearing down the Snakes' resistance.[361]

18 January 1867
EDEN VALLEY *(Paradise Valley, Nevada)*

By the summer of 1866, Indian hostilities had slackened in Nevada, allowing the California Volunteers, who had remained in service more than a year beyond the end of the Civil War, to finally go home. In their place, many Californians, most of whom had worked as miners and styled themselves as "Forty-niners," joined the newly organized Eighth Cavalry in the fall of 1866. The regiment was dispersed throughout Oregon, California, Nevada, Idaho, and Arizona. Company A, organized at the Presidio de San Francisco, was sent to Camp Winfield Scott, a newly built post on Cottonwood Creek, at the north end of present-day Paradise Valley, Nevada, near the eastern slope of the Santa Rosa Mountains.

Patrolling out of Camp Scott, Lt. John Lafferty, a Civil War veteran of the California Cavalry, and fourteen men of Company A came upon a rancheria of Indians, probably Paiutes, in the barren Eden Valley, about sixteen miles southeast of Paradise Valley. Lafferty attacked, killing two Indians and scattering the rest. Sgt. John Kelley took an arrow through his right hand. Lafferty destroyed the rancheria and a large quantity of provisions.[362]

15 February 1867
BLACK SLATE MOUNTAIN *(Golconda, Nevada)*

In early 1867 Capt. Murray Davis, Eighth Cavalry, commanded Camp Winfield Scott, near today's Paradise Valley, Nevada. Following Lt. John Lafferty's successful action in January (see previous entry), Davis sent the aggressive lieutenant out on another scout to search for Indians reported to be in Eden Valley and farther to the south. Lafferty, Sgt. John Kelley, and thirteen soldiers of Company A, Eighth Cavalry, rode out on 11 February with six days' rations.

The patrol moved down the Little Humboldt River to the Humboldt, scouting for two days with no luck. On 15 February, on his way back to Camp Scott, he encountered fifteen Indians on the slopes of Black Slate Mountain, now known as Golconda Butte, about eight miles north of present-day Golconda, Nevada. Lafferty sent Kelley and five troopers around to cover the Indians' most likely escape route, but the soldiers were found out before Kelley could get into place. Nevertheless, Lafferty charged.

The Indians had only two rifles and one pistol among them. One warrior fired his rifle and ran. Another aimed his rifle but it misfired, and a soldier put a bullet in the warrior's head. The cavalrymen chased the Indians until sundown, killing five. The troopers returned to the Indians' abandoned camp, which had winter food stores, grass seeds, fish and rabbit nets, and assorted knives and hatchets, plus several articles Lafferty claimed belonged to whites. The soldiers destroyed the camp and marched back to Camp Scott.[363]

23 February 1867
MEADOW VALLEY/CAMP RENO
(Punkin Center, Arizona)

Prussian-born Capt. Guido Ilges, Fourteenth Infantry, arrived at Camp McDowell from Camp Grant in February 1867. Taking over as commander of the District of the Verde, Ilges immediately prepared to build a new post, to be called Camp Reno. With a thirty-four-man detachment of First Cavalry and Fourteenth Infantry, plus packers and guides, Ilges departed for Meadow Valley in the Mazatzal Mountains on 19 February. The men marched northeast for eighty miles in cold, snowy conditions, keeping an eye out for Indians. Although they saw none, tracks in the snow indicated that the company was being watched.

Camping in Meadow Valley, Ilges began construction of the post, but the Indians had other ideas. At 2 a.m. on 23 February, Apaches sneaked up to the bivouac and fired at the sleeping men. The first volley killed a packer and wounded a soldier. Return fire drove the Indians away, and Ilges moved his command to a hilltop. There were no further attacks.

Deciding he had too few men to build and man the post, Ilges returned to Camp McDowell. All the way back, Apaches harassed the company, with upwards of 200 warriors at a time. The Indians blocked the mountain pass, forcing Ilges to cross the snow-covered ridge and ford an icy stream. On the night of 24 February, Indians again crept near the soldiers' camp, but sentries gave the alarm and the men drove them off.

Ilges reached Camp McDowell the next day, lucky to have taken no additional casualties. Gen. Irvin McDowell was dissatisfied with Ilges's effort, believing that the captain's return showed "an unwillingness to go into, and live, in a rude, rough and uninviting country."[364]

2 March 1867
DATE CREEK *(Date Creek, Arizona)*

Two wagon teams, with two drivers accompanied by five other men, were making their way to Prescott on a road that was considered comparatively safe. On 2 March 1867 they were eight miles west of Date Creek when they were ambushed by about forty Apaches, possibly Yavapais. Firing into the train, the Indians killed the two drivers and one of the passengers. The other four men escaped, but not before two of them were wounded.

Rather than pursue the survivors, the Indians stole what they could carry, destroyed the wagons, and ran off the eighteen mules and four horses. About three hours after the attack, another wagon train approached as the raiders were driving away the stock. Several men on the train went after the Indians, pursuing them into a canyon in the mountains north of the road. There, the Indians turned on them, driving them off and capturing their horses too. The chastened men walked back to their train, buried the dead from the first train, and reported the attack in Prescott. This depredation caused the army to station soldiers in the Date Creek area.[365]

22 March 1867
SOUTH FORK OWYHEE *(Tuscarora, Nevada)*

Capt. Murray Davis, Eighth Cavalry, commanded Camp Winfield Scott in Nevada's Paradise Valley, until he departed the post on the last day of February 1867, leaving Lt. John Lafferty in charge. On 13 March, Paiutes ran off stock from Charles Gagg's ranch, about eight miles south of the post. The next day Lafferty took fourteen men of Company A and left in pursuit. The Indian trail headed east. Despite the fierce snowstorm that obliterated the tracks, Lafferty continued his search. Nine days later he caught up to the raiders near the South Owyhee River, north of present-day Tuscarora, Nevada. In a short, sharp fight, the troopers killed six Indians, captured their weapons, and destroyed their camp.[366]

27 April 1867
SILVIES RIVER *(Burns, Oregon)*

In January 1867, most of the Fourteenth Infantry was transferred to Arizona, but a few companies remained in the Pacific Northwest. Lt. Charles B. Western commanded Camp Logan, Oregon, near the junction of Strawberry Creek and the John Day River. On 28 March Western, with a detachment of seven men of Company F, Eighth Cavalry, attacked a camp of Paiutes on Murderers Creek. He captured three oxen and 2,000 pounds of jerked beef, then destroyed the camp.

Western resupplied at Camp Logan on 20 April, and with thirteen men of Company F, he went on another scout in response to reported

Freight wagon on The Dalles to Canyon City Road, Oregon, 1883 —From authors' collection

Indian depredations at Canyon City, a dozen miles farther down the John Day River. On 24 April he found the Indian trail, which led south into the Aldrich Mountains. Western and his men followed the tracks for two days until the pack train could advance no farther in the rough country. Cutting loose from his train, Western continued on the trail with twelve men and three days' rations. On 27 April the soldiers encountered about fifty Indians on the upper Silvies River north of present-day Burns, Oregon.

The river was running high. Western left three men to guard the horses, and with the remaining troopers he waded in neck-deep water to the opposite bank. The Indians did not expect an attack from the riverside, and Western charged into the camp shooting. After putting up a token defense, the Indians fled.

Six warriors were killed and left behind. The wounded were carried off by their tribesmen. "A number of wounded were also drowned in attempting to cross the river," the army report stated.[367] Western captured thirty-two horses and the camp equipage, including one and a half tons of camas root, which he destroyed.[368]

21–27 June 1867
UNION PACIFIC RAILROAD *(Russell, Kansas)*
During the spring and summer of 1867, Cheyenne and Lakota Indians raided up and down the line of the Union Pacific Railroad, Eastern Division (later the Kansas Pacific). By late June, the rail tracks extended to Fort Harker, near Ellsworth, Kansas. The surveyors, graders, and

construction crews, who worked seventy-five miles or more beyond the end of track, were woefully exposed to hit-and-run Indian raids.

On 23 May a surveying party under Col. W. H. Greenwood was attacked at Monument Station. Indians fought the workers near the latter's camp for more than four hours, stealing thirteen mules before being driven away. The attacks turned deadly on 21 June, when Indians attacked and killed seven workers in a railroad cut a mile west of the North Fork Big Creek, near present-day Victoria, Kansas. The Union Pacific erected a stone monument to the slain workers. (Today, only one chiseled name, Henry McDonney, remains legible.)

On the same day, a grading crew camped near Walker Creek, near present-day Gorham, Kansas, was also attacked. Theodore Goeckler was driving a team of mules, hauling rock from a quarry north of the line. Shortly after noon, Indians attacked. Goeckler managed to unhitch the mules, jump on one, and ride for the relative safety of the camp. Before he could make it there, he was shot and fell to the ground. He got up to run, but a warrior lanced him to death. Afterward, Goeckler's fellows brought his body back to camp and buried it on the west bank of Walker Creek, just south of the railroad.

The next day, Indians killed and scalped three more rail workers. The incident occurred within twenty miles of Fort Harker. John D. Perry, president of the Union Pacific Railroad, Eastern Division, wrote to Kansas governor Samuel J. Crawford complaining that the Indians had driven more than a thousand of his laborers east of Wilson's Creek (present-day Wilson, Kansas). The workers were unarmed, and the nearest soldiers were far to the west of the main work sites, near Fort Wallace. Perry asked Crawford for arms and protection; Crawford forwarded the message to Secretary of War Edwin M. Stanton.

On 24 June Robert M. Shoemaker, a construction contractor for the railroad, also wrote to Governor Crawford and reported that two more workers had been killed in an attack near Bunker Hill. Shoemaker asked for "five hundred stand of the best arms you have, with plenty of ammunition."[369] Four days later, Shoemaker wrote to Crawford again, relating that one of his camps was attacked on the morning of 27 June. Worker John Kessler was killed and another, George Waite, was badly wounded. Shoemaker reported that the workers, now armed, had killed six Indians. After the fight, Shoemaker personally went to Fort Harker to get military guards. The same week, a contractor based at Fossil Creek Station lost three laborers in an Indian attack.

In response to these raids, Governor Crawford received permission to raise a volunteer cavalry force of eight companies. The unit became the Eighteenth Kansas Cavalry Battalion, one of only two state military units raised solely to combat Indians.[370]

23 June 1867
BITTER CREEK *(Bitter Creek, Wyoming)*

In the summer of 1867, the Union Pacific Railroad rapidly expanded westward. Although the tracks extended only into western Nebraska, surveyors ranged hundreds of miles farther to locate and mark the best route. A surveying party under Percy T. Browne, escorted by members of the Second Cavalry, probably from Companies E and L, found the going rough; they were surrounded by unfamiliar country in the Continental Divide Basin known as the Red Desert, in present-day southern Wyoming. In June, Browne, seeking a crossing to the Pacific slope, took an eight-man escort and rode ahead of his company. Andrew Rosewater, a colleague of Browne, recalled, "Mr. Browne was warned not to take these risks but he was full of ambition and zeal."[371]

Browne and his escort rode through the Red Desert's waterless expanse of greasewood and sagebrush for about sixty miles. Having crossed the divide, they were moving down toward the next water source, at Bitter Creek, but they never made it. At midmorning on 23 June, they ran into a force of nearly 300 Lakotas, apparently moving south from the Sweetwater River to the Central Overland Stage route.

Spotting the Indians, Browne raised the alarm. The men dismounted and formed a line, moving steadily back toward high ground as the warriors closed in, firing at them and taunting them. After half an hour, Browne was shot through the abdomen, and he crumpled to the ground with a scream. His companions got him to his feet and retreated a few hundred more feet, but Browne's loss of blood made him stop. He told his companions to shoot him and save themselves, but they ignored his advice. The soldiers dragged him to a small hilltop and set up a defense. The warriors galloped by, shooting and blowing whistles, but this did not panic the resolute defenders.

About noon the soldiers released their horses, hoping this would satisfy their attackers, but after catching the horses the warriors returned. The Indians did not come nearer, but they kept the defenders pinned down under the hot sun until the late afternoon, when they finally rode off.

Browne still insisted that his companions leave him behind, for he knew of only one man who had ever survived a gutshot. Despite his protests, the soldiers waited until nightfall, when they fashioned a litter from a blanket and their carbines and carried Browne away. The men stumbled to the stage road, and after walking a distance, a passing wagon found them and took them fifteen miles to Laclede Station.

Despite his comrades' efforts, Browne died. Gen. Grenville M. Dodge, chief engineer of the Union Pacific, wrote that Browne was "one of the brightest of our young engineers" and that his death was a severe blow to the engineering corps, as well as to Dodge himself.[372]

8 July 1867
MALHEUR RIVER *(John Day, Oregon)*

Built in 1866, Camp Watson, near Rock Creek in present-day Wheeler County, Oregon, was named after Lt. Stephen Watson, who died in a battle with Shoshones at Crooked River, Oregon, in 1864. For much of its brief existence, the camp provided a base for units of the Twenty-third Infantry and First Cavalry.

On 24 June 1867 Capt. Eugene Baker, commander of Camp Watson, left on a scout with Company I, First Cavalry. Baker explored the Harney Lake region then headed north. On 8 July he attacked a village of Indians, probably Paiutes, near the headwaters of the Malheur River and John Day River, about twenty miles southeast of present-day John Day, Oregon. Baker's men killed two warriors and captured fourteen women and children, along with two horses. The company returned to Camp Watson on 24 July, having marched about 700 miles.[373]

15 July 1867
SOUTH FORK MALHEUR *(Venator, Oregon)*

Throughout the spring and summer of 1867, Lt. Col. George Crook conducted a relentless campaign against the Snake Indians. Many small columns combed central and southeast Oregon, giving the Indians little respite. In July Lt. Greenleaf A. Goodale led a detachment of Company K, Twenty-third Infantry, to Camp Wright in the Harney Valley, then waited for instructions from Crook. When Capt. William McKay and his Warm Springs scouts entered the valley, the two men decided to combine forces.

Goodale and McKay moved to a camp on the South Fork of the Malheur River. On 14 July, Goodale took a scout along the west side of Steens

Gen. George Crook —From authors' collection

Mountain. Upon returning later that day, Goodale said he saw Indian signs farther north, between the Middle and South Forks. The companies continued along the Malheur, stopping at 4 p.m. to camp, near present-day Venator. Shortly after making camp, Goodale and McKay decided to make an evening scout. They rounded up eight soldiers, twenty-four Indian scouts, and civilian guides A. J. Boyd and Aaron Hewey to go looking for Weahwewah and his Paiutes.

The search didn't take long, for around twilight the scouts noticed a cave in the mountains and evidence of a camp. When the soldiers and scouts charged in, most of the Paiutes fled except those who had holed up in the cave. Scouts took position around the cave entrance and exchanged fire with those inside. It was dark when a Paiute bullet killed the Warm Springs scout Squalth. Boyd killed the Paiute, and in a final charge, Goodale and McKay's men entered the cave and finished off the defenders.

Goodale reported killing six Indians, wounding one, and capturing two. The Warm Springs Indians carried Squalth's body back to camp and buried him the next day. They stamped down the dirt over the grave and built a fire on it to remove any trace. Goodale returned to Camp Wright on 19 July.[374]

Ca. 1 August 1867
LOVING'S FIGHT *(Loving, New Mexico)*

Charles Goodnight and Oliver Loving, two cattlemen from Texas, were the first to drive large herds of longhorns from Texas to New Mexico, Colorado, and Wyoming, blazing cattle trails that would secure their names in history. During their second season of cattle drives, Loving became impatient with the slow progress of the cattle moving up the

Pecos River. It was late July, and contracts were to be drawn up in August for next year's drive, so he had to get to Denver to make arrangements. He decided to leave the main herd and move ahead on his own. Goodnight cautioned against it, but Loving's mind was made up. He and Bill "One-armed" Wilson saddled up and moved north.

The pair rode by night, passing Pope's Crossing near the present-day Texas–New Mexico state line, then taking the high trail across the Delaware River and over to the Black River. Loving detested night riding, and since they had seen no sign of Indians, he talked Wilson into riding by day. Moving across the open plain north of the Black River, they spotted a large band of Comanches riding fast toward them from the Guadalupe Mountains to the west. The two broke into a four-mile run eastward for the breaks of the Pecos River. They rode about 100 yards to a series of sand dunes that snaked between the bluff and the river. After gathering their weapons, they set loose the horses and took shelter behind the dunes.

One-armed Wilson had Goodnight's six-shot revolving rifle, as well as his own six-shooter, and Loving had a sidearm and a repeating Henry rifle with metallic cartridges. The Indians poured over the bluffs, crossed the river, and surrounded them. Wilson later estimated their number at several hundred. The only gap in the circle of dunes opened toward the river. Loving shot the first Indian who tried to get a bead on them from that angle.

Late in the evening, a voice from the bluffs called to the pair in Spanish, proposing surrender terms. The cowmen suspected treachery, but Wilson wanted to try to talk, asking Loving to cover him. He climbed up the dune with Loving behind him carrying the Henry rifle. As they reached the top, a bullet ripped through Loving's wrist and into his side. The two dove back into the ditch and fired at the charging Indians, driving them back. The cowmen wrapped up Loving's wounds and settled in for a longer siege.

Throughout the next day, the Comanches showered the cattlemen's position with rocks and high-angled arrows, but none of the missiles hit. At one point, Wilson detected movement in the nearby brush. He readied his gun to fire, but the warrior disturbed a rattlesnake and backed off faster than he had crept up.

That evening, Loving was fevered. Sure he was going to die, Loving urged Wilson to get away that night. He said that if Wilson moved downriver, he should run into Goodnight and his cowboys, who were a few days behind them. Loving vowed he would take down as many Indians as he could with his six-gun before putting the last bullet into his own head. If the Indians left, however, Loving would swim a mile downriver to hide and wait for help.

Wilson agreed to go. He took the Henry, as the metallic cartridges were nearly waterproof. Stripping down to his underwear, Wilson waded into the stream. Avoiding a mounted Indian in the middle of the stream, Wilson paddled by along the bank. When he struck deeper water, the one-armed cowboy realized he could not swim with the rifle. He jammed the barrel deep into the bottom sand so the Indians would not find it and swam off weaponless. Farther downstream Wilson climbed out, and by daybreak he was well on his way to Goodnight. Unfortunately, Goodnight had stopped to rest the herd, and he was approximately eighty miles south, twice as far as Wilson had anticipated. Wilson kept on, walking shoeless across the cactus and rocks, for three days.

Ahead of the herd, Goodnight thought he saw someone who appeared to be Indian approaching from a cave near the riverbank. He spurred his horse ahead to take a look. "The river water was red with sediment, and his underclothes were as red as the river itself. But when he beckoned to me, I knew positively that it was Wilson," Goodnight recalled.[375] Wilson could barely talk, his eyes were bloodshot, and his swollen feet left bloody footsteps in the sand. Goodnight lifted his bedraggled friend onto his horse and hurried him back to the outfit. At the camp, when Wilson related his story, Goodnight took six men and raced out to find Loving.

The rescuers rode all night, following Wilson's directions. On the way, they found a page from Loving's journal, reassuring them that they were on the right path. They reached the edge of the bluffs and, believing that the Indians were still there, charged over the bank, fully intending to fight their way in to rescue Loving. The Indians were gone, however, and so was Loving.

Goodnight found the dune where the two cowmen had fought with the Indians. Goodnight remarked that "its banks [were] perforated with probably a hundred arrow shafts. . . . I knew they had not got him, as there was ample evidence that they had been hunting for him everywhere."[376] The rescuers searched downriver but could find no trace of Loving. Where had he gone?

After Wilson left, Loving had fought off his attackers for two more days and nights. The Indians had tunneled through the sand to within feet of him, but they never got to him. On the third night, Loving slipped into the river, but instead of going downstream as he had told Wilson he would do, he went upstream, trying to reach a trail about six miles north, where he hoped to be found by a passerby. Reaching the trail, he lay down in the brush under a small tree. Without food and able only to suck on a water-soaked handkerchief, Loving finally passed out.

Some Mexicans traveling to Texas found the half-dead cowman on the roadside. They fixed him some *atole*, a kind of cornmeal mush, and he regained his senses. He offered them $250 to take him to Fort Sumner, about 150 miles away, and they gladly swung their wagon around. As they headed north, the group met a party of cowmen under Jim Burleson, who rode to Fort Sumner for an ambulance. Loving was retrieved and rushed to the fort. Burleson meanwhile hurried back to check on his cattle. En route he met Goodnight and told him about Loving.

Hearing the good news, Goodnight saddled up his best mule, Jenny, and rode the 110 miles to Fort Sumner in only one day and night. He found that Loving's side wound had healed, but his shattered wrist was infected and gangrene had set in. Loving refused amputation, but Goodnight told the doctor in no uncertain terms that he could either operate or fight. After the amputation was performed, however, the tie on the artery kept breaking open. The doctor retied Loving's artery, but the patient weakened. "I regret to have to be laid away in a foreign country," Loving said to his partner.[377] Goodnight promised to take his remains back to Texas.

Loving died 25 September 1867. He was temporarily buried at Fort Sumner. That winter, when Goodnight finished his business transactions, he set about fulfilling his promise to his partner. He and his cowboys placed Loving's wooden casket inside a sealed tin box packed with powdered charcoal and placed it in a wagon. They left Sumner on 8 February 1868. Six big mules pulled the funeral wagon, with the Texas cowmen riding front and rear. The caravan took the Goodnight-Loving Trail back to Loving's spread at Weatherford, Texas, where they reburied the intrepid cattleman.[378]

11 and 15 August 1867
OWYHEE RIVER *(Jordan Valley, Oregon)*

To safeguard the road from Silver City, Idaho, to Nevada and California, Maj. Gen. Frederick Steele authorized the building of two new posts. In September 1866 Capt. John J. Coppinger, Twenty-third Infantry, built the first one on Soldier Creek, at the southwestern base of South Mountain, near today's Idaho-Oregon border. The post was known variously as Camp Winthrop, Camp Soldier Creek, or Camp Three Forks. Steele had also wanted a blockhouse built about sixteen miles to the southwest, at the Three Forks of the Owyhee River in Oregon, but the area's high canyon walls made building a road impractical, and Coppinger never built the second post.

In the summer of 1867, while hunting hostile bands in conjunction with George Crook, Coppinger left Camp Winthrop with sixty men of Company A and a detachment of Company E, Twenty-third Infantry, and seven scouts. With thirty days' rations, the expedition traveled down Soldier Creek nearly to its junction with the Owyhee, about twenty miles southwest of present-day Jordan Valley, Oregon. On 11 August, the infantrymen struck a small Indian village in the Owyhee Canyon, where they killed two Indians and destroyed their fishery.

Coppinger then marched upstream into Idaho's Red Canyon country. On 15 August, he found and attacked another small Indian band, killing one warrior and capturing a woman and boy. After traveling more than 400 miles, Coppinger's men returned to Camp Three Forks on 19 September.[379]

6 and 8 September 1867
SILVER LAKE *(Silver Lake, Oregon)*

Tennessean Lt. John Foster Small joined the First Cavalry in 1861 and fought in numerous engagements during the Civil War. He was brevetted a first lieutenant for gallant service at the May 1864 Battle of Cold Harbor. In 1867, during Oregon's Snake War, Small commanded Fort Klamath, established in 1863 about eight miles north of Upper Klamath Lake.

Small left the fort on 2 September with fifty-one men of his Company A, First Cavalry, and ten Klamath Indian scouts, taking twenty days' rations. He planned to search for hostile Northern Paiutes in the Silver Lake area, on the California-John Day Road. On 6 September, in the vicinity of present-day Silver Lake, Oregon, Small encountered a small band of Indians. The troopers killed one warrior, captured five women and children, and destroyed the camp.

Two days later, the soldiers came upon a village of considerable size on the shores of Silver Lake. Although Small was outnumbered, he attacked the Indians. His men killed twenty-three Indians, captured fourteen, and destroyed the camp, sustaining a loss of two enlisted men and one Klamath scout wounded. The company returned to Fort Klamath on

22 September. For gallantry in charging a band of Indians and "killing and capturing more of the enemy than he had men," Small was brevetted captain.[380]

17 October 1867
DEEP CREEK *(Moran, Texas)*

Ordered to Texas after the Civil War, the Sixth Cavalry took up several stations across the state. In July 1866 a detachment went to Maxwell's Ranch, on the Clear Fork of the Brazos, where they set up a post called Camp Wilson, which later became Fort Griffin. On 13 October 1867 Sgt. W.A.F. Ahrberg, Company L, led out a scout of forty-five enlisted men of Companies F, I, K, and L and twenty-two Indian scouts, riding in search of raiding Comanches.

Ahrberg and his men rode east through Shackleford, Stephens, and Palo Pinto Counties, then circled back on a southern loop. On the way they found and buried the bodies of five murdered civilians. In southeast Shackleford County, along Deep Creek near present-day Moran, Texas, they finally tracked down the marauders. Ahrberg's men killed three Comanches and captured a woman along with nineteen horses, a mule, and two revolvers. They arrived back at Camp Wilson on 19 October. The stolen horses were returned to their owners.[381]

In November Col. Joseph J. Reynolds, commanding the District of Texas, expressed his appreciation of Ahrberg. General Orders No. 40 stated that Reynolds "takes pleasure in commending the energy and courage displayed by Sergeant W. A. F. Ahrberg, Troop 'L,' 6th U. S. Cavalry, and the detachment under his command, in their recent encounter with a party of Comanche Indians."[382]

4 November 1867
GOOSE CREEK/SHURLY'S FIGHT
(Sheridan, Wyoming)

Lt. Edmund R. P. Shurly, Twenty-seventh Infantry, with forty men of Companies E, G, H, and I, escorted twenty-five empty wagons from Fort C. F. Smith to Fort Phil Kearny. Leaving the post on 28 October, Shurly was six miles north of his destination when he met up with a Wells Fargo supply train escorted by Lt. Florence McCarthy, also of the Twenty-seventh. The two lieutenants agreed to swap trains, with McCarthy taking the empty wagons south and Shurly taking the Wells Fargo train on to C. F. Smith. On 3 November, Shurly had his men store their knapsacks on the lead wagon of the sixteen-wagon train, which contained the ammunition stores. They continued north, but a snowstorm blew in and they made little progress.

The next morning, Shurly got the train moving down Peno Creek (Prairie Dog Creek). East of present-day Sheridan, Wyoming, the party crossed over a divide into the Goose Creek valley. By 11 a.m. the train was strung out, the lead wagons in the valley, the middle negotiating a slippery hill, and the rear nearly out of Shurly's sight half a mile behind the hill. The ammunition wagon was in front, the howitzer was in the rear, and the Wells Fargo teamsters were in the middle with rifles but no ammunition. From a position on the hill, Shurly saw Indians approaching but he could do little.

The Indians, about 300 of them, attacked the front and rear of the train simultaneously. The frightened mules pulling the driverless ammunition wagon bolted, running the vehicle into the hands of the warriors, who leapt on board and drove it out of sight. While the lead wagons made a corral in the valley, Cpl. Peter Donnelly, Company H, fired the howitzer from the rear. As Shurly made his way toward the howitzer, he and seven men were cut off from the rest, but Donnelly worked the howitzer well enough to keep the Indians at bay.

Finally, in order to save the gun, Shurly ordered it limbered up and drove it at all hazards toward the wagon corral. On the way, he took an arrow through the foot. Turning with his revolver in hand, he shot the Indian who had wounded him. Pvt. Harold Partenheimer, Company D, was killed when two arrows pierced his lungs, and Donnelly and Pvt. James McGeever were badly wounded. Cpl. Gordon Fitzgerald, Pvt. Michael Kerr, and civilian William Freeland were also wounded, but less seriously.

Shurly and the others finally reached the corralled wagons, but the corral had been set up hastily in a narrow depression that was within rifle range of the Indians in the surrounding hills and thickets near the creek. With the ammunition wagon gone, Shurly found that the company had only six shots for the howitzer and forty rounds each for the soldiers. Meanwhile the Indians had ransacked three wagons that had been abandoned on the hill, carrying off or destroying much of the 700 sacks of corn they contained and making off with the sutler's stock of red blankets.

The raiders were apparently satisfied with their plunder, for their firing became desultory, and the shooting ended at twilight. Two men rode to Fort Phil Kearny, arriving at midnight with the news. At 1 a.m. Capt. John Green led two companies of Second Cavalry from the fort and reached the besieged train at daylight. The trapped men groaned when they saw what appeared to be more Indians coming over the hill, but the groans turned to cheers when they recognized the horsemen as U.S. Cavalry.

The wagons went on to Fort C. F. Smith while the dead and wounded were taken back to Phil Kearny. Shurly was incapacitated for almost eight months with his arrow wound. Fitzgerald's hand was amputated, and Donnelly and McGeever later died of their wounds. Both were buried in the post cemetery along with Partenheimer. Indian casualties numbered ten warriors killed or wounded.[383]

5 November 1867
CAMP BOWIE *(Bowie, Arizona)*

After terrorizing southeastern Arizona off and on for years, Cochise and his Chiricahuas slipped south into Sonora in late June 1867, and the region around Camp Bowie, near present-day Bowie, Arizona, remained relatively quiet for a few months. Then a one-company post, Bowie was garrisoned by forty-five men of Company G, Thirty-second Infantry, commanded by Capt. John C. Carroll. The soldiers had settled into a daily routine by the time a railroad surveying party came through in November. With his men bored and hungry for news, Carroll invited the surveyors to stay at the post. The next day, William A. Bell, photographer for the survey, was busy taking pictures on Overlook Ridge, just north of the camp, when shots rang out. Bell watched as Carroll and a squad of soldiers went after the Indians and disappeared to the west.

Courier John Slater, who was on his way out of Camp Bowie with the mail when the Apaches showed up, went to ride with the soldiers, figuring he'd use them as an escort at least partway to the next station. Lt. Joseph Lawson, Third Cavalry, with a six-man detachment already out escorting the surveyors, also joined them. The pursuers chased the Indians west through Apache Pass.

All was quiet at the post for several hours until soldiers came drifting back in twos and threes. They never caught the Indians, they reported, but the ones who made it farthest west heard faint shots from the direction of Sulphur Springs valley. When Captain Carroll failed to return, a nine-man search party left the post, taking a shortcut southwest near Helen's Dome. The rescuers found horse tracks and followed them for three miles, at which point they discovered Slater's naked and mutilated body, with his head and long side-whiskers scalped. A little farther along, around nightfall, they found Carroll's mutilated body. They took both bodies back to the post for burial the next morning. Bell snapped a photograph of Camp Bowie with its flag at half-mast.[384]

1–2 December 1867
CRAZY WOMAN CREEK *(Buffalo, Wyoming)*

One of the last supply trains of the season to reach the upper posts on the Bozeman Trail before winter set in were on their way to Fort Phil Kearny. Past Fort Reno the train, escorted by a detachment of Company C, Eighteenth Infantry, under Sgt. George T. Gillaspy, moved into the valley of Crazy Woman Creek, where the party camped on 1 December. That evening, hostile Lakota and Cheyenne surrounded and besieged the train, running off some of the cattle.

The next day, Gillaspy made the best defensive corral he could manage with his small command, but the Indians kept the men pinned down, closing in on a few occasions. The two-day siege saw one soldier killed and three wounded, along with four civilians wounded. No Indians were reported hit. Just as abruptly as they appeared, the Indians left, and Gillaspy was able to bring the train into Fort Kearny.[385]

— 1868 —

16 April 1868
FORT C. F. SMITH *(Yellowtail, Montana)*

Elizabeth Burt, wife of Fort Smith commander Capt. Andrew S. Burt, Twenty-seventh Infantry, left the relative safety of the fort to pick flowers at a nearby spring with abundant ferns and violets. Assured that soldiers were always close by, Mrs. Burt, with her four-year-old son, her sister Katherine Russell, and another army wife, Jane Miller, went out to find the glade. They lost track of time until they were pulled out of their reverie by gunshots and shouts of "Indians!"

Lakotas and Cheyennes were raiding the post's mule herd, and the women were cut off from the fort. The boy's mother and aunt each grabbed one of his hands and, Elizabeth recalled, "gathering up our skirts ran as I believe no women ever ran before."[386] Lt. George M. Templeton and men from Company D double-timed out of the gate, though the soldiers were unaware of the plight of the women. Templeton was riding to rescue John Tewksbury, the fort's hunter, who was holding off about thirty warriors by himself. Tewksbury killed one Lakota, and the soldiers' bullets wounded several Indian ponies. Only one mule from the herd was killed. The Indians rode away empty-handed and without seeing the women and child, who had dashed safely to the fort during the fight.[387]

29 April 1868
DEEP CANYON *(Paradise Valley, Nevada)*

Indian troubles in northern Nevada had eased since the Paiute war of 1865–66 ended, but sporadic raiding continued nevertheless. Camp Winfield Scott had been established in 1866 to secure the area around the Paradise Valley, but in August 1867 James A. Banks, Nevada Speaker of the House, was killed while fishing on Cottonwood Creek, only a few miles from the post. Lt. John Lafferty, Company A, Eighth Cavalry, was fishing just downstream of Banks at the time of the murder. A renegade Indian, possibly a Paiute called Big Foot (a.k.a. Howluck, Oualuck, Oulux), was thought to be responsible.

In November 1867 Lt. Joseph Karge, who had been a colonel in the Second New Jersey Cavalry during the Civil War, was sent to take command of Camp Scott. Lafferty, with several years of frontier experience under his belt, did not get along with the easterner Karge. Several months later, in April 1868, Big Foot and twenty raiders ran off the stock of local rancher M. W. Haviland. Karge ordered the newly arrived Lt. Pendleton Hunter, along with Sgt. John Kelley, Cpl. Thomas Reed, and Pvt. Thomas Ward, to pursue the Indians. Civilian John Rogers joined the patrol. When Lafferty heard about the mission, he confronted Karge, saying that it would be "committing murder" to send a green lieutenant like Hunter out after Big Foot. After a heated argument, Karge finally agreed to let Lafferty gather another squad and join Hunter.

Hunter, meanwhile, tracked Big Foot into Deep Canyon in the Santa Rosa Range, only eight miles from Camp Scott. In his haste to prove himself, Hunter rode into an ambush. Within minutes, Hunter was shot, Kelley and Ward were mortally wounded, and all the horses were hit. Rogers ran for help, leaving only Reed to defend the three wounded men, which he did by doggedly firing to keep the Indians at bay. Rogers safely reached the post, where a relief party was quickly organized. The rescuers reached Deep Canyon about the same time that Lafferty did, and the combined force was able to drive Big Foot's band away.

Hunter recovered from his wound, and Corporal Reed won the Medal of Honor for his valiant defense. It was the only such medal awarded to any soldier during the Indian Wars in Nevada. Lafferty later went with the Eighth Cavalry to Arizona, where, in the Chiricahua Mountains in 1870, he had his jaw shot away by Apaches while trying to retrieve the bodies of fallen comrades.[388]

30 May 1868
SAN CARLOS TRAIL *(Seneca, Arizona)*

In the spring of 1868 commander of the District of Arizona Col. Thomas L. Crittenden, Thirty-second Infantry, directed Lt. Col. Thomas C. Devin, Eighth Cavalry, to hunt for Apaches east of Fort Whipple. On 26 April Devin sent Company B ahead to Camp Lincoln (Camp Verde), on the Rio Verde, with thirty days' rations and followed two days later with Lt. Almond B. Wells and Company L. At Camp Lincoln, Devin picked up some Fourteenth Infantrymen. Now comprising about 150 men and guides, the party headed east.

From the East Fork of the Verde, Devin entered the Tonto Basin. On 29 May Indians fired into the soldiers' camp at midnight, killing a horse. The men of Company L mounted up and tried to follow the raiders in the darkness. By daybreak they had discovered several rancherias, but all were abandoned. From a recently abandoned rancheria on Tonto Creek, the men found a trail leading south toward the San Carlos River.

Resupplying at Fort Whipple, Devin estimated his supply needs. He left the fort with the assurance that his pack mules could travel well carrying 250 pounds each. He soon discovered the animals' limit to be about 200 pounds, however, and found that they could make only ten miles per day. Even at that rate, some of the mules gave out, while others tumbled over cliffs.

Devin halted his southern move and set up camp at the head of Tonto Creek while waiting for more supplies from Camp Lincoln. After replenishing, he continued south through nearly impassable canyons, crossing the Salinas (Salt) River, where the cliff walls rose a thousand feet high. Devin and his men forded the Salinas four times. At one point they attacked a rancheria and killed four Apaches.

South of the Salinas, as the expedition headed toward the San Carlos River, an exploring party on a side trail was ambushed. One soldier and two pack mules were wounded in the skirmish, and two Indians were shot. Devin dispatched another party out for supplies, but it too was ambushed. The pack master, a Mr. Baker, was killed, and the Indians fled before Devin's troops arrived.

Devin took his sixty remaining serviceable horses south on a hard march to the San Carlos River. He reported that even with good guides and eager troops, "I could not get a fight." Reluctantly, he turned back on the long road to Camp Lincoln.[389] He complained that he had been told that he would find a thousand Indians before reaching the San Carlos; instead, he said, "I can at any time find more fresh Indian signs within 50 miles of this post [Fort Whipple] than I found at 200 miles distant."[390]

31 May 1868
CASTLE ROCK *(Juntura, Oregon)*

Constant pressure by Lt. Col. George Crook against the hostile Paiutes and Shoshones finally brought the Snake War to a close in the spring of 1868. On 1 April Crook, assigned as temporary commander of the Department of Columbia, went to the district headquarters in Portland. While he was gone, however, the Indian-hunting expeditions continued. On 24 May Lt. Alexander H. Stanton, First Cavalry, left Camp Harney, on Rattlesnake Creek in Oregon's Harney Lake valley. With him were thirty-seven men of Company F, First Cavalry, and twenty-four Indian scouts. They crossed the Stinking Water Mountains to the South Fork of the Malheur River and hunted along its tributaries.

Camp Harney, Oregon, 1872 —From authors' collection

Working their way north to the North Fork of the Malheur, the scouts found a ten-lodge Paiute camp near Castle Rock, about eighteen miles north of present-day Juntura. They attacked, driving off the Indians and capturing twelve horses. Six Paiute warriors returned and fought a brief skirmish, wounding one soldier. In a quick counterattack, Stanton swept in and captured the warriors.

This minor action had major results. One of the captured Indians was Chief Egan (Ehegante). The Paiute leader Paunina had already been killed at the hands of settlers in April 1867. Now the Paiutes, after years of fighting, were exhausted and starving, and they realized they could not win. They sent word of their desire to surrender to Camp Harney. Crook, who had returned from Portland and was at Camp Warner, traveled north to Harney. On 1 July he met with the Paiutes and the Malheur Shoshones, now led by Chief Weahwewah. During the negotiations, Crook wisely did not force the Indians onto reservations, but simply told them they must return stolen property and stop their killings and depredations. The Indians could live by these terms, and much of the fighting in Oregon came to a close.[391]

24 June 1868
BATTLE CREEK (Riddle, Idaho)
Capt. John J. Coppinger, Twenty-third Infantry, spent much of his service at posts in Idaho Territory, where he participated in several expeditions. On 22 June 1868 Coppinger took forty-five men of Company A and five Indian scouts from Camp Three Forks to escort a surveying party seeking a rail route to the northwest coast.

The expedition had hard traveling through the rough Owyhee country of southwest Idaho, a trip made no easier by threatening Indians. In the vicinity of Battle Creek, in remote terrain west of present-day Riddle, Idaho, Coppinger ran into a small band of Indians. In a short fight, he killed three of them and captured three women and a boy.[392]

19 July 1868
FORT RENO (Sussex, Wyoming)
Companies B and F, Twenty-seventh Infantry, garrisoned Fort Reno in the summer of 1868. As per the April 1868 Treaty of Fort Laramie, soldiers were to abandon all posts along the Bozeman Trail. The Lakotas, however, did not wait for them to go. On Sunday morning, 19 July, Fort Reno commander Lt. Jacob Paulus sent Sgt. William L. Day and eight

privates of Company B out to search for strayed cattle. Only half a mile southwest of the fort, near the Powder River, the detachment spotted five Indians in the brush. Figuring they were warriors from the band of the Lakota Man Afraid of His Horses, Day presumed they were friendly and the soldiers continued walking. Suddenly twenty-five Indians jumped up from a nearby ravine, and the startled soldiers opened fire.

Lt. Edmund R. P. Shurly of the Twenty-seventh Infantry, commanding Company A of the Second Cavalry, happened to be at Fort Reno that day escorting the paymaster to Fort Fetterman. When Paulus heard the shots from upriver, he sent Shurly to Day's aid. With thirty cavalrymen, Shurly spread out in skirmish order along the river bottom, assuming the Indian force was small and hoping to capture them. Near the bluffs by the river, he saw that there were more Indians than he could handle.

Shurly decided to charge the Indians to give Day and his men time to escape. He fought a holding action for a time, but when his flanks were threatened, he sounded a recall. Pvt. George F. Peach was too far out in front to retreat, however, and warriors cut him off, dragged him from his horse, killed him, and cut up his body. Another private, Joseph Miller, was wounded. Shurly halted the retreat and took up a position across a deep ravine three-quarters of a mile from the fort, where he fought for about fifty minutes.

Meanwhile, Paulus had no men available to help Shurly, for at the same time, Indians had appeared on the other side of Fort Reno. The infantrymen sortied out from the post to keep the warriors at bay. Shurly finally disengaged from the Indians and made it back to the fort, where he dismounted his men and sent them out to assist Paulus. The Indians soon pulled back, and the soldiers retreated back to the fort. Later that day, Shurly went out and collected the remnants of Peach's body. His remains were the last to be interred at Fort Reno's cemetery. The post was abandoned in August.[393]

26 July 1868
JUNIPER CANYON *(Silver City, Idaho)*
By the summer of 1868, the major fighting of the Snake War was over, but isolated skirmishes continued. Lt. Col. George Crook had held a successful peace council with Paiutes and Shoshones in July of that year, after the battle at Castle Rock (see Castle Rock, 31 May 1868). With that treaty, Crook believed, correctly, that he had made peace with all the hostile Indians from the Humboldt River to Fort Hall except some of

the Pit River Indians in California and "a few scattering ones between Nevada and the Three Forks of the Owyhee."[394]

Perhaps the last fight of consequence in the Snake War occurred near Camp Three Forks, on Soldier Creek near the Idaho-Oregon border. Lt. George McMannis Taylor, who had fought in the Seventy-third Ohio Infantry in the Civil War and was now a second lieutenant in the Twenty-third Infantry, commanded the post. In July 1868 he led eighteen men of Company E on a scout into the Juniper Mountains, only about twenty miles south of the camp. On 26 July the patrol encountered a band of Indians in Juniper Canyon and attacked, killing five, capturing four, and wounding a number of others. On the way back to camp, as Crook stated in his report, "two prisoners attempted escape and were killed."[395]

20 August 1868
FORT BUFORD *(Buford, North Dakota)*

Fort Buford, established in June 1866 on the left bank of the Missouri, a few miles below the confluence of the Yellowstone, was a magnet for hostile Lakotas seeking to oust the army presence from the upper Missouri. Stock was stolen, herders were killed, and mail riders were harassed on a nearly daily basis. Even large army commands were not immune. On 10 August Lt. Cornelius C. Cusick, Thirty-first Infantry, and fifty men were attacked en route from Fort Buford to Fort Stevenson.

On 20 August at Fort Buford, a fairly strong party of twenty-one men of the Thirty-first Infantry, along with several civilians, were guarding the post's beef herd. More than 150 Lakotas attacked the herd from two sides, stampeding 250 head of cattle. Most of the fort's garrison—detachments of Companies B, E, and G, who were making adobe bricks at the time—seized their weapons and rushed after the raiders. Capt. Charles J. Dickey and Lieutenant Cusick quickly organized the chase, but the Indians fought them off and escaped with the cattle, taking no casualties of their own. Three soldiers were killed in the fight, and four were wounded, including Cusick.[396]

25 August 1868
DIETEMANN MASSACRE *(Kiowa, Colorado)*

The Indian uprising of 1868 hit eastern Colorado and western Kansas hard. Gen. Philip Sheridan reported that from August through October, seventy-nine civilians were killed and nine were wounded, along with six soldiers killed and ten wounded. As was usually the case, settlers bore the brunt of the Indians' animosity, which seemed to target isolated settlements and civilians least able to defend themselves.

A particularly tragic incident occurred along Comanche Creek, Colorado Territory, several miles southeast of present-day Kiowa. About forty settlers lived in the valleys along Kiowa and Comanche Creeks. Two days before the episode, Apollinaris Dietemann and his business partner, Anton Schindelholz, went to Denver to buy supplies and obtain a marriage license for Schindelholz and his sweetheart, Dietemann's sister Maria. On their way back on 25 August, as the two men neared home, Indians, mostly Arapahos who had been raiding earlier in the vicinity of Colorado City (Colorado Springs), appeared on

Gen. Philip H. Sheridan
—From authors' collection

Comanche Creek. Dietemann's ranch hands had seen the Indians early that morning and warned the folks at the house.

Fleeing the house, the Dietemanns thought it best to head up the creek to their nearest neighbors rather than toward Kiowa Station, near where the Indians had been seen. Thirty-one-year-old Henrietta Dietemann took several thousand dollars, $400 of it in gold. About 10 a.m., the family had gone about four miles when Indians suddenly appeared and cut off Henrietta, who was lagging behind. Maria and ranch hand Benedict Marki were carrying Henrietta's three-year-old daughter, Henrietta, and five-year-old son, John. When the Indians grabbed his mother, little John pulled free and ran back to her. A warrior seized him, broke his neck, and shot him full of arrows. While the Indians struggled with the elder Henrietta on the ground, the fleeing settlers realized that their only chance was to change course and head northwest to the Kiowa settlement. They got away, but Henrietta was raped, shot in the right shoulder, clubbed in the face, scalped, and mutilated.

When Apollinaris Dietemann and Anton Schindelholz reached Running Creek Station, several miles west of Kiowa, the news of the raid had already arrived. They unhitched their wagon and rode to Kiowa, where they joined a dozen men who were gathering a search-and-rescue party. They soon found the bodies of Henrietta and her son, but the raiders were gone. The Indians had also raided at least seven other ranches in the area, stealing many horses in the process.

The settlers took the bodies of Henrietta and John to Denver and set them up for public viewing. The exhibition stirred up a major uproar in the region.[397] Acting Colorado governor Frank Hall telegraphed army authorities on 27 August with an urgent message: "The Arapahoes are killing settlers, destroying ranches in all directions. For God's sake, give me authority to take soldiers from Fort Reynolds. The people are arming, and will not be restrained."[398]

9–11 and 13 September 1868
AGUA FRIA/VERDE RIVER *(Cave Creek, Arizona)*

In 1868 Company B, Eighth Cavalry, operated out of Fort Whipple (Fort Prescott), Arizona, and engaged in several fights with the Apaches under the spirited and determined Lt. Rufus Somerby. After serving in Kentucky infantry and cavalry regiments during the Civil War, Somerby was commissioned a lieutenant in the Eighth Cavalry in June 1867 and posted to Arizona. He proved to be a bloodhound in tracking Indians, but his weakness for alcohol landed him in trouble several times.

In September 1868 Somerby took seventeen men of Company B on a whirlwind chase of several Indian bands. On 9 September he attacked a party of Indians identified as Hualapais, killing two warriors and capturing four women. The following day he hit a band of ten Indians near the lower Agua Fria River. In this attack his men killed four warriors, captured three women, and destroyed a large quantity of equipage and provisions.

On 11 September, Somerby's hard-riding troopers crossed the divide between the Agua Fria and Verde Rivers and swept into a Hualapai rancheria, where they killed five Indians and destroyed the camp. As he moved upriver on 13 September, Somerby surprised a band of Tonto Apaches camped at the mouth of the Dragoon Fork of the Verde (Sycamore Creek). The troopers killed two Indians and captured weapons and provisions. Pvt. Charles Gardner was wounded in the skirmish. In total, Somerby's scout resulted in the deaths of thirteen Indians and the capture of seven.

Somerby went on to win two brevets for his work in Arizona, but personal difficulties lay ahead. On leave in 1870, he began drinking heavily. While still in the Eighth Cavalry, he enlisted in an artillery unit. When army brass discovered his deception, Somerby was given a choice between retiring or facing a court-martial. He resigned but reenlisted, this time in the Fifth Artillery. He transferred to the First Cavalry in 1874 and to the Sixth Cavalry in 1881. Alcohol problems always plagued him. The day after Christmas in 1882, at Fort Lowell, Arizona, Somerby picked up his old cavalry carbine and shot himself in the head.[399]

25 September 1868
LA PAZ MASSACRE *(Ehrenberg, Arizona)*

The town of La Paz on the Colorado River, just upstream from present-day Ehrenberg, owed its existence to the discovery of gold in the nearby mountains. By 1868 the gold had become scarce, but the town remained viable as a port for the inland towns of Wickenburg and Prescott.

On 25 September about thirty Hualapais visited La Paz and camped nearby for the night. In town, jittery residents believed the Indians were plotting to kill them. A number of townspeople, including William Wilson, fortified by courage from the local saloons, decided to attack first. Joined by Gustavus Chenowith and his teamsters, who were passing through La Paz with their wagon train, thirteen men attacked the Indians at three o'clock in the morning. Firing into the camp from the darkness, the attackers killed fifteen Hualapais while the remaining Indians, some of them wounded, escaped into the night.

Capt. Samuel B. M. Young, Eighth Cavalry, arrived from Camp Willow Grove with troopers of Company K to investigate. By the time Young arrived, the townsmen and teamsters were gone. Wilson was the only one arrested, for what Young called "a cold-blooded cowardly murder committed by low-lived, drunken, cowardly villains." Local authorities, however, would brook no interference from the military in their jurisdiction. The district judge and the locals thwarted Young's plans, and Wilson "escaped" a few days later.[400]

— 1869 —

Ca. 6 January 1869
BASS CANYON *(Van Horn, Texas)*

Several different mail contractors operated the southern mail lines across Texas after the Civil War. By the fall of 1867 Frederick A. Sawyer and Benjamin F. Ficklin, combining their talents and resources, had their turn. Over the next several months, Indian attacks seemed to get bolder on the lower road, along the Rio Grande and Devil's River, so in the spring of 1868, Ficklin shifted the line to the upper road, which passed through Fredericksburg and went up the San Saba and Middle Concho Rivers. On either route, however, coaches had to take the dangerous road through west Texas.

On 5 January the eastbound stage left El Paso with James Bass driving and Jarvis Hubbell, ex-postmaster of El Paso, the sole passenger. The stage company should have known better, and the two men should have known better. It was practically suicide to attempt such a trip with only two men. Making matters worse, Hubbell was struggling at the time with a badly injured foot, on which he wore a woven slipper.

A capable frontiersman, Hubbell was chagrined at having to be helped up onto the coach. The stage rolled east easily on hard roads carpeted with a veil of snow. The two men passed Fort Quitman and turned northeast into Quitman Canyon then swung southeast. Snow and ice had gathered in the trail ruts along the draw between the Quitman Mountains and Devil's Ridge. The bad weather, the men assumed, meant that the Apaches were probably all huddled up around a warm

Bass Canyon, Texas

campfire. The stage made it to Eagle Springs Station, on the slope of the Eagle Mountains. The workers at the station were the last ones to see Bass and Hubbell alive.

Two days later, line agent Henry Morrell left El Paso with a driver and one passenger. The three had passed Eagle Springs Station and were approaching a pass through the Van Horn Mountains, about nine miles from Van Horn's Well, when they spotted something in the road. The mules shied away and the driver halted them. Morrell inspected the object; it was the battered head of James Bass. The driver hurried the coach on. A short distance later the travelers found a severed arm, and beyond that, a torso. They saw the wrecked stage about half a mile from the road. Arrows pierced the sides like a pin cushion, and bloodstains speckled the interior. On the ground was Hubbell's slipper, but his body was nowhere to be found. Morrell wanted to search the area, but when Apaches appeared in the distance, the travelers sped off for Fort Davis.

At the fort, agent Jim Spears quickly organized an expedition to search the site, but the small cavalry escort he secured turned back after thirty miles, claiming fatigued horses. Spears and the coach driver continued on their own. They buried what was left of James Bass, but they never found any trace of Hubbell. From then on, the pass was called Bass Canyon.[401]

4 February 1869
ARAVAIPA MOUNTAINS *(Klondyke, Arizona)*
Capt. Reuben F. Bernard returned to his Company G, First Cavalry, at Fort Lowell, Arizona, in December 1868, following recruiting duty that had kept him in the East since the end of the Civil War. Shortly after his arrival, he went to Mexico to buy horses, returning on 29 January. Two days later, he was off again on an Indian scout, leaving Fort Lowell with forty men of Company G.

At Camp Grant, Bernard talked to an Indian woman who gave him information regarding the whereabouts of Chiquito's Apache band. He reinforced his expedition with twenty-five men from Company K, seven Indian scouts, four packers, and sixteen mules, and headed south up the San Pedro River. In the Aravaipa Mountains (now called the Galiuros), the party found several abandoned rancherias.

Bernard continued on, through what he called "as hard a snow storm as I ever saw in my life in any country." Still finding no Apaches, he kept twenty-seven men with him and sent the rest back to Camp Grant with

Lt. Alexander H. Stanton. Intended as a ruse, Bernard hoped the move would trick the Apaches into thinking that the entire expedition had left the area. The captain then marched higher into the mountains, in snow fifteen inches deep, letting his intuition guide him "towards the points where there was most certainty of finding Indians or Indian signs."[402]

Bernard's persistence paid off on 4 February, when he spotted smoke in the mountains, then saw nearly forty Indians retreating. Bernard chased them for several miles up and down the snowy slopes. During the pursuit, all of his men emptied their Spencer carbines at least three times each. Along the way, the soldiers crashed through another rancheria, where they killed eight warriors and captured six women and children. On the other side of the mountains, the Apaches finally made their escape. Bernard destroyed their poor camp, which consisted only of a few simple items.

Bernard's only casualty on the scout was a trooper whose horse lost its footing on an icy slope and fell 200 feet. Miraculously both horse and rider suffered only bad bruises. The expedition returned to Fort Lowell on 9 February, after marching about 250 miles.[403]

6 April 1869
LA BONTE CREEK *(Douglas, Wyoming)*

Established in July 1867 near the mouth of LaPrele Creek and the North Platte River, Fort Fetterman was intended to protect emigrant routes through the area and keep hostile Lakota, Cheyenne, and Arapaho Indians in check. As with many western forts, access to good supplies of wood and grass was limited, and the soldiers of Fetterman had to go to the slopes of the Laramie Mountains, anywhere from fifteen to twenty-five miles away, for hay and wood. These small wood- and hay-gathering parties were prime targets for raiding Indians. Pvt. Thomas Bourke, Company K, Eighteenth Infantry, was working at the sawmill near the Laramie Mountains when he became the first Fort Fetterman soldier to be killed by Indians.

Another dangerous task for the soldiers stationed at Fort Fetterman was policing the easily vandalized telegraph lines. In late March and early April of 1869, Sgt. Robert Rae, Company A, Fourth Infantry, led several detachments out to repair the lines, returning each time without incident. But on 6 April an apparently routine repair job proved deadly.

On that day, Rae left Fetterman and headed south with a Corporal Sanders and six privates, taking a six-mule army wagon and two horses.

While they worked on the line near La Bonte Creek, about ten miles south of present-day Douglas, Wyoming, a band of Arapahos attacked and killed Rae and Pvt. Russell B. Emery. Sanders and three men escaped and made it back to the post. The other two men were missing. Cavalry patrols immediately left in search of the Indians, but to no avail. The searchers recovered Emery's body, but Rae's was never found. The two missing men were presumed killed until 9 April, when the exhausted and hungry Privates Babcock and Sullivan stumbled into the fort.[404]

16 May 1869
SALT CREEK PRAIRIE *(Jean, Texas)*
The battle at Salt Creek Prairie was reputedly one of the most desperate fights ever to occur on the Texas frontier. It began as eleven ranchers from Young and Palo Pinto Counties, along with their cook, were gathering cattle along Flint Creek.[405] They had already rounded up about 500 head when they realized that such a large herd would certainly draw Indians. On the damp morning of 16 May, with winds blowing intermittent rain and snow flurries, the cowmen began moving the herd south near Little Salt Creek, about three miles northwest of present-day Jean, Texas.

W. C. Kutch and Shap Carter were driving some strays back to the herd when Henry Harrison's shouts alerted them to Indians. About sixty warriors had surrounded the cowmen. Kutch and Carter were half a mile from the cover of some timber and one mile from their companions. The pair faced a decision. "We can get away without any trouble," Kutch observed, to which Carter responded, "What sort of a tale will we tell when we get home?"[406] Little more discussion was needed.

Kutch and Carter rode hard toward their friends, and a few cowmen charged out to meet them. One of the Lemley boys shouted that they should run to the timber to their west, but Kutch replied that it was too far across "bald prairie." He told them to make for a thicket near a little bluff 300 yards away. The Comanches, however, anticipated their move; when the ranchers neared their potential refuge, Indians popped up and began firing from that very spot. The cowmen veered back onto the open prairie. Their only hope was to dive into a nearby shallow depression in the prairie.

The ranchers abandoned their horses hoping the Indians would take them and leave, but they did not. The depression the cowmen took position in was so shallow they had to lie flat to avoid the Comanches' fire. The defenders were armed only with cap-and-ball pistols, no rifles, while the Indians had long-range rifles and made good use of them. Will Crow was the first rancher killed; Jesse McClain was wounded; George and John Lemley, Rube Secris, Jim Gray, and Carter were each wounded twice; Kutch was hit three times but not killed. Most of the wounds were to the head. Every man was hit except Harrison, Joe Woody, and the ranchers' cook, "Negro Dick." The wounded loaded the weapons while the others kept up a desultory fire.

The fight lasted from about 10 a.m. to about 5 p.m. In the late afternoon, the Comanches gathered on a small hill as if to confer about what to do next. At that point, Ira Graves had all the cowmen stand up, with the badly wounded propped up by their companions. They waved and cheered at the Indians as if daring them to charge. The warriors seemed to have second thoughts about renewing the battle, perhaps believing that despite the long fight, most of their opponents were apparently unscathed. The raiders gathered up the cattle and rode away. Little did they know, their adversaries were down to their last few bullets.

The unwounded Harrison traveled to the Harmison ranch, several miles away, to get help, but before help arrived, John Lemley died in the night. The next day, several cowboys arrived with a wagon to move the wounded and retrieve the dead. The wagon reached the old salt works at present-day Graham, Texas. Carter died before a doctor could be found. Only three men were able to travel home.

Three ranchers had died as a result of the fight, and the cowmen had lost all their cattle, thirty-one horses, and all their supplies and bedding. McClain lived for two more years, but he eventually died from complications of his wounds.[407]

30 May 1869
SPILLMAN CREEK RAIDS *(Lincoln, Kansas)*

After several actions between Cheyenne Dog Soldier Tall Bull and Maj. Eugene Carr's Fifth Cavalry in mid-May 1869, Carr returned to Fort McPherson, Nebraska, to refit, leaving Tall Bull free to aim his vengeance at area settlements. During the last week of May, Cheyennes killed fourteen civilians in north-central Kansas. On Sunday 30 May they turned their attention to Spillman Creek, northwest of Lincoln, Kansas.

About two o'clock in the afternoon, Tall Bull and sixty warriors began their path of destruction down Spillman Creek. The first victims were Eli Zeigler and John Alverson, who were attacked as they headed up the creek to examine an abandoned farm. Zeigler's sister, Susanna

Alderdice, had warned her brother to be careful, having heard recent reports of increased Indian depredations. Near the mouth of Trail and Spillman Creeks, Zeigler and Alverson saw what appeared to be mounted soldiers on the opposite bank. As the figures peeled off toward them, the two men realized that they were Indians. Abandoning their wagon, the pair made for the thickets along Trail Creek. The Cheyennes fired at them for a short time, then occupied themselves with the contents of the wagon.

The raiders next went to a small settlement near the present-day town of Denmark. A couple out tending their garden, Eskild Lauritzen and his wife Stine, were quickly killed, then stripped and scalped. A houseguest of the Lauritzens, Otto Peterson, took off running, but he was soon caught and killed. The Cheyennes next approached the neighboring Christensen home, which the Lauritzen's son happened to be visiting. Here, however, the occupants were armed and ready. A few shots kept the raiders away. After unsuccessfully trying to set fire to the Christensens' outbuildings, the Indians moved on.

Continuing downstream, the Cheyennes next came upon three immigrants, also guests of the Lauritzens, who were out inspecting a possible farmstead. The two men, Fred Meigheroff and George Weichel, fired at the Indians as they and George's wife, Maria, fled south along Spillman Creek. They made it about two miles before they ran out of ammunition. The pursuing Indians quickly killed the men and captured Maria, who was described as a beautiful twenty-year-old.

A mile southeast was the Michael Healy homestead, where Susanna Alderdice and her four children, along with a Mr. and Mrs. Noon, a Mr. Whalen, and Bridget Kine and her daughter, had been staying. When they heard shooting, at about 6 p.m., the Noons and Mr. Whalen quickly made their escape on horseback, leaving the rest of the women and children behind. The abandoned women tried to escape with their youngsters to the thick brush along the Saline River. Clutching her two-month-old daughter, Bridget waded across the river, hiding in the brush on the opposite side. But Susanna, herding her four small children, could not keep up.

The Cheyennes caught Susanna about fifty yards from the river. She sat down, holding her two youngest children, two-year-old Frank and eight-month-old Alice. The Indians shot down five-year-old John with four bullets and put five arrows into Frank, then bashed him against the ground. They shot four-year-old Willis with five arrows and two bullets, then speared him in the back. For some reason they let Susanna keep baby Alice.

Another mile down the Saline, the Cheyennes saw two fourteen-year-old boys, Arthur Schmutz and John Strange. The Indians told the boys they were "good" Pawnees, and a young warrior approached the two. When he was close enough, the Indian smashed his war club into Strange's head. The boy uttered only "Oh Lordy" before he fell dead. Schmutz took off running, but an arrow hit him in the side, piercing his lung. Somehow he kept running, pulling out the shaft. As he fled, two of his brothers, who had heard the commotion and hurried out with rifles, appeared. The Indians retreated. Young Schmutz was taken to Fort Harker for treatment, but he died about ten weeks later.

At the end of that day, the Cheyennes camped on the south side of the Saline near Bullfoot Creek. Coincidentally, they were only about two miles up from the campsite of Lt. Edward Law and his Company G, Seventh Cavalry, who were unaware of the raids until the next day. Upon hearing the news, the soldiers pursued the raiders, but they got away.

Three days after Susanna Alderdice's capture, the Indians, perhaps tired of little Alice's crying, took the baby from her mother and strangled her, hanging the limp body in a tree. Susanna Alderdice and Maria Weichel remained captives until 11 July, when Major Carr caught up with Tall Bull at Summit Springs, Colorado Territory. Just moments before the rescue, Susanna was tomahawked and shot dead. Maria was shot in the chest, but she survived. She later recounted her horrific ordeal as a captive.

Eleven settlers died as a result of Tall Bull's raids along Spillman Creek. Incredibly, when Seventh Cavalry soldiers and some civilians found four-year-old Willis Alderdice the following day, he was still alive. The arrowheads in his body were all removed, including one lodged five inches into his chest. Willis was raised by Susanna's parents and lived until 1920.[408]

4 June 1869
PINAL MOUNTAINS *(Globe, Arizona)*
Capt. George B. Sanford commanded Camp McDowell intermittently from 1866 to 1870. On 20 May 1869, he gathered his own Company E, First Cavalry; Company C, Eighth Cavalry; and a detachment of the Fourteenth Infantry for a scout to the east of the post. They trailed along the Salt River and through the Superstition Mountains to the Pinal Mountains, in the vicinity of present-day Globe, Arizona. Here

Sanford discovered two Apache rancherias hidden in a canyon on either side of a small stream. He divided up his command, sending men along the canyon walls to flank the camp, then he charged down the canyon floor with his main force.

Sanford reported, "The Indians were evidently completely surprised and scattered on all sides, endeavoring to escape up the mountains, and through the canyons and holes."[409] The troops pursued them doggedly in every direction, on horseback and on foot. After a chase that lasted an hour and a half, Sanford recalled his men. He reported twenty Indians slain, including a chief named Squirrel Rifle, and four children captured. One enlisted man was wounded. Sanford returned to Camp McDowell on 8 June.[410]

6–7 July 1869
HARQUAHALA MOUNTAINS *(Salome, Arizona)*

From 1867 to 1877, William Fourr operated a station at Agua Caliente on the Gila River, where raiding Indians constantly harassed him. In June 1869 Yavapai Apaches stole seventy cows from Agua Caliente. Fourr and his friend King S. Woolsey trailed the Indians thirty miles north, where they found that some of the stock had been killed and eaten. Fourr asked for help from the army, and in response came Lt. William McCleave from Fort McDowell with thirty soldiers of Company E, First Cavalry, and Company C, Eighth Cavalry. McCleave had already been searching for raiding Indians operating under the leadership of the Yavapai Wahpooeta, or Big Rump, a suspect in the attack on a mail coach near Wickenburg. Fourr, Woolsey, George Lee, and a former soldier named Shepherd met McCleave and offered to guide him.

The expedition trailed the Apaches north to the Harquahala Mountains and found them near Eagle Tank, in a narrow canyon with the only water in the area. The Indians, who outnumbered the soldiers, would not let them get to the water supply. McCleave dismounted and fought, as Woolsey put it, "[in] Indian fashion, every man from behind a rock." Woolsey surmised that "had they been exposed they would not have lasted ten minutes." At 6 p.m. McCleave ordered a pullout, and when the Yavapais saw this they came out of their positions to chase the soldiers. It was a mistake, for the troopers now had open shots. According to Woolsey, "We hurt more Indians than we had in the previous two hours fighting."[411] Nevertheless, the troopers were unable to get to the water.

The next morning McCleave, desperate for water, attacked at 8 a.m. After an hour of hard fighting the soldiers chased the Apaches away. During the battle, one soldier was severely wounded in the head, but none were killed. McCleave reported killing nine Indians and wounding ten. Big Rump was not among the casualties.

In the end, soldiers were not Big Rump's downfall. About six weeks after the Harquahala Mountains fight, about forty Pimas and Maricopas, under old Maricopa chief Juan Chiveria, ambushed Big Rump and some of his band in Castle Creek Canyon, south of the Bradshaw Mountains. The attackers made short work of the Yavapais. Big Rump ran about 100 yards up a draw in the canyon before he was killed. The Maricopas later brought a party of soldiers under McCleave to the site to prove they had killed the Yavapai chief. McCleave found enough greenbacks and other evidence to prove that Big Rump had indeed taken part in the recent attack on a mail coach near Wickenburg.[412]

Ca. 24 August 1869
NELSON BUCK MASSACRE *(Marion, Nebraska)*

In late July 1869, a party of eleven surveyors under Nelson Buck, who had thirty-four years of experience on the frontier, were on their way to survey along the Kansas-Nebraska line. The men stopped at Fort McPherson, on the Platte River, to secure firearms and an escort for their expedition as they headed south of the Republican River. They waited several days, but no men or arms became available. Buck departed anyway.

By the time Buck and his team reached Red Willow Creek, south of Fort McPherson, they began to have misgivings. Buck sent H. B. McGregor and John R. Nettleton back to the fort to get what they needed. With no luck, McGregor and Nettleton, reluctant to chance the trip back to Buck, simply abandoned their employer and took other jobs.

Around 20 August, Lakota warriors under Pawnee Killer and Whistler were crossing the Republican west of Red Willow Creek when four of them, riding in advance, ran into Buck's surveyors. In a sharp fight, three warriors and one surveyor were killed. The remaining Indian rode back to alert the chiefs, and by the day's end, the Lakotas had attacked Buck's party, killed five more surveyors, and destroyed two wagons. The surviving surveyors made it to Beaver Creek, near the Kansas line. Whether they were going to try to continue their survey or were simply fleeing the area is unknown. The Indians caught up with them and wiped them all out.

On 15 September, unaware of the massacre, Lt. Col. Thomas Duncan, Fifth U.S. Cavalry, with 449 men of Companies B, E, F, L, and M, Fifth Cavalry; Companies B, C, and M, Second Cavalry; some Pawnee scouts; and William "Buffalo Bill" Cody as a guide, left Fort McPherson for the Republican country to hunt raiding Cheyennes. Duncan took the command south and split the men up into detachments to cover the numerous rivers coursing through the area. On 21 September a detachment came upon the remains of Buck's camp on the Beaver River, about ten miles east of Elephant Rock Crossing, near present-day Marion, Nebraska. The men found a surveyor's tripod, a Spencer carbine, a partially demolished wagon, and some broken tools and camp furniture lying about. Thinking little of it, the soldiers went on to continue their scout.

On 26 September, Duncan attacked an Indian village at Prairie Dog Creek. After the fight, he found two more surveyor's tripods. Later, back on the Republican, he met messengers carrying dispatches regarding the missing men. With the couriers was Royal Buck, Nelson Buck's son. Duncan sent Royal with John Nelson, interpreter Cody, and a squad of soldiers under Sgt. Wright, Company I, Fifth Cavalry, back to Prairie Dog Creek, where Duncan had found the tripods, to search the area. No bodies from the survey party were ever found. The only clue was a portion of a letter addressed to one of the surveyors from his sister.

On 2 October an old Lakota woman, either lost or abandoned by her people, was found on the trail between the Beaver and the Republican Rivers. John Nelson, who recognized the woman as a relative of his Indian wife, questioned her about the attack on the surveyors. After first denying any knowledge of it, she finally said that young warriors from the Lakota bands of Pawnee Killer and Whistler brought the tripods into camp one day, but where or how they got them she did not know. Unable to pick up any other Indian trails, Duncan took his command back to Fort McPherson.[413]

5 October 1869
STONE MASSACRE *(Dragoon, Arizona)*

The stagecoach that crossed Sulphur Springs Valley on the afternoon of 5 October carried six men: the driver, a Mr. Kaler; John Finkel Stone, owner of the Apache Pass Mining Company; and four soldiers from Company D, Twenty-first Infantry. Kaler and Stone had made the trip between Fort Bowie and Dragoon Springs many times before, and they

Cochise Stronghold, Dragoon Mountains, Arizona

probably felt little apprehension. They were unaware that a sharp-eyed Chiricahua Apache had spotted them from a high peak in the Dragoon Mountains, and the Apache chief Cochise set a trap for them.

The sun was setting as the coach neared the Dragoon Springs Station. It was common knowledge that Apaches seldom attacked after dark. Just as the stage approached the junction of the Goodwin and Bowie Roads, however, a number of warriors jumped out of a gully beside the road. The Indians blasted the stage with bullets and arrows, killing Kaler and three of the four soldiers in the first volley. The stage careened off the road as the team galloped south toward the mountains, right into another band of mounted warriors. The remaining soldier and passengers discharged only six shots before they were overwhelmed and killed. The Apaches stripped the bodies and donned their clothing.[414]

10 December 1869
CHILSON'S CREEK *(Central Arizona)*

Capt. George B. Sanford led men of his Company E, First Cavalry, and Company A, Eighth Cavalry, on a scout out of Camp McDowell, Arizona Territory, on 9 December. The next day, Sanford reported passing through fine rolling country with good grass and plenty of game, but no fresh signs of Indians. Shortly after that assessment, the command crested a hill and ran into a party of eleven Apache warriors on foot, headed south on a converging trail.

Sanford ordered an immediate charge. The Indians broke and ran, trying to save themselves by fleeing. Realizing they could not outrun the mounted troopers, they tried to conceal themselves in the bushes and rocks. This strategy also failed, and, wrote Sanford, they "made what resistance they could." "The fight was not finished until every Indian of the party, eleven in all, were killed," the captain reported. With only one enlisted man wounded, Sanford returned to Camp McDowell the next day.[415]

— 1870 —

28 January 1870
DRAGOON MOUNTAINS *(Dragoon, Arizona)*

Units out of Fort Bowie had been chasing Apaches for years, especially during the last few months of 1869. When it became too dangerous for Cochise and his people in the Chiricahua Mountains, he moved them west across the valley to the Dragoon Mountains. In mid-January 1970 Fort Bowie commander Capt. Thomas S. Dunn, Twenty-first Infantry, ordered Capt. Reuben F. Bernard, First Cavalry, out to find them. Bernard left the post on 26 January with fifty-five men of his Company G; a detachment of Company G, Eighth Cavalry; five scouts; guide Merejildo Grijalva; and three civilian packers.

Grijalva cut the Indians' trail on the north side of the Dragoons on 28 January and followed it eight miles down the east side of the mountains to where it turned west, toward Cochise's strongholds. Grijalva found a recently abandoned rancheria and a trail headed north toward the western stronghold. The scouts spotted some Apaches high up in the rocks and Bernard charged them, killing two.

Moving quickly on, the expedition found another rancheria in a canyon. In a second charge, Bernard's men crashed through the small village; this time they killed eleven Indians and captured two. In the camp, the soldiers found a bar of gold stolen from John Finkel Stone (see Stone Massacre, 5 October 1869). The rancheria belonged to Cochise's lieutenants, Schoga and Chackone. Cochise himself had temporarily moved north to take refuge in the White Mountains.[416]

24 May 1870
TONTO VALLEY *(Payson, Arizona)*

Still operating out of Camp McDowell, Capt. George B. Sanford took his Company E, First Cavalry, and Company E, Third Cavalry, on a scout through the varied country of central Arizona Territory. The patrol searched for two weeks until they found several large rancherias, possibly in Arroyo Colonida near the Mogollon Rim or on a creek Sanford said the Apaches called "Chivico" [Cibecue?]. One of the rancherias contained large adobe structures and numerous wickiups. Without knowing the Apaches' strength, Sanford sounded a charge and the soldiers galloped in.

In spite of his blind attack, Sanford was successful. With no loss to his command, Sanford killed twenty-two Indians, took twelve prisoners, and captured six horses and mules. In the village, Sanford's men came across considerable stolen property, plus the scalps of two white men. They destroyed large quantities of corn, wheat, and supplies, then returned to Camp McDowell on 2 June.[417]

30 September 1870
MOUNT MARGARET *(Tennyson, Texas)*

On 30 September 1870, Kiowa chief White Horse (Tsen-tainte) and thirty warriors ambushed a mail coach near Mount Margaret, twenty-two miles northeast of Fort Concho, Texas. A Kiowa woman had lost her brother in a previous raid, and since the woman had no nearby relatives to take vengeance, White Horse was selected to "wipe out" the death.

The Kiowas appeared from the brush on the northeast side of the stage road. The driver, Alphonse Prairear, had one army escort. Upon seeing the Indians, Prairear jumped from the stage and he and most of the soldiers ran for their lives. One trooper, Pvt. Martin Wurmser of Company E, Fourth Cavalry, remained at his post inside the coach. As a result of this act of bravery, he was killed, scalped, and mutilated.

Kiowa chief White Horse
—From authors' collection

Soldiers from Fort Concho later arrived on the scene to find the mail scattered on the road and the overturned stage riddled with bullets and arrows. The coach's four-mule team had vanished. The troopers recovered Wurmser's body. The post surgeon at Fort Concho, Dr. Notson, counted sixty-eight arrow wounds on the corpse.[418]

December 1870
CARRIZO SPRINGS *(Carrizo Springs, Texas)*

Continued Indian raiding from the reservations in Indian Territory in the north, and from Mexico in the south, prompted Texas governor Edmund J. Davis to ask the legislature, in June 1870, to approve the organization of twenty ranger companies. Although the rangers usually provided most of their own equipment, this time the state provided them with breech-loading carbines.

By the end of the year, fourteen companies were ready. H. Joseph Richarz, a former Prussian soldier who had established a sheep and cattle ranch west of San Antonio, was awarded the captaincy of Company E. He moved his unit into the abandoned remains of Fort Inge, on the Leona River south of present-day Uvalde, Texas. Richarz complained of his inability to chase Indian raiders into Mexico. "If it were not for this cursed international law," he wrote, "I know very well what to do to clean out these bloody savages on the other side of the Rio Grande."[419]

By 1870 the Indians were mostly targeting ranchers' cattle. When a band stole cattle from a ranch on Turkey Creek, about twenty miles west of Fort Inge, Richarz and Lt. Sevier Vance were out on scouts, so a Sergeant Eckford and the company physician, Dr. Woodbridge, were the only officers on post. Woodbridge led out fourteen rangers, leaving only one man in camp. The rangers arrived at Turkey Creek and found the Indians' trail leading south.

The Indians were a few days and about fifty miles ahead of the rangers, near Carrizo Springs in present-day northwestern Dimmit County. The raiders, who were Comanches and Kiowas, not Lipans or Kickapoos as supposed, struck another place, the Vivian Ranch, where they killed a man and captured a Mexican boy. They also jumped five cowboys, killing one of them. The same Indians then hit Dave Adams's ranch and killed Adams. Half a mile from Carrizo Springs, nine settlers tried unsuccessfully to fight the raiders. Sweeping past them, the warriors chased a wagonload of settlers back to their homes, then continued down the Nueces River.

When the rangers got to Carrizo Springs, local rancher Edward English told Woodbridge that the Indians were two days ahead of them, but he believed they would come back through when they finished raiding. English said he could lead the rangers to a good hideout several miles west of there, off the trail, where they could spot the Indians on their way back. English took the rangers to the suggested spot and they waited overnight.

The next morning, Woodbridge sent English and rangers Doc Quebum and Joe Brierly east to look for signs of the raiders, then sent two more men to the south. These two discovered the Indians driving a herd of stolen livestock, not on the trail they had taken before, but riding right toward them. The men warned Woodbridge, who quickly had his men mount up for a charge.

It was twelve against sixty, but Woodbridge figured the Texans' Winchesters would level out the odds. The Comanches saw them coming and also charged, and the two forces met on the crest of a ridge. The whooping of the warriors panicked two rangers into turning and running, but the ten remaining stood their ground and clashed at close quarters. Ranger Bedinger (or Belleger) was killed by three bullets in the chest. An Indian clubbed Woodbridge in the neck with his bow, knocking him off his horse. Tom Blakeny and John Whitney stood by the stunned doctor, firing their Winchesters furiously until the barrels became too hot to hold. Whitney finally pulled Woodbridge onto his horse and the two made it back to the others.

The Comanches performed dexterous riding and dodging, but the firepower was telling; nine Indians went down. The little knot of men kept firing until they were dangerously low on ammunition, but by then, the Indians had had enough and pulled away, taking Bedinger's and Woodbridge's horses. Bedinger, the only ranger fatality, was scalped.

When English and his party heard firing, they returned to the camp to find the trail of the Indians who had just battled with Woodbridge. They followed it, thinking the rangers had gone after them. Suddenly, twenty-five Comanches encircled English and the two rangers, but they held them off, shooting a scalp-decorated shield from the arm of one warrior. The warriors rode off. The determined English, Quebum, and Brierly followed, however, and waited by the Indians' camp until nightfall. In the dark, they crept up to the camp to look for Woodbridge. Not finding any trace of him, they assumed that the doctor and the rest of the rangers were dead, and they returned to Carrizo Springs. Woodbridge and his rangers later rode in, to the three men's relief. Everyone agreed that without the Winchesters, they would all have been killed.[420]

— 1871 —

1 January 1871
PINAL MOUNTAINS *(Hayden, Arizona)*
Cochise and his Chiricahua Apaches had been at war with the U.S. Army for more than a decade when the aging leader finally began sending out peace feelers. In late summer of 1870 he went to Camp Mogollon, later renamed Fort Apache, and told the authorities there that he wished to stop fighting, remarking that he had killed about as many people as he had lost. In the fall the chief went to Canada Alamosa in New Mexico, ostensibly to consider settling on a reservation there. Many soldiers figured Cochise's actions were just a ploy to gain respite from the fighting. With the onset of winter, he returned to the Chiricahua Mountains.

Before Christmas, a band of Chiricahuas left the mountains and headed north, most likely to raid. On 21 December, Capt. Reuben F. Bernard, with Company G and detachments of Company K, First Cavalry, and Company H, Third Cavalry, left Fort Bowie and cut the Indians' trail, which headed north and west for about 150 miles. On New Year's Day, between the Gila River and the Pinal Mountains, north of present-day Hayden, Arizona, Bernard's men caught up with the Apaches. In the attack on the Indians' rancheria, the cavalry killed nine and wounded many more, taking no losses of their own. The soldiers' round-trip march of about 450 miles in harsh winter conditions proved insufferable for five of the troopers, who deserted shortly after returning to Fort Bowie.[421]

12 February 1871
CHIRICAHUA PEAK *(Portal, Arizona)*
A group of prospectors in the Chiricahua Mountains found more than they bargained for when Apaches attacked them in late January 1871. Two men were wounded, and two others fled north to Fort Bowie to report the attack. Capt. Gerald Russell of the Third Cavalry investigated, but his scouts found no Indian trails. The Apaches, meanwhile, were busy stealing stock. Raiders took fourteen mules and horses from as far away as Silver City, New Mexico Territory, and brought them to

the Chiricahua Mountains, figuring they would not be pursued there by New Mexican troops.

When news of the raids reached Fort Bayard, Capt. William Kelly, Eighth Cavalry, took fourteen men of Company C, one packer, guide Juan Arroyo, and seven civilians from Silver City under James Bullard to follow the Indians' trail. In the Burro Mountains, seven more troopers joined them, and the thirty-one men tracked the raiders southwest. By 12 February, they had entered the eastern Chiricahua Mountains, where they followed what Kelly described as "a well beaten trail to the summit."

At 1 p.m., Bullard found the Indians' camp just southeast of Chiricahua Peak. A heavy snowstorm was blowing, and the Apaches were bundled up in seventeen well-built wickiups. Bullard's men surrounded the camp and poured in a devastating fire. Some of the Indians broke free into the snowy mountains, but fourteen were killed, one was captured, and about twenty were wounded. Geronimo and some Nednhi Apaches may have been present. Kelly and his men confiscated 2,500 pounds of mule and horse meat, some rifles and revolvers, and military papers from a Southern Overland stagecoach. Some of the stolen Silver City stock was also recovered. The rancheria was burned, and Kelly moved out. As he passed through the site again the next day, Kelly saw that some Indians had returned to lay skins and other items around the body of one of the slain, indicating that the fallen warrior had probably been a chief.[422]

28 March 1871
GILA RIVER *(Duncan, Arizona)*
During the winter and spring of 1871, soldiers and civilians hunted Cochise's raiders. On 24 February, John Bullard and thirty civilians found Cochise's camp in the Mogollon Mountains. Bullard was killed in the ensuing fight, while the Arizonans killed Salvadora, son of Mangas Coloradas, and about fifteen other Apaches. In March Apache raiders killed Charles Keerle and his wife at Chocolate Pass in Chihuahua.

On 17 March Capt. Gerald Russell, Third Cavalry, with eleven men of Company K, fought Cochise in the Peloncillo Mountains north of Stein's Peak. He killed three Apaches then returned to Fort Bowie for reinforcements. There Russell gathered thirty troopers and two civilians, and two days later he was off again. In Pedrocito Canyon, Russell came upon an abandoned rancheria, where he found "a gentleman's glove and a small book [as well as a] tress of auburn-colored woman's hair carefully wrapped in paper."[423] Russell believed that the Indians who had camped there were the ones who murdered Keerle and his wife.

Russell continued on the trail, and on 28 March, during a driving rainstorm, he surprised the Apaches south of the Gila Mountains near the Gila River. He divided his force into three squads, then charged into the camp. The soldiers killed fifteen Indians in the attack. Russell believed they would have taken more but for the large number of new recruits in his command; his few veterans had been in the rear with the pack train.

In the debris of the Indian camp, Russell found ration tickets from the Canada Alamosa Reservation. When he returned to Fort Bowie he reported that he thought the number of available troops was insufficient to catch Cochise or to force the Apaches onto the reservations.[424]

8 and 9 June 1871
RYE CREEK/MORTON'S FIGHT *(Payson, Arizona)*

When a band of Tonto Apaches killed herder John Gantt and ran off 137 horses, mules, and cattle from the Bowers ranch on the Agua Fria River, sixteen civilians from Prescott and the surrounding area, under John B. Townsend and Charles B. Genung, rode to the scene. On the trail they ran into Lt. Charles Morton, Third Cavalry, with twenty-nine men from companies A, E, and G, who were heading down from Camp Verde. They joined forces and trailed the raiders easterly toward the Verde River, coming upon some of the Bowers's stolen stock along the way, apparently abandoned by the fleeing Indians.

On 7 June, as the party neared the East Fork of the Verde, guide Jose Ruiz warned that the Indians might set a brush fire to drive the pursuers away. His instincts proved correct. The fire forced Morton and the others off the trail, but within twelve miles they regained the trail at the East Fork, crossed over, and headed upstream. They moved through a canyon with precipitous bluffs hundreds of feet above them, and Genung commented that a few Apaches on top could stop an army with some small boulders.

Although Genung, Townsend, and some of the other civilians held a low opinion of the army's fighting abilities, Morton cooperated with them, and when the civilians ran out of supplies, Morton shared his stores with them. The party camped below the cliffs until 2 a.m. on 8 June, then silently mounted up and moved out. About twelve more miles upstream, near the point where the East Fork changed course from southwest to northeast, Ruiz saw Indian "signal smoke." The men raced ahead, hoping to catch the Indians before they fled. Finding two rancherias, they split up to hit both. Morton's squad killed one Indian, but at the second rancheria the carnage was much higher, with thirty Indians killed and three wounded. Morton had instructed the men not to harm women and children, but he believed the civilians at the second camp shot down one woman and three children regardless. Genung himself was mistakenly shot at by some soldiers in the confusion.

On 9 June the command moved southeast over the Mazatzal Divide to the headwaters of Rye Creek. Just before noon, Ruiz told Morton that they were near another rancheria. The anxious civilians got in the way of Morton's advance, and the charge soon degenerated into a number of individual pursuits into the mountains. Twenty-three Indians were killed in the initial attack, including a woman who was firing at the soldiers. The command destroyed the rancheria and recaptured three horses.

Morton and Townsend stayed hot on the Indians' trail, heading south another four miles. At one point, Townsend took off alone after three Indians, killing one, wounding another, and capturing two horses. Genung caught up with him and killed the third Indian. On the body he found the rifle of John Gantt, proving that these were the Apaches who had raided the Bowers ranch. Townsend's feat so impressed Morton that the lieutenant mentioned him in his official report.

Somewhere near the mouth of Rye Creek, the men realized that they had passed through country that few whites had ever seen. A day and a half more marching brought them to old Camp Reno, where they met a scouting detachment under Capt. Anson Mills. Mills kept up the chase while Morton's exhausted command trekked to Camp McDowell. The fifty-six Indians killed and eight wounded that Morton officially reported made this one of the most noteworthy of all cavalry operations in Arizona Territory.[425]

13 July 1871
CIENAGA DE LOS PINOS *(Pantano, Arizona)*

In July 1871 Capt. Henry E. Smith led most of his Company G, Twenty-first Infantry, from Tucson toward their new station at Camp Bowie. Cochise and his Chiricahua Apaches saw them coming and planned an ambush at the water hole at Cienaga de los Pinos, near present-day Pantano, Arizona. After his men drank, Smith had most of his company move on while the teamsters stayed behind to finish watering the mules.

Waiting until Smith was a couple of miles ahead, Cochise struck the wagons. The wagons' escort held the Apaches off long enough for Smith to hurry back with the rest of G Company. He deployed his men in skirmish order and advanced against Cochise's warriors. The disciplined fire of the infantryman forced the warriors back and eventually broke them. The Apaches abandoned the field, leaving twenty-five dead warriors behind. Smith reported another thirty or more were wounded. One soldier, Pvt. Charles W. Harris, was killed, and three soldiers and one civilian were wounded. Smith, now formed up compactly and ever more watchful, continued on to Camp Bowie.[426]

24 October 1871
HORSESHOE CANYON *(Portal, Arizona)*

Lt. Col. George Crook, Twenty-third Infantry, had come south after a successful campaign against the Paiutes in Oregon to see if he could stabilize the situation in Arizona. He had barely gotten started when the new Indian commissioner, Vincent Colyer, entered the picture to try his brand of peace negotiations with the Indians. Crook had to suspend his operations until Colyer had finished.

The commissioner had hardly left the territory when the "pacified" Indians began raiding again. Seventy or more Apaches attacked ranches near Cienaga San Simon, killing settler Richard Barnes and badly wounding R. M. Gilbert. Gilbert stumbled into Camp Bowie on 22 October and reported the raid. Capt. Gerald Russell assembled twenty-five men of Company K, Third Cavalry, with a few civilians, and marched out that night for San Simon. They buried Barnes's body and followed the Indians' trail south to Horseshoe Canyon, on the eastern slopes of the Chiricahua Mountains.

Russell went up the canyon about three miles to a spring, where he watered his horses about 1 p.m. on 24 October. Waiting among the rocks above the command were about sixty Chokonen and Nednhi Apaches under Geronimo and Juh. The Indians opened fire, and in the first volley they killed civilian guide Robert Whitney. Believing they had killed army scout Merejildo Grijalva, their former captive, the Indians called out "Chivero," their name for Grijalva. The Apaches rejoiced, unaware that Grijalva was in fact with Crook at the time. Standing near Whitney, a Private Blockhaus was severely wounded.

The Indians, certain of victory, closed in a circle around the troopers and blasted them with repeating Henry rifles and single-shot Springfields, which they had previously captured from the army. Russell fought back for four hours, taking no additional casualties. The Apaches stopped firing around 5 p.m., but Russell remained concealed until dark and pulled out during the night. Warriors fired at Russell and his men as they retreated, but the soldiers escaped without further loss and made their way back to Camp Bowie.[427]

— 1872 —

26 August 1872
FORT MCKEAN *(Bismarck, North Dakota)*

Fort McKean, named for Civil War colonel Henry Boyd McKean, sat high atop a bluff overlooking the Heart River at its junction with the Missouri. Indian hostilities had plagued the fort since its establishment on 14 June 1872. On 26 August, about twelve miles from Fort McKean, a war party of about 125 Lakotas attacked a sergeant and six privates—detachments of Companies B and C, Sixth Infantry—and several Arikara scouts. One report indicated that two Arikaras were killed, while others stated that six soldiers and two "citizens" were killed.[428]

3 and 4 October 1872
HEART RIVER *(Almont, North Dakota)*

Col. David S. Stanley, Twenty-second Infantry, commanded military operations for the Yellowstone Expedition, a Northern Pacific Railroad survey expedition seeking a suitable rail route across the Dakotas and Montana. About 550 men of Companies A, B, C, F, H, and K, Eighth Infantry; Companies A, C, and F, Seventeenth Infantry; Companies D, F, and G, Twenty-second Infantry; and some Indian scouts were to serve as escorts for the team of surveyors and engineers, under Thomas L. Rosser. The expedition left Fort Rice, on the Missouri River, on 26 July 1872. They reached the Yellowstone at the mouth of the Powder River on 18 August.

While there, Stanley and several officers encountered Hunkpapas under Chief Gall on the opposite side of the river. As they engaged in a shouting "parley," the Indians opened fire, but none of the officers was hit. The infantry was ineffective in chasing down the mounted warriors. As the expedition moved on, the Indians constantly kept up their harassments.

Meanwhile a similar expedition, under Maj. Eugene Baker, Second Cavalry, left Fort Ellis in Montana to meet up with Stanley on the

Powder River. On 14 August, Baker engaged the Indians in a battle at Pryor's Fork, near Billings. Further Indian troubles forced an early end to Baker's expedition. On 21 and 22 August, Indians skirmished with Stanley at the mouth of O'Fallon's Creek, but there were no casualties. After more half-hearted attempts to proceed with the surveys, Stanley, convinced of the futility of continuing, called it quits and headed back to Fort Rice.

Stanley's command was almost home when, on 3 October, Lakota war parties attacked a couple of detachments that were out hunting beyond White Butte Creek, near the crossing of Heart River. Lt. Eben Crosby, Seventeenth Infantry, and Stanley's own servant, Steven, were killed and scalped. The next day, while parties searched for the two missing men, Lakotas attacked another detachment and mortally wounded Lt. Lewis D. Adair, Twenty-second Infantry. The expedition's failure led Stanley to realize that he must have cavalry to contend with the mounted Lakotas.[429]

2 and 14 October 1872
FORT MCKEAN *(Bismarck, North Dakota)*

Col. David Stanley's Yellowstone Expedition (see previous entry) served to stir up hostilities among the Indians in Montana and the Dakotas. In October 1872, Indians began to harass the garrison at Fort McKean, as they had done about five weeks earlier (see Fort McKean, 26 August 1872). On 2 October, about 300 Hunkpapas attacked the post, then in command of Lt. Col. Daniel Huston, Sixth Infantry. The Indians killed three soldiers and wounded one, all from Company C. The Indians attacked again on 14 October. Lt. Col. William P. Carlin, Seventeenth Infantry, commanding detachments of Company C, Sixth Infantry; Company H, Seventeenth Infantry; and eight Arikara scouts, went out from the garrison to drive away the raiders. Two enlisted men and three Lakotas were killed.[430]

— 1873 —

27 April 1873
EAGLE SPRINGS *(Van Horn, Texas)*

West Texas was a dangerous place in the 1870s, and only large, well-armed parties could hope to travel the area securely. Companies of the Ninth Cavalry, a black regiment, were scattered at posts along the

San Antonio to El Paso Road, as were companies of the Twenty-fourth and Twenty-fifth Infantry, also black regiments. Soldiers at the region's mostly isolated, primitive, and cheerless stations were so often engaged in tedious manual-labor duties that they welcomed the opportunity to go out on escorts and scouts.

On 27 April 1873, some Ninth Cavalrymen under a Sergeant Wilks were carrying mail on the road from Fort Davis to Fort Bliss. Having gotten safely past El Muerto Springs and Howard's Well and through Bass Canyon, they stopped at Eagle Springs Station, on the north slope of the Eagle Mountains, about a dozen miles southwest of present-day Van Horn, Texas. Here a band of Apaches struck. Defending the station was a small detachment of Company B, Twenty-fifth Infantry, from Fort Quitman, under Cpl. E. Parker. The cavalrymen of the mail detail dismounted and joined the infantrymen in a static defense around the station. After a sharp fight, the Apaches melted away into the mountains. The Indians killed two soldiers but reportedly lost "several" warriors.[431]

7 May and 15 and 17 June 1873
FORT ABRAHAM LINCOLN *(Bismarck, North Dakota)*
In November 1872 Fort McKean was expanded and renamed Fort Abraham Lincoln. The army erected new buildings in the valley below the old fort to accommodate the increased cavalry presence. Enlarging the post did not, however, prevent Indian harassment. On 7 May 1873, about 100 Lakotas attacked the fort, which was under the command of Lt. Col. William P. Carlin, Seventeenth Infantry. Detachments of Companies B and C, Sixth Infantry, and Company H, Seventeenth Infantry, repelled the raiders, killing one and wounding three.

In June at Fort Rice, about twenty miles downriver from Fort Lincoln, Col. David Stanley prepared to escort another surveying expedition to the Yellowstone River (see Heart River, 3 and 4 October 1872). His formidable force consisted of ten cavalry and fifteen infantry companies, totaling 1,500 soldiers, along with 400 civilians. Meanwhile the surveyors and engineers of the Northern Pacific Railroad, under Thomas L. Rosser, waited at Fort Lincoln for their escort. On 15 June four of Stanley's companies, under Maj. Edwin F. Townsend, Ninth Infantry, arrived at Lincoln. The same day, the Lakotas attacked the fort again, losing two warriors in the process.

Rather than wait for Stanley's main force, Rosser's survey team departed Fort Lincoln on 16 June with Townsend's Companies B, C,

Fort Abraham Lincoln, North Dakota

F, and H, Eighth Infantry, and a detachment of Seventh Cavalry. The expedition traveled southwest, planning to eventually join Stanley's contingent, which would not leave Fort Rice until 20 June. Only one day out, 150 Lakota warriors jumped the N.P.R.R. crew. Their escort rushed to protect them, and in a short fight, the troopers killed four Lakotas and wounded eight. One soldier and one Arikara scout were wounded.[432]

— 1874 —

9 February 1874
COTTONWOOD CREEK *(Dwyer, Wyoming)*
Nearly a year had passed since Indians had killed anyone on the road between Fort Fetterman and Fort Laramie, Wyoming. The respite ended on 9 February 1874. Lt. Levi H. Robinson, Fourteenth Infantry, had taken out an escort of Fourteenth Infantrymen and Second Cavalrymen to guard a Fort Laramie wood-cutting detail. The wagons rode to the government sawmill just east of Laramie Peak.

When their task was completed, the detail set out for the fort. Along the way, Robinson, with a Corporal Coleman and a private, wandered away from the main body of soldiers. On Cottonwood Creek, about ten miles east of the sawmill and about fifteen miles northwest of present-day Wheatland, Wyoming, a band of Lakotas or Arapahos jumped the three troopers. The private was dismounted at the time and his horse ran off, which distracted the Indians for a moment, allowing him to run into the brush and hide. Robinson and Coleman galloped away, but the Indians were on them in a flash and killed them both.

The sound of the shots brought the main escort racing to the rescue. Their quick arrival saved the life of the private and prevented the scalping of Robinson and Coleman. After this incident, soldiers were ordered to "spare no Indians south of the Platte." The following month, a new fort in northeast Nebraska took the name Fort Robinson in memory of the slain lieutenant.[433]

Ca. 25 August 1874
LONE TREE MASSACRE *(Meade, Kansas)*

The Atchison, Topeka & Santa Fe Railroad hired a twenty-two-man crew to finish its survey in southwestern Kansas. The small expedition left Dodge City in August and divided up on 24 August to cover different regions. Oliver F. Short and his party of six men headed out for Meade County with their wagon and tools. Short, his fourteen-year-old son Daniel, James Shaw, Shaw's eighteen-year-old son Allen, Harry Jones, and John Keuchler were never seen alive again.

Near Spring Creek, about six miles southwest of present-day Meade, Kansas, a band of fifteen or more Cheyennes led by Medicine Water surprised the surveyors in their camp and quickly killed them all. Two days later, another crew saw their wagon and rode up to the scene. The wagon had twenty-eight bullet holes in it, and the oxen were dead in their yokes; the warriors had cut off their hindquarters for food. The party's dog was also dead. Jones and the two Shorts were scalped and had their heads smashed in. Their pockets were turned out and the contents stolen. Medicine Water had also captured Oliver Short's big bay horse.

The six were all buried at the site of their deaths, near a large, lone tree, which served as the massacre's only memorial until 1938, when a Kansas historical marker was erected a mile west of Meade. After her husband's murder, Frances Short petitioned the government for $10,000 in losses. Following much debate, she and Mrs. Shaw eventually received $5,000 each.[434]

7 September 1874
WHITEFISH CREEK *(McLean, Texas)*

By September 1874 the army's Red River campaign against the Indians of the southern plains was in full swing as five columns of troops crisscrossed the Texas Panhandle. Col. Nelson A. Miles, with four companies of his Fifth Infantry and eight companies of the Sixth Cavalry, had recently fought Cheyennes, Comanches, and Kiowas between Mulberry Creek and Tule Canyon. As his supplies began to run low, he decided to send messengers to Camp Supply in Indian Territory.

On the evening of 6 September, Miles sent the reliable Lt. Frank D. Baldwin, Fifth Infantry, and three scouts, Lem Wilson, Harry Wing, and William F. Schmalsle out from his camp on McClellan Creek. The messengers traveled through the night, and at 4:30 a.m. they made it to a secluded spot on Whitefish Creek, in present-day northeastern Donley County, Texas, where they planned to hole up during the day. Soon, in the dawn's red light, an Indian appeared only fifty yards away. The messengers shot him down, perhaps realizing too late that the shots would draw attention to their hideout. Before long, a number of warriors surrounded their position.

Baldwin ordered his men to mount up and break out, and the unexpected charge startled the Indians. The lieutenant and his three scouts rode to higher ground, dismounted, and set up a small defensive perimeter. From there they drove the encroaching warriors back with accurate fire—Wing's "Sporting Rifle" was particularly effective. When the warriors had had enough, they took off, leaving Baldwin and the scouts to continue their journey north.

Baldwin was convinced that they had killed or wounded at least eight Indians. He reported that his party had all acted as calmly as if they were "shooting buffalo," but the fight was "one of the most desperate skirmishes I ever participated in."[435]

21 November 1874
MENARD *(Menard, Texas)*

In the fall of 1874, Capt. Cecil Rufus Perry's Company D, of the newly created Frontier Battalion, camped near the San Saba River in Menard County. About six miles away, two Texas Rangers, William Trewick and Scott Cooley, were hunting stray cattle to slaughter for provisions for their company. The two rangers spotted eleven Comanches heading west. The Indians saw them too, but the warriors did not come after them, which the rangers viewed as peculiar. The pair tried to lure the Indians toward the ranger camp by making a short charge and turning around, but the Indians did not fall for the ruse. Cooley sent Trewick to ride back and get the rest of the company while he tried to "loose-herd" the Indians. Cooley got too close, however, and his horse took a bullet in the leg, so he rode back to camp.

Back at the camp Trewick told Maj. John B. Jones, commander of the Frontier Battalion, about the Indians, and Jones headed out with thirty-five men. Soon Cooley also showed up at the camp and reported to Perry. The captain stayed behind with a few men and sent Cooley out with eleven rangers, under the command of Lt. Daniel W. Roberts. The Indians were riding fast, and Roberts chased them twenty miles before catching up. About fifteen miles south of present-day Menard, Texas, the Comanches turned to fight.

The chief charged at Roberts, firing a Spencer, and hit Roberts's horse. Other Indians were armed with six-shooters. The Texans replied with their Winchesters and a short, sharp fight ensued. Roberts shot and killed the chief, and another ranger killed a warrior nearby. A ranger was shot in the chest. When the Indians had emptied their pistols, they threw them away and went to bows and arrows while they rode off, with the Texans right behind. A few fleeing Indians were hit, and several of their horses were killed.

After a three-mile chase, the Comanches again attempted a stand. Cooley, Charles Bartholomae, and a few other rangers trapped three warriors in a cluster of rocks and brush. Bartholomae fired his last three pistol bullets at a warrior, but all missed. While the Indian nervously tried to nock an arrow, another ranger killed him with a shot from his Winchester. At this point, part of Jones's force, under Lt. L. P. Beavert, got into the action, killing another Comanche and wounding one.

After the long chase, nine of the eleven Indians were dead. A few rangers scalped some of the dead Comanches. Surprisingly, one warrior was captured—taking combatants as prisoners was almost unheard of in Indian warfare. When his horse was killed, the warrior stopped and made signs of surrender. Equally surprising, the Texans took him into custody rather than shooting him, and they prevented the other rangers from killing him later. The captured Comanche was taken to Austin and put on display in the opera house for twenty-five cents' admission. When the adjutant general heard about the exhibition, he put a stop to it and had the Indian placed in prison, where he soon caught a disease and died.[436]

— 1875 —

Ca. 10 February 1875
BEAVER LAKE *(Rocksprings, Texas)*

In the early months of 1875, Comanches raided south into Uvalde County, Texas. Moving down Frio Canyon on 25 January, they stole five horses from a company called Sawyer & Shores. The raiders continued to the Blanco River and moved downstream to its junction with the Sabinal, where they killed and mutilated a Mexican laborer. Northwest of Frio Town, they captured thirty-nine horses from Messrs. Brown, Allen, Gray, and Honeycut. The Comanches then turned back northwest and crossed the Nueces, eventually camping in a dense thicket near Beaver Lake.[437]

Unknown to the raiders, a citizen posse, including Messrs. Humphrey, Green, Patterson, Avant, Sawyer, Blackburn, Goodman, and Wells, had been hot on their trail. Several horses feeding around the thicket attracted the party's attention. When they moved in, they saw an Indian bridling his mount. Avant, Humphrey, and Sawyer fired at him,

Beaver Lake on Devil's River, Texas

297

driving him into the brush. Another Comanche appeared on the other side of the thicket, and Humphrey and Sawyer fired, hitting him in the side. When more warriors emerged from another quarter of the woods, Wells and Goodman, it was reported, "gave them Winchester music to retreat by."[438]

Patterson and Green sped across an opening to block the approach of another band of Comanches, who were bringing in pack mules loaded with meat. Those Indians fled without joining their tribesmen. The Indians in the thicket broke out in all directions, which made it nearly impossible for the small posse to chase them. Patterson cut off one warrior, but his horse stumbled in a rut and threw him to the ground. Four men held the horses while another four charged into the thicket, but the Indians had already scattered.

The tired Texans, who had gone without food for several days, decided to recover what they could and call it quits. They captured thirty-five horses, two Spanish mules, one Indian pony, four shields, several head-dresses, a photograph of "a beautiful white woman," and a light-haired woman's scalp. But what the men found most interesting was a certificate of good conduct, written to Mohecut, or Black Beard, a Kwahadi Comanche chief. It indicated that the chief was using his influence for good and that he promised to remain at peace with the whites. "I ask for him kind treatment at the hands of all with whom he comes in contact," the paper stated.[439] It was dated 1874 and signed by agent J. M. Haworth of the Kiowa and Comanche Agency in Indian Territory. The posse considered the paper to be proof of what Texans already knew to be fact: reservation Indians were being protected in Indian Territory, but they continued to steal and kill in Texas.[440]

— 1876 —

Winter 1875–76
FORT PEASE (Bighorn, Montana)

Fort Pease was situated on the north bank of the Yellowstone River, just downstream from the mouth of the Bighorn. About forty adventurers, under Fellows D. Pease and Paul W. McCormick, built the fort in June 1875, hoping to cash in on the steamboat trade that was expected to follow the building of other forts nearby. Neither the forts nor the river traffic materialized, and the lone Fort Pease became a target for the Lakotas.

Almost from the time the post was built, the Indians essentially held it under siege. The trappers and traders who remained at the post through the winter of 1875–76 became increasingly isolated as the weather deteriorated. After the river froze, supplies became scarce. On many occasions, men who left the fort to hunt or trap were attacked, and several were killed or wounded. On 2 January, a Lakota attack on the post left one man dead and four wounded. One week later, a party of friendly Crows under Bear Wolf ambushed a band of lurking Lakotas, killing seven of them. The last white casualty occurred on 29 January, when Lakotas killed a man from a wolf-hunting party.

On 8 February McCormick rode to Bozeman and asked for soldiers to escort his men from the besieged Fort Pease. Maj. James S. Brisbin left Fort Ellis on 22 February with four companies of the Second Cavalry. On 4 March he reached Fort Pease, which had not been attacked since McCormick left. Brisbin evacuated the nineteen men remaining at the fort, whether they wanted to leave or not, and took all of Pease and McCormick's stock back to Fort Ellis. Six men had been killed and eight wounded during the post's brief existence.[441]

9 June 1876
PRAIRIE DOG CREEK/TONGUE RIVER
(Sheridan, Wyoming)

In the late spring of 1876, Gen. George Crook, leading more than 1,000 men of the Second and Third Cavalry and the Fourth and Ninth Infantry, left Fort Fetterman in search of nonreservation Lakotas and Cheyennes. By 7 June the expedition had moved down Prairie Dog Creek to its junction with the Tongue River, about twelve miles northeast of present-day Sheridan, Wyoming. There the soldiers set up what they thought would be a permanent base camp, where they waited for a group of Shoshone allies.

On 9 June the quiet of the evening was broken by volleys of shots coming from the bluffs to the north, across the Tongue River. Indians had opened fire on a line of soldiers' tents, which, luckily for the troopers, were unoccupied at the time. The company's packers and teamsters fired back into the bluffs, whereupon the Indians pulled back. Though estimates of the Indian numbers ranged from 50 to 900 warriors, in reality, there were only a small number of raiders, Cheyennes fighting under Little Hawk.

Capt. Anson Mills took his battalion of Third Cavalry across the river to engage them. On the left rode Company I, under Capt. William H.

Andrews; taking the left-center was Company E, under Capt. Alexander Sutorius; on the right-center Company M, under Lt. Augustus C. Paul, moved in; and on the far right, Lt. Joseph Lawson led Company A. The cavalrymen dismounted and, leaving one-fourth of the men behind to hold the horses, charged up the bluffs, driving the raiders back over several successive ridges.

The attack was meant as a diversion for a raid on Crook's horse herd, on the other side of camp, south of the Tongue. The plan failed, however, as the horses had just been brought in for grooming. The Indians caught only the pickets, wounding two of them. Despite the great commotion and volume of firing, only two soldiers were wounded, along with several animals hit, while two Indians were reported killed.[442]

7 July 1876
SIBLEY'S SCOUT *(Dayton, Wyoming)*
Following his indecisive 17 June fight with the Lakota and Cheyennes on the Rosebud River, Gen. George Crook stayed in camp on Goose Creek, in northern Wyoming, for nearly three weeks. Twelve days after Lt. Col. George Custer's 25 June defeat at Little Bighorn, Crook finally sent Lt. Frederick W. Sibley to take out twenty-five select men of his Company E, Second Cavalry, and scouts Frank Grouard and "Big Bat" Pourier to try to locate the village of the victorious Indians.

Sibley left the camp at noon on 6 July and headed northwest, along the base of the Bighorn Mountains. He and his men rode about thirty-eight miles to the headwaters of the Little Bighorn before camping for the night. Early the next morning, they ran into parties of Lakotas and Cheyennes who had fought in the Custer battle. Grouard spotted the Indians from afar and hastily led the soldiers off the trail and into the foothills to avoid detection. The cavalrymen had, however, already been seen. Sibley deployed his men in a skirmish line in the timber, about twenty miles northwest of present-day Dayton, Wyoming.

The band Sibley had spotted, approximately nineteen Indians including the Oglala Flying Hawk and the Cheyennes Little Sun and High Bear, were out hunting buffalo. Some other Cheyennes had also seen the soldiers and were maneuvering into a better attack position, but the buffalo hunters charged before the others could get into place. Sibley's men fired at their impetuous attackers, killing High Bear and possibly one other and wounding perhaps five more. As the other warriors arrived and got on three sides of them, the soldiers feared they were doomed. Grouard suggested they tether their horses as bait and move on foot higher into the mountains.

The ruse worked. By the time the Indians attacked, the soldiers were gone, and the warriors spent precious time capturing the horses and equipment rather than chasing Sibley. High in the foothills and carrying nothing but arms and ammunition, the troopers had nearly fifty miles of mountains to traverse to make it back to Crook's camp. Enduring freezing cold at night, Sibley and his men built no fires and ate no food until they finally stumbled back to the Goose Creek camp on 9 July.[443]

1 August 1876
RED CANYON *(Edgemont, South Dakota)*

As part of the Sioux War campaign of 1876, the army established several supply camps in and around the Black Hills. On 17 June Capt. William S. Collier and Company K, Fourth Infantry, out of Fort Laramie, arrived at the southwestern edge of the Black Hills to build a post. Collier constructed the cantonment at the mouth of Red Canyon, about three miles north of the Cheyenne River and about the same distance northeast of present-day Edgemont, South Dakota. The semipermanent post, situated on the road from Fort Laramie to Custer City, was known simply as Camp Mouth of Red Canyon.

Because the camp sat at a minor crossroads, it saw quite a bit of traffic. Sometimes, traveling through the canyon was dangerous. On 16 April 1876, before the post was built, emigrant Charles Metz, his wife, their maid, and several companions had been jumped and massacred by either Indians or white outlaws.

In the late evening of 1 August, sentries reported hearing gunshots from a nearby ranch along the Cheyenne River. Collier sent a detachment of Company K to the scene, where they engaged about twenty Indians trying to run off stock. There was much firing into the deepening twilight, but few combatants were hit. The infantry drove the raiders off, believing they had killed or wounded one warrior, but the Indians got away with several horses.[444]

1 August 1876
HECK REEL'S WAGON TRAIN *(Glendo, Wyoming)*

The summer of 1876 was a fearful time for emigrants, freighters, and settlers on the northern plains. The Battle of the Little Bighorn remained in the news, and Indian attacks increased along the North Platte River.

Near site of Heck Reel wagon train attack, Glendo, Wyoming

Freighters hauling supplies up to Forts Laramie and Fetterman had to be on guard. One of these, A. H. "Heck" Reel, operated a freight outfit out of Cheyenne, Wyoming, under army contract. In late July Reel organized a train of nine wagons in units of three, each unit drawn by twelve to fourteen yoke of oxen and carrying more than 24,000 pounds of freight.

The train left Cheyenne with wagon boss George Throstle, Sylvester Sherman as second in command, and a crew of sixteen men. They headed for Gen. George Crook's camp on Little Goose Creek in Wyoming Territory, where Crook was preparing to chase after the Indians who had defeated George A. Custer. Reel had told Throstle to furnish every man with a .45 revolver and a .44 Winchester rifle. The caravan rode north to the Chugwater River, northwest to Cottonwood Creek, and on to the Overland Trail. On the night of 31 July, they camped on Elkhorn Creek, about eight miles west of present-day Glendo, Wyoming.

Early on 1 August, the wagons started uphill north of the creek, down into the valley of Coffee Creek, then up another set of hills. The bluffs were steep and progress was slow. It was 4 p.m. before they reached level ground, on the divide south of the North Elkhorn River. Throstle and Sherman rode ahead, discussing the ten miles they still had to go before their next campsite, on La Bonte Creek. Suddenly, about thirty Lakotas rode out from a deep draw north of the road. Three bullets hit Throstle, who fell from his horse, dead. Another bullet hit Sherman's saddle and grazed his leg; he spun his horse around and raced back to the wagons.

The Indians were upon the wagon train before the teamsters could begin to corral, and teamster "Irish Pete" caught a bullet in his leg. Then the Indians broke away. The driver of the second unit deserted his post and jumped into the rear wagon of the first unit. The man in charge of the rear unit, knowing there was no chance of getting his wagons into the corral, left them and drove in the abandoned second unit. It appeared that the Indians would get him, but lashing the team with one hand while shooting his pistol with the other, he made it to the corral.

With the wagons now corralled, Sherman looked for the rifles, which were buried in a box under 5,000 pounds of flour. The Lakotas circled around the wagons, shooting beneath their ponies' necks. They did not hit any more teamsters, but they wounded several oxen and saddle horses. When the freighters finally got the Winchesters going, the Indians fell back. In the deepening dusk, Irish Pete saw something move beyond the wagons and fired, killing a teamster's dog.

About 300 yards away, the Indians raided the rear wagons, plundering then burning them. They set 10,000 pounds of bacon on fire, creating flames that rose 200 feet in the air. The oxen yoked to the rear wagons burned to death, while the animals next in line pulled the front wheels off their wagon in a panic. By the light of the fires, the freighters kept close watch, but the Indians made no more charges. The next morning they were gone.

After the Indians left, Sherman organized what was left of the train and got it moving. The teamsters soon found Throstle's body, stripped and scalped, with the heart cut out. The freighters rolled the body in a tarpaulin and threw it in one of the wagons, to be buried later. In addition to the death of Throstle and the wounding of Pete and Sherman, the freighters lost three wagons, ten oxen, four horses, and thousands of dollars' worth of goods.[445]

— 1877 —

8–10 September 1877
SAN FRANCISCO RIVER *(Alma, New Mexico)*
On 2 September 1877, about 300 Apaches under Victorio, Loco, and Pionsenay broke out of the San Carlos Reservation in Arizona. The bands, Mimbres and Chiricahuas, split up into many groups and each took its

own path to old homelands or perceived safety. The breakout coincided with the recent arrival of two scouting parties at Fort Thomas: Lt. Robert Hanna, with Companies B and M, Sixth Cavalry, and Company D of the Hualapai Scouts, from Fort Huachuca; and Lt. John A. Rucker, with eighteen men of Companies H and L, Sixth Cavalry, and twenty-three Indian scouts, from Fort Bowie. In addition, Capt. Tulius C. Tupper, with Company G, Sixth Cavalry, had just ridden in from Camp Grant.

With hardly any time to rest, the combined units, under the command of Captain Tupper, rode out after the Apaches. Es-kin-e-la and his San Carlos Indian Police joined them. With the Apaches splitting up, backtracking, and crossing trails, the pursuit proved difficult. Tupper, with about sixty Indian scouts and seventy soldiers, trailed a large Apache band to the northeast, crossing the Gila Mountains, the Blue River, and the San Francisco Mountains into western New Mexico Territory.

On 8 September just before sundown, Tupper's Indian scouts, ranging ahead of the troopers, caught up with one band of renegades near the San Francisco River, north of present-day Alma. They killed five Apaches and captured seven women and children. The next morning, the Apaches swept through several ranches in the area, stealing stock and killing about twelve men. Then the bands split up again, with Victorio likely heading east toward his old home near Ojo Caliente and Pionsenay heading south toward Mexico.

On 9 September, Tupper's main command reached the San Francisco River and headed downstream in pursuit of Pionsenay's band. As usual, the scouts ranged ahead, and the next day, they fought again with the Apaches, killing seven and capturing six. On 13 September the command crossed the divide to the Gila River, but Pionsenay had gotten away to the south. Tupper and his men followed the Gila back to Fort Thomas.[446]

— 1878 —

6 July 1878
WILLOW SPRING *(Ukiah, Oregon)*

As the Bannock War spread to Oregon in the summer of 1878, Gen. Oliver O. Howard suggested that civilians could accompany the regular troops. Capt. John L. Sperry, sheriff of Umatilla County, organized Company C of Oregon Volunteers on 3 July 1878. Sperry's command of forty-five men, twelve of them mounted, had an assortment of weapons and no training.

With a team and wagon, the company marched south from Umatilla (Pendleton) to slow the various bands of Indians who were heading north and prevent them from joining up with the Umatillas. Sperry reached Willow Spring Canyon, about twelve miles north of present-day Ukiah, at noon on 6 July. With Howard's main force still two days to the south, Sperry would be alone to block about 700 Paiute, Shoshone, and Bannock Indians.

While the volunteers were eating lunch, an advance party of about 150 Indians suddenly attacked. At the first shots, about eleven men bolted, leaving the remainder to fight from a hastily organized defensive position around a sheep shed. The fight lasted six hours. Sperry's desperate men hung on until evening, when the battle sputtered out. Volunteer A. Lamar was killed, and eight others in the party were wounded. Sperry was certain they had killed and wounded a number of Indians, but he could not give an estimate.

At midnight the volunteers pulled out and headed toward Pendleton. They ran into Indians in the darkness three times; each encounter was a haphazard blasting of guns, resulting in unknown Indian casualties, if any. In one of the fights, volunteer Harrison Hale was killed.

Sperry and his exhausted men reached Pendleton on 7 July. Their fights delayed the Indians for one day, allowing the federal troops enough time to prevent the renegades from joining the Indians on the Umatilla Reservation. The volunteers at Willow Spring suffered more casualties than did the regulars in any other fight of the Bannock War.[447]

17 September 1878
BEAR CREEK *(Pinos Altos, New Mexico)*
Lt. Henry P. Perrine, Sixth Cavalry, with detachments of his Companies B and M and Company D of the Indian Scouts, was patrolling in rough country east of Fort Thomas, Arizona Territory. On 13 September, along the Gila River at what was called the Clifton Crossing, the scouts found a small party of three or four renegade Apaches who had left the reservation.

The Apaches bolted, and Perrine began a five-day chase. Their trail led east along the Gila and into New Mexico Territory. North of the Big Burro Mountains, the Apaches left the Gila and went along Bear Creek into the Pinos Altos Mountains. Perrine finally cornered them on 17 September, in Bear Creek Canyon, northwest of Pinos Altos. In a short fight, Perrine killed two Indians and captured four horses and a mule; one enlisted man was killed in the action.[448]

— 1879 —

5 April 1879
MIZPAH CREEK *(Miles City, Montana)*

In the late winter of 1879, in a Cheyenne camp along the Little Missouri River, a domestic quarrel led to Black Coyote killing Black Crane. Chief Little Wolf banished Black Coyote for his deed. Following the warrior into exile was his wife, Buffalo Calf Road Woman, and six of his friends, including Whetstone and Hole in the Breast. This renegade band of eight caused problems along the road between Deadwood and Fort Keogh. On 22 February they killed two white hunters, named Furgeson and Thompson, on the Rapid City Road, and they may have been responsible for killing a stage driver near Fort Keogh.

Chief Little Wolf's people surrendered and came to Fort Keogh on 1 April. Four days later, Black Coyote's band attacked Sgt. Kennedy of the Signal Corps and Pvt. Leo E. Bader of Company E, Second Cavalry, while they were repairing the telegraph line connecting Fort Keogh and Deadwood, near Mizpah Creek, about forty-five miles southeast of the fort. The Indians fired on the two men as they ate lunch. Bader was killed instantly, and Kennedy took a bullet in the hip. The wounded sergeant crawled to a defensive position and held the Indians at bay with his pistol. Finally, civilians traveling along the road drove the Indians away and transported Kennedy to Fort Keogh, where he recovered.

Maj. George Gibson sent out a detachment of Company B, Second Cavalry, under Sgt. T. B. Glover to pursue the renegade Cheyennes. Glover caught up with Black Coyote about eighty miles from the fort, and the Indians surrendered without a fight. Gibson found Bader's horse, carbine, and scalp. The renegades were taken to the fort, where Chief Little Wolf said, "Hang them or [im]prison them for life. I never want to see their faces again." Black Coyote, Whetstone, and Hole in the Breast were tried and convicted of murder. On 7 July, while they awaited execution in the Miles City jail, all three hanged themselves with their belt straps and moccasin cords.[449]

10 September 1879
MCEVER'S RANCH *(Hillsboro, New Mexico)*

Mimbres Apaches under Victorio and Nana bolted from the Mescalero Reservation, where they had long contended that they did not want to live. Heading west to their preferred territory around Ojo Caliente, between the San Mateo and Black Ranges, they attacked men of the Ninth Cavalry, killed civilians, and stole horses. On 4 September the raiders turned south and disappeared into the Black Range.

Despite frantic searching by the army, Victorio's whereabouts were unknown for six days. On 10 September, he suddenly reappeared near the mining camp of Lake Valley, east of the Black Range and about seventeen miles south of present-day Hillsboro, New Mexico. With his marauding Apaches, Victorio descended on the ranch of H. D. McEver. The unsuspecting cowboys didn't have a chance, and seven men were quickly killed. Meanwhile, other Apaches killed two more civilians at nearby Arroyo Seco. As quickly as they had appeared, the Indians were gone. A few weeks later, in October, they returned to burn the McEver ranch to the ground, possibly because the army frequently used it as a base of operations.[450]

— 1880 —

Ca. 5 March 1880
PALOMAS *(Las Palomas, New Mexico)*
About six months after raiding ranches and killing a number of settlers in the fall of 1879 (see previous entry), and shortly after several skirmishes with soldiers, Victorio's Apaches wiped out a civilian wagon train on the trail along the Rio Grande. The region's scattered cavalry units were unable to prevent such hit-and-run raids. Soon after the wagon train attack, two Sixth Cavalrymen from Capt. Curwen McClellan's Company L deserted while on herd duty. Absconding with their guns and horses, the pair rode out with the intention of going to a mining camp in Mexico.

About three weeks later, on 25 March, a Mexican traveler brought McClellan word that the deserters had been killed downriver, near the site of the wagon train massacre. Lt. Thomas Cruse, Sixth Cavalry, was ordered to verify the deaths. With a detachment of troopers, Cruse had ridden downriver about ten miles when the scouts signaled to him, exclaiming, "Damned Chillacagoes [Chiricahuas]!"

The soldiers rode down to find the remnants of the train. Cruse reported, "There were burned wagons, carcasses of animals, graves scattered around for several hundred yards marking where the bodies of people had been hastily covered with earth." Several wagons had apparently been pushed together and set on fire; they had "formed the funeral pyre of several, who either dead or alive, had been thrown thereon and partially consumed."

Cruse believed the train had been attacked as it was crossing the Rio Grande. The Indians were hidden along the steep banks, waiting until some of the wagons had crossed and some were still in midstream. The wagons on the slopes slid down and collided with the others to block the road, leaving the travelers sitting ducks. None escaped. About twenty people were killed, including two or three women and two children. "It was grisly!" wrote Cruse. "I dreamed of it for weeks afterwards."

About two miles farther down the road, Cruse's scouts found the remains of the two deserters. Later investigation revealed that the pair had ridden from Cuchillo to Palomas, where they bought breakfast, sold their carbines and ammunition to civilians for thirty dollars each, and exchanged their army-issued .45-caliber revolvers for .44s like civilians carried. They proceeded to the river crossing, where they saw the remains of the wagon train. Hurrying along and on the alert, they were nevertheless jumped by Apaches, who fired from a small knoll on their left. One horse went down and one of the men was hit in the arm. The other man hoisted his companion onto his horse and tried to gallop away. They got about half a mile farther before the Indians caught up with them and brought down the other horse. Both deserters dropped down among some rocks and, judging from the number of cartridges found at the spot, they put up a good fight. Finally, some warriors crept up to a cluster of cactus about ten yards behind the runaways and fired the final volley into them. Cruse commented, "Deserters as the dead men were, we felt like raising a cheer for the gallant fight they had put up."

There was little left of the bodies to bury. After covering the remains as best they could, Cruse led his detachment back to Palomas.[451]

8 March 1880
ROSEBUD CREEK *(Hysham, Montana)*

In early February of 1880, Lakotas began raiding along the Yellowstone and Tongue Rivers, and several military scouts left Fort Keogh to hunt for them. On 8 March Lt. Samuel W. Miller, with seventeen soldiers from Company E of the Fifth Infantry and some Indian guides, picked up a trail west of the Rosebud River. They followed it until they came upon a Lakota camp about thirty miles west of the river, in the vicinity of Sarpy Creek.

Miller attacked the camp and killed three Lakotas and eight ponies, but the majority of the band got away with most of the stolen horses.

Before escaping, the Indians killed two soldiers and wounded one, leaving a frustrated Miller with little to do but burn the camp and return to Fort Keogh. He sent news of the encounter to Lt. Frank Baldwin, who was on the north side of the Yellowstone. Moving in, Baldwin was able to pick up the Lakotas' trail and recover the rest of the stolen horses.[452]

14 May 1880
OLD FORT TULAROSA *(Aragon, New Mexico)*

Continuing their raiding spree (see Palomas, Ca. 5 March 1880), Victorio and his Apaches moved through New Mexico Territory and into Arizona Territory, apparently heading for the San Carlos Agency. With soldiers on his trail, however, Victorio doubled back east toward old Fort Tularosa, abandoned after the agency there shut down in 1874.

On the evening of 11 May, a rider galloped into the Barlow & Sanders stage station with word that Victorio planned to attack Tularosa, the small settlement near the old post. Sgt. George Jordan and twenty-five men of Company K, Ninth Cavalry, staying at the station that night,

Near site of Fort Tularosa, New Mexico

were getting ready to turn in when the news arrived. Foregoing their rest, Jordan and his buffalo soldiers mounted up and rode through the night for Tularosa.

Arriving exhausted the next morning, the troopers found that so far, the Apaches had killed only one old man in a cornfield. Jordan found no Indians lurking about, so he used the day to fortify Tularosa's buildings and build a stockade around the small settlement. The next day, the townspeople gratefully entered the stockade and waited, but nothing happened. Thinking perhaps it had been a false alarm, some settlers and soldiers left the fortification and were outside when Victorio, with approximately 100 warriors, attacked on 14 May. The Apaches had fired about 100 rounds before everyone could get back inside.

As the Indians made repeated attacks, Jordan's troopers and the armed civilians kept up a heavy defensive fire. Eventually the Apaches grew tired of attacking the stockade and instead went after about 500 head of cattle. Jordan sent ten soldiers to assist the handful of cowboys who were defending the herd. Thus foiled, Victorio figured there was no more use risking the loss of his warriors. He broke off the engagement and headed south. But Victorio was not quite through raiding settlers. The next day, about forty Apaches struck Kelly's Ranch in the Mogollon Mountains and killed three civilians before heading east to the Black Range.

None of Jordan's men were killed or wounded in the Tularosa fight, but it is likely that a few Indians were hit. The townspeople thanked Jordan and his buffalo soldiers for saving them. For his quick thinking and courageous actions, Jordan later received the Medal of Honor.[453]

9 August 1880
QUITMAN CANYON *(Fort Quitman, Texas)*

Apaches led by Victorio, having been raiding in the Southwest for nearly a year, were hounded by United States and Mexican troops (see previous entry). They crossed the border several times while trying to evade capture or death. In August 1880, as the summer rains began, they moved into southwest Texas, moving from water hole to water hole in a game of cat-and-mouse. In the lonely, rugged terrain around Quitman Canyon, just made for ambushes, adversaries could change from mouse to cat in a heartbeat.

Retired Civil War general James J. Byrne, now employed as chief engineer of the Texas & Pacific Railway, had been surveying some tracts of land near Quitman Canyon for his company. On 9 August he was on his way by stage to Fort Davis from Ysleta. Byrne occupied the rear seat of the white canvas-topped buckboard, pulled by two feisty Spanish mules and driven by Ed Walde. On the Quitman and Van Horn Road, after the stage entered a boxlike pass in the canyon, a dozen Apaches attacked the coach.

The first bullets struck Byrne in the hip. He returned fire with his Winchester, but incredibly, he had only two bullets. Walde swiftly maneuvered his mule team to turn and headed back for the shelter of old Fort Quitman. The Apaches rode in closer to the hack and fired again, this time hitting Byrne in the back. One bullet went through Walde's hat, but he drove on at a frantic pace, with the wounded general dangling precariously out of the buckboard. The Indians pursued the stage for two miles, but they were ultimately outdistanced by the speedy mules. Neither Walde nor the mules were scratched, though the stage was riddled with bullets, the canvas was shredded, and three wheel spokes were shot in half.

General Byrne died around 14 August of gangrene resulting from his wounds, and he was buried near Fort Quitman. A letter was discovered on his body, written on 4 August at Ysleta, to his wife, Lilly Loving Byrne, to be delivered in the event of his death. It suggests that he had had a premonition of his doom: "If accident should befall me, this will be my last goodbye, to *all* I love upon this earth. . . . It may be that I have conjured up a horrid dream, but it is too sadly real for that."[454]

Later, Pat Dolan, a close friend of Byrne, drove 600 miles from Fort Worth to take Byrne's remains back to be reinterred there.[455]

17 August 1880
LITTLE MISSOURI RIVER *(Southeastern Montana)*

In 1880 most companies of the Seventh Cavalry were engaged in either guarding construction crews of the Northern Pacific Railroad or patrolling the area between the railroad and the Little Missouri River from the base at Fort Meade, north of the Black Hills. In August Sgt. Edward Davern, with eight men of Company F and three Indian scouts, patrolled south from the railroad into Montana Territory. Davern, as a private and orderly for Maj. Marcus Reno, survived the 1876 Battle of the Little Bighorn. Discharged in 1877, he reenlisted the same day, and he was wounded while fighting the Nez Perces at Canyon Creek on 13 September 1877.

Leading his detachment into the rough country between the Little Missouri and Box Elder Creek, Davern ran into a band of five Lakotas on 17 August. Wounding one Indian, Davern rounded up seven ponies and took them north to Maj. Lewis Merrill. Two newspapers of the time, the *Black Hills Times* and the *Bismarck Tribune*, described the encounter thusly: "Shots were exchanged resulting in two of the Indians making a sudden acquaintance with the happy hunting grounds."[456]

— 1881 —

24 January 1881
CANADA ALAMOSA *(Monticello, New Mexico)*

Even after the death of Chief Victorio in October 1880, Apaches continued to raid in New Mexico Territory. On 14 January around fifty Indians attacked a supply wagon and killed two Mexicans and a white man named Omery Jackson about twelve miles east of Fort Cummings. A few hours later, they attacked a mail stage and killed the driver, James Sweeney, and the passenger, Thomas White. The Apaches then rode north toward the Black Range.

Ninth Cavalrymen out of Fort Cummings pursued the raiders, but heavy snow in the mountains terminated the chase. The Apaches next appeared on 24 January, east of the San Mateo Mountains. Sgt. Madison Ingorman, Company D, Ninth Cavalry, and six privates were escorting a wagon train from Fort Craig to the camp at Ojo Caliente, on the west slope of the San Mateos. Northeast of Canada Alamosa, the Apaches struck. Ingorman and his small command fought back valiantly and drove off the attackers, who rode off to continue their depredations elsewhere. Pvt. William Jones, severely wounded in the skirmish, died the next day in the camp hospital.[457]

18 August 1881
GOLD DUST *(Hillsboro, New Mexico)*

Surviving Apaches of Victorio's band, plus discontented Indians from other Chiricahua bands and a number of Mescaleros, raided up and down the length of the Black Range in the summer of 1881, led by Old Nana. After repelling an attack by the Ninth Cavalry at Cuchillo Negro on 16 August, Nana quickly moved west of the Black Range. In twenty-four hours he traveled about fifty miles through some of the roughest country in New Mexico, coming back to the east side of the range on 18

August. When the Apaches emerged from the mountains, they barreled through the mining camp of Gold Dust, about a dozen miles southeast of present day Hillsboro.

With most of the miners away at the diggings, the Indians boldly shot their way through the tent camp, blasting holes through the canvas covers. The women and children all dove to the floor and escaped the flying bullets. When done with Gold Dust, the raiders turned their attention to the Ousley Ranch, killing Perry Ousley and torching his house and outbuildings. The Indians stopped at the Trujillo Ranch but did no damage, possibly because the Trujillos may have sold food and ammunition to the Indians during the Victorio troubles.

Nana's next stop was southwest of Gold Dust near Lake Valley. They swept into the Irwin Ranch, where Sally Irwin distracted them with a trunkful of colorful ribbons and assorted other items, then grabbed her child and ran for the brush. Mr. Irwin, out tending the cattle at the time, missed the confrontation. Returning to find his house in flames, he was certain that his wife and child were dead. He rode to Lake Valley, where he accused Lt. George W. Smith and his detachment of Ninth Cavalry of sitting idle while citizens were being massacred. He calmed down when Sally walked in with the baby.[458]

2 October 1881
K-H BUTTE *(Bonita, Arizona)*

The Cibecue Uprising of 30 August 1881 led to talk of relocating the Apaches as well as general unrest at the Apache agencies. On 1 October, about 100 Indians of Juh's, Gordo's, Benito's, Naiche's and Geronimo's Chiricahua bands fled the San Carlos Agency heading for Mexico. On the morning of 2 October, the Indians raided a civilian wagon train at Cedar Springs and killed six teamsters. They got away, but soldiers were following right behind.

About six miles southeast of Cedar Springs and eleven miles northwest of present-day Bonita, Arizona, near K-H Canyon on the flank of the Pineleno Mountains, the Indians saw an opportunity in four luckless soldiers. The men, Privates Lindercantz, Company A, Sixth Cavalry, Londall, Company B, Eighth Infantry, and new recruits Ensiner and Welch were out repairing telegraph wire along the Fort Thomas to Fort Grant road. The Apaches quickly killed the men and left their bodies along the trail, where the pursuing soldiers would be sure to see them and halt.

K-H Canyon, Arizona

Around 3 p.m. Lt. Gilbert E. Overton, with Companies A and F, Sixth Cavalry, found the bodies. As soon as the troopers paused, the concealed warriors began to fire. Overton deployed his troops and moved to charge, but the Indians pulled back up the canyon. When Capt. Reuben F. Bernard arrived with Company G, First Cavalry, the combined force moved ahead. Taking cover on a hill called K-H Butte, the Indians pinned the soldiers down with fire from their Springfields. Four soldiers were hit. Bernard took his men around to chase some of the Apaches, but the Indians took defensive positions in the hills. The soldiers could not make further headway against the Chiricahuas, who had the high ground and a good field of fire, and the fight settled into a long-range affair lasting several hours.

By 7 p.m. the soldiers had fired off 4,000 rounds of ammunition and were running low. The men holding the horses were ordered to give up their remaining ammunition for the skirmish line. It was just in time, for at about 8 p.m. the Apaches, harangued by an old warrior into taking the offensive, charged the soldiers. Using their last bullets, the troopers drove the Chiricahuas back. Around 9 p.m., the Apaches, knowing that the soldiers would not follow them in the dark, prepared to escape. To better conceal their movements, they slit the throats of their dogs and light-colored horses, then crept around the army's right flank and fled south across the Aravaipa Valley.

The Indian casualties were unknown but may have been significant. On the army side, in addition to the four soldiers killed earlier in the day, Sergeant Buford, Company F, Sixth Cavalry, was mortally wounded. Pvt. John Hunt, Company F, Sixth Cavalry, and Pvts. William H. Humphreys and Isaac C. Reneard, Company G, First Cavalry, were wounded.[459]

Ca. 1–2 November 1881
DRAVO'S SCOUT *(Fort Apache, Arizona)*
In the chaos that followed the Cibecue Uprising (see previous entry), some cavalry troops chased the fleeing Apaches south toward Mexico, while other detachments remained in the Fort Apache area to hunt down the renegade Apaches, including some defecting scouts, who remained in the north. On 25 October Lt. Edward E. Dravo left Fort Apache with his Company E, Sixth Cavalry, and Lt. Charles Gatewood's Apache scouts on a long-range scouting mission.

The patrol followed various trails north and west, but they caught no Indians until they reached Canyon Creek, above its junction with the Salt River, where they surprised and killed two Apaches. They then crossed to the south side of the Salt and headed east, beyond the junction of the Black River, where they discovered more tracks, which led north of the Black River toward the fort. Dravo sent the scouts forward. Overtaking some Apaches of Sanchez's band, the scouts killed two warriors and captured a woman and child.

After Dravo's men returned to Fort Apache on 5 November, Indian agent Joseph C. Tiffany complained to Gen. Orlando B. Willcox that "my peaceable Indians," whom he described as only old men and cripples, were being unjustly killed by the military.[460]

— 1882 —

1 June 1882
CLOVERDALE CANYON *(Cloverdale, New Mexico)*
In April 1882 Apache chief Loco and several hundred Chiricahuas broke out from the San Carlos Agency, killing about forty settlers on their way to Mexico and fighting several battles with soldiers, including Horseshoe Canyon and Sierra Enmedio. Most of the Indians made it into Chihuahua, where Mexican soldiers under Col. Lorenzo Garcia surprised them and killed seventy-eight men, women, and children.

After their decisive defeat, the Apaches melted into the Sierra Madre. The U.S. forces that were congregated along the border pulled back to their respective bases, but cavalry scouts continued to patrol the area. On 1 June Lt. William Stanton, with detachments of Companies A and C, Sixth Cavalry, and some Indian scouts, ran into a small party of Apaches who had ventured north of the border. In Cloverdale Canyon of the Guadalupe Mountains, in the extreme southwest corner of New Mexico Territory, Stanton attacked the Indians, killing two and driving the others back into Mexico.[461]

— 1883 —

19 April 1883
WILD HORSE LAKE *(Havre, Montana)*

Fort Assiniboine was established in May 1879 on Beaver Creek about four miles above its junction with Milk River and about six miles southwest of present-day Havre, Montana. Troops stationed there were to watch over the Blackfeet in the area and to patrol the U.S.-Canadian line to prevent the Lakotas who had fled into Canada from recrossing the border. Once in October 1880 and again in January 1881, Sitting Bull led small bands across the border to hunt, but each time, soldiers forced him back.

Sitting Bull surrendered in July 1881, but a number of recalcitrant Indians, Nez Perces as well as Lakotas, still wandered the borderlands. On 19 April 1883, near Wild Horse Lake, about thirty-five miles north of Fort Assiniboine, Capt. Randolph Norwood and a detachment of Company L, Second Cavalry, ran into a small band of renegades, killing two of them and driving the others back into Canada.[462]

— 1884 —

15 July 1884
WHITE RIVER/WORMINGTON CANYON
(San Juan County, Utah)

In the early 1880s, trouble began to brew on the Southern Ute (Los Pinos) Reservation in southwest Colorado. The Denver & Rio Grande Railroad constructed a line across part of the reservation, and numerous cattlemen moved in close to the tribe's fine grazing lands. Ranchers and cowboys in the area ran their herds on any free range they could find, including reservation lands. In 1884 a band of Utes killed several cowboys. To help quell the unrest, in June 1884 Companies B and F, Sixth Cavalry, moved from Arizona to Fort Lewis, Colorado, on the La Plata River southwest of Durango and adjacent to Los Pinos Reservation.

One of the region's largest outfits was the Kansas & New Mexico Land & Cattle Company, headquartered in Utah just west of the Colorado border and operated by the Carlisle brothers. Believing that the local Utes and Paiutes were stealing their cattle, the Carlisles complained to the military at Fort Lewis, but the army was slow to respond.

In July some cowboys were rounding up stock in the Blue Mountains of southeast Utah when they ran into a band of southern Utes who had permission to hunt in the area. A dispute erupted when a Ute refused to give up a stolen horse, and one of the cowboys killed him. Another warrior shot a cowboy's horse in the head, and a third tried to knife cowboy Hank Sharp, but Sharp shot him with his pistol. More Utes appeared with rifles and drove the cowboys off.

After this episode, the Carlisle brothers again complained to the officers at Fort Lewis, and Capt. Henry P. Perrine took Companies B and F, Sixth Cavalry, to investigate. Joined by some of the cowboys who had been in the fight, the troopers came upon a dozen dead horses, two dead mules, and several burned wagons. The Ute raiders, along with a Paiute band, had also stolen more than 100 horses from the isolated Garlich Ranch. The troopers and cowboys rode out in pursuit.

In the vicinity of present-day Natural Bridges National Monument, Perrine found himself in some rough and tangled country, with high sandstone cliffs and twisting box canyons. The captain was reluctant to chase the Indians pell mell into their haunts, but a few cowboys, led by a reckless James Rowdy Higgins and army scout and packer Joe Wormington, were eager to continue. Higgins and Wormington persuaded Perrine to let them take ten cowboys ahead to scout for the Indian hideout.

On the White River near Moss Back Butte, the scouting party walked into an ambush.[463] Indian bullets hit Wormington immediately and shot Higgins as he ran back down the butte. Both men were badly wounded. Perrine and the rest rode up, but believing the Indians to be in an impregnable position, Perrine would not risk an assault. The soldiers heard Wormington and Higgins pleading for help while the warriors taunted them from behind the rocks. At nightfall the Indians left, and so did Perrine, thinking it was too great a risk to search for Wormington and Higgins in the dark. Years later, a prospector found the two men's skeletons and buried them.[464]

— 1885 —

9 December 1885

LILLIE'S RANCH *(Pinos Altos, New Mexico)*

Raiding Apaches under Josanie left Mexico in November 1885, fighting in southern New Mexico Territory before heading to the reservation at Turkey Creek near Fort Apache, Arizona Territory. Josanie skirmished near the fort and then moved east into the Mogollon Mountains of New Mexico, where Eighth Cavalry troops under Lt. Samuel W. Fountain and Lt. De Rosey Cabell were scattered. In Silver City, Maj. Samuel S. Sumner received a telegraph regarding the Indians' movements and he alerted Fountain.

Fountain met up with Cabell and made a plan. He took ten troopers, ten Navajo scouts, and two civilian guides, while Cabell stayed in camp. The guide, a man called McKinney, directed Fountain to a high gap on the Mogollon Trail where he said the Indians would have to pass. There the company discovered the Apaches' fires still burning and a fresh trail in the newly fallen snow. McKinney led Fountain to Diamond Creek Canyon, to the north, where they found a fresh trail that crossed the creek near a ranch that had belonged to the Butcher brothers before the Indians killed them the previous June. Fountain hurried toward Lillie's and Papanoe's ranches, hoping to get there before the Indians did.

At Lillie's ranch, Fountain found the outlying buildings had been ransacked. Continuing to the home ranch, five miles farther on, he found a trail leading to Snow (Clear) Creek, which meandered through an isolated, 200-yard-wide valley about forty miles north of Pinos Altos. The ranch, on the far side of the creek, was already ablaze. Some of the raiders had gotten away, but Fountain counted nineteen Indians still loading their horses with plunder. The lieutenant dismounted his men from their tired horses, formed an attack line, and charged across the creek, successfully surprising the Apaches. Only one warrior had time to mount up and attempt to escape, but the troopers shot him dead on his horse. One other running Apache was also killed. The rest got away after a brief chase, but Fountain was able to round up most of their horses.

Searching the smoldering house, soldiers found the body of Thomas C. Prior, who was visiting John Lillie, burned in the ruins. Fountain gathered up the stolen horses and mules and started to herd them across the creek, where Sergeant Moore and Private Beatty were holding the company horses. But Josanie's warriors had returned. The Apaches began firing at the cavalry mounts with Moore and Beatty. Fountain hurried to a point across from Moore and yelled for the sergeant to cover him. As Fountain crossed the valley, gunfire cracked around him, and he fell to the ground; his men thought he had been shot, but the lieutenant had only tripped on the rough ground. He made it across to Moore unscathed, and together they moved the horses to safety. When the guns suddenly fell silent, Fountain figured the Apaches were out of ammunition. The following morning, the troopers discovered the Indians were gone.

Ten horses and two mules were returned to their owners. McKinney was given a big-footed brown horse as a reward. Later, John Lillie was discovered dead in a field some distance from his house.[465]

— 1887 —

25 August 1887
COLOROW'S WAR *(Rangely, Colorado)*
Although the Utes had been removed from northwest Colorado to a reservation in Utah, they continued to hunt in Colorado. Among the hunters was Colorow (actually a Comanche who had lived with the Utes for decades) and his band of eight or ten lodges. In August 1887, two of Colorow's men allegedly stole two horses near Rangely, on the White River, and sold them in Meeker, about eighty miles upstream. The pair then joined Colorow's camp near Buford, about twenty miles east of Meeker. A posse of about seventy men under Sheriff Jim Kendall rode to Colorow's camp to arrest the thieves. An argument started, guns were fired, and Colorow's band of about fifty people fled north to Milk Creek.

After the incident, Kendall rode back to Meeker and warned the townspeople that the Utes were on the warpath and coming to murder them all. As panic swept through the area, Colorado governor Alva Adams called on seven brigades of the Colorado National Guard to rush to Meeker. Meanwhile, Kendall's men trailed the Utes to Yellowjacket Pass. The frightened Indians fled west down the White River. On 22 August nearly 1,000 National Guardsmen converged on Meeker. It then became a contest between Kendall's cowboys and the Guardsmen to see who would catch the Utes first.

On 25 August elements of both groups cornered the Utes at a bend of the White River about eleven miles west of Rangely, only two miles from the Utah border. A muddled two-hour skirmish followed, during which about 100 Utah Utes joined Colorow to help him and his people get away. The fight ended when both sides ran out of ammunition. Four whites were killed, including Kendall's deputy Jack Ward, and five were wounded, while eight Utes were killed. Colorow and the rest got away. The arrival of Lt. George R. Burnett and a few troopers of the Ninth Cavalry, who rode to the scene from Fort DuChesne in Utah, prevented the Coloradans from invading the Indian reservation.

Kendall's posse and the Guardsmen returned to Meeker, almost as mad at each other as with the Utes. The Colorow "war" cost Colorado taxpayers more than $80,000. Chief Colorow died in December 1888, of natural causes.[466]

— 1890 —

7 March 1890
SALT RIVER *(Globe, Arizona)*

In March 1890, just west of the San Carlos Reservation, a small band of renegade Apaches ambushed a freight wagon and killed the passengers. Word of the attack reached Fort Thomas on 2 March, and Gen. Benjamin Grierson gave orders to "capture or destroy the murderers." Lt. Powhatan H. Clarke, Tenth Cavalry, took ten men of Company K out on the search. While on the march, Clarke hooked up with Lt. James W. Watson, Tenth Cavalry, leading troopers of Company L, Fourth Cavalry, and some Indian scouts. The scouts picked up the culprits' trail and determined that there were five of them.

The chase extended across 200 miles of mountain and desert. Sgt. Alexander Cheatham and Company I, Tenth Cavalry, supplied Clarke and Watson along the way, and they never gave up the pursuit. Finally on 7 March, they caught the fugitives in the gorge of the Salt River, near the mouth of Cherry Creek, about twenty miles north of present-day Globe, Arizona. The cornered Apaches hid inside a cave in the cliffs, protecting them from direct fire. The clever Sgt. William McBryar crawled up into a position where he could fire off the rocks, causing the bullets to ricochet into the cave. Two Apaches were killed and the remaining three surrendered.

Watson wrote a recommendation for McBryar, stating that he "demonstrated coolness, bravery, and good marksmanship under circumstances very different from those on the target range."[467] McBryar won the Medal of Honor for his actions. This fight was the last army action against the Apaches in the Southwest.[468]

Summary

Much of the data in the foregoing study came from accounts of military, militia, and ranger encounters with the Indians, although a significant portion came from civilian sources—mountain men, mail riders, emigrants, and settlers. No matter how broad the search, however, it is virtually impossible to compile a complete survey of the nearly countless fights between European Americans and Indians. Nevertheless, conclusions can be drawn. One of the aims of our previous book, *Encyclopedia of Indian Wars*, was to verify that widespread violence occurred across the western states and territories in the years from 1850 to 1890. In this volume, we included more nonmilitary conflicts, and the result serves to amplify our original conclusion—that the frontier was a brutal place. Not only were military casualties high, but the casualty toll among noncombatants was enormous. Far more noncombatants were killed in the Indian Wars than in the Civil War.[469]

In the 1862 Minnesota Uprising, the official count was established at 644 dead white civilians, with about 300 white captives taken. In Kansas and Nebraska, about 400 American citizens were murdered in 1866 and 1867. War Department statistics for Kansas in 1868-69 indicated 158 white civilians murdered, 16 wounded, 48 scalped, 14 women "outraged," and 1 man, 4 women, and 7 children captured. In Nebraska, 52 civilians were killed, wounded, or captured in one ten-day period, 7 to 16 August 1864.

Over the course of the frontier Indian Wars, Indians kidnapped thousands of civilians, nearly all of them women and children. In 1855 the Comanches held 2,000 Anglo and Mexican captives. Between 1860 and 1875, probably about 1,000 American settlers and others were taken captive. In 1850 in New Mexico Territory, Navajos held between 300 and 500 Anglo and Mexican captives.

Arizona and New Mexico were among the most heavily afflicted regions. Superintendent Michael Steck reported in 1863 that in the previous three years, New Mexico Territory suffered 200 civilian deaths and the loss of about half a million sheep. From his Arizona superintendency the same year, Charles D. Poston reported 150 citizens killed. In his 1870 report, Arizona superintendent George L. Andrews stated he could not begin to accurately count the number of lives lost and property destroyed in the previous year, but he provided an example from Pima County alone, where 47 citizens were murdered, 6 wounded, and 1 carried into captivity, plus 500 cattle stolen and $10,000 worth of property damaged or destroyed. Historian Dan Thrapp concluded that the civilian loss in the struggle to claim Arizona and New Mexico "was the most costly, in human lives, of any in the history of America."[470]

Texas was also particularly hard hit during the Indian Wars. From 1865 through the first half of 1867, 35 counties reported 162 settlers killed, 24 wounded, and 43 captured, plus 2,430 sheep and goats, 3,781 horses, and 30,838 cattle stolen. Wise County reported that between 1865 and 1870, it suffered 21 raids, with 12 citizens murdered and 5 captured. One report estimated about 400 whites captured within 100 miles of Parker County, Texas, and Jack County reported 200 citizens killed and captured between 1859 and 1871. Montague County lost 43 citizens killed or captured in 1866 alone. Between 1873 and 1875, 45 settlers were killed, 15 were wounded, and 2 were captured in Texas counties. A compilation showing depredations from 1865 to 1879 shows 407 Texans killed by Indians, 76 wounded, and 81 women and children carried off, with 20,521 horses and mules and 43,392 cattle stolen. The same report stated that 77 Indians were killed, 29 were wounded, and 3 were captured, and that 6,871 horses and cattle were recovered.[471]

In 1796 Congress passed a law to provide compensation to both Indians and whites for depredations committed upon each other. Claims were filed and adjudicated as late as 1920. Poor recordkeeping and lost files make it impossible to determine exactly how many Indian depredation claims whites filed. In 1858, one attorney attempted to get reparations for the murder or capture of 100 civilians in New Mexico, and for stolen property in excess of half a million dollars for 244 others. In Kansas alone in 1867–68, the state legislature took 120 depredation claims in only five counties.

Life and limb were not remunerated—only property—but even so, pitiably few were compensated. From 1796 to 1890, only 3 percent of the claims were paid. In 1867 New Mexico superintendent A. B. Norton complained to the commissioner that from the time the United States acquired the territory, there remained almost $2 million in unpaid Indian depredation claims. Claims numbered in the thousands up to 1891, when all remaining cases were sent from Congress to the Court of Claims to settle. From 1891 to 1920, the court tried 10,841 cases but paid less than 13 percent of the damages claimed.[472]

Untold thousands of white settlers lost lives and property to Indian raids. Compiling the data from both this book and *Encyclopedia of Indian Wars*, we ranked the western states by the number of fights and the total white and Indian casualties from 1823 to 1890:

State	Number of Fights	Total Casualties
Arizona	332	4,621
Texas	332	3,682
New Mexico	209	1,799
Kansas	143	1,268
California	100	1,792
Oregon	97	1,473
Wyoming	88	1,129
Montana	66	1,772
Colorado	56	917
Nebraska	49	750
North Dakota	44	1,122
Idaho	41	1,109
Nevada	39	709
Oklahoma	35	1,416
Washington	23	678
Utah	19	469
South Dakota	9	342

Notes

Full URLs for Internet sources appear in the bibliography.

1823

1   James T. DeShields, *Border Wars of Texas* (Austin: State House Press, 1993), 6-7; J. W. Wilbarger, *Indian Depredations in Texas* (Austin: Hutchings Printing House, 1889), 200-201; Walter Prescott Webb and H. Bailey Carroll, eds. *The Handbook of Texas* (Austin: Texas State Historical Association, 1952), 1:32, 1:355.

2   Robert M. Utley, *A Life Wild and Perilous: Mountain Men and the Paths to the Pacific* (New York: Henry Holt & Company, 1997), 47; Don Berry, *A Majority of Scoundrels: An Informal History of the Rocky Mountain Fur Company* (Corvallis: Oregon State University Press, 2006), 24.

3   Utley, *Life Wild and Perilous*, 47-48; Dale L. Morgan, *Jedediah Smith and the Opening of the West* (Lincoln: University of Nebraska Press, 1964), 63-64; Berry, 24-25.

4   Morgan, 50, 52-57; Utley, *Life Wild and Perilous*, 48-51; Berry, 26, 29-30; William R. Nester, *Arikara War: The First Plains Indian War, 1823* (Missoula, Mont.: Mountain Press Publishing, 2001), 137, 139–42.

5   Stephen L. Moore, *Savage Frontier: Indians, Riflemen, and Indian Wars in Texas*, vol. 1 (Plano: Republic of Texas Press, 2002), 10; Wilbarger, 204-5.

6   Nester, 181.

7   Utley, *Life Wild and Perilous*, 52; Nester, 181.

8   Morgan, 67–70, 77; Nester, 160, 168-74, 179-81; Utley, *Life Wild and Perilous*, 52.

1824

9   Bill Groneman, *Battlefields of Texas* (Plano: Republic of Texas Press, 1998), 15-16; DeShields, 16-17; Wilbarger, 201-2.

10   Jack B. Tykal, *Etienne Provost: Man of the Mountains* (Liberty, Utah: Eagle's View Publishing, 1989), 49-51, 64n34; Utley, *Life Wild and Perilous*, 71-72, 331n7; LeRoy R. Hafen, ed., *Trappers of the Far West* (Lincoln: University of Nebraska Press, 1983), 3-5.

1826

11   A. J. Sowell, *Rangers and Pioneers of Texas* (Austin: State House Press, 1991), 25.

12 Moore, 11-12, 14; Sowell, *Rangers and Pioneers*, 24-25; John Holmes Jenkins III, ed., *Recollections of Early Texas: The Memoirs of John Holland Jenkins* (Austin: University of Texas Press, 1958), 4-5. Discrepencies regarding the date of this fight vary between 1826 and 1829.

13 Jenkins, 5.

1827

14 Utley, *Life Wild and Perilous*, 105.

15 Utley, *Life Wild and Perilous*, 105-7; David J. Weber, *Taos Trappers: The Fur Trade in the Far Southwest, 1540-1846* (Norman: University of Oklahoma Press, 1971), 124-25; Hafen, *Trappers*, 54-55, 106.

16 Utley, *Life Wild and Perilous*, 107; Hafen, *Trappers*, 55; Weber, 125.

17 The trappers were Silas Gobel, Henry ("Boatswain") Brown, William Campbell, David Cunningham, Thomas Daws, Francois Deromme, Issac Galbraith, Polette Labross, Joseph Lapoint, Toussaint Marishall (Marrishall, Marechal), Gregory Ortago, Joseph Palmer, John B. Ratelle, John Relle, Robiseau (Canadian mixed-blood), Charles Swift, John Turner, Thomas Virgin, and two Indian women. Morgan, 236.

18 The men killed were Brown, Cunnigham, Campbell, Deromme, Gobel, Labross, Ortago, Ratelle, Relle, and Robiseau. Morgan, 227, 240.

19 Berry, 191; Morgan, 227-44.

1828

20 Utley, *Life Wild and Perilous*, 96; Berry, 211, 214-17; Morgan, 267–68, 274, 341; John G. Neihardt, *The Splendid Wayfaring* (Lincoln: University of Nebraska Press, 1970), 261, 267. Those killed at the massacre were Thomas Virgin, Toussaint Marishall, Joseph Palmer, Joseph LaPoint, Marion (an Indian boy), Harrison G. Rogers, Martin McCoy, Peter Raney (Ranne), John Gaiter, John Hannah (Hanna), Abraham Laplant (LePlant), Manuel Lazares (Emanuel Lazzarus), Thomas Daw (Daws), Robert Evans, and Charles Swift.

1829

21 Milo Milton Quaife, ed., *Kit Carson's Autobiography* (Lincoln: University of Nebraska Press, 1966), 10.

22 Quaife, 9-10; Thelma S. Guild and Harvey L. Carter, *Kit Carson: A Pattern for Heroes* (Lincoln: University of Nebraska Press, 1984), 35-36; Utley, *Life Wild and Perilous*, 110-11; Weber, 142-43.

1830

23 Quaife, 16.

24 Ibid., 17.

25 Quaife, 13-17; Guild and Carter, 39-42; Utley, *Life Wild and Perilous*, 111-12.

1831

26 The dates of these incidents are in dispute. A Matagorda County historical marker places the events in 1826. Pioneer recollections place it in 1830 or 1831.

27 Jenkins, 161.

28 Wilbarger, 210.

29 Wilbarger, 209-10; Moore, 13; Jenkins, 160-61; Webb and Carroll, 1:238, 1:612.

30 The campsite was probably near the mouth of Calf Creek and the San Saba River, about a dozen miles east of Menard.

31 DeShields, 60-64; Wilbarger, 91-98; William R. Williamson, "Rezin Pleasant Bowie," www.tshaonline.org; Robert S. Weddle, "Los Almagres Mine," www.tshaonline.org.

1832

32 Bradley H. Patterson, Jr., "The Pierre Hole's Fight," in *Great Western Indian Fights*, by Potomac Corral of the Westerners, edited by B. W. Allred and J. C. Dykes (Lincoln: University of Nebraska Press, Bison Books, 1966), 34-37; LeRoy R. Hafen, *Broken Hand: The Life of Thomas Fitzpatrick, Mountain Man, Guide and Indian Agent* (Lincoln: University of Nebraska Press, 1981), 113-16; Utley, *Life Wild and Perilous*, 138–39; David Lavender, *Westward Vision: The Story of the Oregon Trail* (Lincoln: University of Nebraska Press, 1985), 238.

33 Utley, *Life Wild and Perilous*, 141.

34 Bernard DeVoto, *Across the Wide Missouri* (New York: Houghton Mifflin, 1947), 88-89; Berry, 310-12; Utley, *Life Wild and Perilous*, 140-41.

1833

35 Utley, *Life Wild and Perilous*, 142; Berry, 325; John Myers Myers, *The Saga of Hugh Glass: Pirate, Pawnee, and Mountain Man* (Lincoln: University of Nebraska Press, Bison Books, 1976), 114-37, 222-24, 226.

36 Zenas Leonard, *Narrative of the Adventures of Zenas Leonard: Five Years as a Mountain Man in the Rocky Mountains* (Santa Barbara, Calif.: Narrative Press, 2001), 81.

37 Ibid., 85.

38 Bil Gilbert, *Westering Man: The Life of Joseph Walker* (Norman: University of Oklahoma Press, 1985), 127-33; Leonard, *Zenas Leonard*, 83-85; Alpheus H. Favour, *Old Bill Williams: Mountain Man* (Norman: University of Oklahoma Press, 1962), 106-10. Favour believes that the Paiutes had only gathered around the white men out of curiosity. Washington Irving, in his book about Captain Bonneville, depicted Walker's men as white ruffians who killed a "timid and inoffensive race" of Paiutes.

1835

39 Sowell, *Texas Indian Fighters*, 438.

40 John Henry Brown, *Indian Wars and Pioneers of Texas* (Greenville, S.C.: Southern Historical Press, 1978), 16.

41 DeShields, 105-12; Sowell, *Rangers and Pioneers*, 109-14; A. J. Sowell, *Texas Indian Fighters* (Abilene, Tex.: State House Press, 1986), 434-40.

42 Moore, 14.

43 Moore, 16-20; Jenkins, 23; Wilbarger, 218-19; DeShields, 116-17.

44 Jenkins, 182-83, says that the attacking Indians were about 25 Caddos.

45 DeShields, 119.

46 Moore, 42-44; DeShields, 118-22.

1836

47 Wilbarger (*Depredations*, 220) states that Sarah did not see what the Indian did, while DeShields (*Border Wars*, 168) and Webb (*Texas Rangers*, 35) both say that the warrior took the child and "dashed its brains" against a tree.

48 Wilbarger, 220-21; DeShields, 169-70; Walter Prescott Webb, *Texas Rangers: A Century of Frontier Defense* (Austin: University of Texas Press, 1991), 35. Sources vary in the details of Hibbins's escape route.

49 Webb, *Texas Rangers*, 35. Noah Smithwicks 1900 book, *The Evolution of a State*. Much of Hibbins's story comes from Smithwick, who is quoted by Webb.

50 Smithwick quoted in Webb, *Texas Rangers*, 36.

51 Webb, *Texas Rangers*, 37-38.

52 Webb, *Texas Rangers*, 35-38; Wilbarger, 220-21; DeShields, 167-75; Moore, 78–81; Susan and H. D. Orr, "Sarah Creath Howard," www.tshaonline.org.

53 Moore, 94-95.

1837

54 Killed were Joseph Cooper, Alexander Bostwick, Dr. William Sanders, and William Nicholson. Moore, 269-71.

55 Killed were Miles, Lewis P. Sheuster, James Joslen, James Christian, Jesse Blair, and Westley Nicholson (Moore, 273).

56 Moore, 266-78; Wilbarger, 195; Groneman, 79-80.

1838

57 Christopher Long, "Killough Massacre," www.tshaonline.org; Wilbarger, 620-21.

58 Neil's name has been spelled various ways, including Neill and Neal.

59 DeShields, 225-29; Groneman, 80-81; Harry McCorry Henderson, "Battle Creek Fight," www.tshaonline.org.

60 Brown (*Indian Wars*, 51) says the families lived west of the Guadalupe River, opposite the present town of Cuero, in Dewitt County, while DeShields (*Border Wars*, 239) says they lived two miles below Gonzales, in Gonzales County.

61 The number of Putman children, as well as their names and ages, are disputed. Wilbarger (*Depredations*, 2) says that there were four children; DeShields (*Border Wars*, 240) claims there were three, with James being the youngest; Brown (*Indian Wars*, 51) states that there were three, with James four years old and another daughter two and a half.

62 Brown, *Indian Wars*, 51; Wilbarger, 2; Sowell, *Rangers and Pioneers*, 226; DeShields, 239–41.

1839

63 Brown, *Indian Wars*, 51.

64 It is uncertain who the white woman was, but it could have been Jane Crawford, who was still in Comanche hands at this time. The girl was Matilda Lockhart, and the three other children were Mitchell Putnam's.

65 Dorman H. Winfrey and James M. Day, eds., *The Indian Papers of Texas and the Southwest, 1825-1916* (Austin: Texas State Historical Association, 1995), 1:58-59; David F. Crosby, "The Battle of Brushy Creek," *Wild West*,

August 1997; Wilbarger, 2, 3; DeShields, 241; Brown, *Indian Wars*, 51; Sowell, *Rangers and Pioneers*, 226.

66 Brown (*Indian Wars*, 61), Wilbarger (*Depredations*, 146), and Karen R. Thompson ("Battle of Brushy Creek," www.tshaonline.org) say the attack was on 18 February. DeShields (*Border Wars*, 268), Groneman (*Battlefields of Texas*, 84), and Crosby ("Brushy Creek") say the attack was on 24 February. Other sources simply say spring of 1839. Brown antedates the others and is the source for many subsequent histories.

67 Sowell (*Rangers and Pioneers*, 54-55) says that there was another child, an infant son, also placed beneath the floorboards.

68 Sowell, *Rangers and Pioneers*, 55.

69 Wilbarger, 149-50.

70 Jenkins, 56-57, 60, 231; Brown, *Indian Wars*, 61; Sowell, *Rangers and Pioneers*, 54–57; Crosby, "Brushy Creek."

71 Thomas W. Cutrer, "John Bird," www.tshaonline.org.

72 Ibid.

73 Cutrer, "John Bird"; DeShields, 260-63; Jenkins, 179-81; Webb and Carroll, 1:163–65.

74 T. R. Fehrenbach, *Lone Star: A History of Texas and the Texans* (New York: Collier Books, 1968), 455-56; Brown, *Indian Wars*, 65–68; DeShields, 275-80; Webb, *Texas Rangers*, 53-54; Webb and Carroll, 2:265.

75 Brown, *Indian Wars*, 68.

76 Benjamin Dolbeare, *A Narrative of the Captivity and Suffering of Dolly Webster among the Camanche Indians in Texas* (New Haven: Yale University Library, 1986), 2-3.

77 Ibid., 3–7, 27-34. For a more complete story of Dolly Webster, see Gregory and Susan Michno, *A Fate Worse Than Death: Indian Captivities in the West, 1830–1885* (Caldwell, Idaho: Caxton Press, 2007).

1840

78 Winfrey and Day, 1:101.

79 Donaly E. Brice, *The Great Comanche Raid* (Austin: Eakin Press, 1987), 23-24.

80 Rena Maverick Green, ed., *Memoirs of Mary A. Maverick* (Lincoln: University of Nebraska Press, 1989), 38. Matilda's reaction was typical of returned captives. Rape and abuse caused many of them to deteriorate physically and mentally.

81 Rupert N. Richardson, *The Comanche Barrier to South Plains Settlement* (Austin: Eakin Press, 1996), 48-50; T. R. Fehrenbach, *Comanches: The Destruction of a People* (New York: Da Capo Press, 1994), 324-26; Brice, 21-25; Dolbeare, 21, 25; Winfrey and Day, 1:101-2.

82 Webb, *Texas Rangers*, 61.

83 Brice, 28-32, 44–45, 95-96, 99; Craig H. Roell, "Linnville Raid of 1840," www.tshaonline.org; Wilbarger, 27, 32-33; DeShields, 301; Webb, *Texas Rangers*, 60-61; Michno, *Fate Worse than Death*, 73–74.

84 Wayne Lease, *Texas Forts* (Garland: Texas Forts Distributors, 2001), 109; DeShields, 305; Wilbarger, 265-66.

85 The Red Fork Fight is usually said to have taken place near Colorado City, Texas. The prominent hieroglyphics Moore mentioned, however, were probably those located near Paint Rock on the Concho River. This clue, as well as Moore's general description of the country and the distance he said he traveled from the pictographs to the village, points to a battle site much farther downriver. Wilbarger (*Depredations*, 184) believes the fight probably occurred near Ballinger, Texas, which is more likely.

86 Brice, 52–53.

87 Wilbarger, 184-85; DeShields, 310-12; Brice, 50-54; Brown, *Indian Wars*, 83-84; Jenkins, 171-73; Webb, *Texas Rangers*, 45-46.

1841

88 DeShields, 325-27; Wilbarger, 360.

89 DeShields, 331–32.

90 Brown, *Indian Wars*, 86.

91 Ibid., 85–86.

92 Brown, *Indian Wars*, 85-87; DeShields, 330-34, 336; Donald F. Frazier, "Battle of Village Creek," www.tshaonline.org. Denton's remains were found and reburied in the courthouse yard in Denton, Texas, in 1901.

93 James Kimmins Greer, *Texas Ranger Jack Hays in the Frontier Southwest* (College Station: Texas A & M University Press, 1993), 48.

94 DeShields, 340; Webb, *Texas Rangers*, 70-71; Greer, 46-48.

95 Wilbarger, 77-78; Webb, *Texas Rangers*, 71; Webb and Carroll, 1:605; Greer, 50-51.

96 Greer, 51.

97 DeShields, 342-43; Webb and Carroll, 1:569.

98 Utley, *Life Wild and Perilous*, 177-78; "Battle Country," www.ultimate wyoming.com.

99 Utley, *Life Wild and Perilous*, 178.

100 James Mooney, *Calendar History of the Kiowa Indians* (Washington, D.C.: Smithsonian Institution Press, 1979), 278.

101 Mooney, 277-79; H. Bailey Carroll, "Texan Santa Fe Expedition," www .tshaonline.org.

1842

102 DeShields, 361-62.

103 The year of the Gilleland capture is disputed. Webb and Carroll (*Handbook of Texas*), and Handbook of Texas Online indicate that it was in the spring of 1840. The military situation and the reports of the volunteer soldiers, however, suggest that the raid occurred in the spring of 1842.

104 DeShields, 174, 360-63; J. Marvin Hunter, ed., "Mrs. Rebecca J. Fisher," *Frontier Times* 3, no. 8 (May 1926): 16; Webb and Carroll, 1:602-3, 1: 689; Fehrenbach, *Lone Star*, 261.

1843

105 This fight was variously reported to have occurred in 1841, 1842, and 1843. Because many of the rangers were armed with Colt pistols, which were not as readily available in 1841 and 1842, and because it was said that some of Hays's men were in prison in Mexico since the ill-fated Mier Expedition of December 1842, 1843 is likely the correct year.

106 Sowell, *Texas Indian Fighters*, 21-22, 318.

107 Sowell, *Texas Indian Fighters*, 22-24, 809; Greer, 49; Joseph Carroll McConnell, *The West Texas Frontier, or A Descriptive History of Early Times in Western Texas* (pdf, www.forttours.com); Webb and Carroll, 1:105.

108 Webb and Carroll, 2:632; Wilbarger, 53-54; Brown, *Indian Wars*, 92-93.

109 Wilbarger, 55-56; Brown, *Indian Wars*, 93.

110 Wilbarger, 55-58; Webb and Carroll, 2:632.

1844

111 Sowell, *Texas Indian Fighters*, 319–20.

112 Ibid., 321.

113 Ibid.

114 Sowell, *Texas Indian Fighters*, 319-22; Greer, 102-4.

115 Guild and Carter, 131–32; Quaife, 84; John Charles Fremont, *Memoirs of My Life* (New York: Cooper Square Press, 2001), 370-72, 375-76, 409; LeRoy R. Hafen and Ann W. Hafen, *Old Spanish Trail: Santa Fe to Los Angeles* (Lincoln: University of Nebraska Press, 1993), 288-90, 292. Fremont took Pablo Hernandez to Washington D.C., where Sen. Thomas H. Benton cared for and educated him. Pablo showed promise, but he later went back to Mexico, and then to California, where he returned to history as a bandit known as Joaquin.

116 Robert M. Utley, *Lone Star Justice: The First Century of the Texas Rangers* (New York: Oxford University Press, 2002), 12.

117 Winfrey and Day, 2:72-73; Utley, *Lone Star Justice*, 10-12, 306n9; Wilbarger, 75-77; Walter Prescott Webb, *The Great Plains* (New York: Grosset & Dunlap, n.d.), 174.

118 Wilbarger, 601-2; Lease, 97; Catherine G. Alford, "William Oldham," www.tshaonline.org.

119 Sowell, *Texas Indian Fighters*, 132; Greer, 109-10.

1845

120 Greer, 113; Sowell, *Texas Indian Fighters*, 322, 381-82.

1846

121 Greer, 119-20.

122 Sowell, *Texas Indian Fighters*, 369-70; Greer, 118–20, 128-23, 126.

123 Fremont, 490.

124 Ibid., 491. Today a historical marker on Highway 140 commemorates this attack.

125 Dale L. Walker, *Bear Flag Rising: The Conquest of California, 1846* (New York: Forge, 1999), 81-82, 101-03; Fremont, 487, 490-92; Jerry Dwyer, "Fremont in Klamath County," home.comcast.net; Quaife, 98, 100-101. Carson claimed that Fremont did not participate in this battle, but Fremont said he did.

126 Frank McNitt, *Navajo Wars: Military Campaigns, Slave Raids and Reprisals* (Albuquerque: University of New Mexico Press, 1972), 101-2; Joseph P. Peters, *Indian Battles and Skirmishes on the American Frontier, 1790-1898* (Ann Arbor, Mich.: University Microfilms, 1966), 33.

1847

127 Paul I. Wellman, *Death in the Desert: The Fifty Years' War for the Great Southwest* (Lincoln: University of Nebraska Press, 1987), 33.

128 Upon reaching Pueblo, Colorado, Albert met George Ruxton and told him his story, which Ruxton included in his 1848 book, *Wild Life in the Rocky Mountains*. Wellman (*Death in the Desert*) asserts that Turley also escaped, but he was later betrayed by a Mexican he thought was friendly. The Mexican led the Indians to Turley's hiding place and they murdered him.

129 Wellman, 31-37; Bob Scott, *Tom Tobin and the Bloody Espinosas* (Baltimore: PublishAmerica, 2004), 31-34.

130 Lewis H. Garrard, *Wah-to-yah and the Taos Trail* (Norman: University of Oklahoma Press, 1955), 290.

131 William Y. Chalfant, *Dangerous Passage: The Santa Fe Trail and the Mexican War* (Norman: University of Oklahoma Press, 1989), 65-72; Garrard, 289-90; Mooney, 286-87.

132 Chalfant, *Dangerous Passage*, 158; Garrard, 295; Louise Barry, *Beginning of the West: Annals of the Kansas Gateway to the American West, 1540-1854* (Topeka: Kansas State Historical Society, 1972), 686.

133 The casualties were Pvts. Jonathan Arledge, Moses Short, John Dickhart, George Gaskill, and J. H. Blake killed; Sgt. Ben Bishop and Pvts. Henry Vancaster, John Lovelace, Thomas Ward, James Bush (Burk), and Willis Wilson wounded.

134 Chalfant, *Dangerous Passage*, 87-101; Barry, *Beginning of the West*, 694, 700, 705-6.

135 In Company E, William Duncan, Francis Turcott, Ludwick Tanner, Jacob Johnson, Valentine Regg, and Henry Barlow were killed; Benjamin Frost was wounded and scalped but survived. In Company D, Philander Potter and Charles Fuss were killed; Michael McBride, William Warner, and Acuzi Stanley were wounded.

136 Barry, *Beginning of the West*, 691, 705-6; Chalfant, *Dangerous Passage*, 106-8.

137 Barry, *Beginning of the West*, 704; Edwin L. Sabin, *Kit Carson Days*, vol. 2, *Adventures in the Path of Empire* (Lincoln: University of Nebraska Press, 1995), 573; Quaife, 120-21; Chalfant, *Dangerous Passage*, 110-11; Guild and Carter, 170-71.

138 Chalfant, *Dangerous Passage*, 112-18.

139 Barry, *Beginning of the West*, 727.

140 Robert W. Frazer, *Forts of the West: Military Forts and Presidios and Posts Commonly Called Forts West of the Mississippi River to 1898* (Norman: University of Oklahoma Press, 1965), 58; Chalfant, *Dangerous Passage*, 179-81; Barry, *Beginning of the West*, 727; Hafen, *Broken Hand*, 258.

1848

141 Ray Hoard Glassley, *Indian Wars of the Pacific Northwest* (Portland, Ore.: Binfords & Mort, 1972), 23-25; George L. Converse, *A Military History of the Columbia Valley, 1848-1865* (Walla Walla, Wash.: Pioneer Press Books, 1988), 7, 9; Robert H. Ruby and John A. Brown, *Indians of the Pacific Northwest* (Norman: University of Oklahoma Press, 1988), 102-03.

142 Glassley, 27-32; Converse, 9-10.

143 The wounded were James Roop, lanced in the stomach; James Moody, hit by an arrow in the thigh; and J. L. Henry and John C. Slocum, who both had arrow wounds in the shoulder.

144 Barry, *Beginning of the West*, 757-58; Chalfant, *Dangerous Passage*, 212, 215-27.

145 Janet Lecompte, "The Manco Burro Massacre," *New Mexico Historical Review*, October 1966: 312.

146 Lecompte, "Manco Burro," 309-14; Ralph Adam Smith, *Borderlander: The Life of James Kirker, 1793-1852* (Norman: University of Oklahoma Press, 1999), 196; Chalfant, *Dangerous Passage*, 257; Barry, *Beginning of the West*, 756-57.

147 Smith, *Borderlander*, 196-97.

148 After the troopers' return to Fort Mann, it was learned that the boy was named Stephen and had lived at a hacienda of Colonel Quinto in Texas before he became a Comanche captive (Chalfant, *Dangerous Passage*, 237-40).

149 Barry, *Beginning of the West*, 764. The battle site was near the mouth of Day Creek, about eleven miles southwest of present-day Protection, Kansas.

150 Chalfant, *Dangerous Passage*, 240-44.

151 Those wounded, in addition to Eldridge, were Pvts. Philip Kinchlo, G. W. Vance, and James B. Hoover of Company B, and Pvt. Robert Williams of Company A.

152 Chalfant, *Dangerous Passage*, 245-50.

153 Brown, *Indian Wars*, 107-08; Wilbarger, 60-61; Webb and Carroll, 2:946-47.

1849

154 Michael S. Durham, *Desert Between the Mountains: Mormons, Miners, Padres, Mountain Men, and the Opening of the Great Basin, 1771-1869* (Norman: University of Oklahoma Press, 1999), 131, 141-42; Peter Gottfredson, *Indian Depredations in Utah* (Tucson: Fenestra Books, 2002), 18-19.

155 Janet Lecompte, *Pueblo, Hardscrabble, Greenhorn: Society on the High Plains, 1832-1856* (Norman: University of Oklahoma Press, 1978), 238; George W. Webb, *Chronological List of Engagements between the Regular Army of the United States and Various Tribes of Hostile Indians . . .* (New York: AMS Press, 1976), 9.

156 Hubert Howe Bancroft, *History of Washington, Idaho, and Montana, 1845-1889*, vol. 21, *The Works of Hubert Howe Bancroft* (San Francisco: History Company, 1890), 67-8, 80; Ruby and Brown, 123; "Unsettling Events: Fort Nisqually Battle," www.tpl.lib.wa.us.

157 Sowell, *Texas Indian Fighters*, 172-77.

158 In Webb, *List of Engagements*, 10, and Francis P. Heitman, *Historical Register and Dictionary of the United States Army* (Washington, D.C.: GPO, 1903), 2:400, the site of this fight is listed as the San Diego Crossing of the Rio Grande, near present-day Rincon, New Mexico, but recorded narratives indicate that it was near Santa Rita.

159 Daniel C. B. Rathbun and David V. Alexander, *New Mexico Frontier Military Place Names* (Las Cruces, N. Mex.: Yucca Tree Press, 2003), 59; Dan L. Thrapp,

Encyclopedia of Frontier Biography (Lincoln: University of Nebraska Press, 1991), 3:1363; Edwin R. Sweeney, *Mangas Coloradas: Chief of the Chiricahua Apaches* (Norman: University of Oklahoma Press, 1998), 176-78; Dan L. Thrapp, *Victorio and the Mimbres Apaches* (Norman: University of Oklahoma Press, 1974), 23.

160 Percival G. Lowe, *Five Years a Dragoon ('49 to '54) and Other Adventures on the Great Plains* (Norman: University of Oklahoma Press, 1991), 29-31; D. Ray Wilson, *Fort Kearny on the Platte* (Dundee, Ill.: Crossroads Communications, 1980), 33; Webb, *List of Engagements*, 10.

1850

161 Will Bagley, "Murdered Ute's Ghost Haunts Utah History," from *Salt Lake Tribune*, November 5, 2000, http://historytogo.utah.gov.

162 D. Robert Carter, *Founding Fort Utah: Provo's Native Inhabitants, Early Explorers, and First Year of Settlement* (Provo, Utah: Provo City Corporation, 2003), 173.

163 Ibid., 177.

164 The day before the fight, Higbee had a premonition that someone would die in the battle. "It might as well be me as anybody," he said (Carter, *Founding Fort Utah*, 181).

165 Gottfredson, 29-34; Carter, *Founding Fort Utah*, 175-81, 188. The wounded men were Alexander Williams, Isham Flynn, Samuel Kearns (or Carn), Albert Miles, Jabez Nowlin, Thomas (or James) Orr, and Alexander Stephens (or Stevens).

166 Carter, *Founding Fort Utah*, 224.

167 Ibid., 207.

168 Ibid.

169 Ibid., 213.

170 Bagley; Carter, *Founding Fort Utah*, 199–223.

171 Winfrey and Day, 5:81.

172 Ibid., 5:81-82.

173 Thomas T. Smith, *The Old Army in Texas: A Research Guide to the U.S. Army in Nineteenth-Century Texas* (Austin: Texas State Historical Association, 2000), 94, 136; Webb, *List of Engagements*, 10; Winfrey and Day, 5:84.

174 John Salmon Ford, *Rip Ford's Texas* (Austin: University of Texas Press, 1963), 162-64; Smith, *Old Army*, 137.

175 Ford, 166.

176 Ford, 149-50, 165-66; Smith, *Old Army*, 137.

177 Smith, *Old Army*, 138; Webb, *List of Engagements*, 10; Theophilus F. Rodenbough, *From Everglade to Canyon with the Second United States Cavalry* (Norman: University of Oklahoma Press, 2000), 167.

1851

178 Ford, 176.

179 Ibid., 177.

180 Ford, 168, 174-77; Sowell, *Texas Indian Fighters*, 399.

181 H. W. Brands, *The Age of Gold: The California Gold Rush and the New American Dream* (New York: Doubleday, 2002), 314.

182 Benjamin Butler Harris, *The Gila Trail: The Texas Argonauts and the California Gold Rush* (Norman: University of Oklahoma Press, 1960), 147-48; Brands, 312-14; Clifford E. Trafzer and Joel R. Hyer, eds, *Exterminate Them!* (East Lansing: Michigan State University Press, 1999), 23.

183 Lorenzo Sitgreaves, *Report of an Expedition down the Zuni and Colorado Rivers* (Washington, D.C.: R. Armstrong, Public Printer, 1853), 17–18.

184 David Sloan Stanley, *An American General: The Memoirs of David Sloan Stanley* (Santa Barbara, Calif.: Narrative Press, 2003), 62.

185 Sitgreaves, 19.

186 Sitgreaves, 4-20; Stanley, 61-62.

1852

187 Wayne R. Austerman, *Sharps Rifles and Spanish Mules: The San Antonio-El Paso Mail, 1851-1881* (College Station: Texas A & M University Press, 1985), 28-29.

188 Ron C. Tyler, *The Big Bend: A History of the Last Texas Frontier* (College Station: Texas A & M University Press, 1996), 70.

189 Ibid.

190 Tyler, *Big Bend*, 70-71; Wilbarger, 119-23.

1853

191 Robert Wooster, ed., *Recollections of Western Texas, 1852-55, by Two of the U.S. Mounted Rifles* (Lubbock: Texas Tech University Press, 2001), 73-75, 78.

192 Jerry Thompson, *Confederate General of the West: Henry Hopkins Sibley* (College Station: Texas A & M University Press, 1996), 95-98.

193 Wooster, *Recollections of Western Texas*, 78-81, 101.

194 Gottfredson, 43–46.

195 Gottfredson, 46–47, 53, 56, 59, 74–83; Hubert Howe Bancroft, *Hubert Howe Bancroft's History of Utah, 1540-1886,* www.utlm.org, 474, 475n66; Thomas G. Alexander, "Utah, The Right Place," http://historytogo.utah .gov; Tina Kelley and Kathryn M. MacKay, "Wakara," from Utah History Encyclopedia, www.media.utah.edu.

1854

196 Wright said "Baluarta" was a region near a pond that flowed into the Laguna del Madre. This is probably present-day Laguna Salada. Laguna Madre is farther downstream, and not to be confused with the large coastal lagoon of the same name. Wooster, *Recollections of Western Texas*, 69, 86; "Arroyo Baluarte," www.tshaonline.org.

197 Wooster, *Recollections of Western Texas*, 86–87; Smith, *Old Army*, 139.

198 Sowell, *Texas Indian Fighters*, 683–90.

199 Austerman, 56.

200 Sowell, *Texas Indian Fighters*, 563.

201 Austerman, 61.

202 Austerman, 58–62; Sowell, *Texas Indian Fighters*, 563–64.

1855

203 Lawrence John Francell, *Fort Lancaster Texas: Frontier Sentinel* (Austin: Texas State Historical Association, 1999), 39.

204 Ibid., 39–40.

205 Ibid., 42.

206 E. A. Schwartz, *The Rogue River Indian War and Its Aftermath, 1850-1980* (Norman: University of Oklahoma Press, 1997), 94; Stephen D. Beckham, *Requiem for a People* (Corvallis: Oregon State University Press, 1996), 155–56. The latter source says the fight took place on 25 October.

207 Clifford E. Trafzer and Richard D. Scheurman, *Renegade Tribe: The Palouse Indians and the Invasion of the Inland Pacific Northwest* (Pullman: Washington State University Press, 1986), 64–67; Bancroft, *History of Washington, Idaho,* 115; Glassley, 115–16; Converse, 20–21; Webb, *List of Engagements,* 13–14.

1856

208 Bancroft, *History of Washington, Idaho,* 125–32; Ruby and Brown, 152–53.

209 Lynn R. Carson, "The Tintic War and the Deaths of George and Washington Carson," www.carsonfamilyhistory.org, 12.

210 Carson, 10–14; Gottfredson, 102.

211 Carson, 18–19.

212 Ibid., 15–23, 26–27.

213 Glassley, 139–40; Converse, 39.

214 James R. Arnold, *Jeff Davis's Own: Cavalry, Comanches, and the Battle for the Texas Frontier* (New York: John Wiley & Sons, 2000), 90–91; Smith, *Old Army,* 141.

215 William Y. Chalfant, *Cheyennes and Horse Soldiers* (Norman: University of Oklahoma Press, 1989), 41–44; Donald J. Berthrong, *The Southern Cheyennes* (Norman: University of Oklahoma Press, 1963), 134–35; Peters, 34. Conflicting reports date the initial attack on Babbitt's train as 25 August or 26 August.

216 Trafzer and Scheurman, 74.

217 Ruby and Brown, 157; Bancroft, *History of Washington, Idaho,* 168–69; Converse, 39, 41; Trafzer and Scheurman, 74.

218 Bancroft, *History of Washington, Idaho,* 134–37; Ruby and Brown, 159; "Unsettling Events: Port Gamble Battle," www.tpl.lib.wa.us.

1857

219 Lease, 59; Arnold, 172–73; Smith, *Old Army,* 141–42; Webb, *List of Engagements,* 16; Sowell, *Texas Indian Fighters,* 696–99, 778–79.

220 Reports of Jenifer's fight identify the battle site as the North Branch of the Nueces River, but there is no North Branch; the fight probably occurred somewhere between present-day Camp Wood and Rocksprings.

221 Smith, *Old Army,* 142; Arnold, 137; Webb, *List of Engagements,* 16.

222 Austerman, 93–96.

223 Francell, 51–52.

224 Francell, 51–53; A. Ray Stephens and William M. Holmes, *Historical Atlas of Texas* (Norman: University of Oklahoma Press, 1989), 37; Webb, *List of Engagements,* 17.

225 Arnold, 155–56, 163; Smith, *Old Army,* 143; Webb, *List of Engagements,* 17.

226 Webb, *List of Engagements*, 17; Arnold, 163–64. Smith, *Old Army*, 143, lists this engagement as occurring on 28 September.

1858

227 Austerman, 120.

228 Ibid., 117–20.

229 Ida Lasater Huckabay, *Ninety-four Years in Jack County, 1854-1948* (Jacksboro, Tex.: Privately published, 1949), 36.

230 Ibid., 38.

231 Huckabay, 35–39; Doyle Marshall, *A Cry Unheard: The Story of Indian Attacks in and around Parker County, Texas, 1858-1872* (n.p.: Annetta Valley Farm Press, 1990), 80.

232 Marvin E. Kroeker, *Great Plains Command: William B. Hazen in the Frontier West* (Norman: University of Oklahoma Press, 1976), 26–29; Webb, *List of Engagements*, 18; Heitman, 2:403. The date of this battle is recorded in military records as 16 June, but Hazen's account indicates that the fight occurred on 13 June. The location might have been near the entrance to present-day Carlsbad Caverns National Park, about twelve miles southwest of Whites City, New Mexico.

233 Kroeker, 29.

234 Peters, 35; A. J. Bledsoe, *Indian Wars of the Northwest, A California Sketch* (accessed online).

235 McNitt, 331.

236 Ibid.

237 McNitt, 328–31; U.S. Adjutant General's Office, *Chronological List of Actions, etc., with Indians from January 15, 1837 to January 1891* (Fort Collins, Colo.: Old Army Press, 1979), 19.

238 Charles N. Baley, *Disaster at the Colorado: Beale's Wagon Road and the First Emigrant Party* (Logan: Utah State University Press, 2002), 67.

239 Ibid., 1, 4, 15, 31, 35, 59–72, 97.

240 Peters, 35; Bledsoe; "Trinity Rangers," www.militarymuseum.org.

241 Arnold, 217.

242 Charles M. Robinson III, *Men Who Wear the Star: The Story of the Texas Rangers* (New York: Random House, 2000), 116; Arnold, 216–17; Webb, *Texas Rangers*, 169–72; Wilbarger, 442; B. P. Gallaway, ed., *Texas: Dark Corner of the Confederacy* (Lincoln: University of Nebraska Press, 1994), 51–52.

1859

243 Sowell, *Texas Indian Fighters*, 286–88; Smith, *Old Army*, 144. Participant Richard Ware remembered this fight as occurring in 1858, but details match army reports of a fight on 13 February 1859.

244 Kroeker, 30–31; Webb, *List of Engagements*, 20.

245 Arnold, 256.

246 Wilbarger, 442; Arnold, 255–56; Webb, *Texas Rangers*, 170.

247 David V. Alexander, *Arizona Frontier Military Place Names, 1846-1912* (Las Cruces, N. Mex.: Yucca Tree Press, 1998), 39; Adjutant General, 20.

248 Sowell, *Texas Indian Fighters*, 391.

249 Kroeker, 32–35; Sowell, *Texas Indian Fighters*, 386–94; Webb, *List of Engagements*, 20.

1860

250 Arnold, 284.
251 Arnold, 281-84; Smith, *Old Army*, 146.
252 Hafen and Hafen, *Old Spanish Trail*, 248-52; John and William Gorenfeld, "Carlton at Bitter Spring: Punishing the Paiutes," *Wild West*, December 2001, 44-49; Aurora Hunt, *The Army of the Pacific, 1860-1866* (Mechanicsburg, Pa.: Stackpole Books, 2004), 107; Webb, *List of Engagements*, 21.
253 Sweeney, *Mangas Coloradas*, 389-90.
254 Ferol Egan, *Sand in a Whirlwind: The Paiute Indian War of 1860* (Reno: University of Nevada Press, 2003), 252-59.
255 Louise Barry, "The Ranch at Walnut Creek Crossing," *Kansas Historical Quarterly* 38, no. 4 (Winter 1972): 121, 129, 138-40; Ida Ellen Rath, *The Rath Trail* (Wichita, Kans.: McCormick-Armstrong, 1961), 4-5; Gregory F. Michno, *Battle at Sand Creek: The Military Perspective* (El Segundo, Calif.: Upton & Sons, 2004), 26.

1861

256 Austerman, 165-67.
257 In some sources, Zimmer is identified as Anton Brewer.
258 Sweeney, *Mangas Coloradas*, 416-20; Virginia Culin Roberts, *With Their Own Blood: A Saga of Southwestern Pioneers* (Fort Worth: Texas Christian University Press, 1992), 105-16.
259 Roberts, 117.
260 Roberts, 116-17; Edwin R. Sweeney, *Cochise: Chiricahua Apache Chief* (Norman: University of Oklahoma Press, 1991), 185; Sweeney, *Mangas Coloradas*, 420-21.
261 Austerman, 183-84; Morgan Wolfe Merrick, *From Desert to Bayou: The Civil War Journal and Sketches of Morgan Wolfe Merrick*, edited by Jerry D. Thompson (El Paso: Texas Western Press, 1991), 23, 107n53.
262 Roberts, 118-20; Sweeney, *Mangas Coloradas*, 424-26.
263 Peters, 36; Bledsoe.
264 Alvin M. Josephy, Jr., *The Civil War in the American West* (New York: Alfred A. Knopf, 1991), 330-31; U.S. Department of War, *The War of the Rebellion: A Compilation of the Official Records of the Union and Confederate Armies* (Washington, D.C.: GPO, 1880-1901), 8:14-15; "Round Mountain: Civil War Oklahoma," www.americancivilwar.com.
265 Josephy, 331-32; U.S. War Dept., *Official Records*, 8:7-14, 8:17-20; "Chusto-Talasah, Caving Banks: Civil War Oklahoma," www.americancivilwar.com.
266 U.S. War Dept., *Official Records*, 8:22-23.
267 U.S. War Dept., *Official Records*, 8:24-29; Josephy, 332-33.

1862

268 Myron Angel, *History of Nevada* (Oakland, Calif.: Thompson & West, 1881), 166-67.
269 "Arizona's Forgotten Dead: The Story of the Engagement at Dragoon Springs, Arizona," accessed online at Colonel Sherod Hunter Camp 1525, Sons of Confederate Veterans; Sweeney, *Cochise*, 194.
270 Sweeney, *Cochise*, 196.

271 Thomas E. Farish, *History of Arizona* (San Francisco: Filmer Brothers Electrotype, 1915–18), 2:119–20; Sweeney, *Cochise*, 196; U.S. War Dept., *Official Records*, vol. 49, no. 3, 120.

272 Sowell, *Rangers and Pioneers*, 81–87.

273 Sweeney, *Cochise*, 196–98; U.S. War Dept., *Official Records*, 9:558, 9:563, 9:586–87.

274 Angel, 178.

275 U.S. War Dept., *Official Records*, vol. 50, no. 1, 123.

276 Angel, 178; Fred B. Rogers, *Soldiers of the Overland: Being Some Account of the Services of General Patrick Edward Connor and His Volunteers in the Old West* (San Francisco: Grabhorn Press, 1938), 29; U.S. War Dept., *Official Records*, vol. 50, no. 1, 123–25. Angel dates this incident as 1861.

1863

277 Sowell, *Texas Indian Fighters*, 561, 564–65; David Paul Smith, *Frontier Defense in the Civil War: Texas' Rangers and Rebels* (College Station: Texas A & M University Press, 1992), 97.

278 Daniel C. B. Rathbun, *Nevada Military Place Names of the Indian Wars and Civil War* (Las Cruces, N. Mex.: Yucca Tree Press, 2002), 64–65; Angel, 180.

279 Bancroft, *History of Washington, Idaho*, 407, 410–11; William S. Greever, *Bonanza West: The Story of the Western Mining Rushes, 1848-1900* (Norman: University of Oklahoma Press, 1963), 262, 264; U.S. War Dept., *Official Records*, vol. 50, no. 1, 485.

280 U.S. War Dept., *Official Records*, vol. 49, no. 3, 208–10; Richard H. Orton, *Records of California Men in the War of the Rebellion, 1861 to 1867* (Sacramento: State Printing Office, 1890), 181.

281 Rathbun, *Nevada Military Place Names*, 55–56; Orton, 182; Angel, 180–81.

282 Rathbun, *Nevada Military Place Names*, 141; Orton, 182.

283 Michno, *Sand Creek*, 70–71; Thomas Goodrich, *Black Flag: Guerrilla Warfare on the Western Border, 1861-1865* (Bloomington: Indiana University Press, 1995), 62–63; U.S. War Dept., *Official Records*, vol. 22, no. 2, 286.

284 Brigham Madsen, *The Shoshoni Frontier and the Bear River Massacre* (Salt Lake City: University of Utah Press, 1985), 208, says that station keeper William Riley was killed in the initial June raid, but other sources say he was present at the 6 July attack, so apparently he was only wounded in June.

285 Angel, 182; Orton, 567–69.

286 Rathbun, *Nevada Military Place Names*, 41; Orton, 521, 565.

287 U.S. Senate, *Report of the Joint Special Committee on the Condition of the Indian Tribes*, 39th Cong., 2nd sess., 1867, S. Rep. 156, 252; Orton, 670, 674; Peters, 39.

288 U.S. War Dept., *Official Records*, vol. 49, no. 3, 236.

289 Orton, 828, 829; U.S. War Dept., *Official Records*, vol. 49, no. 3, 236.

290 John Ross Browne, *Adventures in Apache Country* (New York: Promontory Press, 1974), 196, 201–2, 216–23.

1864

291 U.S. Senate, *Letter from the Secretary of War*, 50th Cong., 2nd sess., 1888, S. Exec. Doc. 70, 234.

292 U.S. Senate, *Letter from the Secretary of War*, 232–34; Orton, 826, 830; Peters, 41.

293 Daniel Ellis Conner, *Joseph Reddeford Walker and the Arizona Adventure* (Norman: University of Oklahoma Press, 1956), 254.

294 Farish, 4:136–37; Conner, 250–56. Farish says this fight took place in 1864, while Conner dates it as 1865.

295 Micheal Clodfelter, *The Dakota War: The United States Army versus the Sioux, 1862-1865* (Jefferson, N.C.: McFarland & Company, 2006), 160.

296 U.S. War Dept., *Official Records*, vol. 34, no. 3, 168–69; Clodfelter, 160–61; Kurt D. Bergemann, *Brackett's Battalion: Minnesota Cavalry in the Civil War and Dakota War* (St. Paul: Minnesota Historical Society Press, Borealis Books, 2004), 102; Doane Robinson, *A History of the Dakota or Sioux Indians* (Minneapolis: Ross & Haines, 1974), 330; Frank Myers, *Soldiering in Dakota, among the Indians, in 1863-65* (Huron, S. Dak.: Huronite Printing House, 1888), 10–11. Feilner's name is sometimes spelled Fielner. Miner's name is sometimes spelled Minor.

297 Susan Badger Doyle, ed., *Journeys to the Land of Gold: Emigrant Diaries from the Bozeman Trail, 1863-1866* (Helena: Montana Historical Society Press, 2000), 151–53, 208–10, 225, 240–41, 248, 252.

298 Hervey Johnson, *Tending the Talking Wire: A Buck Soldier's View of Indian Country, 1863-1866*, edited by William Unrau (Salt Lake City: University of Utah Press, 1979), 154–55; J. W. Vaughn, *Indian Fights: New Facts on Seven Encounters* (Norman: University of Oklahoma Press, 1966), 6–9; Doyle, 744.

299 Leo E. Oliva, *Soldiers on the Santa Fe Trail* (Norman: University of Oklahoma Press, 1967), 153; U.S. War Dept., *Official Records*, vol. 41, no. 2, 369, 378–79, 413, 445; Louise Barry, "The Ranch at Cow Creek Crossing," *Kansas Historical Quarterly* 38, no. 4 (Winter 1972): 427–34.

300 U.S. War Dept., *Official Records*, vol. 41, no. 1, 212.

301 U.S. War Dept., *Official Records*, vol. 41, no. 1, 212–13; Leo E. Oliva, *Fort Union and the Frontier Army in the Southwest* (Santa Fe: National Park Service, 1993), 307; Marc Simmons, *Following the Santa Fe Trail* (Santa Fe: Ancient City Press, 1984), 146.

302 C. Bernhardt, *Indian Raids in Lincoln County, Kansas, 1864 and 1869* (Lincoln, Kans.: Lincoln Sentinel Print, 1909), 6–13, 16, 24.

303 U.S. War Dept., *Official Records*, vol. 41, no. 1, 212–13; no. 2, 827–29; William H. Ryus, *The Second William Penn* (Kansas City, Mo.: Frank T. Riley Publishing, 1913), 167–73.

304 U.S. War Dept., *Official Records*, vol. 49, no. 3, 389.

305 U.S. War Dept., *Official Records*, vol. 49, no. 3, 386–91; vol. 50, no. 2, 958–59.

306 Charles J. Kappler, *Indian Treaties, 1778-1883* (Mattituck, N.Y.: Amereon House, 1972), 865; Hubert Howe Bancroft, *History of Oregon, 1848-1883*, vol. 30, *The Works of Hubert Howe Bancroft* (San Francisco: History Company, 1883), 507–8; Keith and Donna Clark, "William McKay's Journal, 1866-67: Indian Scouts, Part 1," *Oregon Historical Quarterly* 79, no. 2

(Summer 1978): 127; U.S. War Dept., *Official Records*, vol. 50, no. 2, 1068, 1072–73, 1143–44.

1865

307 U.S. War Dept., *Official Records*, vol. 50, no. 1, 403.

308 U.S. War Dept., *Official Records*, vol. 50, no. 1, 401–3; Orton, 76; Douglas C. McChristian, *Fort Bowie, Arizona: Combat Post of the Southwest, 1858-1894* (Norman: University of Oklahoma Press, 2005), 80.

309 Rathbun, *Nevada Military Place Names*, 73, 75.

310 Rathbun, *Nevada Military Place Names*, 47–48; Angel, 170–72.

311 Michelle Tucker Butts, *Galvanized Yankees on the Upper Missouri: The Face of Loyalty* (Boulder: University Press of Colorado, 2003), 130; Dee Brown, *The Galvanized Yankees* (Lincoln: University of Nebraska Press, 1986), 91.

312 Butts, 123, 130–31; Brown, *Galvanized Yankees*, 91–92.

313 U.S. War Dept., *Official Records*, vol. 48, no. 1, 308, 311–12; Brown, *Galvanized Yankees*, 46–49.

314 U.S. War Dept., *Official Records*, vol. 48, no. 1, 312.

315 Johnson, 262–63; J. W. Vaughn, *The Battle of Platte Bridge* (Norman: University of Oklahoma Press, 1963), 17–18; Agnes Wright Spring, *Caspar Collins: The Life and Exploits of an Indian Fighter of the Sixties* (New York: AMS Press, 1967), 70–71, 76.

316 Orton, 77, 142.

317 Sowell, *Texas Indian Fighters*, 268–69.

318 Sowell, *Texas Indian Fighters*, 269–70, 567; Ruben E. Ochoa, "Martin, Texas," www.tshaonline.org.

319 Farish, 4:125; Constance Wynn Altshuler, *Chains of Command: Arizona and the Army, 1856-1875* (Tucson: Arizona Historical Society, 1981), 41; Constance Wynn Altshuler, *Starting with Defiance: Nineteenth Century Arizona Military Posts* (Tucson: Arizona Historical Society, 1983), 41; Orton, 764.

320 Rathbun, *Nevada Military Place Names*, 155–56; Orton, 185; Angel, 173.

321 Rathbun, *Nevada Military Place Names*, 48. The site of this fight is not certain. There are many Cottonwood Canyons and Cottonwood Creeks in northern Nevada. A likely site, within a week's march of Camp Ruby, is the Cottonwood Creek between the Tuscarora Mountains and Independence Mountains, about a dozen miles north of Carlin. Rathbun places it north of Wells, but that Cottonwood Creek is about 140 miles from Camp Ruby.

322 Rathbun, *Nevada Military Place Names*, 59–60; Orton, 185.

323 Doyle, 346–51, 402–6; LeRoy R. Hafen and Ann W. Hafen, *Powder River Campaigns and Sawyers Expedition of 1865* (Glendale, Calif.: Arthur H. Clark Company, 1961), 320–34.

324 Rathbun, *Nevada Military Place Names*, 156–57.

325 Orton, 381, 383.

326 Sweeney, *Cochise*, 238.

327 Sweeney, *Cochise*, 236–38; Edwin R. Sweeney, *Merejildo Grijalva: Apache Captive, Army Scout* (El Paso: Texas Western Press, 1992), 28–29; McChristian, 84–85.

328 Rathbun, *Nevada Military Place Names*, 30, 86–88; Orton, 185–86; Angel, 174.

1866

329 Rathbun, *Nevada Military Place Names*, 23–27; Orton, 186. The site of this fight is sometimes listed as Fish Creek.

330 Rathbun and Alexander, 37, 131; Orton, 381, 384, 415.

331 Orton, 418, 422–25; Frazer, 4, 6; Webb, *List of Engagements*, 24.

332 Rathbun, *Nevada Military Place Names*, 79–80; Orton, 186–87, 190–91.

333 Bancroft (*History of Oregon*, 518) says the fight occurred between the Owyhee and Malheur Rivers.

334 Bancroft, *History of Oregon*, 518; Thomas M. Anderson, "The Fourteenth Regiment of Infantry," in Theophilus F. Rodenbough and William L. Haskin, eds., *The Army of the United States: Historical Sketches of Staff and Line with Portraits of Generals-in-Chief*, www.history.army.mil; Adjutant General, 23.

335 Farish, 4:104–5; Adjutant General, 23. The latter source lists sixteen Indians killed and dates the fight as 11 April.

336 Altshuler, *Chains of Command*, 55; Farish, 4:138; U.S. Senate, *Letter from Secretary of War*, 310–13.

337 Farish, 4:104–5; Dan L. Thrapp, *The Conquest of Apacheria* (Norman: University of Oklahoma Press, 1967), 33, 35; Altshuler, *Starting with Defiance*, 59–60; Adjutant General, 23. The exact site of the fight is unknown.

338 Austerman, 200–202.

339 Adolph Roenigk, *Pioneer History of Kansas* (Lincoln, Kans.: Lincoln County Historical Society, 1973), 340–46.

340 The attack on the Chinese is thought to have occurred sometime between 19 and 21 May, either on the Jordan River in Oregon or on Battle Creek in Idaho. Pepoon later investigated the massacre and found the bodies scalped and mutilated, with mining picks driven through many of the skulls.

341 U.S. Bureau of Indian Affairs, *Report of the Commissioner of Indian Affairs for the Year 1867* (Washington, D.C.: GPO, 1867), 97; Janine M. Bork, ed., *History of the Pacific Northwest: Oregon and Washington*, vol. 2, www.usgennet.org; "The Snake War, 1864–1868," Idaho State Historical Society, pdf, www.idahohistory.net; "Camp Lyon," Idaho State Historical Society, pdf, www.idahohistory.net; Webb, *List of Engagements*, 25.

342 Bancroft, *History of Oregon*, 522.

343 Austerman, 203.

344 Ibid., 202–3.

345 There are two Rattlesnake Creeks in the area. Don Russell, *One Hundred and Three Fights and Scrimmages: The Story of General Reuben F. Bernard* (Mechanicsburg, Pa.: Stackpole Books, 2003), incorrectly maps the fight in the southeastern Oregon location.

346 Russell, 59–61; Webb, *List of Engagements*, 25; U.S. Senate, *Letter from Secretary of War*, 319–20.

347 Doyle, 433–34, 600, 637, 661; Barry J. Hagen, *"Exactly in the Right Place": A History of Fort C. F. Smith, Montana Territory, 1866–1868* (El Segundo, Calif.: Upton & Sons, 1999), 39–40.

348 Dan L. Thrapp, *Al Sieber: Chief of Scouts* (Norman: University of Oklahoma Press, 1964), 39–40; Adjutant General, 24; Heitman, 1:499.

349 Farish, 4:114; Adjutant General, 24. The latter source claims Hutton killed 33 Indians and wounded 40 at Grapevine Spring.

350 E. R. Hagemann, ed., *Fighting Rebels and Redskins: Experiences in Army Life of Colonel George B. Sanford, 1861-1892* (Norman: University of Oklahoma Press, 1969), 9–10; Adjutant General, 24; Altshuler, *Chains of Command*, 59.

351 Bancroft, *History of Oregon*, 529; U.S. Bureau of Indian Affairs, *Commissioner Report 1867*, 99–100; Adjutant General, 25; R. P. Page Wainwright, "The First Regiment of Cavalry," in Rodenbough and Haskin.

352 U.S. Congress, House, *Report of the Secretary of War*, 40th Cong., 3rd sess., 1868, H. Exec. Doc. 1, 770; Anderson, "Fourteenth Infantry"; Adjutant General, 25.

353 Conner, 207.

354 Thrapp, *Conquest of Apacheria*, 36–37; Conner, 207, 214.

355 Bancroft, *History of Oregon*, 529–30; U.S. Bureau of Indian Affairs, *Commissioner Report 1867*, 92, 100; Adjutant General, 25. The latter source dates this fight as 15 October.

356 Farish, 5:200.

357 Ibid., 5:199.

358 Farish, 5:196–201; Adjutant General, 25.

359 Conner, 289–90; Farish, 3:295—97, 4:137–38.

1867

360 Thomas W. Dunlay, *Wolves for the Blue Soldiers: Indian Scouts and Auxiliaries with the United States Army, 1860-90* (Lincoln: University of Nebraska Press, 1982), 44-46; Carl Waldman, *Atlas of the North American Indian* (New York: Checkmark Books, 2000), 39–41; Charles M. Robinson III, *General Crook and the Western Frontier* (Norman: University of Oklahoma Press, 2001), 89; U.S. Bureau of Indian Affairs, *Commissioner Report 1867*, 85.

361 Dunlay, 47-48; Robinson, *General Crook*, 90-91; U.S. Bureau of Indian Affairs, *Commissioner Report 1867*, 100-01; Clark and Clark, "McKay's Journal, Part 1," 149.

362 Rathbun, *Nevada Military Place Names*, 60-61; Adjutant General, 26; Charles M. O'Connor, "The Eighth Regiment of Cavalry," in Rodenbough and Haskin.

363 Rathbun, *Nevada Military Place Names*, 31-32; Adjutant General, 26; O'Connor.

364 Altshuler, *Chains of Command*, 86-87; Adjutant General, 26.

365 Farish, 5:242-43.

366 Angel, 175; Rathbun, *Nevada Military Place Names*, 177.

367 U.S. House, *Report of the Secretary of War*, 771.

368 Adjutant General, 26, 27; U.S. House, *Report of the Secretary of War*, 770-71; O'Connor.

369 Joseph W. Snell and Robert W. Richmond, "When the Union and Kansas Pacific Built through Kansas: Concluded." *Kansas Historical Quarterly* 39, no. 3 (Autumn 1966): 340.

370 Roenigk, 207-11; Snell and Richmond, 338-41.

371 David Haward Bain, *Empire Express: Building the First Transcontinental Railroad* (New York: Viking, 1999), 375.

372 Grenville M. Dodge, *How We Built the Union Pacific Railway*, 61st Cong., 2nd sess., 1910. S. Doc. 477, 20–21; Bain, 374–75; Rodenbough, 379.

373 U.S. House, *Report of the Secretary of War*, 69; Webb, *List of Engagements*, 31; "Old Camp Watson," http://gesswhoto.com. Adjutant General, 28, indicates that the fight occurred on 8 July.

374 Keith and Donna Clark, "William McKay's Journal, 1866–67: Indian Scouts, Part 2," *Oregon Historical Quarterly 79*, no. 3 (Fall 1978): 272–74; Webb, *List of Engagements*, 31. Webb lists the action as occurring on the 13th, but McKay's daily journal indicates the fight was on the 15th.

375 J. Evetts Haley, *Charles Goodnight: Cowman and Plainsman* (Norman: University of Oklahoma Press 1949), 174.

376 Ibid., 177.

377 Ibid., 183.

378 Haley, 169–84. This incident became the central episode in Larry McMurtry's novel and the television western *Lonesome Dove*.

379 U.S. House, *Report of the Secretary of War*, 69; Webb, *List of Engagements*, 32; "Camp Three Forks," Idaho State Historical Society, pdf, www.idahohistory.net.

380 U.S. House, *Report of the Secretary of War*, 69; Adjutant General, 29; Heitman, 1:892.

381 Frazer, 151; William H. Carter, *From Yorktown to Santiago with the Sixth U.S. Cavalry* (Austin: State House Press, 1989), 137–38; U.S. House, *Report of the Secretary of War*, 712.

382 Carter, *From Yorktown to Santiago*, 138.

383 Hagen, 159–68.

384 McChristian, 95, 97–98; Webb, *List of Engagements*, 34.

385 Webb, *List of Engagements*, 35; U.S. House, *Report of the Secretary of War*, 30; Hagen, 180.

1868

386 Merrill J. Mattes, *Indians, Infants and Infantry: Andrew and Elizabeth Burt on the Frontier* (Lincoln: University of Nebraska Press, 1988), 160.

387 Hagen, 203–04; Mattes, 159–61.

388 Rathbun, *Nevada Military Place Names*, 127–30; Angel, 176.

389 Farish, 5:272–76; Altshuler, *Chains of Command*, 143–44. In Adjutant General, 33, this fight is also called Tonto Basin, though the fighting did not occur in Tonto Basin.

390 Farish, 5:275.

391 U.S. House, *Report of the Secretary of War*, 71–72; George Crook, *General George Crook: His Autobiography*, edited by Martin F. Schmidt (Norman: University of Oklahoma Press, 1986), 158–59; Hank Corless, *The Weiser Indians: Shoshoni Peacemakers* (Caldwell, Idaho: Caxton Printers, 1996), 48; Webb, *List of Engagements*, 37; Robinson, *General Crook*, 100–01.

392 U.S. House, *Report of the Secretary of War*, 71; Webb, *List of Engagements*, 38. Adjutant General, 33, lists eight Indians killed.

393 Hagen, 228–31; Adjutant General, 33; U.S. House, *Report of the Secretary of War*, 31.

394 U.S. House, *Report of the Secretary of War*, 71–72.

395 U.S. House, *Report of the Secretary of War*, 71; Heitman, 1:946; Adjutant General, 34.

396 Frazer, 110; U.S. House, *Report of the Secretary of War*, 35–36; Adjutant General, 34.

397 Jeff Broome, "Indian Massacres in Elbert County, Colorado," *Denver Westerners* 60, no. 1 (January–February 2004): 18–25, 30; Irving Howbert, *Indians of the Pike's Peak Region* (New York: Knickerbocker Press, 1914), 195–96; U.S. House, *Report of the Secretary of War*, 13, 20.

398 U.S. House, *Report of the Secretary of War*, 13.

399 Adjutant General, 35–36; Thrapp, *Encyclopedia of Frontier Biography*, 3:1340–41. Due to variations and duplications in place names, the locations of Somerby's fights are difficult to pinpoint.

400 Altshuler, *Chains of Command*, 148–51; Altshuler, *Starting with Defiance*, 33.

1869

401 Austerman, 228–30. This attack convinced Ben Ficklin to cover his coaches with iron plates, but the extra weight made traveling impractical. The 1967 movie *The War Wagon*, which depicted an armored wagon in the old West, had some historical foundation.

402 Russell, 63, 65.

403 McChristian, 109–10; Russell, 63, 65–66.

404 Frazer, 180–81; Tom Lindmier, *Drybone: A History of Fort Fetterman, Wyoming* (Glendo, Wyom.: High Plains Press, 2002), 26, 36, 53, 69–70; Adjutant General, 39.

405 McConnell. The ranchers were William Crow, John Lemley, George Lemley, C. L. (Shap) Carter, Jesse McClain, W. C. Kutch, J. W. Gray, Henry Harrison, Rube Secris (Segress), and Joe Woody, led by Ira Graves; the cook was called "Negro Dick."

406 McConnell.

407 McConnell; Thomas F. Horton, "Salt Creek Prairie," from *History of Jack County*, www.forttours.com; Wilbarger, 549–51.

408 Bernhardt, 28–31; Jeff Broome, "Libbie Custer's Encounter with Tom Alderdice: The Rest of the Story," in *Custer and His Times*, vol. 4, edited by John Hart (LaGrange Park, Ill.: Little Bighorn Associates, 2002), 75–79, 81–85, 87.

409 Hagemann, 11.

410 Hagemann, 11; Adjutant General, 41.

411 Farish, 8:25.

412 Alexander, *Arizona Frontier*, 67; Adjutant General, 41; Thrapp, *Conquest of Apacheria*, 61; Farish, 8:24–25; "William Fourr Biography," Hayden Library Special Collections, Arizona State Library, files.usgwarchives.org.

413 Thomas Duncan, "Report of Lt. Col. Thomas Duncan, 7 October 1869," File 437 DR, U.S. War Department, Records of U.S. Army Commands, RG 98, National Archives and Records Administration, Washington, D.C.; Thomas Duncan, "General Duncan's Journal, 22 November 1869," File 540-0 DR V6 IPV 3, 1869, U.S. War Department, Records of U.S. Army Commands, RG 98, National Archives and Records Administration, Washington, D.C.; W. H. Emory, "Republican River Expedition, Report of Col. W. H. Emory, 22 November 1869," U.S. War Department, Records of U.S.

Army Commands, RG 98, National Archives and Records Administration, Washington, D.C.; Rollin C. Curd, *A History of the Boundaries of Nebraska and Indian-Surveyor Stories* (Chadron, Neb.: Boundaries Publishing, 1999), 105–9; Louis A. Holmes, *Fort McPherson, Nebraska, Fort Cottonwood, N.T.: Guardian of the Tracks and Trails* (Lincoln, Neb.: Johnsen Publishing, 1963), 40; William F. Cody, *The Life of Hon. William F. Cody, Known as Buffalo Bill, the Famous Hunter, Scout, and Guide* (Lincoln: University of Nebraska Press, Bison Books, 1978), 275. The surveyors killed were Nelson Buck, J. L. Logan, J. C. Haldeman, H. L. Levi, F. C. McFarland, W. McCulloch, James Walteman, J. V. Brown, Linden L. Crocker, and Stanley Meecham.

414 Sweeney, *Cochise*, 267–68.

415 Hagemann, 11–12; Adjutant General, 43. This fight is also called Mount Buford.

1870

416 McChristian, 118–19; Sweeney, *Merejildo Grijalva*, 50–51.

417 Hagemann, 12; Alexander, *Arizona Frontier*, 118; Adjutant General, 45. The latter source dates the fight as 25 May.

418 Austerman, 253; Wilbur Sturtevant Nye, *Carbine and Lance: The Story of Old Fort Sill* (Norman: University of Oklahoma Press, 1969), 118; H. Allen Anderson, "White Horse," www.tshaonline.org; Webb, *List of Engagements*, 56; Clayton W. Williams, *Texas' Last Frontier: Fort Stockton and the Trans-Pecos, 1861-1895* (College Station: Texas A & M University Press, 1982), 139.

419 Utley, *Lone Star Justice*, 137–39.

420 Sowell, *Texas Indian Fighters*, 204, 239, 277–79, 552, 571–73.

1871

421 McChristian, 123–25; Sweeney, *Merejildo Grijalva*, 52; Russell, 79–80.

422 Sweeney, *Cochise*, 305–6; Adjutant General, 47.

423 Sweeney, *Cochise*, 307.

424 Sweeney, *Cochise*, 306–8; Alexander, *Arizona Frontier*, 95.

425 Britt W. Wilson, *Lieutenant Morton's 1871 Scout from Camp Verde, Arizona Territory* (Banning, Calif.: privately published, 1997), 2–18; Farish, 8:171–87; Adjutant General, 49.

426 McChristian, 133; Webb, *List of Engagements*, 59; Adjutant General, 49. Several sources date this fight as 13 July, while McChristian dates it 18 July. McChristian also writes that Smith reached Camp Bowie on the night of the fight, but that would seem impossible, since the post was about 70 miles away.

427 Crook, 167–68; McChristian, 136–37; Sweeney, *Merejildo Grijalva*, 54–55.

1872

428 Robinson, *History of the Dakota*, 402; Webb, *List of Engagements*, 62; Adjutant General, 52.

429 Robinson, *History of the Dakota*, 402; Heitman, 1:151, 1:340; Mark H. Brown, *The Plainsmen of the Yellowstone: A History of the Yellowstone Basin* (Lincoln: University of Nebraska Press, 1969), 197, 202–03; C. St. J. Chubb, "The Seventeenth Regiment of Infantry," in Rodenbough and

Haskin; Oskaloosa M. Smith, "The Twenty-second Regiment of Infantry," in Rodenbough and Haskin.

430 Robinson, *History of the Dakota*, 402; Webb, *List of Engagements*, 62; Adjutant General, 52; Peters, 33–34. Casualty reports vary in different accounts. Some sources say the men killed in the 2 October fight were Arikara scouts, not soldiers. Similarly, some sources list the two soldiers killed in the 14 October fight as civilians.

1873

431 Arlen F. Fowler, *The Black Infantry in the West, 1869-1891* (Norman: University of Oklahoma Press, 1996), 21–23; Smith, *Old Army*, 155–56; Williams, 167; Adjutant General, 54.

432 Webb, *List of Engagements*, 65–66; Adjutant General, 54–55; Peters, 35; Lawrence A. Frost, *Custer's Seventh Cavalry and the Campaign of 1873* (El Segundo, Calif.: Upton & Sons, 1986), 48–49, 113, 214 n1. Casualty counts vary in different accounts.

1874

433 Lindmier, 72; Webb, *List of Engagements*, 68–69.

434 Craig Miner, *West of Wichita: Settling the High Plains of Kansas, 1865-1890* (Lawrence: University Press of Kansas, 1986), 22, 24; Arlene Feldman Jauken, *The Moccasin Speaks: Living as Captives of the Dog Soldier Warriors, Red River War, 1874-1875* (Lincoln, Neb.: Dageford Publishing, 1998), 56, 194. The historical marker states that the massacre occurred 11 miles southwest of the marker and that the men were buried 5 miles to the south.

435 Frederick W. Rathjen, *The Texas Panhandle Frontier* (Lubbock: Texas Tech University Press, 1998), 168.

436 Sowell, *Texas Indian Fighters*, 642–44; Wilbarger, 575; McConnell.

1875

437 The official report indicates a different spot for the Indians' camp, but it was most likely near the divide between the Dry Devil and the South Llano Rivers, in present-day northwest Edwards County.

438 Winfrey and Day, 4:370.

439 Ibid., 4:371.

440 Ibid., 4:369–71.

1876

441 John S. Gray, *Centennial Campaign* (Fort Collins, Colo.: Old Army Press, 1976), 40–41; John S. Gray, *Custer's Last Campaign: Mitch Boyer and the Little Bighorn Reconstructed* (Lincoln: University of Nebraska Press, 1991), 125–30; Paul L. Hedren, *Fort Laramie and the Great Sioux War* (Norman: University of Oklahoma Press, 1998), 41.

442 Gray, *Centennial Campaign*, 114–15; J. W. Vaughn, *With Crook at the Rosebud* (Harrisburg, Pa.: Stackpole Company, 1956), 17–19.

443 Gray, *Centennial Campaign*, 199–200; Jerome A. Greene, *Lakota and Cheyenne Indian Views of the Great Sioux War.* (Norman: University of Oklahoma Press, 1994), 74–75, 77; Adjutant General, 61.

444 Hedren, 76–77, 108, 139; Adjutant General, 62.

445 Vaughn, *Indian Fights*, 167–75.

1877

446 Thrapp, *Victorio*, 195–98; Carter, *From Yorktown to Santiago*, 191–92; Webb, *List of Engagements*, 80–81.

1878

447 Mark V. Weatherford, *Bannack-Paiute War: The Campaign and Battles* (Corvallis, Oreg.: Privately published, 1957), 35–40.

448 Webb, *List of Engagements*, 84; Carter, *From Yorktown to Santiago*, 199.

1879

449 Brown, *Plainsmen of the Yellowstone*, 321–22; John H. Monnett, *Tell Them We Are Going Home: The Odyssey of the Northern Cheyennes* (Norman: University of Oklahoma Press, 2001), 164–65, 170–71.

450 Rathbun and Alexander, 115–16; Thrapp, *Victorio*, 363; Adjutant General, 70.

1880

451 Thomas Cruse, *Apache Days and After* (Lincoln: University of Nebraska Press, 1987), 67–70.

452 Webb, *List of Engagements*, 88; Brown, *Plainsmen of the Yellowstone*, 325. The fight has been recorded as Rosebud Creek, although it probably took place near Sarpy Creek. Some sources date it as 5 March.

453 William H. Leckie, *The Buffalo Soldiers: A Narrative of the Negro Cavalry in the West* (Norman: University of Oklahoma Press, 1967), 220–21; Monroe Lee Billington, *New Mexico's Buffalo Soldiers, 1866–1900* (Boulder: University Press of Colorado, 1991), 95–96; Art T. Burton, *Black, Buckskin, and Blue: African-American Scouts and Soldiers on the Western Frontier* (Austin: Eakin Press, 1999), 160–61; Adjutant General, 73; Thrapp, *Conquest of Apacheria*, 198. Thrapp suggests that the Kelly's Ranch fight in Adjutant General, *Chronological List of Actions*, may be the same as Cooney's Camp on Mineral Creek.

454 Williams, 245. Various sources list different dates for Byrne's death, ranging from 9 August to 22 August.

455 James B. Gillett, *Six Years with the Texas Rangers, 1875–1881*, edited by M. M. Quaife (Lincoln: University of Nebraska Press, 1976), 180–81; Williams, 244–45; Thrapp, *Encyclopedia of Frontier Biography*, 3:203. Thrapp believes the attacking Indians might have been Mescaleros.

456 Melbourne C. Chandler, *Of Garryowen in Glory: History of the Seventh U.S. Cavalry Regiment* (Annandale, Va.: Turnpike Press, 1960), 78, 428; Robert Lee, *Fort Meade and the Black Hills* (Lincoln: University of Nebraska Press, 1991), 72, 74; Ronald H. Nichols, ed., *Men With Custer: Biographies of the Seventh Cavalry* (Hardin, Mont.: Custer Battlefield Historical & Museum Association, 2000), 79; Webb, *List of Engagements*, 90; Adjutant General, 73.

1881

457 Billington, 101; Adjutant General, 74.

458 Stephen H. Lekson, *Nana's Raid: Apache Warfare in Southern New Mexico, 1881* (El Paso: Texas Western Press, 1987), 28–29; Rathbun and Alexander, 15, 73–74.

459 Larry L. Ludwig and James L. Stute, *The Battle at K-H Butte: Apache Outbreak, 1881, Arizona Territory* (Tucson: Westernlore Press, 1993), 3, 5, 7–12, 64, 81; Jason Betzinez and Wilbur Sturtevant Nye, *I Fought with Geronimo* (Lincoln: University of Nebraska Press, 1987), 49.

460 Charles Collins, *Apache Nightmare: The Battle at Cibecue Creek* (Norman: University of Oklahoma Press, 1999), 193, 259 n35.

1882

461 Webb, *List of Engagements*, 93; Adjutant General, 76; Angie Debo, *Geronimo: The Man, His Time, His Place* (Norman: University of Oklahoma Press, 1976), 153.

1883

462 Frazer, 79; George Kush, "In the Great Mother's Land: The Mounted Police and the Sioux," Sixth Annual Symposium, Custer Battlefield Historical & Museum Association, 1992, 84–85; Webb, *List of Engagements*, 93.

1884

463 In the official reports, the battle site was identified as Wormington Canyon, which was incorrectly placed in Colorado.

464 Carter, *From Yorktown to Santiago*, 253; Richard K. Young, *The Ute Indians of Colorado in the Twentieth Century* (Norman: University of Oklahoma Press, 1997), 31–32; Frazer, 38; Robert L. Foster, "Cowboys, Indians, and the Fight in White River Canyon," *Wild West*, February 2007, 30–33; Webb, *List of Engagements*, 93; Adjutant General, 77.

1885

465 John M. Carroll, ed., *The Papers of the Order of the Indian Wars* (Fort Collins, Colo.: Old Army Press, 1975), 83–87; Rathbun and Alexander, 106; Webb, *List of Engagements*, 94.

1887

466 Marshall Sprague, *Massacre: The Tragedy at White River* (Lincoln: University of Nebraska Press, 1980), 326–28; "Blood and Scalps," *Western Star*, September 3, 1887, www.rootsweb.com.

1890

467 Burton, 197.

468 Burton, 196–97; Heitman, 2:448. Webb, *List of Engagements*, 95, and Adjutant General, 79, date this fight as 11 March.

Summary

469 James F. Brooks, *Captives and Cousins: Slavery, Kinship, and Community in the Southwest Borderlands* (Chapel Hill: University of North Carolina Press, 2002), 180, 191, 249, 326, 354; Michael L. Tate, "Comanche Captives: People between Two Worlds," *Chronicles of Oklahoma* 73, no. 3 (Fall 1994): 244; Marvin H. Garfield, "Defense of the Kansas Frontier 1866-67," *Kansas Historical Quarterly* 1, no. 4 (August 1932): 344; Garfield, "Defense of the Kansas Frontier 1868-69," *Kansas Historical Quarterly* 1, no. 5 (November 1932): 471-72; Robert Wooster, *The Military and United States Indian Policy, 1865-1903*, 213.

470 U.S. Bureau of Indian Affairs, *Report of the Commissioner of Indian Affairs for the Year 1865* (Washington, D.C.: GPO, 1865), 472-74; U.S. Bureau of Indian Affairs, *Report of the Commissioner of Indian Affairs for the Year 1862* (Washington, D.C.: GPO, 1862), 397; U.S. Bureau of Indian Affairs, *Report of the Commissioner of Indian Affairs for the Year 1867* (Washington, D.C.: GPO, 1867), 196; U.S. Bureau of Indian Affairs, *Report of the Commissioner of Indian Affairs for the Year 1870* (Washington, D.C.: GPO, 1870), 115; John S. Watts, *Indian Depredations in New Mexico* (Tucson: Territorial Press, 1964), 65; Averam B. Bender, *The March of Empire: Frontier Defense in the Southwest, 1848-1860* (New York: Greenwood Press, 1968), 263n15; Thrapp, *Conquest of Apacheria*, 366.
471 Winfrey and Day, 4:235-36, 4:314, 4:330, 4:390, 4:438; Marshall, 18; Brooks, 354.
472 Larry C. Skogen, *Indian Depredation Claims, 1796-1920* (Norman: University of Oklahoma Press, 1996), 32, 120, 151-52, 195, 212.

Bibliography

Books and Periodicals

Alexander, David V. *Arizona Frontier Military Place Names, 1846-1912.* Las Cruces, N. Mex.: Yucca Tree Press, 1998.

Altshuler, Constance Wynn. *Chains of Command: Arizona and the Army, 1856-1875.* Tucson: Arizona Historical Society, 1981.

———. *Starting with Defiance: Nineteenth Century Arizona Military Posts.* Tucson: Arizona Historical Society, 1983.

Angel, Myron. *History of Nevada.* Oakland, Calif.: Thompson & West, 1881.

Arnold, James R. *Jeff Davis's Own: Cavalry, Comanches, and the Battle for the Texas Frontier.* New York: John Wiley & Sons, 2000.

Austerman, Wayne R. *Sharps Rifles and Spanish Mules: The San Antonio-El Paso Mail, 1851-1881.* College Station: Texas A & M University Press, 1985.

Bain, David Haward. *Empire Express: Building the First Transcontinental Railroad.* New York: Viking, 1999.

Baley, Charles W. *Disaster at the Colorado: Beale's Wagon Road and the First Emigrant Party.* Logan: Utah State University Press, 2002.

Bancroft, Hubert Howe. *The Works of Hubert Howe Bancroft.* Vol. 30, *History of Oregon, 1848-1883.* San Francisco: History Company, 1883.

———. *The Works of Hubert Howe Bancroft.* Vol. 21, *History of Washington, Idaho, and Montana, 1845-1889.* San Francisco: History Company, 1890.

Barry, Louise. *The Beginning of the West: Annals of the Kansas Gateway to the American West, 1540-1854.* Topeka: Kansas State Historical Society, 1972.

———. "The Ranch at Cow Creek Crossing." *Kansas Historical Quarterly* 38, no. 4 (Winter 1972): 416-44.

———. "The Ranch at Walnut Creek Crossing." *Kansas Historical Quarterly* 37, no. 2 (Summer 1971): 121-47.

Beckham, Stephen D. *Requiem for a People.* Corvallis: Oregon State University Press, 1996.

Bender, Averam B. *The March of Empire: Frontier Defense in the Southwest, 1848-1860.* New York: Greenwood Press, 1968.

Bennett, James A. *Forts and Forays: A Dragoon in New Mexico, 1850-1856.* Edited by Clinton E. Brooks and Frank D. Reeve. Albuquerque: University of New Mexico Press, 1996.

Bergemann, Kurt D. *Brackett's Battalion: Minnesota Cavalry in the Civil War and Dakota War.* St. Paul: Minnesota Historical Society Press, Borealis Books, 2004.

Bernhardt, C. *Indian Raids in Lincoln County, Kansas, 1864 and 1869.* Lincoln, Kans.: Lincoln Sentinel Print, 1909.

Berry, Don. *A Majority of Scoundrels: An Informal History of the Rocky Mountain Fur Company.* Corvallis: Oregon State University Press, 2006.

Berthrong, Donald J. *The Southern Cheyennes.* Norman: University of Oklahoma Press, 1963.

Betzinez, Jason, and Wilbur Sturtevant Nye. *I Fought with Geronimo.* Harrisburg, Pa.: Stackpole Company, 1959. Reprint, Lincoln: University of Nebraska Press, 1987.

Billington, Monroe Lee. *New Mexico's Buffalo Soldiers, 1866–1900.* Boulder: University Press of Colorado, 1991.

Bledsoe, A. J. *Indian Wars of the Northwest: A California Sketch.* San Francisco: Bacon & Company, 1885. Reprint, Olympia, Wash.: Bayside Press, 1990.

Brands, H. W. *The Age of Gold: The California Gold Rush and the New American Dream.* New York: Doubleday, 2002.

Brice, Donaly E. *The Great Comanche Raid.* Austin: Eakin Press, 1987.

Brooks, James F. *Captives and Cousins: Slavery, Kinship, and Community in the Southwest Borderlands.* Chapel Hill: University of North Carolina Press, 2002.

Broome, Jeff. "Indian Massacres in Elbert County, Colorado." *Denver Westerners* 60, no. 1 (January–February 2004): 3–30.

——. "Libbie Custer's Encounter with Tom Alderice: The Rest of the Story." *Custer and His Times,* vol. 4, edited by John Hart, 63–93. LaGrange Park, Ill.: Little Bighorn Associates, 2002.

Brown, Dee. *The Galvanized Yankees.* Lincoln: University of Nebraska Press, 1986.

Brown, John Henry. *Indian Wars and Pioneers of Texas.* Austin: L. E. Daniell, 1880. Reprint. Greenville, S.C.: Southern Historical Press, 1978.

Brown, Mark H. *The Plainsmen of the Yellowstone: A History of the Yellowstone Basin.* Lincoln: University of Nebraska Press, 1969.

Browne, John Ross. *Adventures in the Apache Country.* New York: Harper & Brothers, 1871. Reprint, New York: Promontory Press, 1974.

Burton, Art T. *Black, Buckskin, and Blue: African-American Scouts and Soldiers on the Western Frontier.* Austin: Eakin Press, 1999.

Butts, Michelle Tucker. *Galvanized Yankees on the Upper Missouri: The Face of Loyalty.* Boulder: University Press of Colorado, 2003.

Carroll, John M., ed. *The Papers of the Order of the Indian Wars.* Fort Collins, Colo.: Old Army Press, 1975.

Carter, D. Robert. *Founding Fort Utah: Provo's Native Inhabitants, Early Explorers, and First Year of Settlement.* Provo, Utah: Provo City Corporation, 2003.

Carter, William H. *From Yorktown to Santiago with the Sixth U.S. Cavalry.* Austin: State House Press, 1989.

Chalfant, William Y. *Cheyennes and Horse Soldiers.* Norman: University of Oklahoma Press, 1989.

——. *Dangerous Passage: The Santa Fe Trail and the Mexican War.* Norman: University of Oklahoma Press, 1994.

Chalfant, William Y. *Without Quarter: The Wichita Expedition and the Fight on Crooked Creek.* Norman: University of Oklahoma Press, 1991.

Chandler, Melbourne C. *Of Garryowen in Glory: History of the Seventh U.S. Cavalry Regiment.* Annandale, Va.: Turnpike Press, 1960.

Clark, Keith, and Donna Clark. "William McKay's Journal, 1866–67: Indian Scouts, Part 1." *Oregon Historical Quarterly 79*, no. 2 (Summer 1978): 121–171.

———. "William McKay's Journal, 1866–67: Indian Scouts, Part 2." *Oregon Historical Quarterly 79*, no. 3 (Fall 1978): 269–333.

Clodfelter, Micheal. *The Dakota War: The United States Army Versus the Sioux, 1862-1865.* Jefferson, N.C.: McFarland & Company, 2006.

Cody, William F. *The Life of Hon. William F. Cody, Known as Buffalo Bill, the Famous Hunter, Scout, and Guide.* 1879. Reprint, Lincoln: University of Nebraska Press, Bison Books, 1978.

Collins, Charles. *Apache Nightmare: The Battle at Cibecue Creek.* Norman: University of Oklahoma Press, 1999.

Conner, Daniel Ellis. *Joseph Reddeford Walker and the Arizona Adventure.* Norman: University of Oklahoma Press, 1956.

Converse, George L. *A Military History of the Columbia Valley, 1848-1865.* Walla Walla, Wash.: Pioneer Press Books, 1988.

Corless, Hank. *The Weiser Indians: Shoshoni Peacemakers.* Caldwell, Idaho: Caxton Printers, 1996.

Crook, George. *General George Crook: His Autobiography.* Edited by Martin F. Schmidt. Norman: University of Oklahoma Press, 1986.

Crosby, David F. "The Battle of Brushy Creek." *Wild West*, August 1997.

Cruse, Thomas. *Apache Days and After.* Caldwell, Idaho: Caxton Printers, 1941. Reprint, Lincoln: University of Nebraska Press, 1987.

Curd, Rollin C. *A History of the Boundaries of Nebraska and Indian-Surveyor Stories.* Chadron, Neb.: Boundaries Publishing, 1999.

Debo, Angie. *Geronimo: The Man, His Time, His Place.* Norman: University of Oklahoma Press, 1976.

DeShields, James T. *Border Wars of Texas.* 1912. Reprint, Austin: State House Press, 1993.

DeVoto, Bernard. *Across the Wide Missouri.* New York: Houghton Mifflin, 1947.

Dolbeare, Benjamin. *A Narrative of the Captivity and Suffering of Dolly Webster among the Camanche Indians in Texas.* Clarksburg, Va.: M'Granaghan & M'Carty, 1843. Reprint, New Haven: Yale University Library, 1986.

Doyle, Susan Badger, ed. *Journeys to the Land of Gold: Emigrant Diaries from the Bozeman Trail, 1863-1866.* Helena: Montana Historical Society Press, 2000.

Dunlay, Thomas W. *Wolves for the Blue Soldiers: Indian Scouts and Auxiliaries with the United States Army, 1860-90.* Lincoln: University of Nebraska Press, 1982.

Durham, Michael S. *Desert between the Mountains: Mormons, Miners, Padres, Mountain Men, and the Opening of the Great Basin, 1771-1869.* Norman: University of Oklahoma Press, 1999.

Egan, Ferol. *Sand in a Whirlwind: The Paiute Indian War of 1860.* Reno: University of Nevada Press, 2003.

Farish, Thomas E. *History of Arizona*. 8 vols. San Francisco: Filmer Brothers Electrotype, 1915–18.

Favour, Alpheus H. *Old Bill Williams: Mountain Man*. Norman: University of Oklahoma Press, 1962.

Fehrenbach, T. R. *Comanches: The Destruction of a People*. New York: Da Capo Press, 1994.

———. *Lone Star: A History of Texas and the Texans*. New York: Collier Books, 1968.

Ford, John Salmon. *Rip Ford's Texas*. Edited by Stephen B. Oates. Austin: University of Texas Press, 1963.

Foster, Robert L. "Cowboys, Indians, and the Fight in White River Canyon." *Wild West*, February 2007.

Fowler, Arlen L. *The Black Infantry in the West, 1869–1891*. Norman: University of Oklahoma Press, 1996.

Francell, Lawrence John. *Fort Lancaster Texas: Frontier Sentinel*. Austin: Texas State Historical Association, 1999.

Frazer, Robert W. *Forts of the West: Military Forts and Presidios and Posts Commonly Called Forts West of the Mississippi River to 1898*. Norman: University of Oklahoma Press, 1965.

Fremont, John Charles. *Memoirs of My Life*. New York: Cooper Square Press, 2001.

Frost, Lawrence A. *Custer's Seventh Cavalry and the Campaign of 1873*. El Segundo, Calif.: Upton & Sons, 1986.

Gallaway, B. P., ed. *Texas: Dark Corner of the Confederacy*. Lincoln: University of Nebraska Press, 1994.

Garfield, Marvin H. "Defense of the Kansas Frontier, 1866–67." *Kansas Historical Quarterly* 1, no. 4 (August 1932): 326–44.

———. "Defense of the Kansas Frontier, 1868–69." *Kansas Historical Quarterly* 1, no. 5 (November 1932): 451–73.

Garrard, Lewis H. *Wah-to-yah and the Taos Trail*. Norman: University of Oklahoma Press, 1955.

Gilbert, Bil. *Westering Man: The Life of Joseph Walker*. Norman: University of Oklahoma Press, 1985.

Gillett, James B. *Six Years with the Texas Rangers, 1875–1881*. Edited by M. M. Quaife. Lincoln: University of Nebraska Press, 1976.

Glassley, Ray Hoard. *Indian Wars of the Pacific Northwest*. Portland, Ore.: Binfords & Mort, 1972.

Goodrich, Thomas. *Black Flag: Guerrilla Warfare on the Western Border, 1861–1865*. Bloomington: Indiana University Press, 1995.

Gorenfeld, John, and William Gorenfeld. "Carleton at Bitter Spring: Punishing the Paiutes." *Wild West*, December 2001.

Gottfredson, Peter. *Indian Depredations in Utah*. 1919. Reprint, Tucson: Fenestra Books, 2002.

Gray, John S. *Centennial Campaign*. Fort Collins, Colo.: Old Army Press, 1976.

———. *Custer's Last Campaign: Mitch Boyer and the Little Bighorn Reconstructed*. Lincoln: University of Nebraska Press, 1991.

Green, Rena Maverick, ed. *Memoirs of Mary A. Maverick*. San Antonio: Alamo Printing Co., 1921. Reprint, Lincoln: University of Nebraska Press, 1989.

Greene, Jerome A. *Lakota and Cheyenne Indian Views of the Great Sioux War.* Norman: University of Oklahoma Press, 1994.

Greer, James Kimmins. *Texas Ranger Jack Hays in the Frontier Southwest.* College Station: Texas A & M University Press, 1993.

Greever, William S. *The Bonanza West: The Story of the Western Mining Rushes, 1848-1900.* Norman: University of Oklahoma Press, 1963.

Groneman, Bill. *Battlefields of Texas.* Plano: Republic of Texas Press, 1998.

Guild, Thelma S., and Harvey L. Carter. *Kit Carson: A Pattern for Heroes.* Lincoln: University of Nebraska Press, 1984.

Hafen, LeRoy R. *Broken Hand: The Life of Thomas Fitzpatrick, Mountain Man, Guide and Indian Agent.* Lincoln: University of Nebraska Press, 1981.

———. *Powder River Campaigns and Sawyers Expedition of 1865.* Glendale, Calif.: Arthur H. Clark, 1961.

Hafen, LeRoy R., ed. *Trappers of the Far West.* Lincoln: University of Nebraska Press, 1983.

———, and Ann W. Hafen. *Old Spanish Trail: Santa Fe to Los Angeles.* Lincoln: University of Nebraska Press, 1993.

Hagemann, E. R., ed. *Fighting Rebels and Redskins: Experiences in Army Life of Colonel George B. Sanford, 1861-1892.* Norman: University of Oklahoma Press, 1969.

Hagen, Barry J. *"Exactly in the Right Place": A History of Fort C. F. Smith, Montana Territory, 1866-1868.* El Segundo, Calif.: Upton & Sons, 1999.

Haines, Joe D., Jr. "'For our sake do all you can': The Indian Captivity and Death of Clara and Willie Blinn." *Chronicles of Oklahoma* 77, no. 2 (Summer 1999): 170-83.

Haley, J. Evetts. *Charles Goodnight: Cowman and Plainsman.* Norman: University of Oklahoma Press, 1949.

Harris, Benjamin Butler. *The Gila Trail: The Texas Argonauts and the California Gold Rush.* Norman: University of Oklahoma Press, 1960.

Hedren, Paul L. *Fort Laramie and the Great Sioux War.* Norman: University of Oklahoma Press, 1998.

Heitman, Francis B. *Historical Register and Dictionary of the United States Army.* 2 vols. Washington, D.C.: GPO, 1903.

Hoig, Stan. *The Kiowas and the Legend of Kicking Bird.* Boulder: University Press of Colorado, 2000.

———. *The Sand Creek Massacre.* Norman: University of Oklahoma Press, 1961.

Holmes, Louis A. *Fort McPherson, Nebraska, Fort Cottonwood, N.T.: Guardian of the Tracks and Trails.* Lincoln, Neb.: Johnsen Publishing, 1963.

Howbert, Irving. *Indians of the Pike's Peak Region.* New York: Knickerbocker Press, 1914.

Huckabay, Ida Lasater. *Ninety-four Years in Jack County, 1854-1948.* Jacksboro, Tex.: Privately published, 1949.

Hunt, Aurora. *The Army of the Pacific, 1860-1866.* Glendale, Calif.: Arthur H. Clark, 1951. Reprint, Mechanicsburg, Pa.: Stackpole Books, 2004.

Hunter, J. Marvin, ed. "Mrs. Rebecca J. Fisher." *Frontier Times* 3, no. 8 (May 1926).

Jauken, Arlene Feldman. *The Moccasin Speaks: Living as Captives of the Dog Soldier Warriors, Red River War, 1874-1875.* Lincoln, Neb.: Dageford Publishing, 1998.

Jenkins, John Holmes, III, ed. *Recollections of Early Texas: The Memoirs of John Holland Jenkins.* Austin: University of Texas Press, 1958.

Johnson, Hervey. *Tending the Talking Wire: A Buck Soldier's View of Indian Country, 1863–1866.* Edited by William Unrau. Salt Lake City: University of Utah Press, 1979.

Josephy, Alvin M., Jr. *The Civil War in the American West.* New York: Alfred A. Knopf, 1991.

Justus, Judith P. "The Saga of Clara H. Blinn at the Battle of the Washita." *Research Review* 14, no. 1 (Winter 2000): 11–20, 31.

Kappler, Charles J. *Indian Treaties, 1778–1883.* Mattituck, N.Y.: Amereon House, 1972.

Kroeker, Marvin E. *Great Plains Command: William B. Hazen in the Frontier West.* Norman: University of Oklahoma Press, 1976.

Lavender, David. *Bent's Fort.* Lincoln: University of Nebraska Press, 1972.

——. *Westward Vision: The Story of the Oregon Trail.* New York: McGraw-Hill, 1963. Reprint, Lincoln: University of Nebraska Press, 1985.

Lease, Wayne. *Texas Forts.* Garland: Texas Forts Distributors, 2001.

Leckie, William H. *The Buffalo Soldiers: A Narrative of the Negro Cavalry in the West.* Norman: University of Oklahoma Press, 1967.

Lecompte, Janet. "The Manco Burro Pass Massacre." *New Mexico Historical Review,* October 1966: 305–18.

——. *Pueblo, Hardscrabble, Greenhorn: Society on the High Plains, 1832–1856.* Norman: University of Oklahoma Press, 1978.

Lee, Robert. *Fort Meade and the Black Hills.* Lincoln: University of Nebraska Press, 1991.

Lee, Wayne C., and Howard C. Raynesford. *Trails of the Smoky Hill.* Caldwell, Idaho: Caxton Printers, 1980.

Lekson, Stephen H. *Nana's Raid: Apache Warfare in Southern New Mexico, 1881.* El Paso: Texas Western Press, 1987.

Leonard, Zenas. *Narrative of the Adventures of Zenas Leonard: Five Years as a Mountain Man in the Rocky Mountains.* Santa Barbara, Calif.: Narrative Press, 2001.

Lindmier, Tom. *Drybone: A History of Fort Fetterman, Wyoming.* Glendo, Wyom.: High Plains Press, 2002.

Lowe, Percival G. *Five Years a Dragoon ('49 to '54) and Other Adventures on the Great Plains.* Norman: University of Oklahoma Press, 1991.

Ludwig, Larry L., and James L. Stute. *The Battle at K-H Butte: Apache Outbreak, 1881, Arizona Territory.* Tucson: Westernlore Press, 1993.

Madsen, Brigham. *The Shoshoni Frontier and the Bear River Massacre.* Salt Lake City: University of Utah Press, 1985.

Marshall, Doyle. *A Cry Unheard: The Story of Indian Attacks In and Around Parker County, Texas, 1858–1872.* N.p.: Annetta Valley Farm Press, 1990.

Mattes, Merrill J. *Indians, Infants and Infantry: Andrew and Elizabeth Burt on the Frontier.* Lincoln: University of Nebraska Press, 1988.

McChristian, Douglas C. *Fort Bowie, Arizona: Combat Post of the Southwest, 1858–1894.* Norman: University of Oklahoma Press, 2005.

McNitt, Frank. *Navajo Wars: Military Campaigns, Slave Raids and Reprisals.* Albuquerque: University of New Mexico Press, 1972.

Merrick, Morgan Wolfe. *From Desert to Bayou: The Civil War Journal and Sketches of Morgan Wolfe Merrick*. Edited by Jerry D. Thompson. El Paso: Texas Western Press, 1991.

Michno, Gregory F. *Battle at Sand Creek: The Military Perspective*. El Segundo, Calif.: Upton & Sons, 2004.

——. *Encyclopedia of Indian Wars: Western Battles and Skirmishes, 1850-1890*. Missoula, Mont.: Mountain Press, 2003.

——, and Susan Michno. *A Fate Worse Than Death: Indian Captivities in the West, 1830-1885*. Caldwell, Idaho: Caxton Press, 2007.

Millbrook, Minnie Dubbs. "The Jordan Massacre." *Kansas History* 2, no. 1 (Winter 1979): 219-30.

Miner, Craig. *West of Wichita: Settling the High Plains of Kansas, 1865-1890*. Lawrence: University Press of Kansas, 1986.

Monnett, John H. *Tell Them We Are Going Home: The Odyssey of the Northern Cheyennes*. Norman: University of Oklahoma Press, 2001.

Mooney, James. *Calendar History of the Kiowa Indians*. Washington, D.C.: Smithsonian Institution Press, 1979.

Moore, Stephen L. *Savage Frontier: Rangers, Riflemen, and Indian Wars in Texas*. Vol. 1. Plano: Republic of Texas Press, 2002.

Morgan, Dale L. *Jedediah Smith and the Opening of the West*. Lincoln: University of Nebraska Press, 1964.

Myers, Frank. *Soldiering in Dakota, Among the Indians, in 1863-65*. Huron, S. Dak.: Huronite Printing House, 1888.

Myers, John Myers. *The Saga of Hugh Glass: Pirate, Pawnee, and Mountain Man*. Lincoln: University of Nebraska Press, Bison Books, 1976.

Neihardt, John G. *The Splendid Wayfaring: The Story of the Exploits and Adventures of Jedediah Smith and His Comrades . . . from the Missouri River to the Pacific Ocean, 1822-1831*. Macmillan, 1920. Reprint, Lincoln: University of Nebraska Press, 1970.

Nester, William R. *The Arikara War: The First Plains Indian War, 1823*. Missoula, Mont.: Mountain Press Publishing, 2001.

Nichols, Ronald H., ed. *Men with Custer: Biographies of the Seventh Cavalry*. Hardin, Mont.: Custer Battlefield Historical & Museum Association, 2000.

Nye, Wilbur Sturtevant. *Bad Medicine and Good: Tales of the Kiowas*. Norman: University of Oklahoma Press, 1962.

——. *Carbine and Lance: The Story of Old Fort Sill*. Norman: University of Oklahoma Press, 1969.

Oliva, Leo E. *Fort Union and the Frontier Army in the Southwest*. Santa Fe: National Park Service, 1993.

——. *Soldiers on the Santa Fe Trail*. Norman: University of Oklahoma Press, 1967.

Orton, Richard H. *Records of California Men in the War of the Rebellion, 1861 to 1867*. Sacramento: State Printing Office, 1890.

Peters, Joseph P. *Indian Battles and Skirmishes on the American Frontier, 1790-1898*. Ann Arbor, Mich.: University Microfilms, 1966.

Potomac Corral of the Westerners. *Great Western Indian Fights*. Edited by B. W. Allred and J. C. Dykes. Lincoln: University of Nebraska Press, Bison Books, 1966.

Potter, Mrs. W. R. *History of Montague County, Texas.* Salem, Mass.: Higginson Book Company, 1957.

Quaife, Milo Milton, ed. *Kit Carson's Autobiography.* Lincoln: University of Nebraska Press, 1966.

Ramsay, Jack C., Jr. *The Story of Cynthia Ann Parker: Sunshine on the Prairie.* Austin: Eakin Press, 1990.

Randall, Kenneth A. *Only the Echoes: The Life and Times of Howard Bass Cushing.* Las Cruces, N. Mex.: Yucca Tree Press, 1995.

Rath, Ida Ellen. *The Rath Trail.* Wichita, Kans.: McCormick–Armstrong, 1961.

Rathbun, Daniel C. B. *Nevada Military Place Names of the Indian Wars and Civil War.* Las Cruces, N. Mex.: Yucca Tree Press, 2002.

——, and David V. Alexander. *New Mexico Frontier Military Place Names.* Las Cruces, N. Mex.: Yucca Tree Press, 2003.

Rathjen, Frederick W. *The Texas Panhandle Frontier.* Revised edition. Lubbock: Texas Tech University Press, 1998.

Richardson, Rupert N. *The Comanche Barrier to South Plains Settlement.* Austin: Eakin Press, 1996.

Roberts, Virginia Culin. *With Their Own Blood: A Saga of Southwestern Pioneers.* Fort Worth: Texas Christian University Press, 1992.

Robinson, Charles M., III. *General Crook and the Western Frontier.* Norman: University of Oklahoma Press, 2001.

——. *The Men Who Wear the Star: The Story of the Texas Rangers.* New York: Random House, 2000.

——. *Satanta: The Life and Death of a War Chief.* Austin: State House Press, 1997.

Robinson, Doane. *A History of the Dakota or Sioux Indians.* Minneapolis: Ross & Haines, 1974.

Rodenbough, Theophilus F. *From Everglade to Canyon with the Second United States Cavalry.* New York: D. Van Nostrand, 1875. Reprint, Norman: University of Oklahoma Press, 2000.

Roenigk, Adolph. *Pioneer History of Kansas.* Lincoln, Kans.: Privately published, 1933. Reprint, Lincoln, Kans.: Lincoln County Historical Society, 1973.

Rogers, Fred B. *Soldiers of the Overland: Being Some Account of the Services of General Patrick Edward Connor and His Volunteers in the Old West.* San Francisco: Grabhorn Press, 1938.

Ruby, Robert H., and John A. Brown. *Indians of the Pacific Northwest.* Norman: University of Oklahoma Press, 1988.

Russell, Don. *One Hundred and Three Fights and Scrimmages: The Story of General Reuben F. Bernard.* Mechanicsburg, Pa.: Stackpole Books, 2003.

Ryus, William H. *The Second William Penn.* Kansas City, Mo.: Frank T. Riley Publishing, 1913.

Sabin, Edwin L. *Kit Carson Days, 1809-1868.* Vol. 2, *Adventures in the Path of Empire.* Lincoln: University of Nebraska Press, 1995.

Sager, Catherine. *The Whitman Massacre of 1847.* Fairfield, Wash.: Ye Galleon Press, 2004.

Schwartz, E. A. *The Rogue River Indian War and Its Aftermath, 1850-1980.* Norman: University of Oklahoma Press, 1997.

Scott, Bob. *Tom Tobin and the Bloody Espinosas.* Baltimore: PublishAmerica, 2004.

Simmons, Marc. *Following the Santa Fe Trail.* Santa Fe: Ancient City Press, 1984.

Bibliography

Sitgreaves, Lorenzo. *Report of an Expedition down the Zuni and Colorado Rivers.* Washington, D.C.: R. Armstrong, Public Printer, 1853.

Skogen, Larry C. *Indian Depredation Claims, 1796-1920.* Norman: University of Oklahoma Press, 1996.

Smith, David Paul. *Frontier Defense in the Civil War: Texas' Rangers and Rebels.* College Station: Texas A & M University Press, 1992.

Smith, Ralph Adam. *Borderlander: The Life of James Kirker, 1793-1852.* Norman: University of Oklahoma Press, 1999.

Smith, Thomas T. *The Old Army in Texas: A Research Guide to the U.S. Army in Nineteenth-Century Texas.* Austin: Texas State Historical Association, 2000.

Snell, Joseph W., and Robert W. Richmond. "When the Union and Kansas Pacific Built through Kansas: Concluded." *Kansas Historical Quarterly 39,* no. 3 (Autumn 1966): 334-52.

Sowell, A. J. *Texas Indian Fighters.* Austin: State House Press, 1986. First published as *Early Settlers and Indian Fighters of Southwest Texas,* 1900, by Ben C. Jones & Company.

———. *Rangers and Pioneers of Texas.* 1884. Reprint, Austin: State House Press, 1991.

Sprague, Marshall. *Massacre: The Tragedy at White River.* Boston: Little, Brown, 1957. Reprint, Lincoln: University of Nebraska Press, 1980.

Spring, Agnes Wright. *Caspar Collins: The Life and Exploits of an Indian Fighter of the Sixties.* New York: AMS Press, 1967.

Stanley, David Sloan. *An American General: The Memoirs of David Sloan Stanley.* Santa Barbara, Calif.: Narrative Press, 2003.

Stephens, A. Ray, and William M. Holmes. *Historical Atlas of Texas.* Norman: University of Oklahoma Press, 1989.

Sweeney, Edwin R. *Cochise: Chiricahua Apache Chief.* Norman: University of Oklahoma Press, 1991.

———. *Mangas Coloradas: Chief of the Chiricahua Apaches.* Norman: University of Oklahoma Press, 1998.

———. *Merejildo Grijalva: Apache Captive, Army Scout.* El Paso: Texas Western Press, 1992.

Tate, Michael L. "Comanche Captives: People between Two Worlds." *Chronicles of Oklahoma 73,* no. 3 (Fall 1994): 228-263.

———. *The Frontier Army in the Settlement of the West.* Norman: University of Oklahoma Press, 1999.

Tatum, Lawrie. *Our Red Brothers and the Peace Policy of President Ulysses S. Grant.* Lincoln: University of Nebraska Press, 1970.

Thompson, Jerry. *Confederate General of the West: Henry Hopkins Sibley.* College Station: Texas A & M University Press, 1996.

Thrapp, Dan L. *Al Sieber: Chief of Scouts.* Norman: University of Oklahoma Press, 1964.

———. *The Conquest of Apacheria.* Norman: University of Oklahoma Press, 1967.

———. *Encyclopedia of Frontier Biography.* 3 vols. 1988. Reprint, Lincoln: University of Nebraska Press, 1991.

———. *Victorio and the Mimbres Apaches.* Norman: University of Oklahoma Press, 1974.

Trafzer, Clifford E., and Joel R. Hyer, eds. *Exterminate Them!* East Lansing: Michigan State University Press, 1999.

Trafzer, Clifford E., and Richard D. Scheuerman. *Renegade Tribe: The Palouse Indians and the Invasion of the Inland Pacific Northwest.* Pullman: Washington State University Press, 1986.

Tykal, Jack B. *Etienne Provost: Man of the Mountains.* Liberty, Utah: Eagle's View Publishing, 1989.

Tyler, Ron C. *The Big Bend: A History of the Last Texas Frontier.* College Station: Texas A & M University Press, 1996.

U.S. Adjutant General's Office. *Chronological List of Actions, etc., with Indians from January 15, 1837 to January 1891.* Fort Collins, Colo.: Old Army Press, 1979.

Utley, Robert M. *A Life Wild and Perilous: Mountain Men and the Paths to the Pacific.* New York: Henry Holt & Company, 1997.

——. *Lone Star Justice: The First Century of the Texas Rangers.* New York: Oxford University Press, 2002.

Vaughn, J. W. *The Battle of Platte Bridge.* Norman: University of Oklahoma Press, 1963.

——. *Indian Fights: New Facts on Seven Encounters.* Norman: University of Oklahoma Press, 1966.

——. *With Crook at the Rosebud.* Harrisburg, Pa.: Stackpole Company, 1956.

Waldman, Carl. *Atlas of the North American Indian.* New York: Checkmark Books, 2000.

Walker, Dale L. *Bear Flag Rising: The Conquest of California, 1846.* New York: Forge, 1999.

Watts, John S. *Indian Depredations in New Mexico.* Washington, D.C.: Gideon, 1859. Reprint, Tucson: Territorial Press, 1964.

Weatherford, Mark V. *Bannack-Paiute War: The Campaign and Battles.* Corvallis, Oreg.: Privately published, 1957.

Webb, George W. *Chronological List of Engagements between the Regular Army of the United States and Various Tribes of Hostile Indians which Occurred during the Years 1790 to 1898, Inclusive.* St. Joseph, Mo.: Wing Printing & Publishing, 1939. Reprint, New York: AMS Press, 1976.

Webb, Walter Prescott. *The Great Plains.* 1931. Reprint, New York: Grosset & Dunlap, n.d.

——. *The Texas Rangers: A Century of Frontier Defense.* Austin: University of Texas Press, 1991.

——, and H. Bailey Carroll, eds. *The Handbook of Texas.* 2 vols. Austin: Texas State Historical Association, 1952.

Weber, David J. *The Taos Trappers: The Fur Trade in the Far Southwest, 1540–1846.* Norman: University of Oklahoma Press, 1971.

Wellman, Paul I. *Death in the Desert: The Fifty Years' War for the Great Southwest.* Lincoln: University of Nebraska Press, 1987.

White, Lonnie J. *Hostiles and Horse Soldiers: Indian Battles and Campaigns in the West.* Boulder, Colo.: Pruett Publishing, 1972.

Wilbarger, J. W. *Indian Depredations in Texas.* Austin: Hutchings Printing House, 1889.

Williams, Clayton W. *Texas' Last Frontier: Fort Stockton and the Trans-Pecos, 1861-1895*. College Station: Texas A & M University Press, 1982.

Wilson, Britt W. *Lieutenant Morton's 1871 Scout from Camp Verde, Arizona Territory*. Banning, Calif.: Privately published, 1997.

Wilson, D. Ray. *Fort Kearny on the Platte*. Dundee, Ill.: Crossroads Communications, 1980.

Winfrey, Dorman H., and James M. Day, eds. *The Indian Papers of Texas and the Southwest, 1825-1916*. 5 vols. Austin: Texas State Historical Association, 1995.

Wooster, Robert. *The Military and United States Indian Policy, 1865-1903*. Lincoln: University of Nebraska Press, 1995.

——, ed. *Recollections of Western Texas, 1852-55, by Two of the U.S. Mounted Rifles*. Lubbock: Texas Tech University Press, 2001.

Young, Richard K. *The Ute Indians of Colorado in the Twentieth Century*. Norman: University of Oklahoma Press, 1997.

Public Documents

Dodge, Grenville M. *How We Built the Union Pacific Railway*. 61st Cong., 2nd sess., 1910. S. Doc. 477.

U.S. Bureau of Indian Affairs. *Report of the Commissioner of Indian Affairs for the Years 1861-1871*. Washington, D.C.: GPO, 1861-71.

U.S. Congress. House. *Report of the Secretary of War*. 40th Cong., 3rd sess., 1868. H. Exec. Doc. 1.

U.S. Congress. Senate. *Report of the Joint Special Committee on the Condition of the Indian Tribes*. 39th Cong., 2nd sess., 1867. S. Rep. 156.

——. *Letter from the Secretary of War*. 50th Cong., 2nd sess., 1888. S. Exec. Doc. 70.

U.S. Department of War. *The War of the Rebellion: A Compilation of the Official Records of the Union and Confederate Armies*. 128 vols. Washington, D.C.: GPO, 1880-1901.

Archive Collections

Duncan, Thomas. "General Duncan's Journal, 22 November 1869." File 540-0 DR V6 IPV 3, 1869. U.S. War Department. Records of U.S. Army Commands. RG 98. National Archives and Records Administration, Washington, D.C.

——. "Report of Lt. Col. Thomas Duncan, 7 October 1869." File 437 DR. U.S. War Department. Records of U.S. Army Commands. RG 98. National Archives and Records Administration, Washington, D.C.

Emory, W. H. "Republican River Expedition, Report of Col. W. H. Emory, 22 November 1869." U.S. War Department. Records of U.S. Army Commands. RG 98. National Archives and Records Administration, Washington, D.C.

Manuscripts and Papers

Kush, George. "In the Great Mother's Land: The Mounted Police and the Sioux." Sixth Annual Symposium, Custer Battlefield Historical & Museum Association, n.p., 1992.

Unrau, William E. "The Role of the Indian Agent in the Settlement of the South-Central Plains, 1861-1868." PhD diss., University of Colorado, 1963.

Internet Sources

Alexander, Thomas G. "Utah, The Right Place." http://historytogo.utah.gov/utah_chapters/american_indians/thewalkerwar.html.

Alford, Catherine G. "William Oldham." http://www.tshaonline.org/handbook/online/articles/OO/fol16.html.

Anderson, H. Allen. "White Horse." http://www.tshaonline.org/handbook/online/articles/WW/fwh81.html.

"Arizona's Forgotten Dead: The Story of the Engagement at Dragoon Springs, Arizona." Colonel Sherod Hunter Camp 1525, Sons of Confederate Veterans. http://members.tripod.com/~azrebel/page21.html.

"Arroyo Baluarte." http://www.tshaonline.org/handbook/online/articles/AA/rba63.html.

Bagley, Will. "Murdered Ute's Ghost Haunts Utah History." From *Salt Lake Tribune*, November 5, 2000. http://historytogo.utah.gov/salt_lake_tribune/history_matters/110500.html.

Bancroft, Hubert Howe. *Hubert Howe Bancroft's History of Utah, 1540–1886.* http://www.utlm.org/onlinebooks/bancroftshistoryofutah_contents.htm.

"Battle Country." http://www.ultimatewyoming.com/sectionpages/sec5/extras/battlecountry.html.

"Blood and Scalps." From *Western Star*, September 3, 1887. http://www.rootsweb.com/~kscomanc/indians_3sept1887.html.

Bork, Janine M., ed. *History of the Pacific Northwest: Oregon and Washington.* Vol. 2. 1889. Republished online, Portland, Ore.: North Pacific History Company, 1999–2003. http://www.usgennet.org/usa/or/county/union1/1889vol2/volumeIIpage21-31.htm.

"Camp Lyon." Idaho State Historical Society Reference Series. No. 357 (0357.pdf). http://www.idahohistory.net/.

"Camp Three Forks." Idaho State Historical Society Reference Series. No. 358 (0358.pdf). http://www.idahohistory.net/.

Carroll, H. Bailey. "Texan Santa Fe Expedition." http://www.tshaonline.org/handbook/online/articles/TT/qyt3.html.

Carson, Lynn R. "The Tintic War and the Deaths of George and Washington Carson." http://www.carsonfamilyhistory.org/books/TinticWar/TinticWar.html.

Carter, D. Robert. "Utes' Amazing Escape into the 'House of God.'" http://www.rockcanyonalliance.org/godhouse.php.

"Chusto-Talasah, Caving Banks: Civil War Oklahoma." http://www.americancivilwar.com/statepic/ok/ok002.html.

Cutrer, Thomas W. "John Bird." http://www.tshaonline.org/handbook/online/articles/BB/fbi15.html.

Dwyer, Jerry. "Fremont in Klamath County." http://home.comcast.net/~jcfremont/jcfklp1.htm.

Frazier, Donald F. "Battle of Village Creek." http://www.tshaonline.org/handbook/online/articles/VV/btv1.html.

Henderson, Harry McCorry. "Battle Creek Fight," http://www.tshaonline.org/handbook/online/articles/BB/btb1.html.

Horton, Thomas F. "Salt Creek Prairie." From *History of Jack County.* http://www.forttours.com/pages/saltcreek.asp#saltcreek.

362

Kelley, Tina, and Kathryn M. MacKay. "Wakara." From *Utah History Encyclopedia*. http://www.media.utah.edu/UHE/w/WAKARA.html.

Long, Christopher. "Killough Massacre." http://www.tshaonline.org/handbook/online/articles/KK/btk1.html.

McConnell, Joseph Carroll. *The West Texas Frontier, or A Descriptive History of Early Times in Western Texas*. 2 vols. Palo Pinto: Texas Legal Bank & Book Company, 1939. pdf. www.forttours.com/pages/mcconnellbook.asp.

Ochoa, Ruben E. "Martin, Texas." http://www.tshaonline.org/handbook/online/articles/MM/hrmbb.html.

"Old Camp Watson." http://gesswhoto.com/watson.html.

Orr, Susan and H. D. "Sarah Creath Howard." http://www.tshaonline.org/handbook/online/articles/HH/fhoat.html.

Peterson, John A. "Black Hawk War." From *Utah History Encyclopedia*. http://historytogo.utah.gov/utah_chapters/american_indians/blackhawkwar.html.

Reeve, W. Paul. "The Circleville Massacre: A Tragic Incident in the Black Hawk War." From *History Blazer*, September 1995. http://historytogo.utah.gov/utah_chapters/american_indians/circlevillemassacre.html.

Rodenbough, Theophilus F., and William L. Haskin, eds. *The Army of the United States: Historical Sketches of Staff and Line with Portraits of Generals-in-Chief*. New York: Maynard, Merrill & Company, 1896. Republished online, http://www.history.army.mil/books/R&H/R&H-FM.htm.

Roell, Craig H. "Linnville Raid of 1840." http://www.tshaonline.org/handbook/online/articles/LL/btl1.html.

"Round Mountain: Civil War Oklahoma." http://www.americancivilwar.com/statepic/ok/ok001.html.

"The Snake War, 1864–1868." Idaho State Historical Society Reference Series. No. 236 (0236.pdf). http://www.idahohistory.net/.

Thompson, Karen R. "Battle of Brushy Creek." http://www.tshaonline.org/handbook/online/articles/BB/btb2.html.

"Trinity Rangers." http://www.militarymuseum.org/TrinityRangers.html.

"Unsettling Events: Fort Nisqually Battle." http://search.tpl.lib.wa.us/unsettling/unsettled.asp?load=Fort+Nisqually+Battle&f=indian.bat\ftnisqua.bat.

"Unsettling Events: Port Gamble Battle." http://search.tpl.lib.wa.us/unsettling/unsettled.asp?load=Port+Gamble+Battle&f=indian.bat\ptgamble.bat.

Weddle, Robert S. "Los Almagres Mine." http://www.tshaonline.org/handbook/online/articles/LL/dkl5.html.

"William Fourr Biography." Hayden Library Special Collections. Arizona State Library. http://files.usgwarchives.org/az/yavapai/bios/fourr.txt.

Williamson, William R. "Rezin Pleasant Bowie." http://www.tshaonline.org/handbook/online/articles/BB/fbo46.html.

Index of Fights by State

General Index

About the Authors

Husband and wife **Gregory F. Michno** and **Susan J. Michno** are Michigan natives and both are Michigan State University graduates. Greg, an award-winning history author, has written dozens of articles and numerous books about the American West as well as World War II. His books include *USS Pampanito: Killer-Angel*; *Death on the Hellships: Prisoners at Sea in the Pacific War*; *Battle at Sand Creek: The Military Perspective*; *Deadliest Indian War in the West: The Snake Conflict, 1864-1868*; *The Mystery of E Troop: Custer's Gray Horse Company at the Little Bighorn*; *Lakota Noon: The Indian Narrative of Custer's Defeat*; and *Encyclopedia of Indian Wars: Western Battles and Skirmishes, 1850-1890*. He also contributed to the DVD history *The Great Indian Wars, 1540-1890*.

Susan Michno has collaborated with Greg for many years and has published several articles of her own. She and Greg coauthored *A Fate Worse than Death: Indian Captives in the West, 1830-1885*, and they recently completed a new book, *Circle the Wagons: Indian Attacks on Wagon Trains in Hollywood and History*. The couple lives in Longmont, Colorado.